TAMING TIBET

Taming Tibet

Landscape Transformation and the Gift of Chinese Development

Emily T. Yeh

Cornell University Press
Ithaca & London

Foundation Books

FOUNDATION
BOOKS

Foundation Books is an imprint of Cambridge University Press, India.

Cambridge House, 4381/4 Ansari Road, Daryaganj, New Delhi 110 002

www.cambridgeindia.org

This edition was published by arrangement with Cornell University Press.

First South Asia edition 2014

Printed in India at Replika Press Pvt. Ltd.

ISBN 978-93-82993-99-5 Paperback

To RS and the people of Lhasa

Contents

List of illustrations viii
Preface ix
Note on Transliterations and Place Names xv
Abbreviations and Terms xvi

Introduction 1
A Celebration 26
1. State Space: Power, Fear, and the State of Exception 29
Hearing and Forgetting 52

PART I. SOIL

The Aftermath of 2008 (I) 57
2. Cultivating Control: Nature, Gender, and Memories of Labor in State Incorporation 60

PART II. PLASTIC

Lhasa Humor 95
3. Vectors of Development: Migrants and the Making of "Little Sichuan" 97
Signs of Lhasa 126
4. The Micropolitics of Marginalization 129
Science and Technology Transfer Day 161
5. Indolence and the Cultural Politics of Development 163

PART III. CONCRETE

Michael Jackson as Lhasa 191
6. "Build a Civilized City": Making Lhasa Urban 195
The Aftermath of 2008 (II) 228
7. Engineering Indebtedness and Image: Comfortable Housing and the New Socialist Countryside 231

Conclusion 264

Afterword: Fire 269
Notes 273
References 295
Index 313

Illustrations

Maps

1. Tibet Autonomous Region 22
2. Lhasa *Chengguanqu* and Lhasa Municipality 23
3. Social-spatial relations in a peri-urban village 152

Figures

1. "Marching upon wasteland" 55
2. Vice Premier Chen Yi helping plant apple seedlings at the July First State Farm 75
3. Plastic greenhouses in Lhasa's peri-urban landscape, 2001 93
4. The new urban landscape 189
5. Michael Jackson as Lhasa 191
6. Sacred City Flower Garden brochure 208
7. Resettlement houses of those relocated from the Economic and Technological Development Zone, 2007 219
8. Posters of Chinese leaders adorn a sitting room, 2007 248
9. Image engineering, 2007 249
10. Flags atop a Comfortable House, 2007 250

Preface

In March 2008, Tibetan protestors set fire to, damaged, and destroyed roughly one thousand shops run by Han and Hui migrants in Lhasa, killing nineteen people and sending much of the capital of the Tibet Autonomous Region up in flames. The violent unrest, which fueled a nationalist backlash across China, became the subject of starkly competing interpretations premised on fundamentally different understandings of development, migration, and the place of Tibet within the People's Republic of China (PRC). The transnational Tibet Movement views Han migration as a key component of a deliberate policy of "cultural genocide." In contrast, the state and most Chinese citizens view these same migrants as a natural and inevitable part of the process of economic development, modernization, and progress that began with the "peaceful liberation" of Tibetans in 1951. A week after the March 14 riot, a *New York Times* reporter interviewed a Han Chinese businessman, one of whose Tibetan trinket shops had been smashed and burned. "Our government has wasted our money in helping those white-eyed wolves," he said, referring to Tibetans. "Just think of how much we've invested . . . Is this what we deserve?" This comment stood out for its mildness among the Han in Lhasa, who consistently described Tibetans as "lazy and ungrateful for the economic development they have brought."[1]

The angry sentiments of Han migrants in the aftermath of the unrest drew directly from state discourse about the benevolence and generosity of the state and its Han citizens toward Tibet. Indeed, PRC legitimation of its sovereignty over Tibet has always rested heavily on the presumption of Tibetan gratitude, first for liberation from the cruel, barbaric, and feudal pre-1950s "old society" and then, starting in the 1980s, for the bestowal of the gift of development, through the skills brought by Han migrants as well as the provision of large-scale infrastructure and massive subsidies from the government. In this narrative, all but a few radical separatists are grateful for this largesse. Thus, the official explanation of the 2008 unrest is that it was instigated and masterminded by the Fourteenth Dalai Lama and a "conspiracy of the Dalai clique and Western anti-China forces."[2] From this vantage point, Tibetan citizens, grateful for development brought by the state and their "older brother" in the Chinese nation-family, the Han, would not protest unless they were duped and manipulated by evil forces abroad, intent on destroying China's territorial sovereignty.

The violence in Lhasa was exceptional among the more than one hundred protests and demonstrations across Tibetan areas in the spring of 2008, the vast majority of which were peaceful. However, the March 14 incident in Lhasa, or simply "3-1-4" as it has become known, quickly became a flashpoint within China. A severe crackdown followed the protests, with de facto martial law, greatly heightened surveillance, large numbers of arrests, and in Lhasa a dramatic militarization of the city. Several years later, People's Armed Police were still stationed around the clock at intersections throughout the city, and armored vehicle and daily helicopter patrols became part of the urban landscape. Tibetans across the PRC began to face new forms of discrimination, as they were routinely turned away from hotels and restaurants and subjected to extensive background checks and questioning at airports and hotels. In Lhasa, ethnic tensions sharpened considerably following the state response to the unrest, creating new fault lines in spaces such as government offices. Ordinary Han Chinese continued several years later to express bewilderment and resentment at the apparently inexplicable ingratitude of the Tibetans.

The dynamics set in place in the decades before the 2008 protests continue unabated. In response to protest, state authorities intensify restrictions on the one hand and offer visible forms of material development on the other. The provision of goods, infrastructure, and GDP growth is meant to deepen Tibetans' conviction of and gratitude for belonging to the PRC. After 2008, many Tibetan areas were targeted by a Gratitude Education campaign, in which households receiving everything from posters of Chinese Communist Party leaders to new houses and tents were asked to show gratitude to the state and Party by opposing separatism, criticizing the Dalai Lama, and strengthening national integrity. The ongoing intensification of the processes and struggles that have led to multiple forms of violence suggests the urgent need to analyze their dynamics in the hopes of future resolution.

Taming Tibet provides a critical analysis of the modes of power that have produced the landscapes of struggle, compromise, and violence afflicting Tibet today. Focusing on Lhasa, I illuminate the production of state power, tracing attempts to foster and improve Tibetan livelihoods by expanding markets, subsidizing the building of new houses, and shaping Tibetans as subjects who desire development. I also show how these efforts have worked together at different points in time with the control over movement and space, and the exercise of the sovereign right to take life, and how they are experienced in everyday life. This approach helps to clarify the limits of the oversimplified explanatory frameworks that dominate discourse about the Tibet Question for various publics by highlighting the complexity of development, which works as a form of state territorialization. Development processes, particularly of agrarian change, Chinese migration, and urbanization, produce both the material landscape and contradictory Tibetan subjectivities.

Ethnographic analysis is a powerful way to open up the specificities of the everyday production of state power, as well as of the encounter between the market rationality posited and fostered by projects of development and selves shaped by multiple and contested forms of value. It is also useful for understanding spatiality and the production of place. Studies of contemporary Tibet have tended to adopt conventional assumptions about space as a backdrop or container rather than as a social product, and about places as isolated rather than produced through relationships with other places and through embodied everyday practices. Statist accounts defend government actions in Tibet by arguing, "it's the same as everywhere else in China." In this view, citizens of different ethnicities, classes, or origins interact with each other and are positioned relative to each other in the same way regardless of geographical location. This fails to account for the way in which past social relations create the particular spaces in which new social relations unfold and are spatialized. In contrast, my analysis is deliberately geographical, emphasizing the active social production of place and space.

Taming Tibet privileges ethnographic moments in the decade between 1998 and 2009, relying heavily on nine months of field research from 2000 to 2001. My interest in Tibet was first sparked, perhaps unusually, not by a fascination with Tibetan Buddhism, nor by the momentum and visibility of the transnational Tibet Movement's political campaigns in the late 1990s, but rather by an interest in development, a chance trip to Lhasa as a tourist in 1993, and the opportunity to work as a project officer in China's Agenda 21 Office in Beijing from 1995 to 1996. During that time, I visited Tibet again, realized that the "sustainable development" we were discussing in Beijing had very little to do with what I saw in Lhasa, and began to question what it meant to be engaged in development. Then, as a language student at Tibet University from 1998 to 1999, I noticed Lhasa's plastic-covered landscape and discovered that its plastic greenhouses had been set up by Han migrant farmers to grow the vegetables I bought in the city's markets from Chinese retailers. At that time I also first encountered Tibetans who told me that they rented their land out to these migrants because they themselves were "too lazy" to grow vegetables for the market. These experiences inspired my desire to understand the relationship between development, landscapes, markets, hegemony, and the place of Tibet within the PRC.

I returned to conduct research for nine months in 2000–2001, and again in the summer of 2002. Although I had originally planned to conduct an in-depth single village study, this proved impossible given pervasive concerns about "stability" and security, and the surveillance and internalized self-surveillance these produced in everyone I encountered. These conditions significantly shaped the form and methods of my research, as well as my embodied understanding of the experiences of state power. Instead of living in a village, I lived in urban Lhasa and commuted daily to nearby villages and state farms, where I interviewed Han farmers who were cultivating vegetables on subleased land; Tibetan families and farm workers who were renting out their land to Han farmers; other Tibetan peasants, as well as village and township leaders; retired workers on the state farms; and urban officials and scientists. In addition to semistructured interviews and oral and life histories, I also conducted informal market surveys and village mapping, and attended some village meetings. Among the places where I worked was the village I call Kyichuling (all village names are pseudonyms), to which I return throughout the book to trace state territorialization and development as they have been experienced and worked through the landscape from the 1950s through 2009.

In 2004, I worked with the Sichuan Academy of Social Sciences to conduct forty interviews with returned Han migrants in Shuangliu and Mianyang, Sichuan, to deepen my understanding of the migrants' perspectives and the political economy of migrant sending areas. Follow-up visits to Lhasa each year between 2005 and 2009 focused on processes of urbanization and the Comfortable Housing Project of the New Socialist Countryside. The analysis in this book is based on over two hundred semistructured interviews and many informal conversations and observations over roughly a decade. The conditions of research and the constraints on access were restrictive, capricious, and ambiguous, leading to a great deal of self-surveillance. My own embodied position, first as a Chinese born in America who was frequently mistaken for being Tibetan, and later as a researcher married to a Tibetan born in Nepal, shaped my research and others' interactions with me in ways that were often unpredictable, beyond my control, and indeed even outside of my awareness.

These same conditions mean that I cannot acknowledge by name those to whom I owe the greatest debt: the many people of Lhasa who generously gave their time, shared their knowledge, and patiently answered my many questions. This includes elderly Tibetans who shared their life stories, villagers young and old, close friends, language teachers, cadres and scholars, office workers, tour guides, and many others who not only made my work in Lhasa possible and interesting but also inspired me with their integrity and generosity. I dedicate this work to them.

This project has been so long in the making that I am certain I have not remembered all whose assistance I should acknowledge here. Among those I cannot forget, however, are my teachers at the University of California, Berkeley, who have my deepest respect and thanks. Nancy Peluso was and is a model of scholarly research and writing for me. Thomas Gold, David Germano, and Michael Watts provided encouragement and critical feedback. Also formative in my research and thinking were Donald Moore, Gillian Hart, and Kevin O'Brien, whose intellectual influence should be clear in these pages. I am grateful to the faculty of the Energy and Resources Group for creating such a unique and productive intellectual community. Among the many ERGies I would like to thank are Reuben Deumling, Navroz Dubash, Dennis Kelso, and Simone Pulver.

Outside of ERG, many other friends at Berkeley also provided comments and critique. Among these were members of several writing groups in which I participated, including Suraya Afiff, Lea Borkenhagen, Dan Buck, Claudia D'Andrea, Ken Foster, Amy Hanser, Bill Hurst, Kun-chin Lin, Seio Nakajima, Eileen Otis, Jennifer Sokolove, and Jennifer Sowerwine, as well as Lis Grinspoon, Jake Kosek, Celia Lowe, Anand Pandian, and Janet Sturgeon. In addition to making the maps that appear in this book, Mark Henderson has been a wonderful and patient collaborator on a number of teaching and writing projects during and since graduate school.

Since I arrived at the University of Colorado Boulder in 2003, I have found a very supportive intellectual community. Joe Bryan, Elizabeth Dunn, Najeeb Jan, Tim Oakes, and Rachel Silvey have all shaped my writing and thinking in significant ways. I am also grateful to other faculty and graduate students at CU who have offered feedback at different stages, including Holly Gayley, Mara Goldman, Abby Hickcox, Carole McGranahan, and Nicole Willock. I have learned a great deal from all of my graduate students, but am especially indebted to Kabzung and Yonten Nyima, for their insights on contemporary Tibet and for their assistance with later parts of the research. Undergraduate Hu Zhuying also provided valuable assistance. Geography colleagues beyond Colorado have kindly offered advice, as well as feedback on presentations and parts of the manuscript. Among them are Jason Cons, Leiba Faier, Cindy Fan, Andrew Grant, You-tien Hsing, Nathan Sayre, and Joel Wainwright. My thanks to all.

Tibetan studies colleagues, near and far, have also shaped the research and manuscript in crucial ways. I am particularly grateful to Robert Barnett for being a fount of endless knowledge about contemporary Tibet, and to Charlene Makley, whose thinking has been very influential. Ralph Litzinger has been a constant source of support and encouragement. Many other Tibetan studies scholars have also generously offered feedback or shaped this project in other ways, including Geoff Childs, Susan Costello, Kabir Heimsath, Karl Ryavec, and the late Andre Alexander. I would be remiss in not mentioning my fortune in sharing time in Lhasa with Jeff Lodas, Mike Parent, Lhakpa Sherpa, Antonio Terrone, Chris Walker, and Ben Wang. I thank Jeff for drawing the initial hand sketch of the village map found in this book. This project would never have been possible without Tibetan friends in the United States who helped me get started in research in Tibet. Of these I particularly thank Dechen, Konchok, Lobsang Choephel, Pema Drolkar, Pema Wanggyal, and Tsedan Tashi.

Thank you to Roger Haydon at Cornell University Press for being an advocate of the book and shepherding it through the publication process, and to Charlene Makley and an anonymous reviewer for the press for providing much needed guidance. Their input has significantly improved the final shape of this book, as have the sharp eyes and meticulous attention of the manuscript editor, Susan Specter, and the copy editor, Gavin Lewis.

This work would not have been possible without the generous support of a number of institutions. An EPA STAR fellowship, a Social Science Research Council International Dissertation Research Fellowship, and a UC Berkeley Chancellor's Dissertation Fellowship provided critical support. Further field research was made possible through funding from a John D. and Catherine T. MacArthur Foundation Research and Writing Grant, the Tibet Heritage Fund, and an IMPART award from the University of Colorado at Boulder. I also received a Social Science Research Council Book Fellowship, which provided me with helpful advice from Leslie Kriesel, and time away from teaching to write through a CU Boulder Center for Humanities and Arts Faculty Fellowship as well as a CU Boulder Faculty Fellowship.

Portions of chapter 5 were previously published in "Tropes of Indolence and the Cultural Politics of Development in Lhasa, Tibet," *Annals of the Association of American Geographers* 97, no. 3 (2007): 593–612. Copyright 2007 by Association of American Geographers, reprinted by permission of Taylor & Francis on behalf of the Association of American Geographers. Portions of chapter 6 were previously published in Emily T. Yeh and Mark Henderson, "Interpreting Urbanization in Tibet: Administrative Scales and Discourses of Modernization," *Journal of the International Association of Tibetan Studies*, no. 4 (2008): 1–44, THL #T5563, 2008.

Finally, I thank my family both extended and immediate. Ding Shizhang, Liu Ruixin, John Ting, and Randy Yeh provided places to stay and logistical assistance in China. Thanks to my mother and father, Susan Ting and Hsiang Tao Yeh, for their love and continued support over so many years. This project has been part of my life for the entire duration of my relationships to date with Kunga, Osel, and Seldron. I am grateful to Kunga for his love, patience, good humor, and willingness to read far too many chapter drafts, to our son Osel for the joy and laughter that he brings to my life, and to our daughter Seldron, whose arrival at the end of this project marks a new beginning.

Note on Transliterations and Place Names

The Wylie transliteration system is very useful for preserving original Tibetan spellings, but it produces results that are very difficult for those not able to read Tibetan to pronounce or make sense of. Given my hope that this text will reach a wide audience, I have chosen in most cases to use the THL (Tibetan and Himalayan Library) Simplified Phonetic Transcription system created by David Germano and Nicolas Tournadre, which both adheres to some basic principles of Wylie and indicates pronunciations in standard Lhasa Tibetan. For certain terms where precision or etymology are key to the argument, as in chapter 6, and in most cases in the notes, I give Wylie transliterations.

For Chinese words and names in general, I use the standard pinyin system. For Tibetan places, I generally provide Tibetan rather than Chinese names. For Chinese places and for cross-referencing of some Tibetan places, especially in the context of official documents, I provide names in Chinese using pinyin.

Abbreviations and Terms

AAHD	Agriculture and Animal Husbandry Department
ABC	Agricultural Bank of China
CCP	Chinese Communist Party
Ch.	Chinese
chang	traditional Tibetan beer
Chengguanqu	county-level administrative area of Lhasa
chupa	Tibetan robe, traditional Tibetan dress
hukou	household registration
minzu	Chinese term roughly translating as "nationality" or "ethnic group"
mu	one-fifteenth of a hectare
neidi	inner China; used in Tibet to refer to Han areas of China
PLA	People's Liberation Army
PRC	People's Republic of China
PSB	Public Security Bureau
RMB	Renminbi, the PRC currency (or yuan)
suzhi	Chinese term roughly translating as human "quality"
TAR	Tibet Autonomous Region
Tib.	Tibetan
tsampa	Tibetan staple of roasted barley flour

TAMING TIBET

Introduction

Sunlight pierces through the thin air above the Tibetan plateau and reflects off the golden roof of the Jokhang Temple, the religious center not just of Lhasa, but of all Tibet. Buddhist chronicles envision the Tibetan landscape as a gargantuan supine demoness, and Tibet's conversion to Buddhism as her taming by a set of temples that bolt her to the earth across vast expanses of territory. At the center is the Jokhang, the temple that pins down her heart. It is the destination of a lifetime for Tibetan pilgrims, who set out many months earlier from their village homes hundreds of miles away, making their way to Lhasa one prostration at a time, laying the full length of their bodies, arms outstretched, over fifteen-hundred-foot passes and sodden muddy tracks. Pilgrims and city residents—those who are not students, Chinese Communist Party members, or employed in any way by the government, that is—spend hours prostrating themselves in front of the massive doorway to the temple.

Behind the doorway is the object of their prostrations, the Jowo Rinpoche, statue of the Shakyamuni Buddha at age 12. It was brought to Lhasa in AD 641 by the Chinese Tang dynasty Princess Wencheng, as the residents of Tibet are frequently reminded. Her marriage to King Songtsen Gampo, who consolidated the Tibetan Empire in the seventh century and moved its capital to Lhasa, was used after the Tibetan uprising in Lhasa in 1959 as proof of Chinese claims to sovereignty over Tibet, Songtsen Gampo's senior, Nepalese wife conveniently forgotten. Today Wencheng is still constantly evoked to symbolize the close past and future intertwining of the Tibetan and Han peoples, the apotheosis of the unity of the nationalities, for which all citizens of the People's Republic of China must strive.

Since the "peaceful liberation of Tibet" in 1951, the Chinese state has sought to win the hearts and minds of Tibetans, to convince them to think of themselves as citizens of the People's Republic of China. Two narratives, one based on history and the other on gratitude, undergird the discursive work of state incorporation. The first is that Tibet has always been part of China and that any suggestions otherwise are meddlesome attempts by foreign imperialists to dupe and goad an isolated few Tibetan "splittists"—separatists who attempt to "split" the otherwise seamless fabric of the Chinese Motherland. Tibet's historical status is central to the Tibet Question, as both Chinese state authorities and Tibetans have reconceptualized past imperial relationships in terms of modern territorial sovereignty, anachronistically projecting the modern nation-state form backwards in time to make their claims. The naturalization of the nation-state as a container marks the centrality of Western concepts of sovereignty and territory in geopolitical disputes over Tibet.

The Chinese state and most of its citizens interpret the ongoing troubles over Tibet through the lens of China's Century of Humiliation, which began with the nineteenth-century Opium Wars, as illegal Western imperialist efforts to challenge Chinese sovereign rule over its own territory. Until the mid-1980s, official history traced the oneness of Tibetans and Chinese back to the marriage of Tang Princess Wencheng to Songtsen Gampo, founder of the Tibetan Empire. This was not a particularly compelling claim to unified political status, as a century later a descendant of Songtsen Gampo's briefly occupied the capital of the Chinese Tang dynasty.

Since the mid-1980s, the official narrative has dated Tibet's incorporation into China to the Sakya leaders' submission to the Mongol Yuan dynasty (1279–1368). Tibetans point out that the Tibetan-Mongol relationship, like the latter relationship between Tibet and the Qing Empire, was not one of pure subordination but rather a priest-patron relationship of equals between spiritual and temporal powers. They further point out that China does not today claim numerous other territories that were once part of the Yuan Empire, and that neither the Yuan nor Manchu rulers identified as Chinese.

The second narrative of the inevitability of Chinese rule in Tibet is that the Sino-Tibetan relationship has long been characterized by generous Chinese giving, which ought therefore to be reciprocated by Tibetan gratitude. A twenty-part television drama produced by Chinese Central Television in 2000 and aired incessantly in Lhasa credits Princess Wencheng with bringing not only the Jowo Rinpoche statue, but also Buddhism, technologies, music, manners, and even agriculture to Tibet, in other words, of giving Tibetans the gift of civilization itself. Idioms of tribute, offering, and gifts characterized the imperial relations between Chinese and Tibetan political centers over many subsequent centuries.[1]

With the incorporation of Tibet into the territorial boundaries of the PRC as a modern nation-state, the performance of gratitude became a demand on citizens rather than just a ritual between rulers. Government authorities framed state incorporation as the liberation of Tibetan serfs from their cruel and barbaric local leaders and their exploitative religious institutions, enabling Tibetans to throw off their chains of oppression to become forward-looking socialist citizens. Tibet before 1951, renamed the "old society," is described as a "poor, backward, isolated, and stagnant feudal serf society":

> Cruel oppression and exploitation by the feudal serf-owners, and especially the endless consumption of human and material resources

> by religion and monasteries under the theocratic system and their spiritual enslavement of the people, had gravely dampened the laborer's enthusiasm for production, stifled the vitality of the Tibetan society and reduced Tibet to a protracted state of stagnancy.[2]

Tibetans thus became indebted to the state for socialist liberation from this brutish old society.

With the death of Mao in 1976 and the subsequent introduction of market reforms in the 1980s, and particularly since the deepening of marketization in the 1990s, economic development and its provision of commodity goods came to overshadow liberation as the master discourse of sovereignty. "Development is the hard truth," declared Deng Xiaoping in his famous Southern Tour of 1992 that jump-started China's transformation to a "socialist market economy," an economy dominated primarily by capitalist relations of production but that retains considerable state ownership and management, a one-party political system, and elements of socialist ideology such as the absence of private landownership.

In Tibet, this newer narrative of development as the "hard truth" insists that Tibetans would still be stuck in their 1950s state of technological backwardness and poverty were it not for the Chinese state's benevolent gift of development. The emphasis on economic growth, investment, and consumption intensified further after the launch of the Open Up the West (*Xibu da kaifa*) campaign in 2000. Legitimization of PRC sovereignty now rests heavily on Tibetan gratitude for the gift of development bestowed by the generous beneficence of the party-state. To question this gift is to challenge the legitimacy of Chinese rule in Tibet—a mark of splittism and the ultimate manifestation of ingratitude, one that dangerously threatens to undo arduous processes of territorialization.

On a summer day in 2001, I stroll past the Jokhang and its tourists and prostrating pilgrims with a friend who grew up in a rural village but has been a Lhasa resident for the past decade. His government paycheck makes him a member of Lhasa's new elite, whose ability to purchase spacious new homes and consumer goods may or may not compensate for the fact that since 1996, they have been ordered not to practice religion. We stop at the two long lines of wooden stalls in the square in front of the Jokhang to haggle over khataks, or ceremonial scarves. Khataks sell very well because they are used in so many occasions in everyday Tibetan life. Tibetans drape them on altars, thrones, and other sacred sites in monasteries and temples, and along the circumambulation routes around them. They present them to friends who are departing on a journey, or who have returned from a trip, and to decorate at New Years. They also present them to monks or other important guests, and at graduations, weddings and other celebrations.

Khatak giving is a ubiquitous and uniquely Tibetan practice. The Han have not adopted it. It therefore comes as a bit of a surprise when, on closer inspection, one realizes that the long rows of khatak sellers are all Han migrants. There isn't a single Tibetan seller of khataks in downtown Lhasa.

Indeed, since the deepening of economic reforms in the early 1990s, Han migrants have come to dominate virtually all new economic activities in Lhasa, whether tailoring, taxi driving, restaurant ownership, or vegetable sales. The intensified marketization and state investment into development projects brought by the Open Up the West campaign in 2000 further accelerated the arrival of migrants, as did the completion of the Qinghai-Tibet Railway in 2006. A Chinese construction crew built my friend's spacious new house, and after it was done, he hired Chinese carpenters to complete its interior decorations. Many Tibetans in Lhasa now live on an economy of Han rents. In the Lhalu neighborhood, Tibetans whose farmland has been expropriated for urbanization make a living renting out their courtyard space and houses to Chinese migrants, who run shops and businesses. Thus, they joke, "We used to raise cows for a living; now we raise Chinese for a living."

One block west of the square in front of the Jokhang we come to Yuthok Road, named for the turquoise-covered bridge that once marked the western boundary of the city of Lhasa. The watery marsh that Yuthok Bridge crossed having been filled in long ago, Yuthok Road is now at the heart of the rapidly expanding city. Though a religious, cultural, and political center for centuries, Lhasa has been deterritorialized and reterritorialized as a backward periphery of the PRC that urgently needs to be developed. Efforts to improve Lhasa, such as the makeover of Yuthok Road from its drab high socialist days as People's Road to a pedestrian shopping arcade with flashing neon lights, green and yellow plastic coconut trees, electronics stores, and clothing boutiques, are inscribed on the landscape.

The golden roof of the Jokhang Temple is not the only glittering surface in Lhasa. It is joined by the tinted blue glass windows of the new China Mobile building, metallic dragon sculptures, and globular clusters of metallic tendrils that shoot lights every night like flashing Christmas trees with Chinese characteristics. And then there is the smooth, sparkling Golden Yaks sculpture, a present for Tibet at the fortieth anniversary of its 'peaceful liberation,' permanently fixed at a busy intersection just beyond the Potala Palace. Lhasa's many gleaming exteriors tend to reflect back whatever story is projected on them, whether of exotic spirituality and ancient wisdom, Han colonization and Tibetan victimization, or development and Tibetan prosperity. Yet such ways of seeing Lhasa's landscape obscure the complex processes of its production. Beneath its alluring surfaces, scraping away at development's economy of appearances, Tibet is a place of ambiguity and puzzling contradictions.

Territorialization and Puzzles of Landscape Transformation

This book is about the production and transformation of the Tibetan landscape from the 1950s to the present, as catalyzed by development as a state project that is presented as a gift to the Tibetan people, and as it works to territorialize Tibet. By territorialization, I mean the process of securing the naturalization of Tibetans' association with the Chinese state and of the borders of the PRC as a spatial container for Tibetans. My argument, that development works to territorialize Tibet through the making of particular landscapes and subjects, presumes an analytic that challenges the realist framework in which territory simply exists. Rather than a preconstituted, naturalized geographical unit or container of social, cultural and political-economic relations, state territory is the product of an ongoing process of territorialization through which the "'spatial relations' that make a given state-society ensemble hegemonic" are worked out.[3] Territory is the fundamental form of space of the modern nation-state.[4] This book explores the process of territorialization in Tibet from the 1950s to the end of the first decade of the twenty-first century, with a particular focus on development in the making of hegemonic social-spatial relations.

Territorialization is a deeply material and embodied process that involves the transformation of both subjectivities and landscapes. From the 1950s through the 1980s, this embodied process was framed as both cause and effect of Tibetan gratitude for socialist liberation, whereas since the 1980s, the framing has shifted toward one of Tibetan gratitude for the gift of development. Throughout, the transformation of the material landscape of Tibet has often been enacted through the labor of Tibetans themselves, transforming their subjectivities in ways that help naturalize Tibetans' association with the PRC even as they may simultaneously resist this association. The exploration of state territorialization in Tibet brings into view the contradictory and complex nature of development and belonging in ways that are not immediately apparent from a surface reading of the landscape.

Taming (*'dul ba*) is central to Tibetan conceptions of self as well as landscape, and is thus particularly resonant with territorialization. In the Tibetan Buddhist view, the ego must be tamed in order to obtain liberation from cyclic existence; *'dul ba* is also the name for the rules of monastic discipline. Tibetan rituals seek to tame and civilize disorderly and destructive aspects of reality, including place-based deities, while Buddhist practitioners work to tame their own mental consciousness. To tame is to self-discipline, to cultivate a particular type of subjectivity and craft a desired self. At the same time, Tibetan historiography asserts that Buddhism tamed the Tibetan landscape through the impaling of the supine demonness and subjugation of local deities. In the Tibetan origin story, Tibet first became a "field of conversion" for Avalokitesvara, *bodhisattva* of compassion, patron and protector of the land of Tibet, when he introduced grain cultivation to the children of a *bodhisattva*-ape and a rock-ogress, turning these ancestors into humans. A tamed Tibet in this view is one that is cultivated with barley and populated by Buddhists, particularly religious teachers who tame malevolent spirits in the landscape and who help disciples tame their egos. The remaking of Tibetan selves and landscapes by the PRC through territorialization threatens to undo this earlier process of taming through a new project of civilization, cultivation, and conversion.[5]

Three key landscape transformations form the trajectory of state territorialization in Tibet from the 1950s to the present. First, state farms and communes were introduced in the 1950s and continued through the high socialist period until the early 1980s. Tibetan laborers and commune members worked the soil, producing a new socialist landscape through their toil. Second, in the 1990s, the project of development, market reforms, and a shift from socialist liberation to economic development allowed Han Chinese migrants to enter Tibet in large numbers. They quickly dominated new economic activities, including greenhouse vegetable cultivation, which has literally covered the peri-urban agricultural landscape of Lhasa in plastic. Finally, urbanization and the intensified expansion of the built environment in the 2000s marked a new round of development and landscape transformation that emphasized new concrete structures as gifts of development from the state.

Each of these material transformations, discussed in the three main parts of the book, reveals the complexities and contradictions of Tibetan agency with respect to projects of state building and development. In the early 1950s, two state farms on the edge of Lhasa were key sites through which the state initially established territorial control. Lower-class Tibetans, particularly women, were recruited to join the farms, where they worked together with People's Liberation Army (PLA) soldiers, growing the grain and vegetables that nourished the troops both physically and psychologically, and enabling them to begin the task of state incorporation. In addition to feeding the troops, these state farms also served as sites for the introduction of new crop varieties and agricultural inputs that marked the start of scientific agriculture and modernization, key elements of the improvement and progress that today constitute the gift of development for which Tibetans should be grateful. The organization of Tibetan agriculture into both state farms and communes transformed nature through that period's dominant environmental imaginary, or way of imagining the proper human relationship with nature. At the same time, state farms and communes attempted to remake Tibetans into socialist subjects and Chinese citizens through the transformative act of labor. Memories of collective labor during this period in turn shaped Tibetans' practices of labor and participation in the market after economic reform.

In contrast to the campaigns that characterized agriculture during the Maoist period, the turn to markets and the selective use of neoliberal ideology after economic reforms allowed Han migrants to participate in the project of development and its transformation of the landscape through the "freedom" of the market. These migrants do not arrive in Lhasa through a program of deliberate transfer—indeed, most migrants have no intention of staying more than a few years and do not claim Lhasa as home. Nevertheless, state authorities insist that migrants should be welcomed with open arms as vectors of development, who bring much-needed progress to Tibet. Thus, Han migrants' ability to better position themselves vis-à-vis state and market than local Tibetans and to benefit from economic reform and the massive investment of central government funds into Tibet becomes, in the "apparatus" of state development, something that Tibetans should appreciate, for, among other things, its purported educative effects on their own subjectivities.[6]

Many of these Han migrants are market gardeners. After arriving in Lhasa, they sublease plots of land from Tibetan villagers, signing one- to three-year contracts, and paying roughly double what Tibetan peasants would otherwise earn growing barley or winter wheat. Han farmers then build greenhouses with bamboo poles and plastic sheets, and grow vegetables year-round. Until the gradual saturation of the market in the late 1990s, Han migrants reported net profits many times what they paid in rent. Tibetan villagers who rent out their fields have been generally unable to earn much income from alternative uses of their labor time, such as small-scale business or wage labor on construction projects.

Despite political and ethnic tensions in Lhasa, and dissatisfaction with state policies that have enabled large-scale Han migration, Tibetans willingly rent out their land to the Han rather than engaging in greenhouse farming themselves. Why is this the case, when Tibetan villagers could make significantly greater profits by growing vegetables? In other words, why do Tibetan villagers apparently reproduce their own economic marginalization by ceding economic activities with higher profit-earning potential to Han migrants? The first time I asked a Tibetan farmer why there seemed to be no Tibetans growing vegetables, in 1998, he replied, "To plant vegetables, you must have a lot of patience. You must get up very early in the morning and stay up until late at night. Tibetans don't like to get up early in the morning to do this work." His answer was not unique. Again and again I heard that Tibetans "don't like to work," "can't work as hard as the Chinese," and in short, are "lazy." Why do these Tibetans invoke a trope of Tibetan indolence to explain their own nonparticipation in this and other new economic activities? How should we understand the close resemblance of their explanations of their inability to participate in the new market opportunities brought by development with a state discourse about Tibetans' "psychology of idleness"?[7]

My attempts to answer these questions quickly revealed that Tibetan participation in the reshaping of the landscape is not shaped only by economic considerations, nor are speech acts about patterns of labor merely transparent reflections of embodied habits of work. Instead, both are produced by a conjuncture of sedimented histories, memories of the collective past, and experiences of development as a hegemonic project that is both desired and resisted. The covering of the peri-urban landscape in plastic laid down by Han migrants renting land from Tibetan villagers is a visually striking inscription of development on the material landscape, one made possible only through a particular formation of Tibetan subjectivities by processes of territorialization and development.

After the launching of the Open Up the West campaign in 2000, urban expansion accelerated, displacing these plastic greenhouses concentrically outward to villages further from Lhasa. State authorities came to see urbanization as an urgent task for Lhasa's development, the "only way out" of Tibet's ever-backward status. As these development efforts have intensified, so too has the role of both gift and spectacle, whether in city apartment blocks and shopping malls that seem to spring up overnight, or the large-scale state investment in the construction of new houses in the Comfortable Housing Project of the New Socialist Countryside. State investments in the building of these structures are increasingly made with the expectation of shows of gratitude, as made clear by the explicitly named Gratitude Education (*gan en jiao yu*) campaign with which they have been accompanied. However, there is noticeably more intensive investment in orderly and impressive lines of houses along the sides of major roads and in major cities, rather than in more remote villages. Local residents dub this phenomenon "image engineering," an idiom that encapsulates a view of development as a spectacle meant to conjure up the performance of their loyalty to the state. At the same time, many Tibetan villagers have also participated in the engineering of this image in the particular choices they have made in building new houses.

The establishment of the state farms, the rise of Han migrant vegetable farming, and the expansion of the built urban and rural environments all contribute to securing the naturalization of Tibetan belonging to the PRC. Embodied, material practices of landscape transformation are, in other words, central to the production of state territory. As Mukerji notes, the material manipulation of land "imprints the political order onto the earth, making it seem almost an extension of the natural order."[8] I pay particular attention to the work of ordinary people, exploring the fact that the material manipulation of the landscape of Tibet is not imposed by a purely external force that hovers above and apart from local society. Rather, it is carried out in part through the agency—conceived of not as sovereign will but as the capacity for action enabled by geographically and historically specific relations of power—of those whose relationship to territory is being fundamentally altered.[9] In other words, I explore how Tibetans were recruited at specific points in time into hegemonic projects that became flashpoints for more open struggle and resistance at other times.

In brief, then, this book examines the play of subjection and agency, desire and fear, as various forms of territorialization, particularly development, work on and through the Tibetan landscape. How, in the 1950s, were some Tibetans recruited to work on the state farms that proved critical to maintaining the lives of the PLA soldiers and thus to solidifying the PRC's early control over Tibetan territory? Why did peri-urban villagers through the 1990s and beyond sublease their land, forgoing opportunities to earn greater income and ceding an economic niche to the resented Han migrants, while blaming their own indolence? And why, after 2005, did Tibetan villagers voluntarily take out loans for new house-building projects even while claiming that they greatly feared indebtedness? These puzzles suggest that pervasive narratives about pure Tibetan victimization are flawed, denying—much as do narratives of Tibetans being duped and manipulated into the 2008 protests—the possibility of agency. This agency, or capacity for action, produces the changing landscape.

In their use of the term "image engineering," Tibetans recognize what has been called the duplicity of landscape, its tendency to obfuscate and erase the social conditions of its production.[10] In reaction to older Sauerian studies of landscape that focused on the cultural determinants of the morphological form of landscapes, Marxian geographers such as Stephen Daniels and Denis Cosgrove shifted attention in the 1980s to landscape representation and landscape as an ideological way of seeing, which maintains capitalist social relations and reinforces capitalist strategies of appropriation and control by making them seem natural and invisible.[11] More recently, geographical studies of landscape have emphasized the importance of landscapes as simultaneously representational and material, socially produced through both discourse and embodied labor.[12] Not only does labor produce the landscape, but at the same time, the representations of the products of that labor as a landscape impose a view in which the domination and control of that labor is naturalized.[13]

Above, I stressed the duplicity of the Lhasa landscape, the surfaces and spectacles that reflect easy narratives of progress or victimization, to set the stage for a critique of not only transformations of the land during the period of high socialism and state capitalist development since the 1980s, but also of ways of seeing the Tibetan landscape that efface the cultural politics of Tibetan involvement in its production, as Tibetans negotiate their desires, interests, and values. I do so in the belief that to understand the production of landscape requires understanding the subject positions of those who live and work within it. Furthermore, as Don Mitchell suggests, landscapes are social products that become "naturalized through the very struggles engaged over [their] form and meaning." Drawing on Bruno Latour's concept of quasi-objects, he argues that landscapes are both material realities and embodiments of the relations, arguments, and struggles that go into making them, despite their appearance as inert or "natural." Only by investigating the struggles that go into making landscapes can relations of power that obfuscate landscapes be understood. Moreover, struggles over landscape are historically sedimented and create trajectories that shape, though they do not completely determine, the future. As Mitchell puts it, "the look of the land becomes at least partially determinate in the struggles that are to follow."[14] These struggles, I will demonstrate, are as much cultural as they are political and economic. I show how the mutual constitution of the cultural, the political-economic, and the socio-spatial creates the contradictory nature of development as a hegemonic project as it works on its subjects and the landscape they produce.

Cultural Politics and Political Economy of Development

To explore this contradictory nature in parts 2 and 3 of this book, I develop an analytic of development—the name of a process that differentially changes access to resources and conditions of material production and livelihoods—as fundamentally both a political-economic and a cultural project. Struggles over cultural identities and meanings are not incidental to "development" in the sense of either deliberate schemes of improvement or of processes of differentiation brought by the expansion of capitalist relations. Instead, I show how culturally and historically informed experiences of development shape meanings and dispositions that in turn alter access to and control over income opportunities and decisions about production and reproduction. One of my central arguments is that culturally specific idioms of development are key to shaping its political-economic outcomes.

Antonio Gramsci's insights are particularly relevant here. Seeking to understand why there was a communist revolution in Russia but not Italy, Gramsci developed in his prison writings an "analysis of situations," a method to examine how diverse, geographically and historically specific forces come together to create political conjunctures and their associated politics of the possible. In their interpretation of Gramsci's ouevre cultural theorists, particularly Raymond Williams and Stuart Hall, have demonstrated how cultural formations can be important in maintaining hegemony, without crudely reducing culture to a form of false consciousness. Subjects do not have singular objective interests determined by locations within monolithic structures.[15] Instead, an "analysis of situations" can show how interests and actions such as the apparently contradictory decision by Tibetan farmers to sublease their land to Han migrants despite both loss of potential profits and their resentment over Chinese migration, are a result of the coming together of a specific set of elements, rather than false consciousness.

To use a term philosopher Louis Althusser took from Freud and introduced to Marxism, situations are *overdetermined* by cultural, political-economic, and socio-spatial factors. Profoundly influenced by Gramsci, Althusser rejected economistic interpretations of Marx, reductionist accounts in which the economic base determines outcomes in the last instance. Seeking to explain the Russian Revolution, Althusser used "overdetermination" to argue that the apparently simple contradiction between the forces and relations of production is never actually simple, but rather "always specified by the historically concrete forms and circumstances in which it is exercised" including the superstructure, the internal and external historical situation, traditions, and context. Historical events, in other words, are always conjunctural and never purely determined by an economic base.[16]

Though very different from Althusser's structural Marxism in his attentiveness to the experience of ordinary people, cultural theorist Raymond Williams built on these conceptualizations and employed "overdetermination" to work against economism and distance himself from interpretations of determination that isolate autonomous categories (such as the economy) to predict outcomes in the last instance. Used to recognize multiple forces as structured within particular historical and geographical situations, the concept of overdetermination signals the refusal to "illegitimately suppress the complexity, specificity and interdependence that obtains in actual political-economic relations."[17] Furthermore, it means recognizing that cultural identities and meanings are not epiphenomenal reflections of the material base, but are real, material and constitutive forces in and of themselves.

The concept of development gains its power in part from its dual reference both to the immanent unfolding of what is natural, and to a process of active intervention.[18] In the sense of a national project of achieving modernity (and "development" is almost always imagined on the nation-state scale) the term refers both to the achievement of capitalist value production and to a deliberate, planned project of improvement devised and guided by those in positions of expertise and trusteeship. These two sides of development, sometimes referred to as "little d" and "big D" development, are related to each other through a Polanyian double movement as opposing tendencies that characterize the dynamics of capitalism, where the dispossession that is integral to the uneven expansion of capitalist relations leaves in its wake the need for new projects of improvement and intervention by experts.[19]

At the same time, development as a project of government also works to shape the desires of its subjects, and the actions that stem from those desires. As such, the status of being developed becomes a "moral horizon of a project of self fashioning" where the work that is done on the self to achieve development involves bodies, desires, habits, and emotions.[20] The close relationship between development and capitalist value production, or what geographer Joel Wainwright has called "the sublime absorption of capitalism into the concept of development" means that the work on the self that is called forth seeks to intensify a particular "instrumental reason that is disposed to exchange-value production," creating an infrastructure within which certain kinds of economic conduct are intelligible and compelling, while others are seen as irrational and nonsensical.[21]

However, the work of self-fashioning that is incited acts on a self that is not a blank slate or a standardized and universal *homo economicus*, but rather one that is the product of multiple cultural traces and sedimentations. This is why culture matters, and how the cultural politics of development co-constitutes its political economy. Persistent layers of meaning produced by specific histories and geographies shape the selves on which development projects work. This produces contingent and often unexpected or contradictory outcomes given development planning's presumption that it acts on and simultaneously has as its goal the making of *homo economicus*. As geographer Vinay Gidwani puts it in a study of agrarian development in India, market rationality, or a mode of action normatively oriented to the production of capitalist value "is always contaminated and in danger of being interrupted by other rationalities."[22] These other rationalities are alternative understandings, culturally and historically constituted, of self, labor, moral worth and identity, of the good life and the life worth living. The product of these multiple forces at work in the constitution of the self and its desires always exceeds both the intentions of development planning and the boundaries of singular interests or subject positions.

In exploring the production of the Tibetan landscape through the project of development since the 1980s, I analyze development as a hegemonic project. The contradictions of Tibetans' roles in enabling Chinese greenhouse vegetable farming and participating in the construction of new houses are the outcomes of overdetermined struggles over cultural identity, access to resources, and subject formation that result from hegemony. It is important to stress again that hegemony is not the same as false consciousness. Developed by Antonio Gramsci and reinterpreted by Stuart Hall, Raymond Williams, Paul Willis, and other cultural Marxists as a way to understand how and why subordinate groups seem to consent to their own oppression, the concept of hegemony refers to a pervasive, lived experience of power relations, always simultaneously ideational, including meanings and values that constitute a sense of reality, and material. It is never static or totalizing, but rather processual, unstable, and constantly fought over and maintained on many sites and at different levels, requiring ongoing effort.[23]

For Gramsci, hegemony was an always unstable combination of coercion and consent, which produces subaltern contradictory consciousness: an unpredictable, mutable amalgam of common sense and good sense. Common sense is that which is adopted uncritically from the past; it is "not a single conception, identical in time and space," but rather, even within the mind of single individual always "fragmentary, incoherent, and inconsequential, in conformity with the social and cultural position of those masses whose philosophy it is." Opposed to it is good sense, a "coherent and systematic philosophy," or a conception of the world worked out consciously. Good sense criticizes and goes beyond common sense, but can nevertheless also be limited by it.[24] The concept of contradictory consciousness helps us steer between the simplistic notions of false consciousness and romantic views of resistance that plague common interpretations of Tibetans and their relationship with the Chinese state, which generally consider only economic growth or the politics of culture, but not how the two are interwoven.

Gramsci was concerned with the combination of coercion and consent, rather than with a situation of pure coercion or repressive sovereign power. To what extent does this analytic work in contemporary Tibet? Consent, as I interpret it, is another way of naming the securing or conducting of conduct, of guiding the action of subjects who retain the capacity to act otherwise.[25] The balance of coercion and consent in the application of state power in Tibet varies not only according to sphere of social life but also in time and space. Coercion characterizes the regulation of those actions deemed to originate from a religious motivation much more than those concerned with secular profit making, for example. The decade leading up to the protests of 2008 was characterized by a relatively lighter application of sovereign power than the years immediately afterward; such cycles also characterized the contrast between the 1980s until the Lhasa protests of 1987, and the period after martial law was imposed in 1989.

In exploring the cultural politics of Tibetan agency in the production of the landscape, much of this book focuses on development, a form of government that tries to accomplish rule by creating governable subjects and governable spaces.[26] In developmental regimes, ruling powers claim progress as a goal, a defined people or population as the object of improvement, and adopt an ideology of science that offers techniques and principles to both achieve and measure progress.[27] As such, development is a form of what Michel Foucault called biopower, a form of power concerned with the fostering of life rather than the command over death. This departs from the common image of state power in Tibet as being absolutely repressive or violent sovereign power, concerned with the taking of life. However, the rise of biopower does not replace sovereign and disciplinary modes of power. Rather, all three modes are applied in different combinations at different times, and reinforce rather than contradict each other.[28]

Thus, in focusing on development, I do not ignore the ever-present threat of state violence, which plays a vital role in shaping and severely limiting the terrain of possible forms of mobilization and struggle. This threat forecloses the possibility of an outright, organized call for boycotts of Han migrant–run businesses in Lhasa, for example, because of the close identification of the Han with the People's Republic of China, despite the PRC's official designation as a "multinational state" (*duo minzu guojia*), where all fifty-six *minzu* (nationalities or ethnic groups) are simultaneously distinct and united into a singular supernationality: the Chinese nationality (*Zhonghua minzu*), which belongs naturally to the state whose space is defined by the boundaries of the PRC. It is this overarching Chinese (*Zhonghua*) nationality or nation that claims the territory of the PRC as its rightful and natural space to occupy.

The singular Chinese nationality is imagined as a giant, harmonious family of siblings, in which the elder brother Han solicitously takes care of and leads the other minority *minzu*. This familial harmony between the Han and minorities is referred to as the unity of the nationalities (*minzu tuanjie*), both a state of being that is presumed to always already exist and an exhortation, invoked to call itself into existence. It works as a form of coercive amity in that all challenges to it are labeled "national splittism," a political crime of splitting the natural oneness of the fifty-six *minzu* of the larger Chinese family.[29] Within this logic, demands for greater autonomy or greater acceptance of difference between minorities and the Han than is already provided are interpreted as splittism. Within the discourse of unity and harmony, then, lies the unchallengeable premise of Han superiority over minority groups, and the identification of the Han with China.[30] The pecking order of sibling *minzu* cannot be openly challenged without inviting accusations of threatening the state's territorial sovereignty. The threat of state violence forecloses the possibility of certain types of action, while state power simultaneously produces subjects that both desire and resist certain forms of improvement offered in the name of the gift of development.

Development as Gift

Polarized, dominant narratives about Tibet take the prevalent discourse of development as a gift at face value, that is, they interpret claims about the gift through the ideology of a pure gift. On the one hand, the Chinese state and most of its citizens have interpreted development in Tibet as the delivery of a pure gift: a series of acts of altruism and generosity, bringing benefit and generating positive sentiment. A banner strung across Lhasa's Jiangsu Road in 2006, the year the Qinghai-Tibet Railway opened, proclaimed, "Many Thanks for the Help and Support of the Central Government and the People of the Whole Country!" The granting of massive quantities of aid to Tibet contributed to the Chinese nationalism that burst out following the 2008 riots in Lhasa in a violent rage at the Tibetans' incomprehensible failure to act properly grateful for the generous bestowal of goods. On the other hand, the transnational Tibet movement rejects the idea that development has been a pure gift, and thus that it has been a gift at all. From this perspective, the gift of development is a farce, an easily dismissed notion clearly at odds with the facts. There have been no gifts for Tibet.

I suggest a different approach. Instead of accepting or dismissing the idea of the development gift as a pure gift, I propose taking it much more seriously, as something deserving of critical analysis. Doing so can help illuminate what work development does, and with what effects. This means analyzing the nature of the gift as a double-edged sword: although gifts may appear free and disinterested, they are actually always constraining and interested, entrapping their recipients in a relationship of obligation.

In *The Gift*, his classic work on the subject, Marcel Mauss demonstrated the Janus-faced nature of the gift, a term that in its etymology in Germanic languages means both "present" and "poison."[31] Gifts always establish relationships or bonds, as well as their accompanying obligations to give, receive, and reciprocate.[32] Thus, the act of giving contains within it two opposite movements: it is an act of both generosity and violence, of sharing and of debt. To be given a gift is also to lose some measure of autonomy and freedom.[33]

When gifts cannot be fully reciprocated, they establish, express, or legitimize relationships of power and inequality. The recipient who cannot give back becomes beholden to the donor, creating conditions of lasting asymmetry and dependence.[34] The giving of gifts in asymmetric situations produces what Pierre Bourdieu calls symbolic domination, an unrecognized form of violence that obscures and euphemizes hierarchies and dependence.[35] Because asymmetric giving often involves the allocation of material goods that recipients need or desire, it is an especially effective practice of symbolic domination, one that transforms a donor's status from that of the dominant to the generous. The recipient implicitly acquiesces to the social order that produces the gift; "he or she becomes *grateful*.... It is this active complicity on the part of the recipient that gives the practice of unreciprocated giving its social power."[36]

The development relationship is very clearly one of asymmetry and dependence, but it has not for the most part been the subject of the extensive anthropological literature on the gift, which focuses instead on gift exchange among individuals and social groups.[37] Studies that have considered development through the lens of the gift have generally taken as objects of inquiry foreign aid chains and relationships between states vis-à-vis international aid, rather than development as a national project.[38] In reconceptualizing foreign aid as a practice of symbolic domination that transforms material domination into gestures of gratitude and generosity, Tomohisa Hattori argues that methodologically, "the agency of states can be approached in a similar manner as the agency of individuals ... the state is ontologically 'real.'"[39] It is this assumption, Hattori argues, that allows the application of theories of the gift from anthropology and sociology, based on the study of social relations among individuals and groups, to the state.

Yet, the assumption that states are ontologically real is deeply problematic. Attempts to locate the edges of the state, the boundaries of the state as a coherent and discrete object set cleanly apart from society, inevitably result in ambiguities that reveal the impossibility of the exercise. Instead, the state is an abstraction, not a discrete thing, real in its effects, but lacking presence outside of those effects.[40] Moreover, the notion of a nation-state as a singular stable subject with straightforward motivations is deeply ideological, presupposing homogeneity and fully rational policymaking. This does not mean, however, that we must choose between dismissing the narrative of the gift altogether, or assuming that states are ontologically similar to individuals.

I argue that the implications of development as gift in the state-citizen relationship hinges centrally on the way in which gifts are implicated in identity and recognition. Gift giving is a strategy of seeking to constitute and cultivate the identities of the subjects involved, an intersubjective practice.[41] Both giver and receiver must recognize the gift as a gift, and themselves in their roles as giver and receiver. It is this element of recognition that leads Jacques Derrida to argue that the gift is an impossibility, and that Mauss in fact wrote of everything but the gift. The fundamental aporia of the gift refers to the fact that once recognized as a gift, it is no longer a gift, but an obligation that has to be reciprocated. Derrida writes, "The simple consciousness of the gift right away sends itself back the gratifying image of goodness or generosity, of the giving-being who, knowing itself to be such, recognizes itself in a circular, specular fashion, in a sort of auto-recognition, self-approval, and narcissistic gratitude."[42] To be a true gift, the gift cannot appear to be or signify, either consciously or unconsciously, a gift to the individual or collective subject doing the giving. At the moment this recognition takes place, as it must, the pure gift ceases to exist. This is the case, Derrida argues, even if the gift is refused, because the perception or recognition of a gift has already occurred. The very grammar of the gift positions the giving-being of the (impossible) gift as a subject with an identity as giver. Derrida argues:

> In our logic and our language we say it thus: someone wants or desires, someone intends-to-give something to someone. Already the complexity of the formula appears formidable. It supposes a subject and a verb, a constituted subject ... a subject identical to itself and conscious of its identity, indeed seeking through the gesture of the gift to constitute its own unity and, precisely, to get its own identity recognized so that that identity comes back to it, so that it can reappropriate its identity: as its property.[43]

The development gift is thus a process through which the state as giver comes to be recognized as if it were a concrete entity, a thing, a constituted subject with its own distinct identity. The giving and receipt of development reinforces the state effect, an effect in which a state that lacks ontological presence in and of itself comes to appear as a clearly bounded, unified actor, definitively delineated from the nonstate. It consolidates recognition of the state, asserting a separation between the state, which does the developing through giving, and its populace, the object and recipient of the development gift.[44] Thus, receiving a gift of development becomes an act of recognition by Tibetans of the Chinese state as their state and of PRC territory as a space within which they are bound, that is, a process of state territorialization. This is key to how and why the gift of development for Tibetans becomes both present and poison.

It should be clear that my analysis of development as gift is heuristic, not ethnographic. My concern here is not with the gift as an ontological category for Tibetans or Chinese. Though, as I will show, culturally and historically specific meanings of personhood, value, and labor are crucial for understanding how development is experienced, received, and negotiated, my focus on the gift is not about delineating the cultural constructions of personhood in Tibetan or Chinese society. This is not a comparative work on gift giving, and thus I do not turn to the Chinese literature on the gift, which like the broader literature focuses on intersubjective relations. Instead, as a heuristic, following Bourdieu and Derrida's insights, the concept of development as gift illuminates not only development's ambiguities and contradictions for its recipients, but also how it territorializes Tibet by making the state seem real and thing-like.

The Place of Lhasa in the Tibetan Landscape

Located on the north bank of the middle reaches of the braided Kyichu River, a tributary of the Yarlung Tsangpo (which becomes the Brahmaputra River), Lhasa is situated in a valley at 3,650 meters altitude. Surrounded by mountain ranges to the north and south, the valley is also the site of several hillocks, among them Red Hill, on which sits the Potala Palace, first built by Songtsen Gampo when he moved the capital of the newly consolidated Tibetan Empire to Lhasa. A millennium later, in 1642, the Great Fifth Dalai Lama rebuilt the Potala to become the residence of the Dalai Lamas, and turned Lhasa once again into a seat of government administration. By then, the three great Gelukpa monasteries of Drepung, Sera, and Ganden, surrounding Lhasa, had been centers of religious learning for some two centuries, attracting monks from far-flung regions across Tibet.

The city of Lhasa was long defined by three nested circumambulation circuits: the Nangkor, or inner circuit within the walls of the Jokhang temple; the Barkor, or intermediate circuit, a one-kilometer cobbled path around the Jokhang, lined with shops and stalls that form a lively market and tightly packed residential area; and the Lingkor, the roughly eight-kilometer outer path that encircles the Barkor neighborhood as well as the Potala Palace. By the seventeenth century, the Barkor had become a bustling market for goods from around the world, including glass bottles, copper, coins made in Nepal,

Kashmiri saffron, Persian turquoise, European amber, and coral gathered from the Mediterranean and polished in workshops in Italy.[45] Lhasa, in short, had become a political, religious, economic, and cultural center and would remain so for the next three centuries. Although it was a political capital only of central Tibet, its economic and cultural significance spanned the Tibetan plateau.

Tibetan regions constitute almost one-quarter of the PRC's land area, which helps explain why the demand on the part of the Tibetan government-in-exile for true autonomy for a single administrative region of "Greater Tibet" is viewed as such a threat by the PRC to its territorial sovereignty. Tibetan cultural geography today sees Greater Tibet as comprised of the three provinces of U-Tsang (corresponding very roughly to the present-day Tibet Autonomous Region—TAR), and the northeastern and southeastern regions of Amdo and Kham.[46] From the perspective of PRC political geography, however, Greater Tibet does not exist; the area that corresponds to it is divided into the TAR and parts of the provinces of Qinghai, Sichuan, Yunnan, and Gansu. The TAR, of which Lhasa is the capital, corresponds very roughly to the area under direct control of the Tibetan government in Lhasa in the early twentieth century, but covers slightly less than half of the total area of what has been called ethnographic or cultural Tibet, and is home to less than half of the total Tibetan population within the PRC.

These vast areas that make up cultural Tibet were not politically united for any significant length of time since the demise of the Tibetan Empire in the mid-ninth century, and Tibetan society as a whole was not historically characterized by a strong centralized state.[47] Nevertheless, practices such as long-distance trade and pilgrimage produced a relative coherence to Tibetan cultural identity across this extensive region, including a common literary language, a sense of shared history, aspects of genealogy, myth, religion, and folkloric notions such as the identification of Tibetans as eaters of *tsampa,* the main staple consisting of roasted barley flour.[48] However, a modern national identity emerged only in the twentieth century. This sense of unity has been strengthened both by the situation of exile, and ironically within the PRC by state policies and practices that stress the belonging of Tibetans to the larger Chinese nation-state while simultaneously recognizing all Tibetans as sharing the same "nationality" as *Zang zu* (Tib.: *pörik*; Wylie: *bod rigs*). These dynamics of ethnic governance within the PRC, including the invention and recognition of *minzu* and calls for the unity of the nationalities, more than any primordial national identity, are reflected in lyrics of popular contemporary songs such as Kham singer Kunga's popular "Lhasa Bar" which, sung in Chinese with a Tibetan chorus, links the malaise of contemporary Lhasa with a broader Tibetan identity:

> In Lhasa's bars
> There are all kinds of people.

The only one missing is the one I love.
She told me
That she doesn't love me
Because I have no money....
Because I am a big drunk....
Because I am a drifter singer.
Tibetan chorus: We are all Tibetan brothers
We are all Tibetan brothers
We are all Tibetan brothers....

Lhasa is not representative of a singular, reified Tibetan culture. Instead, its importance lies in its privileged position in the imagined geography of the Tibetan nation and its place as a powerful symbol of Tibetan cultural identity. Recognition of these symbolic valences has also made Lhasa the site of the most intense application of state policies aimed at enforcing "harmony" and quelling dissent. This provides a diagnosis of broader patterns of state power that have, since the unrest of 2008, become more visible in their application across cultural Tibet.

In addition, Lhasa's significance lies in its role as the administrative center of the TAR, and historically as the seat of the Tibetan government. As such, Lhasa was home before the 1950s to a small group of between 150 and 200 aristocratic households, who held one or more estates and from whose ranks lay government officials were recruited. From the mid-eighteenth until the mid-twentieth century, most land in central Tibet was organized into estates, held variously by these aristocratic families, by the government in Lhasa, and by monasteries and incarnate lamas.[49] Politically, central Tibet was divided into districts, each of which was governed by one lay and one monastic district commissioner appointed by the Tibetan government. Villages near Lhasa were under the control of the *Zhölpa Lekung*, a government office that managed eighteen districts and estates.

The commoners who formed the majority of the agricultural population of Central Tibet were known as *mi ser*, and were further divided into taxpayer households and "small households."[50] Taxpayers had their own plots of agricultural land, which were hereditarily maintained and over which they held all rights except for the right of disposal. These plots were called "tax basis" land, because it was on their basis that taxpayers paid taxes in labor and grain, to the estate lord, and to the government in Lhasa. Taxpayers could not be evicted if they fulfilled these obligations, but neither could they leave their land permanently. Many leased their plots to "small households" and had servants of their own.

"Small households," by contrast, had neither land nor tax obligations associated with landholding. Constituting about two-thirds of the Tibetan population by the early twentieth century, many landless families had been taxpayers in the recent past or in previous generations, but relinquished the status after being unable to fulfill tax obligations. Small households included those who made yearly payments to their lords in exchange for release from labor requirements, allowing their members to move around to other estates and sell their labor for wages; those assigned to work for taxpayer families in return for a small daily wage; and those given small, noninheritable plots of land on an estate in exchange for cultivating the lord's demesne fields. Finally, there were also various kinds of servants, who did not own land, but were provided with food and clothing in return for their labor.[51] Whether because of inability to pay taxes, exorbitant labor demands, or other reasons, *mi ser* sometimes ran away from their lords. Because Tibet was characterized by labor shortage and a surplus of uncultivated land, flight was a relatively easy option. By the early twentieth century the number of runaways had reached significant proportions, and as we will see, many of the earliest workers on Lhasa's July First and August First State Farms in the 1950s were runaways from small households.[52]

The incoming Chinese Communist Party (CCP) interpreted this system of social organization as a brutal, feudal one, from which Tibetans needed and deserved liberation. The PLA defeated the Tibetan army in Chamdo in 1950, leading to the signing of the Seventeen Point Agreement (referred to as Tibet's "peaceful liberation") in 1951, which officially recognized Chinese sovereignty over Tibet in exchange for a series of conditions including a promise not to alter the political system of central Tibet. Later the same year, the PLA marched into Lhasa. What followed was an uneasy period of attempted cooperation between the CCP, which tried to negotiate with the traditional aristocratic ruling class, and the Tibetan government. This early period of incorporation in which the basic governing system was not supposed to change, described in detail in chapter 2, came to an end after the March 10, 1959 uprising that led to the exile of the Fourteenth Dalai Lama and some eighty thousand Tibetans. The Dalai Lama subsequently repudiated the Seventeen Point Agreement and the Chinese government also negated its conditions, embarking quickly on full-scale reform including the expropriation of land from monasteries, the aristocracy, and the Tibetan government, and its redistribution to the *mi ser*. Those who did not flee were assigned new class labels to create new identities as socialist subjects of the PRC, and as described in chapter 2, collectivization and communization quickly followed.

A new administrative geography was overlaid on the Tibetan landscape previously conceptualized as the impaled demoness, and in Lhasa, the three nested circumambulation circuits. In 1965, the Preparatory Committee for the Autonomous Region of Tibet became the Tibet

Autonomous Region, which was divided into six prefectures and Lhasa Municipality, a prefectural-level city covering almost thirty thousand square kilometers (see map 1). Within Lhasa Municipality are seven counties and the Lhasa *Chengguanqu*, or "Metropolitan District," a county-level administrative unit that encompasses both the actual built-up area of Lhasa as well as four rural townships: Ngachen (Ch.: Najin), Tsalgungtang (Caigongtang), Dogde (Duodi) and Nyangre (Nyiangra) (see map 2).[53]

The term "Lhasa" thus has three distinct, nested spatial referents: a prefectural-level municipality (Ch.: *Shi*), a county-level *Chengguanqu* that includes rural townships, and the actual urbanized area. The latter is the only one that does not exist as an administrative entity, but is the one imagined by Tibetans and Han alike when they use the term "Lhasa" on its own. It is the one that peri-urban Tibetan farmers who are administratively part of the Lhasa *Chengguanqu* refer to when they speak of the city of Lhasa spoiling their children. Thus, it is also what I mean when I use the term "Lhasa" by itself.[54] This area, too, has changed over time. Through the late 1950s, the thirty-thousand-some residents of urbanized Lhasa could be found mainly in a three-square-kilometer area of densely packed alleyways branching off from the Barkor path; the Potala and the village of Zhöl below it, now downtown Lhasa, were considered separate from the city. Today, the built-up area of the city is rapidly expanding in the production of a new landscape of development discussed in part 3.

Whereas Lhasa was for centuries a political, economic and cultural center, it has today become—despite its rapid urbanization—a periphery, a backwater, a place of little economic importance and no political power in China, one with "a very, very long way to go," as the *People's Daily* puts it.[55] The ongoing project of PRC state incorporation through development has transformed Lhasa from a Tibetan center into a Chinese periphery: Tibet's territorialization has been simultaneously a process of peripheralization and marginalization. Peripheries do not simply exist, but rather are produced and reproduced as components of state-building projects. The ever-backward status of Tibet as a place in need of continual development is co-constitutive of state formation. Because development efforts in Tibet work to reproduce marginality, Tibet is a particularly useful place from which to study Chinese state formation, for as Das and Poole have put it, "margins are a necessary entailment of the state, much as the exception is a necessary component of the rule."[56] Margins are simultaneously spaces of exclusion and inclusion, of being both inside and outside.[57] This topological character of inclusion by exclusion and exclusion by inclusion characterizes the differential treatment of Tibetan citizens, as well as the processes of working on the state farms, renting land to migrants for vegetable cultivation, and urbanization.

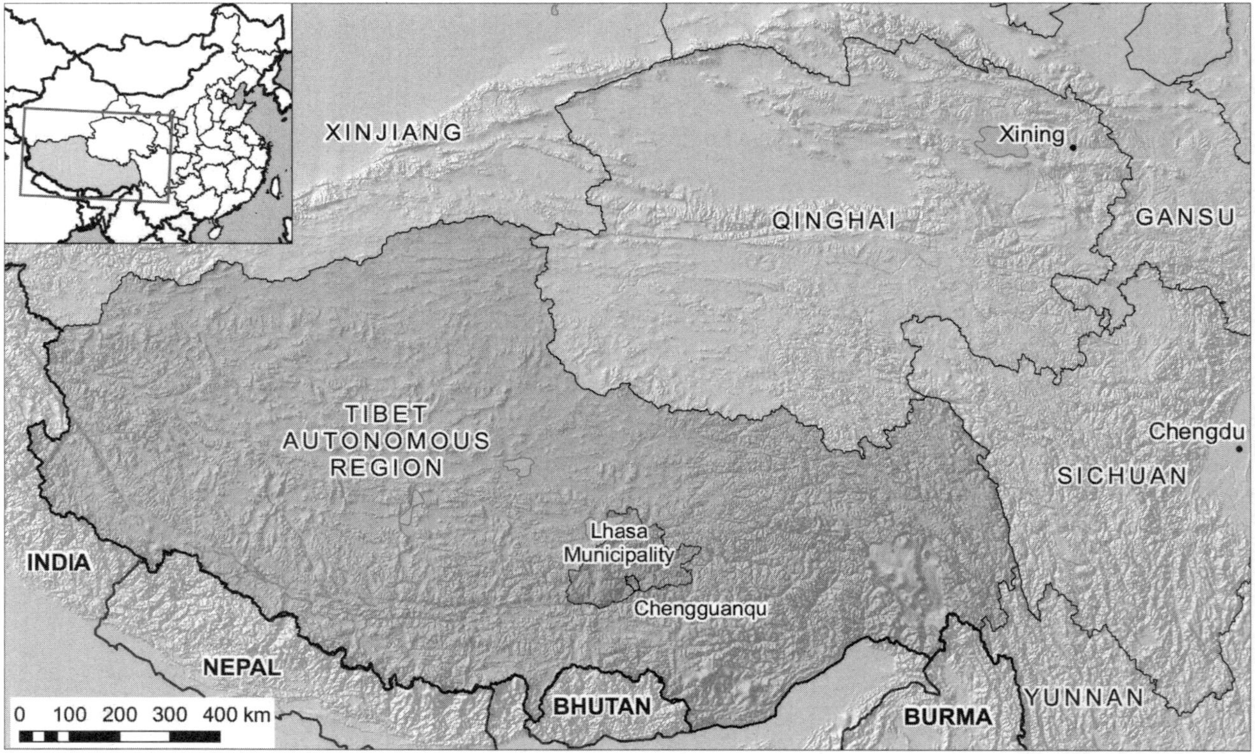

Map 1. Tibet Autonomous Region, with surrounding territories, Lhasa Municipality, and position within the People's Republic of China. Map by Mark Henderson.

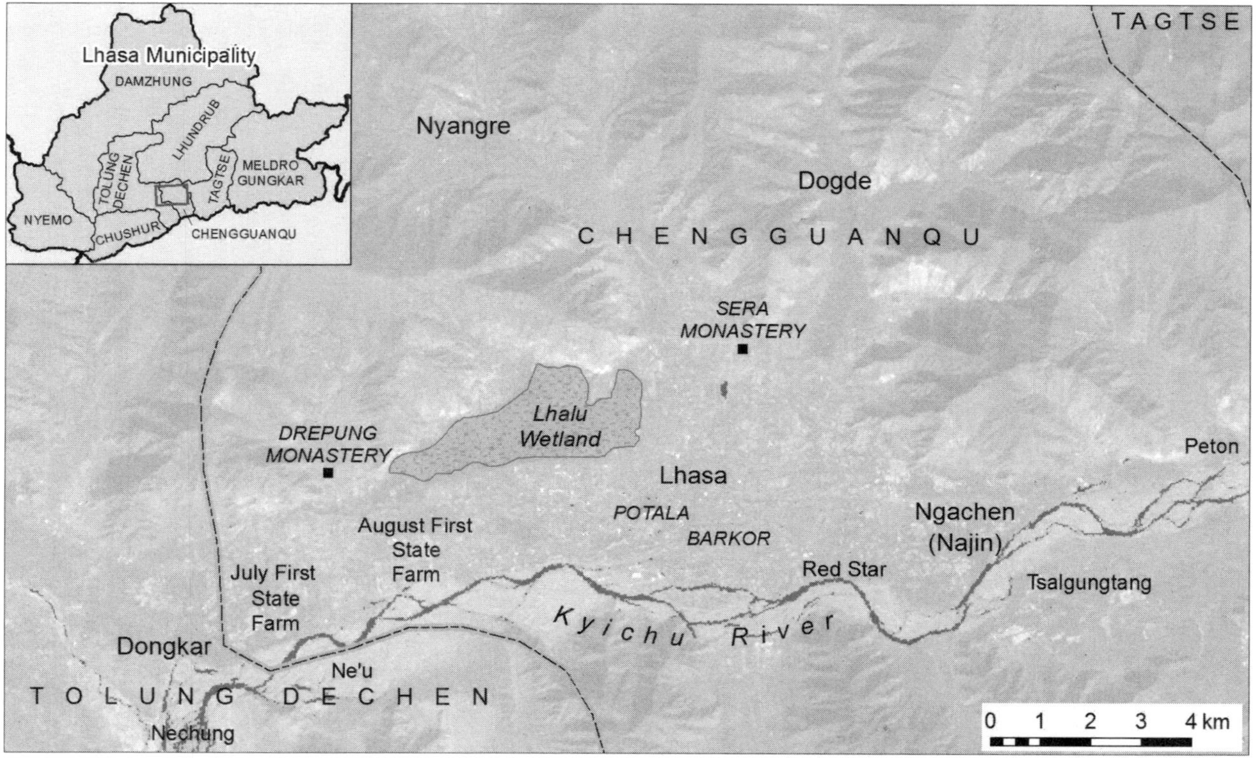

Map 2. Lhasa *Chengguanqu* and Lhasa Municipality. Map by Mark Henderson.

Plan of the Book

Chapter 1 examines the dramatic difference between embodied Tibetan spatial practices and the production of state space. In so doing, it explores the more coercive forms of disciplinary and sovereign power that condition the experience of everyday life in Lhasa and shape the politics of the possible. Particular spatial techniques, such as the freezing and circulation of mobility, work together with the gift of development to reify the state. Key disciplinary techniques rely on a pervasive inculcation of an internalized politics of fear and its twin, a fear of politics, while sovereign power differentially targets Tibetans, placing them in a permanent state of emergency. This strongly conditions the way in which Han migrants and local Tibetans can maneuver within the shifting political economy of development.

The three parts of the book correspond to the three major landscape transformations. Part 1, "Soil," focuses on grain and vegetable agriculture in the crucial period of the 1950s when the PRC first asserted and established control over Tibet and imposed a new socialist vision of the proper relationship between people and nature. In particular, the state farms are discussed as key sites of state territorialization in the 1950s, demonstrating how nature was enrolled into the process of state formation, and exploring why in these farms' early stages Tibetan female workers voluntarily joined the state farms, helping the process of state territorialization.

Part 2, "Plastic," turns to the production of the Lhasa landscape after decollectivization, when liberation was superseded by development, and high socialism was replaced by a selective neoliberal ideology of free movement of goods and people, enabling Han migrants to move into Lhasa and grow vegetables in plastic greenhouses. Chapter 3 is concerned with the Han migrants who have come to dominate visible economic activities in Lhasa, making it "little Sichuan." Since the early 1990s, official development discourse in the TAR has welcomed migrants with open arms as vectors of development, bearers of "quality," or *suzhi,* that they bring to the benefit of Tibet. As a result, these Han migrants are positioned to be the major beneficiaries of the massive development subsidies that flow into the TAR, yet they themselves are resentful at what they see as the state's unfair allocation of resources to Tibet.

The following chapter shifts the focus to local Tibetans and their interactions with migrants over the land that they sublease for vegetable cultivation. It shows how Tibetan nonparticipation in vegetable farming is overdetermined by political economy, cultural politics and social-spatial relations. Chapter 5 then considers the cultural politics of development with an ethnographic account of two pervasive idioms through which development is experienced, contested, and negotiated: the tropes of indolence and of being spoiled. The argument of the previous chapter continues, demonstrating that such idioms are not "merely cultural," but rather are mutually constitutive of the political economy of development. The macro and micro political economy of development shapes the cultural idioms through which development is understood, and these in turn constrain and shape the possibilities for future maneuver.

Part 3, "Concrete," turns to the production of new urban and built landscapes in the first decade of the twenty-first century as deepening processes of state territorialization. Chapter 6 explores Lhasa's urbanization, setting it within a larger shift across China since economic reform, in which the urban has come to be valorized as the privileged site of progress and development. Tracing the paving over of former vegetable-cultivating villages with the outward expansion of the city, I examine the building of new luxury houses for the middle class as well as the expropriation of farmland from villagers in a process of accumulation by dispossession. I argue that urbanization is not only a technical matter of construction and the increased density of people and buildings, but also the imposition of a new grid of legibility and territorial ordering of space.

The final chapter turns to the Comfortable Housing Project, a gargantuan development program in the form of house building across the rural Tibetan landscape. The spectacular nature of this wave of new rural construction is exemplary of the importance of the visual image in development in Tibet. The building of new houses is conceptualized as a gift and as a "breakthrough point," foundational to changing residents' "ways of thinking," which will in turn motivate them to become proper self-developing subjects. The reactions of villagers in Lhasa Municipality to the house-building project have been contradictory and ambiguous. As they take on debt to build new houses, the project binds Tibetans more deeply into a relationship with the state and thus furthers the project of territorialization.

A Celebration

Late one night in the summer of 2001, I arrived in Lhasa, grimy and enervated after the fifty-six-hour bus ride from Xining, Qinghai. After a few months away, this was to be the beginning of a three-month stay to continue my fieldwork. Things had already gone awry. My promised research permission had been pulled abruptly a few days before I left home for China, a situation that was resolved eventually only through creative finagling. In the interim, I waited anxiously.

My anxiety was greatly heightened by the anxiety of Lhasa residents at the time. Soon after I arrived I began to hear rumors about a massive celebration that would happen at some undetermined time in the near future. May 23, 2001 marked the fiftieth anniversary of the signing in Beijing of the Seventeen Point Agreement, officially the "Agreement of the Central People's Government and the Local Government of Tibet on Measures for the Peaceful Liberation of Tibet," which acknowledged PRC sovereignty over Tibet. July 1, 2001, was the eightieth anniversary of the founding of the Chinese Communist Party. Although both anniversaries had passed by the time I arrived in Lhasa, neither had yet been celebrated. I learned that both would be commemorated simultaneously in a grand celebration on an unannounced day "sometime soon," with prominent guests including CCP General Secretary and PRC President Hu Jintao, who had presided over the imposition of martial law in Lhasa in 1989, during his tenure as TAR party secretary from 1988 to 1992. The uncertainty over when the celebrations might occur fueled a crackling tension and slowed down the passage of hours and days, holding life in suspension. Tibetan friends counseled me to leave Lhasa and return only after the celebrations were over. "This is not a good time," they said, "things are very tight right now." One friend apologized for not warning me not to come when she heard about the celebrations, but said she had been too nervous to send an email even mentioning the subject.

Although only a handful of top leaders knew when the celebration was to be held, there were clues that the time was approaching. State memory work geared up and went into overdrive. Soon there was not a single pair of lampposts along Lhasa's outer ring road that had escaped having a banner emblazoned with a political slogan, or a string of miniature flags commemorating the fiftieth anniversary, stretched across it. All shops, public buildings and restaurants were also given commemorative flags, and urban residents were given Chinese flags to fly on their rooftops. In one work unit, all staff members were assigned to work in pairs on two-hour security shifts until the celebrations were over. They were to report all suspicious activities. When not on shift, they had mandatory sessions to practice singing patriotic Chinese songs.

At the same time, tourism was severely curtailed and the visibility of the state security apparatus increased dramatically. Regular and plainclothes police appeared at all intersections, and the police made surprise visits to apartment buildings under the control of neighborhood committees to check that all Tibetans had Lhasa residence permits. Those who did not were temporarily cleared out of the city, along with beggars and pilgrims. Tibetans were to carry their national identification cards with them at all times. Local officials held meetings to warn urban residents that any breach of conduct would result in imprisonment with no questions asked and no appeals heard until after the celebrations were over. Some were warned that they might face arrest if they ventured out at night at all during the celebration period. They were not, however, informed of when that might be.

The fact that the day of the celebration was a secret was the subject of much talk. I heard repeatedly that "even some of the top TAR leaders don't know when it's going to be!" According to one college professor, "you see, the Chinese leaders are afraid of the Tibetans." Others asked, "Whose celebration is this anyway?" Still others surmised that the day was not going to be announced out of the fear that someone might set off a bomb during the celebration.

During the build-up period, a huge viewing podium for the visitors was built directly below the Potala Palace, the imposing thousand-room, thirteen-story palace rising out of Red Hill that had been the home of the Dalai Lamas and the seat of the Tibetan government. The visual supremacy of the Potala Palace, the highest structure in Lhasa, was to be challenged after the celebration in 2001 when Hu Jintao laid the foundation stone for a thirty-seven-meter monument directly across from the Potala to commemorate the fiftieth anniversary and celebrate national unity. The podium faced Potala Square, which had been built in 1995, after the relocation of much of the historic Zhöl neighborhood, to celebrate the thirtieth anniversary of the founding of the TAR. Like Beijing's Tiananmen Square, this monumental space was designed for grand ceremonies and parades such as the celebration to be held soon, spectacular events whose message is performed through the arrangement of extravagant numbers of bodies in space more than through the content of the speeches given.

The viewing podium for visiting dignitaries embodied the contradictions of state power, while also condensing and producing the concreteness of the state's existence. Some residents claimed that underground tunnels had been dug from the viewing podium to a safe area inside the Potala, to which the dignitaries could quickly escape "in case anything happens." At the same time as such rumored elaborate precautions betrayed the nervousness of the state and its effects on its citizens, the podium became a clear visual manifestation of state power. Hundreds of Tibetan pilgrims and (mostly elderly) residents of Lhasa and nearby villages circumambulate the Potala every day, spinning prayer wheels in one hand and counting prayer beads in the other, or prostrating themselves along the entire length of the route. The spot directly in front of the center of the Potala's façade is an important site where circumambulators frequently stop to perform prostrations toward the palace. This was precisely the spot at which the viewing podium was built. From their vantage point, the pilgrims could not see the Potala at all, only the several-story-high podium. This created the striking image over the next few months of pilgrims prostrating themselves to the garish viewing podium itself.

In the meantime, between work unit patrols, singing practice, and riot police with water cannons and soldiers with machine guns riding atop armored vehicles, everyday activities ground to a halt. Everyone I knew gave me the same advice: avoid gatherings of people. In fact, just stay home now and don't venture out until it's over. A mahjong-loving retired worker in his early forties advised:

> I'm just going to stay home all day, for five days, for a week, for however long they're going to celebrate. I say, "you do your thing. I'm just going to sit home and watch TV. I'm not even going to leave the house! Then you can't accuse me of doing anything at all." That's right. I'm just going to stay right here at home and watch television the entire time.

To avoid state surveillance and the ever-present possibility of being accused of a political crime, he immobilized himself, confining himself within the space of his home. Not wanting to jeopardize my research, I too participated in the same self-disciplinary practices by not venturing out of my residence for almost a week.

During the day of the actual celebration, selected representatives from work units and nearby villages performed songs and dances for the visiting officials from Beijing. For all other Tibetans in Lhasa, this period was one of enforced idleness, exhortations to economic productivity notwithstanding. Not only did normal work activities grind to a halt, but because no one knew when the celebration would be, it was also impossible to plan ahead. Several main thoroughfares were blocked, making navigation around the city difficult, and the knowledge and visible evidence of heightened security and identification checks further encouraged self-surveillance. Most Tibetans confined themselves to their homes. The city was partitioned into spaces that were sanctioned and spaces that were not; at night, the allowable space was reduced to one's home.

1 State Space

Power, Fear, and the State of Exception

> And of course it is the State which declares the state of siege and therewith ensures Leviathan's special effects, the fetish-power of the State-idea where the arbitrariness of power butts the legitimation of authority, where reason and violence do their little duet. "The tradition of the oppressed," [Walter Benjamin] wrote at the end of the 1930s, "teaches us that the 'state of emergency' in which we live is not the exception but the rule". . . our notions . . . of certainty . . . now appear as a state of sieged dream-images, hopelessly hopeful illusions of the intellect searching for peace in the world whose tensed mobility allows of no rest in the nervousness of the Nervous System's system.
>
> —Michael Taussig, *The Nervous System*, 1992

In late January 2001, I traveled to Shigatse, the second largest city in the TAR, for the local New Year (Tsang Losar), celebrated a month earlier than Tibetan New Year in Lhasa. My friend and I failed to awaken early enough to join the majority of pilgrims on their predawn trek to the summit of Drolma Ri, the main peak overlooking Shigatse, and back down to the lower part of the hill; perched on its summit are the ruins of a fort, which according to local legend looked like a distorted Potala Palace because its copied design had been carved on a radish that shrank on the journey home. By the time we started our climb, a long sinuous line of thousands of pilgrims was already working its way down a narrow path from the summit, where the pilgrims had burnt juniper incense, and made offerings of tsampa and tea leaves, also called chömar. They had also planted new prayer flags on the summit, to replace those from the year before.

We passed by a young man, baseball cap on backward and sporting sunglasses, blue jeans, and a long black trenchcoat, with a two-pouch tsampa and incense holder slung over his shoulder. Like the many other young men and women we saw, he was covered in the white tsampa that all were throwing at each other. We came upon several circles of men and women picnicking and enjoying thermoses of yak-butter tea and green plastic jugs of home-brewed chang, near the saddle of the lower hill. Right on the saddle were several cairns, incense burners, and prayer flags. From there we watched lines of five to ten Tibetans—often strangers, sometimes mixed groups of men and women, others all men or all women—form spontaneously by the cairns, facing the ruins of the fort. Everyone dipped into their tsampa pouches with their right hands, and soon, on some cue I could not detect, the line of propitiators raised their right arms in unison. Their arms swung upward as the celebrants shouted "kyi kyi so so!," letting just a bit of tsampa fly up into the air at the top of the trajectory and the end of the phrase.[1] *Then they lowered their arms and raised them three more times while calling " lha gyal lo! lha gyal lo! lha gyal lo!"—"Victory to the gods!" At the very last syllable, the entire line of propitiators simultaneously threw their tsampa into the air. The mood was festive and light, men exercising their vocal cords in the brisk air with jubiliant, cacaphonous shouts of "Gyi hee hee!" and all present throwing tsampa into the air, toward the gods and at each other.*

Pilgrims on their way to and from the fort also stopped momentarily on the path to trade tsampa with strangers traveling in the opposite direction. One opens his tsampa bag in offering. The person who happens to be crossing in the other direction at this very moment takes a small pinch of tsampa from the other's pouch, puts a pinch in her mouth, and then three times tosses the rest over her shoulder, or to the side in a circular motion, signifying the three Precious Jewels, the Buddha, Dharma, and Sangha. She then takes another pinch of the offerer's tsampa and smears it on his right shoulder, a way of wishing that person good fortune. As I was heading down the mountain a few hours later, three young men, completely covered with tsampa, came running past me. One saw my pouch, stopped short, and asked me politely, "Miss, please give me a bit of chömar." I opened my pouch, he took a handful and threw it at his friends. A few seconds later a young girl of perhaps ten or twelve approached me and very politely asked the same thing. Again, I opened the pouch, she took a handful, and then launched the flour mixture into my face. Everyone around us burst into good-natured laughter, leaving me feeling foolish but happy to participate in the day's festivities.

The most prominent religious practices in which, until very recently, virtually all Tibetans have participated at some point in their lives, circumambulation and pilgrimage, connect persons and places by the physical as well as metaphysical relationship formed between participants and the landscape. As such, circumambulation and pilgrimage are also ubiquitous Tibetan forms of place making. Indeed the Tibetan term for pilgrimage, *nèkor* (Wylie: *gnas skor*), contains within it the term for "place" (*gnas*), understood as both a physical place and the residence of powerful deities in or of that place.

Michel de Certeau has argued that "footsteps weave places together"[2]—that place making is a deeply embodied process of bodies moving through space, as bodies are always emplaced rather than free-floating. The walking of many circumambulation routes is hard physical work, and the physical connection between person and place that is forged in pilgrimage is highlighted by the fact that the most meritorious way of performing circumambulation is to prostrate oneself the entire length of the route, so that one's whole body touches every inch of the ground along the way. The relationship between the body and physical landscape is created not just by seeing and touching the landscape, but also by positioning the body in relation to the place, by vocalizing and listening, as the vignette above describes, and by collecting and sometimes consuming substances from a place.[3]

In addition to creating a relationship between bodies and the landscape, pilgrimage and circumambulation are also key sites for the reproduction of Tibetan sociality. The practices not only bring families, friends, and villagers closer together in a day of fun and entertainment, but also bring Tibetans into direct social contact with others who dwell far away, forming new social relations that stretch across wide geographical expanses and deepening bonds of loyalty in old ones. Dharma companions (*chö trog*), strangers from sometimes far-flung places, whom one may meet and befriend on an important and arduous pilgrimage, form lifelong bonds and become friends for life. Thus, pilgrimage and circumambulation create broader senses of home and place. Indeed, as a ubiquitous social-spatial practice, pilgrimage historically created a sense of a common Tibetan identity across the vast Tibetan plateau, in the absence of a strong centralized state.[4]

Today, circumambulation continues to be essential to the ongoing reproduction and cohesiveness of Tibetan communities at multiple sociospatial scales. Spaces of circumambulation are specifically Tibetan places: the circumambulation route from Pabongka to Dogde on the Dharma Wheel Festival is one of the rare public space-times in or near Lhasa in which basically only Tibetan is spoken. In addition to the merit gathered, such occasions are also opportunities for catching up on gossip and family news, and conducting trade and business.[5] They are also, quite simply, lots of fun. Picnics follow circumambulation, with food, sweet and butter tea, *chang*, and conversation leisurely shared among friends, relatives, villagers, and strangers. Indeed the explicit religious, merit-making meanings of these practices often seem subordinated to their social roles, and Lhasa residents joke about the old grannies who faithfully circumambulate the Lingkor every morning before dawn, turning their prayer wheels with one hand, counting prayer beads in the other, and gossiping the entire time.

Up through the 1950s, Lhasa residents' spatial practices were marked strongly by their bodily movements along the three nested circumambulation routes of the Nangkor, Barkor, and Lingkor, and by other embodied practices such as the viewing and visiting of the gargantuan *thangka* (Tibetan Buddhist scroll painting) at Ganden Monastery on the fifteenth day of the sixth Tibetan month, making offerings at the unveiling of the great *thangkas* at Drepung and Sera Monasteries during the summer Yoghurt Festival, or the traverse of mountain ridges between the Nyangre and Dogde valleys on the Dharma Wheel Festival. These and farther-flung pilgrimages to and circumambulations around the temples with which Buddhism tamed the Tibetan landscape by pinning down the supine demoness continue to be crucial spatial practices today. However, since the 1950s, they have been circumscribed as the state seizes space. During the Maoist period these practices were largely banned. The 1980s saw a revival of religious practice, including those of pilgrimage and circumambulation, but the movement of Tibetan bodies in particular patterns through space has been once more greatly curtailed at times since then, most notably after 2008 when the state's control over space corresponded with the increasing normality of a state of exception in Tibet.

This chapter explores space as the "privileged instrument," the open secret of the production of state power.[6] Analyzing how state power has been produced through the control over space since the 1950s sets the stage for the discussion of territorialization through material transformations of the landscape in the rest of this book. As Henri Lefebvre has suggested, the production of state space is a production of territory. Territory enables state action, and state action produces territory. While the modern state attempts to "pulverize" space into an abstract grid, social forces attempt to defend, create, and reproduce spaces of everyday life and social reproduction, for example through practices of circumambulation and pilgrimage.[7]

The State Effect and Modes of Power

The state, sociologist Philip Abrams demonstrated decades ago, "is not the reality which stands behind the mask of political practice. It is itself the mask which prevents our seeing political practice as it is."[8] As a social fact and a structural effect, however, the state is exceedingly powerful and a compelling object of analysis. Throughout this book, I use the term "the state" to refer to this effect and the way it is experienced. Here I explore ethnographically how it has come to be manufactured and imagined in post-1950s Lhasa as a translocal and almost transcendental entity through specific spatial practices and arrangements. I examine the production of state power through control over space: the everyday techniques, practices, and arrangements through which the state becomes reified, appearing coherent, unified, and autonomous from society.

Key to state reification is what Michel Foucault called disciplinary power or disciplines, microphysical methods of order that generate power out of "the meticulous organization of space, movement, sequence and position . . . complex hierarchies of command, spatial arrangement and surveillance."[9] The command of space, characterized by a Cartesian attitude, a view of space as an abstract grid, is central to the production of state power and the state effect. In Lhasa, the spatiality of the state is characterized by control over mobility, strict regulation of movement, and the arbitrary freezing and releasing of the circulation of citizens through the city. Michel de Certeau characterized actions that originate from such command over space as strategies, in opposition to tactics, which are arts of the weak that take advantage of opportunities. The analytical distinction between a strategy, a characteristic of state space, and a tactic does not mean that subalterns are incapable of "strategizing" in the sense of planning or thinking logically about courses of action, but rather that the terrain on which action occurs has been organized and set out in advance.[10]

Another key process in the production of the state effect is the employment of practices of visibility, or what de Certeau calls the "mastery of places through sight." Disciplinary power, generated in part by surveillance and self-surveillance, is characterized by the principle of vision. Architecturally, its apotheosis is Bentham's Panopticon, which induces a state of permanent visibility that makes power and surveillance permanent in their effects. Surveillance is internalized, so that the effect of surveillance remains even during moments when there is no actual external conduct of surveillance. As a result, the Panopticon becomes "a machine for creating and sustaining power relations independent of the person that exercises it . . . [so] that the inmates should be caught up in a power situation of which they themselves are the bearers."[11]

The disciplinary practices and arrangements of control over space and the principles of visibility traced here include elements that are common across China's territory, and indeed to statist techniques of government more generally. However, they are employed to an exceptional degree and through exceptional means in the Tibet Autonomous Region. The mantra that Tibetan residents of the TAR repeat in reference to the political conditions that shape their lives is "Tibet is special." Indeed, as I will demonstrate, the TAR, and increasingly also the Tibetan areas of Qinghai, Sichuan, Yunnan, and Gansu provinces, are zones of exception, where laws apply through their suspension. This is the case not just when martial law has formally been declared, but also during times when state officials insist that all is normal.

In his prominent theorizations of sovereign power, philosopher Giorgio Agamben argues that the once-extraordinary state of exception has become a paradigm for contemporary government, whether democratic or authoritarian. The state of exception is a condition in which law and violence, as well as biological and political life become indistinguishable. The state's violent response to the 2008 protests across Tibet is testament to the ever-present possibility of being reduced to bare life, of being abandoned by the law and killed without it being considered a homicide or celebrated as a divine sacrifice. Agamben provides us with a way of thinking about this increasingly permanent state of emergency in which the sovereign assertion of the exception becomes the rule.[12]

However, Agamben's project is an ontological rather than a geographical or historical one. His assertion that "we are all virtually *homines sacri*" now marks a lack of concern with the embodiment of difference and the specific geographies of exceptionalism that make certain groups reducible to bare life. As feminist and other critical human geographers have pointed out, this approach not only ignores biological constructions of difference and their connections to citizenship, but also elides the uneven production of space. Yet exceptions and states of emergency, even as they become the rule in the contemporary world, are always applied differentially, not uniformly. Exceptionality is embodied and emplaced, not free-floating and placeless.[13] As a specifically marked subset of citizens of the PRC in a contested national space, Tibetans in the TAR are made exceptional in their relationship with the law, by the spatial practices, discourses, and techniques through which the state gains form.

In Lhasa, these practices include not only rules of spatial partitioning, segmentation, and registration, and controls on mobility but also the heightened visibility of the state's capacity for violence, displayed through the more than dozen military and paramilitary garrisons sitting within the urbanized core of the city. Just across the Kyichu River, Pumburi Hill is a popular and frequent destination for Lhasa residents to burn incense and hang prayer flags on auspicious days; on the hike up, it is hard to avoid seeing the army compound directly to the west, with its lines of cannons pointing directly at the city. Military convoys of trucks carrying troops, fuel, and equipment are a common sight, as are nightly patrols by armored jeeps with flashing lights. These reminders of sovereign power are everyday parts of the Lhasa landscape even in "normal" times, so that, as Walter Benjamin also suggested, the state of emergency is no longer the exception but the rule.

These signs of the potential for violence inspire fear—of employment loss, brutal treatment, detention, and incarceration both for oneself and one's family members—an affective state that provokes self-policing. Self-surveillance and policing in turn intensify the experience of the state as an external, unified object. Above all what is feared is being marked as having a "political problem," of being guilty of splittism. To have a "political problem" is to be relegated to a state of abandonment, a condition in which, Agamben writes, one "is not, in fact, simply set outside the law and made indifferent to it but rather *abandoned* by it, that is, exposed and threatened on the threshold in which life and law, outside and inside, become indistinguishable."[14]

There is no clear line between what is "political" and what is not; the boundary between the two is a zone of indistinction. This results in what I call a fear of politics and a politics of fear that characterize the spatiality of the state in Lhasa. Efforts to avoid anything that might risk being construed as "political," to stay clear of the wide margins and murky borders of that zone of indistinction, produce self-surveilling subjects and the effect of a state that is everywhere listening and watching for infractions of its arbitrary rules.

Spatial Circumscription

Every political anniversary, whether of the "peaceful liberation" or of the founding of the PRC, TAR, or CCP, is occasion for an official celebration and thus for control of public movement through space, to ward off the possibility that citizens might disrupt the planned celebratory spectacles, diminishing the lessons of the state's awe, might, and splendor that they are designed to instill. The circulation of bodies through space is arrested not only during political anniversaries that reinforce narratives of state legitimacy, but also during non-anniversaries, that is anniversaries of protests or other oppositional moments. Such dates are occasions for what become simultaneously an enforced forgetting and a vivid reminder of the event. Concerned about the possibility of citizens commemorating such days of dissent, officials impose heavy security and restrictions on mobility. The reminder of the putative nonevent ironically reveals the nervousness of state power.

In the TAR, the most important non-anniversary has long been the date of the March 10, 1959 uprising in Lhasa that led to the exile of the Dalai Lama and about eighty thousand Tibetans. Starting long before the 2008 unrest, which in Lhasa began on March 10 when monks walked from Drepung Monastery to the city center to demand the release of monks previously detained for celebrating the award of the U.S. Congressional Gold Medal to the Dalai Lama, early March was a period of visibly heightened security and immobility. In the winter of 2008–9, teachers in Lhasa were ordered to report back from their long winter holidays by March 1 even though classes would not start for another week, because all travel into Lhasa might be blocked in anticipation of the anniversary.

The space-time of the state is marked by another round of restrictions in early October, given both China's National Day and the anniversaries of three 1987 demonstrations that sparked a wave of more than one hundred protests between then and 1989, when martial law was imposed in Lhasa. In 2009, TAR residents, like all PRC citizens, had eight days off for the combination of Mid-Autumn Festival and National Day, one of the "Golden Week" holidays declared in 2000 to boost the domestic tourism market and leisure culture, and to allow people to make long-distance family visits. In the TAR, though, work unit employees were not allowed to travel or host visitors from elsewhere during the holiday. Security guards were posted around the clock at each work unit gate and stricter ID checks were imposed.

While the summer months tend to be more relaxed than March and October, they too are punctuated by periodic restrictions, including the May anniversary of the 1951 "peaceful liberation" and the September founding of the TAR. Like the celebrations of the former in 2001, the thirtieth anniversary of the latter in 1995 was marked by a grand spectacle of disciplinary power, meticulously managed and involving the painstakingly detailed organization of space, movement, and position. At a Barkor Neighborhood Committee meeting in preparation for the upcoming celebration, residents were instructed:[15]

> The 30th anniversary is an auspicious day. Those with political problems can't attend [the gathering]. . . . Hundreds of thousands will be there, so we can't wander around at will. Drink a little less tea in the morning [of the ceremony]. The exact situation is not yet clear. You might have to go to the bathroom, but find you have to wait in line, or you may not be able to find one at all. If you need to go and they won't let you, an argument could start. But quarreling there is a political problem. . . . We are requested to wear Tibetan dress. Wear your newest and best. If anyone deliberately wears patched clothes that day, it'll be a political problem. It'll be difficult for the person concerned.

These sartorial concerns and careful advice to regulate participants' bodily functions constitute a form of disciplinary power targeted at the micro-organization of individual bodies, suggesting the importance of attention to the scale of the body in revealing dimensions of state power.[16]

Also punctuating the summer months are other enforced nonevents, as well as religious holidays that have been increasingly marked by restrictions on mobility. One is *Trunglha Yarsol*, the celebration of the Dalai Lama's July 6 birthday. In the 1980s and again in the mid-1990s, Tibetans gathered at a traditional site in Trunglha village along the banks of the Kyichu River, then just east of the urbanized downtown area, to celebrate *Trunglha Yarsol* by burning incense and throwing *tsampa*, the symbol of Tibetan identity, into the air.[17] In 1999, however, public notices and announcements warned Lhasa residents that this celebration had been criminalized. The village was renamed, and Public Security Bureau (PSB) officers and People's Armed Police soldiers manned checkpoints to prevent entry to the celebration site on that day.[18] The following year security forces were stationed not only at the village but also at incense burners around the city, to prevent any performance of respect for the Dalai Lama, and in 2001, PSB officials fined a group of youth 500 RMB for picnicking in a nearby park on that day, accusing them of celebrating the Dalai Lama's birthday despite their protests to the contrary about the meaning (or lack thereof) of their picnic.[19]

Bans on particular places at particular times have expansionary effects that further constrict mobility. One fall day in 2001, months after the sensitive birthday had passed, I walked by Trunglha village with a Tibetan friend, on the way to an interview elsewhere. When I told him the name of the village he suddenly realized where we were and became visibly nervous, saying that it would do no good for anyone to find out that he had been here, since he had a good job and wanted to keep it. The entire space had become, for him, a zone of fear. By merely passing through a space associated with restricted presence on a certain day of the year, he feared that he was already guilty, or had the potential for guilt, of a political crime for which he might forfeit employment. Here, as Agamben puts it, "guilt refers not to transgression, that is, to the determination of the licit and the illicit, but to the pure force of the law, to the law's simple reference to something."[20] Tibetans are marked as always already guilty, a state of being that has intensified since the nationalist backlash against the unrest of 2008.

Differential Guilt and the Immobilization of Tibetan Place-making Practices

The Chinese Constitution guarantees all *minzu* (nationalities or ethnic groups) equal rights, and the protection of each group's legal rights for the mutual benefit of all.[21] On top of fundamental equality, the state also claims to provide minority groups such as Tibetans with additional rights through provision of autonomy and through the special favors, solicitous care, and assistance offered to them by preferential policies. There are indeed legal differences in provisions such as the birth control policy, in which minorities are generally allowed more children than the Han. At the same time, however, there are many spheres in which the law is differentially applied to Tibetans, not through special concessions but rather through differential abandonment. This differential guilt is a technique of sovereign power that helps produce the state effect. As geographer Anna Secor argues in a study of the Turkish state, the production of the state "coincides with the methodical production of difference, inequality and injustice . . . it is a process of differentiation, enacted in the repeated, multiple, and incessant hailings and turnings, appeals and suspensions, through which state, space and the subject are constituted."[22]

Numerous extralegal bans that apply only to Tibetans and that restrict Tibetan mobility and use of space are in force in Lhasa. They are extralegal not only in the sense of going clearly against or lying outside of the rights of PRC citizens as defined by the Chinese Constitution, but also in being shadowy in administrative origin. Many are unpublished and difficult to trace; yet, they are widely implemented and enforced.

One such rule that differentiates Tibetans from other PRC citizens is the extreme difficulty they face in obtaining a passport. The receipt of a passport is supposed to be a routine affair, as befits a document that signifies citizenship: one fills in an application, pays a nominal fee, and a passport is in hand a short time later. In the TAR, most passport applications are denied, even when extensive and time-consuming background checks reveal no "political problems." Only those with state employment traveling on official, government-sanctioned business are generally able to obtain passports with any kind of timeliness. Others wait years, making weekly visits to the PSB to check on the status of their applications, only to be told month after month, year after year, that no decision has been made, or that their applications have been denied, no reason given. Being held in suspension, waiting for indeterminate lengths of time for a decision, is characteristic of the space-time of the state on its margins.[23] The endless runaround, the seeming indifference with which citizens are set in motion and then stopped in their tracks, form a spatiotemporality in which the promise of justice is suspended.[24] Mobility is frozen, not in general, but specifically for Tibetans—to prevent them from traveling beyond China's borders, in a kind of spatial incarceration to prove the natural belongingness of Tibetans to the territory contained within the PRC. Tibetans are well aware that they are always treated as a special case, unable to enjoy the full rights of citizenship precisely because of the nervousness in the state apparatus about their desire for that citizenship and identity with China.

A more explicitly spatial ban in Lhasa is the unwritten one that prevents Tibetan monks and nuns from entering most official compounds, including the campus of Tibet University, without special permission. Tibetan monks and nuns are thus always already visibly marked as guilty subjects. As Robert Barnett notes, there is no legal basis on which an entire profession or social group can be prevented from having the same rights to public (or semipublic) space as other citizens. Barnett interprets this ban by noting that monks and nuns are also visibly marked as traditional and thus the embodiment of the opposite of the state's project of development and modernization. He suggests that their (perceived) defiant antimodernism is coded as a disease that must be quarantined by spatial barriers in order to contain its threat to the progress and development of the rest of the population.[25] This organization and partitioning of space and the distribution of bodies in Lhasa into the secular, developed, and advanced and the dangerous, guilty, backward, and religious is accomplished by practices of disciplinary power that work to further reinforce the production of the state effect.[26] By producing zones of exclusion within the city and drawing boundaries between the life spaces of the privileged and the banned, such spatial strategies erase and dismiss certain kinds of people.[27]

Another widely implemented restriction that is targeted specifically at Tibetans applies to a much wider swath of society: the ban on religious activities for all students from first grade through college and beyond—and cadres, anyone who receives a government salary. Given the structure of the urban economy in the TAR, where government and party administration (concentrated in urban areas, especially Lhasa) accounts for more than 13 percent of total economic activity in the region and more than 50 percent of the tertiary sector, these restrictions apply to a very large proportion of Lhasa's Tibetan residents.[28] Those who receive government salaries and who are thus targets of these bans include not only officials but also teachers, bank workers, librarians, and custodial staff for government offices, as well as their family members.[29]

Banned activities include wearing cords blessed by lamas, visiting temples and monasteries, and circumambulations of all kinds. Schoolchildren are threatened with expulsion, and government salaried employees with losing their jobs, if they are caught circumambulating the Barkor or Lingkor, or visiting monasteries or temples. However, Barkor residents also claimed that shortly after the crackdown that followed the March 2008 unrest, when government officials were determined to prove that Lhasa had "returned to normal," retirees were paid and ordered to circumambulate the Barkor to produce the visual images to back up those claims. Indeed, on March 18, 2008 Chinese Central Television station claimed that "life in Lhasa is returning to normal. . . . Many shops that [were] not heavily damaged have reopened."[30] But Tibetan residents of the Barkor claimed about the same time that "usually retired cadres are not allowed to circumambulate at all. But when the government said to go, they had to go . . . at a time when nobody dared to go out on the street, never mind to the Barkor, all of the shops remained open because officials came and said: open your shop or we'll fine you. . . . They staged an old man to look like he was buying things in a shop, and then posted the photograph on a website." State power manifests itself through the control over mobility and presence or absence of particular citizens' bodies in particular spaces; the spatiality of the state is characterized by "referral and deferral, circulation and arrest; it is the power both to set in motion and to suspend the circulation of people, documents, money and influence."[31]

When asked how anyone would know if they had circumambulated or visited monasteries or temples, Lhasa residents affected by the ban mostly reply that there are surveillance systems in place, that people are paid to look for schoolchildren or work colleagues engaged in acts of circumambulation or religious visits. Indeed, after the protests that shook Lhasa from 1987 to 1989, there was a deliberate shift in policy that called for more active surveillance by the State Security Bureau (secret police), video technology, and funding for paid informant networks.[32] As much as if not more than actual surveillance, though, spatial bans work through self-surveillance, the fear of the possibility of surveillance that imposes what Foucault describes as "a principle of compulsory visibility . . . of being able always to be seen, that maintains the individual in his subjection"[33] in relation to an imagined all-seeing state. This self-surveillance encourages the spatial restrictions to have an expansionary effect, as in the case of one retiree with heart disease who told me that she had embarked on a program of taking walks for several hours each morning, but would go out of her way to avoid the Lingkor circuit around the city, despite its convenience and ideal length, so that her exercise could in no way be construed as religious practice.

Tension around the ban on religious activities is heightened on religious holidays associated with particular sites and circumambulation routes, such as the circumambulation of the Lingkor and almsgiving on *Sagadawa*, the fifteenth day of the fourth Tibetan month.[34] Prior to these dates, schoolchildren and government workers are warned not to participate, again upon threat of expulsion or loss of employment, and in some cases work units require their employees to show up early in the morning, or even stay at the office the night before, to prove they are not circumambulating. One cadre explained to me that her family had been afraid to leave the house during *Sagadawa* and the days preceding it; they stayed at home as much as possible, confining themselves so that their movements in the city could not be mistakenly construed as having anything to do with the forbidden religious use of space.

These restrictions are significant not only because of the religious importance of these events but also because circumambulations, pilgrimage, and religious festival sites are spatial practices that play a central role in the reproduction of Tibetan sociality. Thus it is not only religion, but also these embodied practices of place making, community building, and cultural reproduction that are increasingly denied by the encroachment of state space on Tibetans who have any stake in broader PRC society, whether through participation in compulsory education or higher education, or through earning a salary. This ban applies only to Tibetans, not to Han or members of other ethnic groups living in Tibet. Chinese officials and residents are generally unaware of the ban, as are tourists. The ethnic differentiation of the ban suggests, as Anna Secor writes of Turkey, that the "abstract guilt of the individual before the law, enacted through its strategic space-time of control, is not evenly distributed across a homogenous population of citizen-subjects."[35] Instead, the production of the state is a process of differentiation in which some groups are presumed guiltier than others, producing differentiated processes of subjection. The ban has probably never been published, even internally, but instead was likely conveyed to Party leaders in each government unit and from them to non-Party staff (and from teachers to students, as if students were also government employees).[36]

A number of issues stand out. First, applying only to ethnic Tibetans, it targets particular racialized bodies. In addition, the ban applies only to Tibetan Buddhism, and is technically illegal given that the Chinese Constitution guarantees all citizens the freedom of "normal religious belief."[37] Indeed, Robert Barnett notes that within the Chinese legal system the ban is theoretically impossible: "no available explanatory formula or discourse exists to make sense of it among the range of such statements in China."[38]

The impossibility of the ban that is nevertheless applied points to the topology of the state of exception, the enactment of which is the foundation of sovereign power, a threshold between violence and law. The apparatuses of state security, the State Security Bureau, the Public Security Bureau, and the quasi-military People's Armed Police, subject Tibetans in Lhasa to this precarious condition of being both inside and outside the law. The institution of the police in particular, writes Agamben, is the point at which the "almost constitutive exchange between violence and right that characterizes the figure of the sovereign is shown more nakedly and more clearly than anywhere else."[39] They embody the state of exception, challenging the possibility of justice.[40] Always perceptible, the police presence was acutely exacerbated in the aftermath of the March 2008 unrest in Lhasa, intensifying the pulverization of the spaces of everyday life and social reproduction and the production of state power.

Intensifying Applications of Sovereign Power

After the unrest of 2008, the presentation of identification cards became a recurring theme in everyday Tibetan life. National identification cards announce their bearer's *minzu* category, thus exposing Tibetans to widespread discrimination. In the lead-up to the 2008 Beijing Olympics, hotels in Beijing did not accept Tibetan (or Uighur) guests. Taxi drivers often refused to take Tibetans and some restaurants in cities such as Chengdu refused to serve Tibetans. In the type of racial profiling familiar now in the post-9/11 United States, Tibetan travelers at airports are frequently pulled aside for extra security checks, while those returning home from abroad are subject to extra questioning and sometimes checks of their belongings. At an international anthropology conference held in Yunnan Province more than a year after the unrest, I witnessed a Tibetan scholar, an invited participant delivering an academic paper, present his national identification card at the conference hotel. His Tibetanness marked on the card triggered a fifteen-minute investigation by the front desk, by phone and computer, before he was allowed to check in. These are incessant reminders of the differential guilt of ethnically marked citizens, despite formal equality before the law. Complaints of unequal treatment have no legal recourse as the measures are taken in the name of social stability and security, of the need to root out those guilty of destroying the unity of the nationalities, during a state of emergency of indefinite duration.

After the violence in Lhasa in March 2008, the Karma Kunsang neighborhood and the Barkor teemed with soldiers and became clogged with checkpoints. Soldiers were posted at the entrance of every courtyard in the Barkor. Long-term Lhasa residents whose household registrations were elsewhere, even those who owned houses and had been residing there for years, were required to show a national identification card, a temporary residence permit, and another card from the *Chengguanqu*, to be allowed to enter or leave, indeed to move at all.

Identification checks penetrated the private space of the home as the city was purged of Tibetan nonresidents. Residents whose relatives were visiting, whether from Kham, Amdo, or the nearby countryside, found their relatives forced to leave Lhasa a day or two after arriving, denied permission to stay in their own family members' homes. "My uncle came to visit. He had nowhere else to go, but they wouldn't let him stay at our house. The authorities made him leave Lhasa and go back home. No one tells the Han that they can't stay, that they have to go home," remarked one Tibetan in 2009 about the injustice of differential rights to the city. "The government says that all fifty-six *minzu* are equal, but there is no equality. If I wanted to rent my downstairs space to a Han there would be no problem. No one would say anything. But to rent it to a Tibetan brings a lot of problems, constant investigations, questioning." Tibetans from Kham and Amdo, even those with government employment in Lhasa, spoke of the new necessity of always having to carry and show one's national identification card.

Beyond the space of the home and the local street, identification checks were also installed at roadblocks on major roads leading into Lhasa. The road to Phenpo, forty kilometers north of Lhasa, was frequently blockaded, likely because hundreds of ordinary villagers, young and old, participated in protests there in spring 2008. For several months after the unrest there were three to four checkpoints along the one-hour car route from Lhasa, at which identification cards were very closely scrutinized. Rural village farmers, especially older ones, who had never gone through the process of applying for an identification card and who had relied in the past on the practice of getting a letter of introduction from the township government on the rare occasions they needed to travel, found themselves immobilized and scrambling to apply for identification cards, a process subject to much waiting and delay. This imposed increased legibility and extended the spatiotemporality of the state into rural spaces. The checkpoints were withdrawn for a time but reappeared again before *Sagadawa*. Monks and nuns from Phenpo were completely forbidden from traveling to Lhasa, even if they showed valid identification.

The "Nervous System," as Michael Taussig calls the state, equates nervousness with guilt. Anyone who appears nervous before the law is abandoned by it, exposed to the threshold where inside/outside and life/law are no longer distinguishable.[41] In the run-ups to the Olympics and to the fiftieth anniversary of the 1959 uprising, this meant preventive detention of at least a thousand Lhasa residents, including students and monks, particularly those recently expelled by state authorities from their monasteries, rounded up off the streets seemingly randomly and held in military detention camps.[42] The very arbitrariness of preventive detention, of guilt as fate rather than transgression, work together with control over mobility and space in a strategy that produces affective states of fear and uncertainty, and these in turn help concretize the effect of a coherent, unified, powerful state and of its space as territory.

Politics of Fear/Fear of Politics and Spaces of Surveillance

Writing about her fieldwork in Beijing in the early 1980's, Mayfair Yang describes a powerful and pervasive culture of fear that constrained everyday speech and action by instilling durable habits of wariness and self-protection that persisted even in the absence of any direct threats.[43] Such habits still characterize Tibet, maintained in part through its ubiquitous political slogans, the frequent class cancellations for political study, and the policemen who sit in Barkor Square every day, yelling through bullhorns at anyone who congregates in groups of greater than two. These and other throwbacks to a much earlier political era across China are consistently explained as Tibet's "special circumstances" (*teshu qingkuang*). Deep disparities between China's east and west are not only economic but also political. The palpable difference in tension, in the whispers, in the frequency with which residents look over their shoulders to see who might be listening, mark the TAR as a political zone of exception.

The politics of fear is created by surveillance and by a subtle threat of terror made more threatening by its unpredictability. Rules are mostly unwritten and can be broken. One can find oneself "getting away with" quite a lot, a position that already requires an interpellation into guilt, or suffer for doing little or nothing. Tibetans take many risks—where a risk makes sense as such only after one has been made subject to a particular set of rules—often without material consequence. But uncertainty leads to fear and self-monitoring; surveillance becomes self-surveillance, which in turn creates more fear. The politics of fear are those of the Panopticon—set in motion by visible surveillance cameras and helicopters and the knowledge of the existence of paid informants working for the State Security Bureau, but maintained by self-monitoring. This imposes a principle of compulsory visibility on its subjects, regardless of actual surveillance. It is this fact of always being able to be seen, of having the potential to be seen, which maintains subjection. One of the most common effects of this self-surveillance is the conviction among many Tibetan residents of Lhasa that their phones are tapped. This leads them to monitor very carefully what they say on the phone, contributing to an experience of the state as thing-like, powerful, and omniscient.

Internalized surveillance encourages Tibetans to make a distinction between dangerous public spaces and safe private spaces, generally of the home. The guarded private space of the household is thus the primary site for counternarratives about both history and contemporary development. As we sat in the living room of the house from which she would soon have to move, Lhamo, an elderly woman in Kyichuling village, began our conversation about the new apartment blocks that were being built for the village by saying, "the leaders say the new houses are very, very good." She continued, "except in our own homes, no one dares to say anything except 'the Chinese Communist Party is very good and the government is very good.' If we go outside and say that the government is bad, they'll arrest us right away." Her daughter-in-law chimed in, after our conversation turned to some of their negative feelings about the new houses, "You would never say these things in a restaurant, because there are listening devices everywhere. When you go to parks, there are often listening devices on the trees. Even circumambulating the Lingkor. They hire all sorts of people, young women, old grannies, to walk behind other people and listen to what you are saying." Lhamo explained that on her daily circumambulation of the Lingkor, which thanks to her arthritic knees now takes her six hours to complete, "I only go with people I really trust, and if they say something bad about the government, I look around in both directions to make sure no one is listening." Her daughter-in-law concluded, "Lhasa is very scary."

Lhasa's teahouses, ambiguous sites of risk taking, form a dangerous but beloved liminal zone. Dark and noisy, they often serve only Tibetan sweet tea and yak-butter tea, though sometimes also simple bowls of Tibetan noodles, none of which appeal much to Han tastes. Their walls decorated with posters of Indian pop stars, Western food spreads, or pastoral scenes of Swiss dairy cows, teahouses have a layout and atmosphere distinct from Han restaurants or Chinese-style teahouses that serve jasmine or green tea; they are a distinctively Tibetan space, possibly the only space other than circumambulation routes where Tibetan is exclusively spoken. They are popular gathering places not only for Tibetan cadres on frequent breaks from their work units, but also for older men and women who gather to rest and chat after morning circumambulation. Indeed, they seem to be constantly full in the middle of the day, attesting to the state of unemployment and underemployment of Tibetans in the local economy.

Teahouses are sites of all manner of Tibetan talk. I was frequently told that if I wanted to hear the gossip of the town, I should visit the teahouses. But others warned me to stay away: "Sometimes plainclothes State Security

Bureau officers start conversations, with openers like 'the situation these days in Lhasa is not very good,' and wait for someone to take the bait," marking them to be taken away later. Another friend offered me more advice: "You should never talk to anyone you don't know in a teahouse. Just because someone says something bad about the government doesn't mean you should agree with him. In fact, if someone says something negative, chances are it's a State Security Bureau person in disguise." Despite these cautions, teahouses are somewhat unusual spaces where self-surveillance is sometimes momentarily suspended. At the same time, even the private space of the home is not completely immune to surveillance. One woman reported that not long before she left Tibet in the late 1990s, two friends, whom she did not realize worked for the State Security Bureau, had been sent to check up on her. Only several months afterward did one apologize for coming to her house to monitor her as part of his job. She reported feeling shocked: "We were old friends. I thought they were just coming to visit me after my son was born, and to play mahjong. We played a lot of mahjong together."

Beyond spaces of the home and teahouse, self-surveillance reinforces the differentiation and divide between Tibetans and their "older brother" Han, creating multiple barriers for the latter's understanding of local events and perspectives. A well-established Beijing-based professor of politics with no particular experience in Tibet conducted a short trip to Lhasa in 2009, hoping, as many other Chinese scholars did, to find out more about just why the unrest had happened, and whether "it was really so simple as outside instigation." But, he told me, he found the restrictive atmosphere and evident control both surprising and an obstacle to the understanding he had hoped to achieve.

These dynamics are not new. In 1999, in advance of the Dalai Lama's birthday, not only were university students, both Tibetan and foreign, warned strictly against participating in or watching any activities that locals might hold on the day, but travel agents offered to take tourists on a free tour to the countryside that day, to remove them from Lhasa. On July 5, a couple of enthusiastic tourists from Fujian walked into a popular tourist restaurant where I was eating. One asked the Tibetan proprietor, "Are there any festivals coming up?" "No," he replied. "Really? But we heard there is one tomorrow." "Really? I don't know about it," he insisted. Finally, the Fujianese tourist exclaimed, "Yes, we heard it was to celebrate the Dalai Lama's birthday. Is it true?" Judging from his earnestness and the prayer beads he wore on his wrist, I imagined he might be a practitioner of Tibetan Buddhism, and that he was genuinely interested in a religious event. But the proprietor responded only, "Really? How ridiculous. How pointless (*wu liao*). Who would want to do something like that?" That was the end of the conversation, though I knew that the proprietor knew perfectly well both about the following day, and that Lhasa residents were likely to try to celebrate by burning incense at the traditional, though now forbidden site in Trunglha. Furthermore, from what I knew about him, as a Tibetan Buddhist he did not in fact find it "pointless" at all. Nevertheless, he clearly calculated that talking about the subject to a couple of Chinese tourists could be construed as "political" and bring far more trouble than it was worth.

Their lives saturated with politics through a constant stream of campaigns, restrictions, messages, and meetings, Tibetans in and around Lhasa are finely attuned to the blowing of political winds. The constant exposure wears them down while simultaneously hypersensitizing them to certain phrases and images marked inside the realm of the "political." Yet the category of the "political" is always ambiguous, producing an expansionary effect. A nebulous field of uncertainty surrounds a whole host of actions and words: Are they "political" and thus forbidden, or not? No one knows for sure.

"Politics" thus has a way of metastasizing into all arenas of life. The summer of 2009 witnessed the worst drought the Lhasa area had seen in many decades. Day after day of blistering sun, heat, and no hint of rain withered the crops and brought the young and the young at heart out into the alleyways of the Barkor and even along Beijing Road with buckets of cold water with which to douse each other. Two people would grab hold of a friend or a stranger, holding the victim still while a third poured an entire bucket of cold water on her head. Or a person with a bucket would chase someone only to switch direction suddenly and drench an unsuspecting passerby instead. This was a drought special, a way of asking for and hoping that the rains would come. The good-natured whoops and screams of those who had been chased and drenched filled the air, giving Lhasa an almost festive feel, pockets of normalcy in a state of emergency. I was grateful to have narrowly escaped, along with my cellphone and laptop, being doused several times.

The fun lasted for a few days. Soon, though the rains still did not come, the watering stopped and the streets became quiet once again. Meetings had been held and a new rule announced: throwing water is a "political" statement, and is not allowed. Along with this, I was told, residents were reminded that even small gatherings of groups of people of any kind on the streets must be avoided. On the declaration that throwing water is actually a "political" act, one person remarked, "Soon they'll be telling us we're not allowed to eat. Of course, we can't say that out loud."

The spread of the forbidden category of "politics" to infect the splashing of buckets of water during a drought was somewhat unanticipated even by hypersensitized Lhasa residents. More frequently, the expansionary fear of politics led to self-surveillance and self-censorship of any kind of public criticism. Early in my fieldwork, I made occasional social visits to a retiree whom I had met while studying Tibetan several years earlier. When she called, she refused to say her name on the phone. At her house, she would often make what sounded to me like the most innocent of statements, but quickly follow them with her favorite gesture: crossing two index fingers in an X in front of her lips, a symbol that she was keeping quiet, and a warning to me to keep silent as well. Once, after making this gesture of silencing, she explained, "I'm old, I don't really care about what happens to me, but *nyinje* ("compassion"—"poor things"), my children are still young and have their whole lives ahead of them. It would be terrible for them to go to jail. I worry about them." The incriminating statement? She had told me that she did not like attending political study meetings.

The fear of politics stifles initiative and creativity, as anything out of the ordinary becomes suspect. One cadre who tried to start some civic-minded volunteer activities before being warned by his work unit to stop said in resignation, "There's nothing that can be done. One is happiest here if one has no ambition and no ideas and just sits around. It's best to sit in a teahouse, have fun, and be carefree. There is nothing that can be done." This is particularly the case when any foreign person or organization is involved, given the nervousness about territorial sovereignty and incomplete territorialization that underlie logics of governance. These dynamics were heightened after the unrest of 2008, when anyone communicating with the outside world was liable to be charged with passing along state secrets and threatening national security.

Accountability

The fear of politics also makes "politics" a category that is sometimes invoked as a talisman to ward off problems and responsibility. Over dinner in a village with a family I had gotten to know quite well, the mother remarked in a studiedly offhand way, "Some people ask us: 'Aren't you afraid of having this girl asking all these questions? Aren't you afraid something will happen, that there will be trouble later?' But you're not asking anything *political*." This was a statement, but also a request for reassurance. The half-question, half-statement, "but you're not asking about anything *political*," was repeated to me countless times during my fieldwork along with multiple warnings not to get involved in "politics."

These warnings stemmed from a fear of politics, but there was also a sense in which lecturing against political involvement was a way of distancing oneself from the possibility of being accused of such involvement, of having a "political problem." This reflects a more general principle by which accountability is used to create control, not by a monolithic state hovering above society, but through the micropolitics of power and the propagation of fear down the bureaucratic ranks, from one level to the next in the state apparatus.

At each level of government, officials are held accountable for any actions taken by their subordinates, as well as for any unusual events such as demonstrations. This provides a strong incentive for officials to make sure nothing happens on their watch. TAR Party secretaries, appointed by the central government, strive to ensure that protests and other forms of open dissent do not break out during their reigns. Keeping tight control can make the difference between promotion and demotion for high-level officials. At lower levels of government, it can make the difference between having and losing one's job. For Tibetan officials the stakes are particularly high. Furthermore, the porous boundary that separates the "political" from the acceptable is as ambiguous for officials, especially lower-level ones, as for ordinary residents. This nurtures extreme conservatism and an expansion of the "political" realm that again appears to solidify the state and expand state space.

This became clear to me when I was put in the very uncomfortable position of being dispatched as one of four local interpreters for a large bilateral development project in a rural agricultural county where experts from the foreign partner country were visiting. The local Party secretary in charge of overseeing the project implementation was an "Aid-Tibet" cadre (sent to the TAR from another province as part of a program launched in 1994) whom I will call Mr. Hu. After a few days of work, he called the four of us to a meeting, at which he warned us not to reveal certain types of information, or to translate questions about certain topics:

> All of you must take care about sensitive issues. For example, birth control . . . if some villagers say things . . . then you must take care to adjust it a bit, you understand. You will have to be very vague about some sensitive issues and policies. After all, there are some things we cannot tell foreigners. I'm sure all of you understand.

Mr. Hu went on to call on us to actually ensure that the foreign experts asked nothing sensitive or "political," a category that according to him included questions about not only birth control, but also infectious diseases, human rights, the Dalai Lama, and military districts. Instead, we should stick strictly to topics explicitly stated in the project mission statement. Otherwise, he lamented, "I might receive a phone call in a week or two and find out suddenly that there has been some problem." At that point, he warned, "Everyone, all of you and I as well, will have trouble." He went on to explain,

> Actually, I should count as someone who is relatively familiar with politics, but even I don't know sometimes what kinds of things will suddenly become a problem. . . . You must avoid sensitive issues, especially politics. You should also avoid talking about resettlement. For example, our resettlement programs are often meant to help poor

> villages and poor families but sometimes it is not so clear to foreigners why resettlement is being done. Then there will be a big problem, for example a situation like what happened recently in Qinghai.[44]

Despite his experience and rank, Mr. Hu claimed that he could not accurately predict what might later be labeled a "political" issue by even higher-level officials. The fear of job loss, disgrace, or worse, encourages cadres like Mr. Hu to take a hard line toward "politics," regardless of their personal beliefs or circumstances. The incentive structure encourages officials to protect themselves from any responsibility also for events that may *later* be declared "political." The fact that the porous boundaries between the acceptable and the "political" are ambiguous and in flux serves to keep the fear of politics in place. In the absence of clear rules about what constitutes sensitive and "political" subjects, Mr. Hu cast a wide net. This in turn widens the scope of the fear of politics and the politics of fear. Accountability is a political technology through which individuals regulate their own and others' conduct, building state power.

Accountability works in other ways too to reify the state and imbue it with power. Guilt by association is increasingly employed, as parents, siblings, and children are held accountable and detained along with anyone accused of a political crime. Children in Lhasa with immediate families, or aunts and uncles, who were accused of participating in the March 2008 unrest, were told they would not be eligible to sit for high school or college examinations. Such regulations further reinforce the surveillance and self-surveillance of discipline, while also blurring the boundaries between violence and law, and revealing the arbitrariness and nervousness of power.

Opportunistic Space-times

State control over space is not complete. Circumambulation and pilgrimages continue to take place, as do everyday practices of walking, of mundane movements of bodies through space, which constitute "tricky and stubborn procedures that elude discipline without being outside the field in which it is exercised."[45] Subalterns deploy tactics, opportunistic actions that reproduce other forms of sociality and spatiality than those of state space. Though not performed by self-sovereign subjects, tactics are products of agency. This is important to recognize, given a tendency among some observers of the 2008 unrest to portray Tibetans who participated as being duped and manipulated victims of foreign conspirators, a vanguardist stance that frames Tibetans as incapable of agency.

One such opportunistic space-time was formed by the two twenty-ninth days of the twelth month of the Tibetan calendar in 2001. Tibetans perform a ritual on the twenty-ninth day of the twelfth month to eliminate all of the obstacles and bad omens of the previous year. After cleaning the house thoroughly, each person takes a handful of barley dough, kneads it a bit, and touches it briefly on various parts of his or her body. The family then gathers all of the pieces of dough and throws them out at three-way intersections or, in rural areas, in the fields.

The astrological calculations on which the lunar Tibetan calendar is based call for the omission of inauspicious dates and the doubling of auspicious ones in some years. In 2001, state authorities announced on television, radio, and in the newspapers that the twenty-ninth should be celebrated on the first, not the second of its double occurrence that year. According to television broadcasts, this was because the astrological calculations showed that the first was the more powerful and important of the two double days, and thus the proper time to celebrate—a seemingly inexplicable intervention into Tibetan religious ceremony by an atheist state that has done much to discourage religious practice. It also happened that the first of the two twenty-ninths was a Wednesday, the day on which the Dalai Lama's birth sign falls, and therefore an especially auspicious day for him. Thus, I was told that conducting the celebration—which is about "throwing out" old obstacles and inauspicious omens—on a Wednesday would be to symbolically "throw out" the Dalai Lama. Among other things, the incident exemplifies the degree to which politics in Tibet is conducted on a symbolic level.

Because of this Wednesday problem, the actual question of whether or not the twenty-ninth should, according to astrological calculations, be celebrated on the first or second day became somewhat beside the point, and many Tibetans, especially those who lived further from the city and were thus under less direct surveillance and pressure, did not comply with this government announcement. After celebrating the New Year in a village whose residents openly celebrated on the second twenty-ninth, I returned to Lhasa. A cadre friend invited me to dinner at his home. While we were walking down the street, I asked him what had happened with the two twenty-ninths. He chuckled nervously and said curtly, "many people celebrated it on the second one." I asked why. "That is the custom." However, when we reached his home, he contradicted his statement on the public street, saying that according to custom the celebration should in fact have been on the first of the two double days, but that this year it was a problem because it fell on the Dalai Lama's "soul day," thus "no one would celebrate it on the first day." In this symbolic struggle, the state strategy was predicated primarily on a temporal rather than spatial ordering, providing an opportunity for a tactical response. Such tactics, however, are deployed from positions of insecurity, their form shaped by rather than removed from the state effect.

This chapter has focused on the production of state space through disciplinary and sovereign modes of power. The ambiguous and expansionary category of the "political" inculcates practices of self-surveillance that reify the state. Together with the circumscription of mobility, the microregulation of position and attire of individual bodies in certain space-times, and the release and circulation of movement, surveillance and self-surveillance are techniques of disciplinary power that allow the state to be imagined as a transcendental, coherent entity.

While disciplinary power is characterized by control over space and the mobility of individual bodies, the application of sovereign power is rendered clear through the state of exception and through the differential standing and guilt of citizen-subjects before the law. Even as the state of exception forms the paradigm of modern government and the basis of modern sovereignty, abandonment by the law is differential across bodies, spaces, and territories, and this differentiation is part of how sovereign power is exercised. The selectivity of the "Nervous System" in its permanent state of emergency plays an important role in differentiating the ways in which Han migrants and local Tibetans can maneuver within the shifting political economy of development. In addition, the years after 2008 saw a new articulation of sovereign power with development, as I discuss in chapter 7.

The production of state space differs dramatically from quotidian Tibetan understandings and experiences of space, formed by practices such as pilgrimage and circumambulation. These embodied place-making practices historically produced a broad regional sense of Tibetan identity, facilitated trade, and created deep connections between individuals and the landscape as both sacred sites and territory; it is precisely their importance that strengthens the contemporary imposition of state space and attempts to remake space as a homogenous grid rather than an inseparable component of social reproduction. However, these attempts are not completely successful, and everyday practices of mobility and tactics that take advantage of opportunities continue to reproduce spaces of everyday Tibetan life.

Hearing and Forgetting

While spending some time with a peasant family who lived about an hour outside of Lhasa, I learned that there would be a township meeting about the year's surplus grain sale quotas. I asked if I could come along to the meeting and what time it would start. My middle-aged host replied, "They said to come at 10 a.m., but no one will actually show up until later. Maybe 12 or 1 p.m. People don't listen with their ears anyway. They sit up there and talk and we sit lower down and can't hear what's going on, so we just talk amongst ourselves. I don't want to go." She added, "you can go in my place."

> Despite the loudspeaker, it was very difficult to hear him. . . . The Party Secretary began to talk about how important this meeting was. Very few people were paying attention. A group of men sitting next to me had a large green plastic jug full of home-brewed chang. They had brought their own cups and drank throughout the entire meeting, straight through the Party Secretary's lecture about why villagers should not sit around, waste time, and drink chang. A woman sitting next to me threw small objects in various directions, hitting people all around with pebbles and sunflower seed shells. Almost everyone was cracking sunflower seeds, leaving the shells strewn all over the ground. A few men and women were spinning wool, and many women were knitting. People talked, joked amongst themselves, and threw things at each other.
>
> After the Party Secretary stopped reading his talk—about 75 minutes into the meeting, which lasted for 2 hours—he announced, "Now I'm done but I know that none of you have any idea about the contents of what I've just said." Then he admonished the villagers . . . for not listening, reminding them again that this meeting was very important.
>
> *(Field notes, November 24, 2000)*

When I asked a few villagers afterward to clarify various issues discussed at the meeting, they professed to have no idea. I began to wonder if I had been the only person among the hundreds in attendance who had actually tried to listen and remember. The Party secretary and other township officials expected the villagers not to listen. With such a poor loudspeaker, they seemed not even to make the effort to have people be able to hear. The leaders of the township approached the speech as a matter of responsibility; once it was done, their duty was fulfilled and everyone involved could now carry on. For both the leaders and the villagers, participating in the performative act of the meeting as political ritual was more important than the constative meanings of what they said.

Tibetans in Lhasa spend a lot of time in meetings. They spend a lot of that time reading novels, taking naps, snacking on watermelon and sunflower seeds, and drinking *chang*. This gives them what seemed to me an extraordinary ability to walk out of meetings without remembering a single word that had been said. The art of hearing and not remembering is not a very oppositional tactic. Unlike some forms of humor, sarcasm, and irony, it does not directly challenge state memory work or other authoritative discourses. Yet at the same time, it contributes the least to the reproduction of the state effect. While one can only directly challenge authoritative discourses in circumscribed spaces of the home, reinforcing a terrain set out in advance by state control of space, one can be forgetful anywhere.

I

Soil

Figure 1. "Marching upon wasteland." From a feature on the Learn from Dazhai campaign in *Minzu huabao* [Nationality pictorial] 1 (1966). The original caption says: "The organized Tibetan people of Pali [Phagri, in Yadong (Dromo) County] continue to march upon the wasteland, opening up greater amounts of land every year."

The Aftermath of 2008 (I)

I managed to visit friends in Lhasa for a couple of weeks in the winter. I wanted to see what had become of the city, and of my friends, before it was closed off again for all of the coming anniversaries. What I found was a city under siege. Posted at every intersection throughout the city were four to seven People's Armed Police officers, bearing rifles and riot shields, standing on duty twenty-four hours a day. Armored vehicles circulated the streets at night, shining bright lights, accomplishing their intended tasks of intimidation, instilling fear, and ensuring that the streets were clear of people, of anyone but themselves.

What I also found was a palpable simmering rage, of a kind I'd never experienced since I first started visiting Lhasa fifteen years before. A friend who lived in the Barkor said to me, "I looked out my window and saw more than ten people killed with my own eyes. The streets were flowing with blood, there were streams of blood everywhere I looked. . . . The saddest thing is that many families had members who were killed in the spray of random bullets that came from the tanks that rolled down the recently widened alleyways, but they couldn't even tell anyone that their loved ones had died, for just admitting to having a dead family member would subject one to further scrutiny, further political trouble." Guilt stemmed not from transgression of the law, but simply from the misfortune of being exposed to the law. Being interpellated by the law, if only through the miserable luck of having a sibling or parent struck by a stray bullet, was enough to condemn one to guilt.

This statement was from a friend who has never struck me as particularly political. He cares far more about the local lama in his home village than about the Dalai Lama, whom I've heard him obliquely criticize in the past for not putting enough resources into what he sees are the truly important things for the development of Tibetan culture. He's never seemed particularly angry. But things are different now. In the future, he tells me, China will become just like the United States. China will have its terrorists, its September 11. No doubt about it, because Tibetans are holding too many things in their hearts. Right now, he says, they think about the Dalai Lama and they decide to forbear, to tolerate, to have compassion for his sake. But when he's gone, my friend tells me, nothing will hold Tibetans back.

I found this narrative everywhere among Tibetans, of all political persuasions, from all walks of life. It's so tragically different from the hardened position that has become common sense among the Chinese public, according to which the Dalai Lama is the source of all problems, the cause of all violence, the figure on whom everything can be blamed. This narrative, which has blended so powerfully into the nationalist backlash, fails to take into account not only the influence of Gandhi and Buddhist modernism on the Dalai Lama, but also the fact that it's precisely the Chinese state's attempt to demonize him that has invested him with more political, cultural, moral, and religious authority than any of his predecessors.

Walking back to my hotel one evening I came upon an incongruous sight. At the entrance to the Tsomonling neighborhood was a group of six young Han soldiers, standing in formation. A couple had their riot shields raised, others held rifles slung loosely from their shoulders, with the muzzles facing the street. Within four feet of them, a young Tibetan man and two young women had strung up parallel ropes to jump. They laughed loudly as if they had no care in the world and were not standing within arm's reach of gun-toting People's Armed Police. They were defiantly cheerful, trying to carve out a space of normalcy in a state of emergency.

I had dinner at an elegant restaurant with a group of friends, well-placed cadres and intellectuals, educated in inland China. They tell me that, as a Tibetan, it's almost impossible now to get a hotel room in Beijing or Shanghai, unless you have special "back door" connections. "They take one look at your ID, see you're Tibetan, and tell you that they're full." Their experiences in taxis and restaurants are often similar, though with no ID required, they've taken to telling people they are some other minority group, anything but Tibetan. It really doesn't seem like we're "daughters of the same mother," jokes one of them, referring to the ubiquitous song about the unity of the nationalities. "I was at the post office in Shanghai mailing a few things home," said another. "Everything was fine. I was having a perfectly normal conversation with the clerk, in perfectly normal Chinese, when I had to write my address. Of course, I had to write Tibet. That's where I live! When the clerk saw it, she suddenly became very weird. It was as if she felt like she had to speak special Chinese to me, a Tibetan, and I could no longer understand her, though just moments before, we were having a completely normal conversation."

During the unrest, they said, the Karma Kunsang neighborhood, where we were eating, was just like Baghdad. Every few feet there was another group of three soldiers, standing back to back, guns cocked, ready to fire. Lockdown. Immobility. Armored vehicles occupying the narrow alleyways. There was a checkpoint every ten steps, and no way to move past without producing three different identification cards. Everyone was confined at home. Space closed in, there was nothing to do but sit between four walls and wait.

There were meetings before the Olympic torch relay went through Lhasa in June. It was announced: The torch is coming; don't even think about leaving your house. The streets were empty. "We were prisoners." Those in work units who were assigned to participate were told to show up at 6 a.m., not a minute late, wearing their finest, newest Tibetan clothes. If you don't wear new clothes, they were told, we'll make a note of it, and deal later with your political problem.

While I was being told about all this, one man pointed up at the restaurant wall and said, "Hey, isn't that one of those listening devices?" It was a joke, except that it wasn't.

2 Cultivating Control

Nature, Gender, and Memories of Labor in State Incorporation

> The frontiers . . . between the past and the present, are [not] so easily fixed . . . we need only poke beneath the subsoil of [the earth's] surface to discover an obstinately rich loam of memory.
>
> —Simon Schama, *Landscape and Memory*, 1995

The first problem faced by the People's Liberation Army after it marched into Lhasa in October 1951 was how to accommodate and feed its more than eight thousand troops. One of the provisions of the Seventeen Point Agreement was that the PLA would be "fair in all buying and selling and shall not arbitrarily take a single needle or thread from the people." Due to the extreme difficulty of transporting goods from the east, the troops were entirely dependent on local supplies. The sudden introduction of this large number of soldiers into Lhasa badly shook the local economy, and according to the Indian representative in Lhasa at the time, rapidly "affected the livelihood of the poor man, whose share of food and daily necessities has been ruthlessly whittled down."[1]

General Zhang Guohua, commander of the 18th Division of the PLA, asked the two acting prime ministers of Tibet to sell the Tibetan government's grain reserves to the PLA. They refused, on the grounds that the surplus was needed for the coming winter. A serious misunderstanding occurred when one of the prime ministers stated, "It was bad to lose a war, but it is worse to let [the Tibetan] people starve." However, Zhang Guohua took this to mean that the Tibetans deliberately planned to starve the PLA troops, a misinterpretation that provoked a great deal of resentment among Chinese commanders. Many Tibetan aristocrats did start to sell grain to the PLA from their own estates but this was not enough to feed all of the troops, some of whom were on the edge of starvation. Food prices went up dramatically, to the consternation of the PLA commanders, who believed that the two prime ministers were deliberately engineering both price increases and food shortages to promote anti-Chinese feelings. These pressures on food supply were partially alleviated by the establishment of a Grain Procurement Board in 1952, through which the Chinese government gave interest-free loans to Tibetan businessmen and aristocrats to import food from India.[2]

Another important response to the food shortage was the establishment of Tibet's first two state farms in 1952. Named for the dates they were founded, the July First and August First State Farms were established just west of Lhasa to grow both grain and vegetables to feed the hungry PLA troops (see map 2). In addition to laying the groundwork for a network of state farms across the TAR, they were key sites of state incorporation. Through vegetable cultivation and mechanized agriculture, they fostered a new environmental imaginary of nature as battleground, producing a new Tibetan landscape. The production of this landscape also transformed the laborers, resulting in the cultivation not only of vegetables but also of new subjectivities. Recruitment of early farm workers was most effective among impoverished Tibetan women who became a kind of "surrogate proletariat" for the process of socialist transformation. State farms offered them a way to transcend class and gender obstacles, but in turn they were interpellated as proper modern subjects of the PRC who played a role in territorial consolidation.

Despite the involvement of top military commanders and the importance of the farms in the early political history of what became the TAR, the establishment of these state farms has been ignored in Western as well as exile Tibetan historiography.[3] Here I tell the story of labor on these farms as a key component of state territorialization in the 1950s. Vital to the process was the way in which the conquest of nature, imagined in a Maoist framing as separate from society and untouched by local historical agency, constituted state power. This was a transformative process in which both the agents and the nature they worked on emerged simultaneously. The importance of Tibetan women on the state farms also makes clear the gendered nature of early state incorporation as an emasculating process.

While the state farms were key sites of territorialization in the early Maoist period, their total area was tiny in comparison to that of communes throughout Tibet. Thus, the remainder of the chapter turns to the labor that produced the new landscape of collectives beginning in 1960, through the communes, and then through decollectivization, using the peri-urban village of Kyichuling, to which I return again in parts 2 and 3, as a focal point.

These accounts of labor and the production of landscape on both state farms and communes are based on elderly Tibetans' memories of the past. Such narratives are not transparent reflections of objective truth but rather are produced in the context of present power relations and circumstances. Given the centrality of the cultural politics of labor and work in contemporary development, state officials' insistence that Tibetans need to "work harder" to cultivate themselves as proper subjects of development, and Tibetans' insistence that they are too "lazy," it is not surprising that the quality and forms of labor during the Maoist period constitute a key narrative through which the present is understood. Tibetan workers on communes, which were formed only after the state farms had played a large role in securing state control, remember their experiences of life and labor very differently than do the early workers on the state farms. After decollectivization, many state farm workers were nostalgic for their historic roles on the farms, whereas former commune members expressed a sense of relief that the collective period was over and celebrate their freedom from compulsory socialist labor in the present. These divergent narrative qualities are a product both of different current circumstances, with early workers on the July First State Farm in particular doing well economically in retirement, as well as of differences in processes of subject formation in the 1950s. Despite the differences, both were forms of socialist labor that produced a new Tibetan landscape and contributed to state territorialization.

Struggling Against Nature: Founding the State Farms

During the seventh-century reign of Songtsen Gampo, the four-hundred-some-hectare area that became the July First and August First State Farms was known as Lho nup la wa tsel (Wylie: *Lho nub gla ba tshal),* indicating its location south *(lho)* and west (*nub*) of the Potala Palace, and that it was covered with gooseberry shrubs (*gla ba tshal*).[4] Later its common name became Nordölingka (Wylie: *Nor stod gling kha*) indicating that it was to the west past *(stod)* the Norbulingka, the summer palace of the Dalai Lama. The northern part of the area abutted the Lhalu wetland. The sand channel of Lhasa, which directed the seasonal, sediment-laden flows of the Nyangre and Dogde rivers, also flowed through part of this area, depositing a great deal of silt. The southern part of the area lined the north bank of the braided Kyichu River and was thus full of river stones and sand and rather unsuitable for agriculture.[5] Much of the area was also covered with thorny shrubs and was used to graze the Tibetan government's sheep. In addition, taxpayers from some estates, including those of Kyichuling village, were required to cut and haul shrubs from the Nordölingka every year, which were then stored for usage as fuel during the yearly Great Prayer Festival. Like the adjacent wetland, it was a lived landscape, imbricated in and produced by social relations.

The PLA purchased the land from the Tibetan government for forty thousand *dayuan* (silver dollars, the former currency of Nationalist China), in order to grow vegetables and grain for the army, as well as to introduce and develop new crop varieties.[6] Work on the farms began in the early months of 1952. In addition to PLA soldiers, Tibetans from nearby villages were also hired as temporary wage laborers (called *xiao gong*, or "small laborers") on both state farms. By autumn of 1952, some sixty-six hectares of land had been "opened up" and cultivated on the August First State Farm alone, producing one hundred thousand kilograms of grain. The following year, workers and soldiers expanded the area of grain farming, and cultivated cucumbers, melons, peppers, tomatoes, peas, cabbage, and other vegetables.[7]

Exile Tibetan historiography is silent on how the Tibetan government decided on the land sale, leaving only Chinese accounts to draw on. An official history of agricultural reclamation in the TAR seethes with anger at the Tibetan government while leaving no question of how important the farms were for securing control and beginning the process of state territorialization:

> The imperialists of the upper levels of the Tibetan [government] on the one hand gloated over [the PLA soldiers'] misfortune, and on the other hand, implemented a tight grain blockade on our soldiers. [They] coerced our Tibetan brothers, and did not permit them to sell grain to the Liberation Army, and also said, "If we can't chase the PLA away, we'd better force them to leave by starving them.". . . As a result, the very first responsibility placed before our army was how to solve the problem of food. After there was food to eat, then we would have feet firmly planted on the ground in Tibet, and would be able to bear the burden of defending the frontier and fulfill the glorious responsibility of constructing the frontier.[8]

Another official history of the July First State Farm written to celebrate its fortieth anniversary strikes a similar tone while conveying an environmental imaginary in which the land is seen as waste:

> . . . at that time, because of the reactionary local Tibetan government's obstruction in every imaginable way, there was no way to select an appropriate place for an experimental farm. In the end [the PLA bought] the Tibetan government's wasteland *(huangdi)* for grazing sheep. . . . On this piece of land, there was not a single house, nor one *fen* of arable land. With crisscrossing gullies, overgrown brambles, and gravel everywhere, the conditions were extremely arduous. However . . . our country's People's Liberation Army Northwest Division officers and soldiers and the technical personnel acted in accordance with Chairman Mao's guiding principle of "the army entering Tibet should not take local resources" . . . Carrying out difficult struggles with a spirit of self-reliance, starting in the spring of 1952 they began to open up this piece of wasteland.[9]

The state farms encapsulated the dominant environmental imaginary of the Maoist period, in which land without agriculture was seen as empty, uninhabited, and desperately in need of civilization. Rallying cries of the time included calls to "attack the grasslands" and "wage war against the earth," and state media praised young people "courageously going to the virgin lands of the Motherland that have not yet been plowed up [to] turn the empty lands into an earthly paradise."[10] This view of nature was rooted in part in imperial Chinese imaginaries, expressed in their descriptions of the northern grasslands using terms such as "waste" (*huang*), "barbaric" (*ye*), and "empty" (*xu*).[11] This historical view was combined with a new emphasis on the voluntarist human capacity to triumph over nature in the pursuit of production through sheer willpower, the mobilization of massive amounts of labor, and correct socialist thinking.[12]

Military slogans and songs linked the conquest of nature and transformation of the landscape with the incorporation of Tibet into the PRC and the defense of Chinese territory. The first Military District Party Committee meeting in February 1952 invented a new strategy summarized by the slogan, "Reclaim Wasteland and Produce, Be Self-Reliant, Stand Firmly on Your Feet, Construct Tibet, Defend the Border." Soldiers were also instructed to study the slogan, "The Army Must Advance on the Wasteland, Demand Grain from the Soil, Demand Vegetables from the Desert."

In February and March of 1952, 50–70 percent of the PLA soldiers and officers stationed in Lhasa were sent to "open up the wasteland" and create fields on the state farms. The efforts of these soldiers were celebrated as patriotic and heroic. Their toil was enlisted in the task of transforming the "waste" into blossoming agricultural fields:

> At last, after much struggle, a piece of desert wasteland on the banks of the Lhasa River was finally bought from the hands of the Tibetan government's upper levels. . . . Lhasa's riverbanks were strewn with stones everywhere, and overgrown with thistles and thorns. [The soldiers] had to very quickly turn the land that for thousands of years had been a completely barren desert into fertile farmland . . . it was extremely difficult to suddenly turn over that cold and hard soil, which was so hard that the spades couldn't dig into it. Using pickaxes they could barely even scratch a few shallow marks. The soldiers' hands became severely cracked and covered with blood blisters. . . . People nowadays cannot imagine the difficulty of life back then. But the soldiers who battled to reclaim the wasteland had high morale and were afraid of neither suffering nor difficulty.[13]

Doing such intense labor at the high altitude must have been very difficult at first for the soldiers. One former soldier from Chongqing recalled that his nose bled frequently. "In the afternoon, I often had to close my eyes because I was so dizzy and couldn't stand the sun." Accounts about officials in Tibet in the 1990s and 2000s often emphasize the extreme bodily hardships of living at high altitudes, a reason many give for spending time outside of Tibet. However, official accounts of the state farms do not mention the effects of altitude on Han soldiers. For the early troops, conquering and controlling their bodies' reactions to the altitude and new climate was part and parcel of controlling labor and nature. Descriptions emphasized the wild and desolate nature of the landscape rather than its effects on the health of Han soldiers. Their labor was glorified and idealized. For example, while "opening up the wasteland," the soldiers are described as singing songs with lyrics such as these, which resonate with Mao's invocation of the legendary "Foolish old man who moved the mountain" to exhort peasants to turn mountains into plains:

> The military reclamation soldiers are heroes,
> Opening up wasteland and producing on the plateau.
> The sound of the song of labor flies to the clouds.
> Millions of spades and picks make the mountains shake and fall.
> Even if the earth is as hard as steel,
> Even if our sweat soaks through our shirts,
> We will turn these barren sands into cropland.[14]

The theme of conquering nature appeared repeatedly in this period. In May 1952, the Kyichu River flooded the newly reclaimed land, giving army leaders an opportunity to demonstrate their ability to battle nature, framed as an external object. As the event was later described, "General Tan jumped into waist-deep water to direct the fight against flooding. In a battle lasting more than thirty hours, they forced the rising waters to retreat."[15] Picture books published about the early years of the TAR reinforce the idea that the proper way to engage with nature is through battle. A pictorial collection about the TAR between 1954 and 1984, entitled *Golden Bridge*, features captions and statements such as "At a road construction site, a battlefield to conquer nature," "Conquering the treacherous Najin River," "The army and the people unite as one to conquer natural barriers," and "Make the mountains bow their heads and the rivers give way."

Such framings of the voluntaristic human capacity to battle against and triumph over nature differed significantly from the environmental imaginaries of both historical Tibet and the post-Mao reform era. Though Tibetans celebrated the "taming" of the Tibetan landscape through the pinning down of the supine demoness and the conversion to Buddhism, they also praised the quality of being wild and uncultivated in numerous contexts, including the Tibetan origin myth.[16] Tibetan poetry expresses an affinity for open, expansive, unfarmed landscapes, as do continuing cultural practices of hermitage and retreat, and there is no Tibetan equivalent of the "Foolish Old Man who moved the mountain." After economic reform, and particularly beginning in the late 1990s, the protection of nature became a dominant new environmental imaginary, differing significantly from the Maoist trope of battling nature, though still based in a view of a fundamental separation of humans from nature.

Returning to the 1950s, land reclamation by soldiers soon extended beyond Lhasa. By 1954, soldiers sent to Shigatse, Chamdo, Dingye, Bomi (Kongpo) and Ngari reclaimed more than twenty-six hundred hectares of "wasteland" for agriculture. In addition, a history of agricultural reclamation tells us that during this period soldiers planted more than 150,000 trees and dug more than 110 irrigation canals. Tibetans, it is said, composed paeans about their gratitude for wasteland reclamation, singing: "Tens of thousands of [*mu* of] plateau wasteland, which nobody has tilled for tens of thousands of years; But ever since the new Han people arrived, the wasteland has rolled over and everyone is smiling," and "The plains on which not even grass grew in the past—today trees grow in rows; the wasteland which in the past nobody wanted, now has the fragrance of grain crops everywhere."[17]

The struggle to conquer nature continued long after initial land reclamation. The national Learn from Dazhai Campaign, launched in 1964 when Mao Zedong called on the entire country to imitate the Dazhai Production Brigade in Shanxi Province, made its mark on the Tibetan landscape. In addition to fervent study of Mao Zedong thought, the campaign called for attacking nature and forcing it into submission in various ways: "encircle the rivers, build land," "destroy the forests, open the wastelands," "on flatlands, construct terraces," resulting across China in large-scale land reclamation, terrace construction in ecologically inappropriate locations, and severe environmental consequences.[18] As a national model, Dazhai was a quintessential example of a Maoist spectacle, a concentrated spectacle in Guy Debord's terms, as opposed to the more diffuse spectacle of the postsocialist period marked by the pursuit of commodities and material goods. The leader of the Dazhai Brigade, Chen Yonggui, became the object of national adulation, with mass rallies in which thousands of performers arranged themselves in his image, devoted to him through the late 1970s. Debord remarks that such concentrated forms of spectacle "must be accompanied by permanent violence";[19] in Mao-era China this took the form of violence against both other humans and nature.

Tibetans on both state farms and communes were subjects of this spectacle. Tibetan state farm leaders were sent to Dazhai on study tours in the early 1970s, and Chen Yonggui also visited Tibet. The campaign in Tibet focused on land reclamation, tree planting, large irrigation canals, and the consolidation of small fields into larger ones that could be more easily plowed by tractor. On the July First State Farm, as part of the campaign, workers spent two years reclaiming pasture on the banks of the Kyichu River, ultimately abandoning the effort because of continual flooding. In keeping with Debord's observation of the concentrated spectacle that "the imposed image of the good envelops in its spectacle the totality of what officially exists," many exaggerated and unrealistic claims were made about the triumph of labor over nature.[20] The Nepalese consulate in Lhasa at the time reported for example, that "Army men in one land reclamation center harvested 3.75 tons of rice per hectare [in 1972] despite drought. They cut a 7 kilometer canal across a hanging cliff to lead in water from distant snow-capped mountains to create large tracts of paddy fields."[21]

The struggle against nature through labor during the Learn from Dazhai campaign was explicitly linked to the struggle against "class elements" (the formerly wealthy) and against "superstition," a term with which Tibetan religion was maligned and attacked. One of the slogans promoted on the August First State Farm during the campaign was, "Struggle Against the Earth, Struggle Against the Sky, Struggle Against the Class Elements, to the Utmost Extreme."[22] Learn from Dazhai also served as a vehicle for attacks on religious traditions. On the Phenpo State Farm, in Lhundrub County just north of Lhasa, trees that grew near natural springs were logged during the campaign, with the slogan, "Who Says Sacred Springs Can't Be Moved? Who Says Sacred Trees Can't Be Cut?" The leveling of the landscape undertaken by the Learn from Dazhai campaign was also a leveling of traditions. Attacking and transforming what was envisioned as empty wasteland helped dismantle the meanings and social relations, whether of pre-1950s tax payments to estate lords and the Tibetan government in Lhasa, or of sacred springs and trees that existed in sympathetic relations to particular households or monasteries, that had constituted previous socionatures. With the erasure and dismantling of previous socionatural histories, new relationships with nature such as modern mechanized agriculture—with its new inputs, irrigation, and crop varieties—could come to dominate. Tibetans were expected to be grateful for the introduction of such forms of modernization. These landscape transformations thus helped establish hegemony and bind the land more firmly into the territory of the newly formed PRC.

Labor and the Making of Socialist Subjects

One of the first major actions of the PRC in Tibet was thus a massive and backbreaking transformation of the landscape for the growing of grain and vegetables to feed Han soldiers. This new landscape was produced not only by PLA soldiers, but also, beginning in 1952, by Tibetans. When the August First State Farm opened, its work force consisted of about a hundred PLA soldiers and a dozen young Tibetan men and women, some from Kham and others from landless "small households" in central Tibet, who were taught Chinese and worked alongside the soldiers. Soon the farms also hired temporary wage laborers from nearby villages. The Tibetan workers (other than Tibetan female workers who married Han soldiers) ate separately from the soldiers, calling themselves the "*tsampa*-eating August

First State Farm workers" and were all paid the same salary of two *dayuan* per day of work. They purchased their *tsampa* from noble families who were willing to sell grain reserves to the army, or from markets in Lhasa on their days off from work. There was a popular saying at the time in Lhasa that the Chinese showered Tibetans with *dayuan*: "The Chinese Communist Party is our parent to whom we are grateful. [With the CCP] it rains silver *dayuan*."

There was no shelter on the farm until soldiers and workers began to build mud brick houses and dormitories in 1953; until then, they lived in tents. Initially without tractors, the soldiers and workers used shovels and hoes to reclaim land during the first years. Retired workers remembered removing thorny shrubs by digging around the roots, tying ropes around the base of the shrubs, and pulling them out of the ground. Once they had removed them, they burned most of the shrubs for fuel. The years before 1955 were particularly arduous. Together with the soldiers, the Tibetan workers reshaped the landscape, hauling soil from marshy patches and nearby mountains to fill pits and sandy areas. Workers filled willow baskets with soil and hung them from two ends of strong wooden shoulder poles, which they carried long distances. Retired workers said that their shoulders became crooked from all of this earth-transforming labor. As one elderly Tibetan woman put it, "Our pens were shovels, our books were the fields. As a result we are all bent-over people. Our legs are crooked. Our backs are bent over."

Men and women labored together in twelve-person squads, organized in military fashion and responsible for fulfilling certain duties each day. These were arranged into larger platoons, later renamed teams, which specialized in particular production tasks. In 1955, many of the early Tibetan workers became formal state farm workers. This reduced their salaries, but gave them the right to eat together with the soldiers in the dining hall. They were issued thick cotton clothes, pants, and woolen shoes for the winter, as well as a set of summer clothes, and recalled that they could eat their fill of the plentiful food on the farm.

By 1959, there were more Tibetan workers than Han soldiers on the August First State Farm. However, after the uprising that March, some of the laborers returned to their villages because they qualified for the new class category of "poor peasants" and were thus entitled to receive food and other goods redistributed from the estates and those classified as "representatives of feudal lords." Those who remained on the farm would be considered state employees and thus ineligible for redistributed goods. The workers who left were replaced by a new batch of workers: "reformed" prisoners of war. Immediately after the flight of the Dalai Lama in March 1959, those who had participated or were accused of participating in the uprising were labeled counterrevolutionaries and arrested. Many of these prisoners were sent to reform-through-labor camp at the Najin hydroelectric power plant near Lhasa.[23] After the hydroelectric plant was completed, prisoners in poor health and those who were considered to have "reformed" their errant ideological ways were sent to work on different branches of the August First State Farm.[24] Prisoners were assigned the heaviest labor, including digging, harrowing, and flattening out land in preparation for regular workers who then did the actual cultivation.[25]

Prisoners and ordinary workers alike participated in land reclamation, grain and vegetable cultivation, construction, and the digging of irrigation canals on the farm. They also participated in the attempted reclamation of the Lhalu wetland, adjacent to the August First State Farm. Before 1959, this wetland covered over ten square kilometers northwest of Lhasa. It was managed by local villagers, under the direction of Tibetan government officials, for the production of marsh reeds, which were used as fodder for horses owned by the government. Villagers also dug marsh turf for fuel. After 1959, however, the wetland was viewed through the new dominant environmental imaginary as unproductive waste, leading to the attempt to reclaim it for agriculture. More than fifty workers on the August First State Farm, including many prisoners, were sent to dig canals that crisscrossed the wetland. One former prisoner of war recalled that the workers were required to dig the canals as wide and deep as the span of a person's outstretched arms. After the wetland had been partially drained, the farm put up signs indicating the names of various designated fields within it. However, after three years of failed grain cultivation, the PLA Logistics Department took over the project, eventually abandoning it in the late 1960s, but not before significantly draining the wetland.[26]

More than just a battle against nature, the transformation of the "barren desert" and "cold hard soil" of the Nordölingka into the state farms, like the transformation of the "wasteland"/wetland by PLA soldiers and reform-through-labor prisoners was also a struggle over the inclusion of Tibetan territory and people into the Chinese nation-state. In the process of their conquest of an externally conceived nature, Tibetan laborers were to be transformed into proper socialist subjects and Chinese citizens, grateful for their liberation and the paternal care of the Chinese state. This is clear in the logic of "reform through labor," but it operated as well in the Tibetan laborers who joined the farm voluntarily. Through their own labor, these early state farm workers transformed not only nature, but also their own bodies and sensibilities as they produced the landscape. They came to think of themselves in new ways, as heroic laborers whose hard work was improving and modernizing Tibet. Through their embodied labor on the farms, they were recruited into hegemonic projects of state incorporation.

The early laborers on the two farms were in the early 2000s much more nostalgic about the past, especially the 1950s, than their counterparts who experienced the communes. Though all describe the Maoist, collective period as a time of toil and difficult physical labor, the state farm workers recall and retell their labor proudly. They remember their labor as useful and productive, part of a worthwhile endeavor, rather than recalling it primarily as a period of intense drudgery with no redeeming qualities. This is particularly true for the July First State Farm workers who have been treated much better in their retirement because of the farm's eventual reorganization into a scientific institute.

One retired July First State Farm worker recited one of several poems eulogizing the difficulty of labor in the 1950s:

> It's not easy to be a worker on the July First State Farm.
> Just after the sun rises over Mount Utse,
> One needs a throat made of iron
> And lips made of copper.[27]

This referred to the fact that because workers had to jump out of bed in the morning to begin working, there was no time to leisurely sip one's morning tea; hence a "throat of iron" and "copper lips" were necessary to avoid being scalded. Another worker, Tseyang, was nostalgic for the work ethic of the early days on the farm. Back in the 1950s, she recalled, workers were only required to work eight hours a day but many volunteered to do more. In fact, although work at night was purely voluntary at that point, both men and women went anyway "because our minds (*sem*) were so good at the time." Likewise, Lhamo was proud of how July First State Farm workers such as herself built embankments in the middle of the night when they worried that the Kyichu River might flood its banks. "Sometimes we slept with our clothes on. Back then we could accomplish as much work in one day as it takes three days to do now! Really!" Another retired worker compared the results of her labor in the past favorably against the current status of the farm:

> Back then, people were good. Everybody helped each other. Everybody worked hard, not like now. . . . We made all of the fields. [Around 1963–64] all of the fields were really in excellent condition. . . . These days people only care about money, and not about the fields.

Cultivating Control

The early struggles against nature and the reshaping of the landscape of the state farms through labor facilitated the establishment of Tibet as Chinese territory in a number of ways. First and foremost, it fed the invading army's troops, enabling them to stay. The provision of grain and vegetables was integral to the key strategy of "not eating the local place"—establishing military self-reliance in order to reduce local resentment and increase the odds of winning Tibetans' willingness to think of themselves as belonging to the PRC. Even while focused on winning over the ruling class in the 1950s, the CCP maintained a keen sense of the importance of not taking from poor residents. As a result, in the early 1950s, there was a "genuine feeling that the Chinese had come to 'modernize' Tibet" as the majority of Tibetans "began to see China as the center of technology and modernity."[28] The strict discipline among the PLA troops, together with an emphasis at the time on respecting local traditions, worked very well for the new regime in establishing a foothold in Tibet.

Whereas grain was needed to survive, vegetables were required to keep the troops happy and willing to stay in Tibet. According to official histories of the August First State Farm, it was through the cultivation of vegetables that the farm planted "the seeds of hope, the seeds of unity, and the seeds of flourishing prosperity on the snowy and windy plateau."[29] In addition to growing vegetables outdoors, July First and August First State Farm workers constructed rudimentary greenhouses—long, shallow pits in the ground with peat and mud walls. They laid wooden sticks on top, sewed together old clothes, and tossed these over the wooden frame to insulate the vegetables at night.

The cultivation of these vegetables on the "cold barren wasteland" enabled state control. Vegetable cultivation is credited with having

> . . . greatly inspired the troops who had entered Tibet to stay for the construction of Tibet, as well as inspiring them to consider the frontier their home, and their courage and their faith. It also dealt a heavy blow to the imperial upper levels of the Tibetan government's enormous arrogance, and received the sympathy, support, and faith of the patriotic Tibetan people. . . . Our Tibetan brethen saw from the fruits of the bountiful harvest that the CCP leaders' PLA really is the brother of each nationality and in fact came to help the people of Tibet develop production and improve their livelihoods.[30]

In official history, the introduction of vegetable cultivation is associated not only with a blow to "imperial" arrogance but also, deploying the metaphor of Chinese nation as family, with Tibetan gratitude for the care of the elder brother Han's assistance.

The troops invented their own slogan, "With a gun in one hand and a pickaxe in the other, [we] will defend the frontier, construct the frontier, and turn the roof of the world into a heaven on earth." The August First State Farm not only fed the army for survival, but also provided troops with the type of food that convinced them to stay, laying "the foundation for the troops to stand steadily on two feet in Tibet."[31] Similarly, an official history of the July First State Farm states that "The successful planting of . . . vegetables, fruit, and melons not only improved the Tibetan people's livelihood conditions, but also greatly inspired the Han cadres' work morale, firming their determination to construct Tibet over the long term."[32]

At its establishment in August 1952, the August First State Farm was managed by the Production Division of the Logistics Department of the Tibet Military District. In April 1960, the farm formally came under a new unit, the Tibet Military Production Department, a main task of which was agricultural reclamation. By that time, the department had overseen the reclamation of thirty-three hundred hectares of land and established numerous other farms across Tibet under military management. Not only was the labor of August First farm workers organized in military fashion, but they also contributed to actual war efforts. In 1962, workers were sent from the farm to the MacMahon Line, the contested border with India in eastern Tibet, with horses carrying ammunition and dry food because the roads near the border were impassable. This supplied the troops for the brief Sino-Indian war of October 1962, which ended with a swift military victory for China.[33]

In 1965–66, Han cadres, workers, and nineteen hundred "support the borders" youth volunteers were transferred to work on various military state farms in Tibet, including the main branch of the August First State Farm. However, most only stayed for two to three years. Children of prominent TAR leaders, such as the daughter of Tian Bao, one of the few Tibetans who had joined the Long March, also worked on the August First State Farm for short periods of time as a way of proving their revolutionary credentials.[34] The system overseeing the farms was reorganized in 1970, becoming the Tibet Military District Production and Construction Division, under dual military and civilian administration, and after the Cultural Revolution ended in 1976, production on many of the farms was diversified beyond grain agriculture to include wheat grinding, the production of soy sauce, liquor, and handicrafts, and natural resource extraction.

The August First State Farm itself also opened a number of new branches that turned into grain production bases, but the original 160-hectare main branch in Lhasa remained the PLA's primary vegetable production base in Tibet for more than three decades, until the beginning of economic reform. Retired Tibetan workers recalled regularly loading up army trucks with the vegetables they had grown. The labor of Tibetan vegetable growers on the August First State Farm nourished the PLA, helping it establish state control in Tibet. This remained the case until 1979 when both the August First State Farm and the network of other state farms were taken out of military control and placed under the civilian Agricultural Reclamation Department. This department governed the farms while experimenting with a financial contracting system that gradually made these farms responsible for their own profits and losses.

Vegetable cultivation on the July First State Farm cultivated state hegemony in a different way. Unique among all state farms in the TAR, the July First State Farm was quickly turned over to civilian administration and designated for scientific functions. Thus, it eventually came under the jurisdiction of the Lhasa Municipality government rather than the Agricultural Reclamation Bureau. The farm was given the responsibility to develop new seed varieties, and to advance the scientific level of the civilian government and the region's farmers. As such, the July First State Farm laid the foundation for the development of "scientific agriculture," which is said to have "had a very large use in politics. . . . It was also a powerful counterattack against the reactionary upper levels' futile attempt to destroy the unity of the nationalities, and the reactionary propaganda to split the Motherland."[35] The emphasis on science and "scientific agriculture" against cultural practices designated as "superstition" became an important terrain of struggle, one that would several decades later influence Tibetan farmers' decisions not to compete with Han migrants by growing vegetables. On the July First State Farm, ground zero for scientific agriculture in Tibet, the discourse of science was very clearly linked from the very beginning with Chinese state sovereignty over Tibet in the language of the "unity of the nationalities."

The July First State Farm served as the main showcase for Chinese agricultural achievements in Tibet. One former worker recalled that Chinese reporters and officials frequently visited the farm during the harvest to take pictures of the workers: "For the harvest, we had to put on our new clothes. Then one Tibetan would stand on one side, and one Tibetan on the other side, and in the middle two Han cadres would stand." The farm was also frequently promoted to foreign visitors to justify Chinese presence in Tibet through the spectacle of progress. During an agricultural exhibition held in Lhasa in 1954 on PRC National Day, watermelons cultivated on the farm were served to specially invited guests from India, Sikkim, and Nepal. Nepalese consulate staff members were also brought to the July First State Farm on visits in 1972 and 1974, where they reported being impressed by its achievements.[36]

Small, rudimentary glass-pane greenhouses were first introduced on the July First State Farm in 1954.[37] Several young female workers recalled the painstaking labor required of them in caring for these vegetables. They took turns rising at 4 a.m. to light a small fire near one end of a greenhouse to slowly raise the temperature inside, tending to it until 7am. Remnants of the walls of these earliest greenhouses were still visible in 2001, including the painted slogan, "Oppose American Imperialism!" As one farm official pointed out, "This farm really reflects the history of Tibet." Vegetable production on both farms continues to be interwoven with the master narrative of gratitude and state legitimacy. According to an article that appeared in the *China Daily* celebrating the fiftieth anniversary of the "peaceful liberation":

> Asked to compare today with the years prior to democratic reform in 1959, Yangzom said the changes are 'beyond measurement.' Before liberation, the slaves survived on *tsampa*, or roasted barley, the Tibetan staple, and they seldom had their fill. Today, Yangzom and her peers have a regular supply of rice, wheat flour, and fresh vegetables available to them.[38]

The importance of the July First State Farm in the early establishment of PRC control in Tibet is also indicated by the frequent visits of high-level military, Party, and government leaders. The 1953 training of the farm's first batch of sixty-three Tibetan students in agricultural technology was marked by the participation of Generals Zhang Guohua and Fan Ming, leaders of the PLA's Southwest and Northwest Military Regions, respectively, during the initial takeover. In the 1950s and 1960s, visitors also included Tan Guansan, vice Party secretary of the Tibet Work Committee and political commissar of the PLA Tibet Military Commission; PRC Deputy Premier Chen Yi, who planted apple seedlings that he had brought with him in the farm's first orchard (see figure 2); Ren Rong, deputy political commissar of the Tibet Military Commission; and Pasang, deputy secretary of the TAR CCP. When the first national-level delegation from Beijing came to Tibet in 1956 for the establishment of the Preparatory Committee for the Autonomous Region of Tibet, which preceded the formal formation of the Tibet Autonomous Region in 1965, members of the delegation stayed on the farm. In 1995, when General Fan Ming and his wife returned to Lhasa for a visit to celebrate the thirtieth anniversary of the founding of the TAR, they made a special visit to the July First State Farm, during which the general spoke emotionally about the difficulties of life in the early days of the farm, when there was "nothing to eat but weeds." Moreover, former Vice Premier Li Peng is said to have personally penned a verse about the farm when he visited it for its twentieth anniversary: "The Academy of Agricultural Sciences under the dry white mountains has pears, peaches, and melons and fruits, all/Over-wintering barley is the direction/Bringing benefit to Tibet's new achievements."

A final way in which the July First State Farm was significant for advancing the process of state territorialization was the fact that it cultivated its young workers to become officials and leaders; many later went on to hold key government and Party posts throughout the TAR. The farms were places to incorporate Tibetans into the new national political structure, promoting their sense of belonging. Many officials who served in the 1990s, including county deputy party secretaries and heads of government departments at the regional level, had spent part of their youths on the July First State Farm. Other early workers were selected to become mountain climbers and other

Figure 2. Vice Premier Chen Yi (second from left) helping plant apple seedlings he has brought from Beijing at the July First State Farm. Photograph from *Xizang Zai Qianjin* [Tibet is progressing] (PLA Illustrated Magazine Publishing House, 1956). The original caption states that by planting the seedling, Chen Yi was "wishing for bumper harvests for the Tibetan people."

symbols of Chinese national pride. Perhaps the most famous of the early July First State Farm workers was the actor Wangdu, who played the serf Jampa in the influential 1963 film *Serf* (*Nongnu*). In response to his severe abuse by what is portrayed in the film as the evil, corrupt, and oppressive pre-1951 Tibetan society, Jampa becomes mute, recovering his ability to speak only after the "peaceful liberation."

This film shaped to an extraordinary degree the national Chinese imagination about Tibet for more than three decades, and Wangdu became a celebrated actor, head of the Tibetan Drama Theater, and recipient of a special allowance from the State Council after retirement. Wangdu's own personal history is portrayed in the form of the "speaking bitterness" narratives of the Maoist period as one of being a serf who ran away and joined a monastery where he "went through hardships" and was ill-treated, until he ran away again and joined the state farm as a cart driver. "That was the happiest time I had known; I had enough to eat and warm clothes and no one abused me," he is quoted as saying.[39]

Gender and Social Mobility in the Early Years of the State Farms

How were early workers like Wangdu recruited, and why did they join? The early workers on both the July First and August First State Farms were from poor "small households" (*dud chung*) in nearby villages such as Damba and Dongkar, who were recruited to work as day laborers, or young runaway small householders from estates around central Tibet. In addition, there were also a number of impoverished Khampas (Tibetans from the southeastern region of Kham), who had come to Lhasa on pilgrimage and were still there when the PLA marched in. Early state farm workers were uniformly from among the lower strata of traditional Tibetan society, making their trajectories on the farm stories, in class terms, ones of upward mobility. By chance as well as hard work, these formerly impoverished and landless peasants managed to do quite well under the new regime. Their own personal mobility was integral to the process of state incorporation.

Norbu, for example, was born in Nangchen, a culturally Kham area in what is now Yushu Prefecture in Qinghai Province. He traveled to Lhasa on pilgrimage in 1950, ran out of funds, and decided to stay to earn some money for the trip home. However, this coincided with the "peaceful liberation." He and his friends were camped by the Kyichu River with many other Tibetans when one day a Han soldier asked them if they wanted to work for pay. They did. The soldier led the five of them to the PLA Logistics Department, where they unloaded supply trucks and occasionally helped to cook. As he told the story, because he was the hardest-working among his group of friends, the army made him an informal leader of the group. Shortly afterward, however, a new rule was instituted that Tibetans were no longer allowed to work in the Logistics Department. His friends, from different parts of Tibet, all left for home, but thinking his home was too far away he instead asked a minor official in the department to help him find work. This man informed him that he might find some work on the August First State Farm, and gave him a letter of introduction with a seal. On the farm, he became leader of a squad that hauled night soil from Lhasa's latrines to the state farms. He joined the Party, and in 1970, became a vice team leader for the vegetable cultivation team. The next year he was promoted to team leader, a post that he held for eight years. He then served as the Party secretary of the farm's "sideline industry" work team for five years, before retiring in 1984. In his retirement, he described his choice to stay on the farm by saying, "How to put it? I was very young. I was far from home. I had no choice but to work hard. . . . It was not a question of liking or not liking." Despite his ambivalent narrative in the 2000s, his decision to seek out employment on the farm, as well as to join the Party and become a team leader suggest both that working on the farm seemed a better option to him than returning home, and that he was rewarded for his choices through his promotions on the farm.

Other early workers, like Nyima, were from Lhasa. His father had worked as a bodyguard for the Dalai Lama, and his mother was from Lhoka. When he was young, Nyima was a servant for monks in the *Namgyal Tratsang*, the monastery in the Potala Palace. While working there, he heard from a friend about the Communists on the state farm. He knew very little about them other than what he was told: that there was no difference between leaders and workers, that the food was good, and that they showed movies at night. He decided to run away and join what he thought would be the good life. He recalled that when he first arrived at the July First State Farm, in 1955, he removed his hat, scratched his head, and made other gestures of polite deference. The person registering him checked his health and asked him his age, and then told him the rules of the farm: listen to the Communist Party leader, pay attention to the unity of the nationalities, and don't get into fights. When he first started, he had Sundays off. Every Sunday he rose early to walk to Lhasa, bringing some food in a basket to visit his parents. However, he and his friends were always careful to put their *chupas* (Tibetan robes) back on for the day, otherwise Tibetans in town would know that he was working for the state farm and call him "someone who surrendered to the Chinese" or yell at him, "you've turned into a Chinese person." He remembered being particularly worried that he might run into his former boss, a high-ranking monk-official, on his trips to Lhasa, but that never happened. Like other older workers, one of his most emphatic memories of his early years on the farm was that the food was very good. He was only around seventeen years old at the time, and he and his friends particularly enjoyed the army movies, which they watched regularly. In 1958, Nyima became the fourth Tibetan to learn how to drive a tractor. In retirement, he continued to enjoy a good pension, and professed a great love for the state farm as well as fondness for his early days on it.

In addition to being landless, the early Tibetan work force was also highly skewed toward women. The stories of the early state farm workers are ones in which the promise of economic and gender mobility could be effective in countering other loyalties in the recruitment of workers who produced Tibet's new landscape. Nyima's wife, Lhamo, for example, was born in the town of Markham in Kham where her father had been stationed as a soldier in the Trapchi Regiment of the Tibetan army, but came to Lhasa when she was a toddler. In 1955, she was planning to go to the post office where, she had heard, young Tibetans could sign up to attend school in China. While she was on her way there with another young Tibetan woman, a horse cart from the July First State Farm passed by, and its driver asked if they would like to go to the state farm. Farm leaders told Lhamo that she had a lot of potential, convincing her to stay there.

On the night soil runs, in which many early workers took part, both men and women encountered verbal abuse, but the women were especially harassed by Tibetan men on these trips. Female Tibetan workers who joined the farm during this period told stories of being taunted with epithets such as "Chinese shit transporters!" "Chinese shit eaters!" and "Chinese shit pickers!" Tibetan men in Lhasa yelled at them, "You're just like the Chinese!" Several told me that when they were digging out the latrines, other Tibetans sometimes deliberately tried to urinate and defecate on them from above. The Tibetan wife of one Han soldier on the August First State Farm enrolled briefly in the Tibetan Cadre School (now Tibet University) but quit because she was frequently taunted on the road to school by monks with threats such as "We'll peel off your skin!" for collaborating with the Chinese.

The early women workers recalled the *dap dop* ("fighting monks") and the Dalai Lama's bodyguard corps at the Norbulingka as being particularly troublesome.[40] One retired female worker from the July First State Farm blamed the harassment on the fact that she was young and had done what the farm had told her to do—cut her hair short and wear the Chinese clothes provided by the farm, rather than keeping it long in Tibetan style, and wearing Tibetan dress. The few times that she walked past the Norbulingka with other Tibetan women from the farm, the bodyguards slapped her in the face, calling her a traitor, "one who has surrendered to the Chinese." Lhamo, also retired from the July First State Farm, similarly recalled that when two women went together to the latrines, carrying shoulder poles with buckets for the night soil, they had to fill the buckets up quickly because soldiers of the Tibetan army pointed guns at them, ordering them to hurry up with the work and leave.[41] Lhamo recalled that one day, several *dap dop* chased her and another young female farm worker. The pair ran and hid in an elderly Tibetan woman's home nearby until they felt it was safe to go back to the farm. Often, Tibetan men and women workers went together to gather night soil, which women considered safer because most of the men were Khampas, with a reputation for being tough fighters. As a result, the Lhasa men did not usually harass them.

During these same early years, the pressure on PLA soldiers to be on their best behavior was intense. Soldiers were warned repeatedly to respect local people and customs in every way. Doctor Zhang, a Han soldier from Chongqing who joined the PLA in 1949 to escape poverty and marched with the Logistics Department of the 18th Division to Lhasa beginning in 1950, recalled that the soldiers were given a bowl of butter tea to drink every day. If anyone refused to consume this common Tibetan drink, the army "would give you a hat to wear"—that is, accuse the soldier of being unpatriotic and having a "political problem." Upon entering Lhasa, the soldiers were forbidden from entering monasteries, fishing, and killing birds, and were frequently reminded to respect local customs.

In addition to exercising discipline and restraint when dealing with local people, soldiers were also heavily pressured to stay in Tibet.[42] This pressure to stay was encapsulated in a slogan, which along with a small drawing of the Potala Palace, was printed on soldiers' towels, cups, thermoses, and bags: "Construct Tibet for the Long Term; Make the Frontier Your Home."[43] They were actively encouraged to marry local women and settle down in Tibet, an internal policy summarized as "Grow Roots, Flower, and Bear Fruit."[44] One Han soldier recalled that he had originally expected to be in Tibet only for three years, but suddenly the policy changed and he was expected to settle down there. Han PLA soldiers who didn't want to marry local women made up their own ditty about how they planned to avoid that fate: "Tibet, Tibet, rotate every three years. If we don't rotate in three years, we'll become monks."[45]

If a Han soldier did find a Tibetan girlfriend, he was to report the matter immediately to the PLA Political Department, who checked both the woman's physical health and her designated class status. Soldiers were only allowed to marry Tibetan women if they were classified as "middle farmer" or below. Aside from this restriction, it was very easy to obtain permission for such marriages because the army wanted to encourage Han soldiers to settle down in Tibet. Doctor Zhang, for example, married a woman from a poor servant family in Tagtse County, who ran away from home and came to Lhasa in 1955 where she found work as a custodian at the No. 19 Military Hospital. She met Zhang there, and they married the following year, after which she joined him working on the August First State Farm. Many Han soldiers married local women, not only because they believed they might not ever be allowed to go home, but also as a way of proving their loyalty to the military and to the country during those intensely political years. Many of these marriages ended in divorce after the soldiers retired and wanted to return home. Many of their wives refused to move, while others went but then returned to Tibet. Doctor Zhang was quite unusual in deciding to retire with his wife in Lhasa.[46]

In addition to marriage, Han soldiers and officials were also pressured to be on their best behavior, particularly with Tibetan female workers on the farms. Many retired Tibetan workers from both the July First and the August First State Farms described the 1950s as a time when the Han and ethnic relations were particularly good. Their memories of Han cadres at that time are always set in implicit or explicit opposition to the Chinese officials and vegetable farmers who live in Tibet now. Without any prompting to talk about ethnic relations, several told me, "The Han (*gyarig*) back then were so good!" and "Back then, the Han-Tibetan unity was real, not like now." One said, "Nowadays if you look for Han as good as the ones back then, you wouldn't be able to find any." Another retired worker from the July First State Farm began his narrative about the farm with this statement: "Back then, the Han were so good [thumbs up gesture]. These days you can't find good Han like that. There aren't any more." A retired female August First farm worker recalled, "Back then, the leaders looked after the Tibetans very well. They really took care of us. The leaders paid a lot of attention to unity. They told us, 'if anyone calls you a *lao zang min* ("old Tibetan") that's an insult and you should call them *lao han min* ("old Han") back.'"

Among the retired workers, it is the women who seem to most deeply appreciate "the goodness of the Han back then." One recalled, "The Han back then were better than one's own parents." Tseyang, who was very young when she joined the early workers on the July First State Farm, told me that farm leaders came to check on the younger workers every night, to ask if they had enough blankets. Furthermore, she claimed that because the soldiers were under such strict disciplinary rules at that time, "Nothing ever happened to Tibetan girls, even those who were sixteen, seventeen, eighteen years old—they didn't even dare to make jokes with innuendos." Tseyang had no doubts about why this was the case, explaining, "They were very strict because they were worried about not being able to put their roots down here in Tibet."

Tseyang exemplifies the recruitment of Tibetan women into the new political structure in the 1950s, and the opportunities for social mobility that joining a Lhasa state farm afforded them. Born into a landless family in Damba village, just below Drepung Monastery, she joined many other Damba villagers at age twelve, in 1952, on the nearby July First State Farm. For two years, as a temporary laborer, she participated in construction of houses on the farm. Even though she earned two silver dollars per day as a temporary worker, she recalled that she was still quite hungry from lack of food at home, so much so that she sometimes stole leftover steamed buns that had been thrown out and were ready to be dumped in the pig pens. The cooks also scraped the rice from the bottom of the pots and wrapped it in paper to give to her and other younger workers to eat. In 1954, the workers of Damba village were given the option of joining the farm as formal workers. Twenty-eight villagers, including Tseyang, decided to join while many more decided to remain temporary workers. Although the salary was lower for formal than for temporary workers, Tseyang recalled that the overall situation was much better. She was quite happy because the meals were free, and included four cooked dishes and soup each day. Furthermore, she remembered that "we could eat as much as we wanted" and that someone from the farm cleaned up after them. The farm had its own hospital as well, and workers received free health care.

Because she was quite young, farm officials encouraged her to go to school. While she was still deciding whether or not to go to school, Chinese

Central Television came to make a small program about her life, following her transition from Damba to being a temporary worker and then a full-time worker. Of all of the villagers from Damba, the farm only sent her and one other young woman to school in China, in 1957. In her assessment, she was extremely lucky to have had a mother who was open-minded enough to allow this, "or in any case, [a mother who] had decided that the Chinese were here to stay." Her mother asked a lama from nearby Drepung Monasery to perform a divination about her daughter's schooling. Again, she was lucky; the lama said that it would be okay to send her daughter to school in China.

Tseyang did very well. After the 1959 uprising, she was sent back to the TAR and eventually became a deputy Party secretary, a post she held for about a decade. The other Tibetan woman who was sent to school in 1957 married a Han man and moved to Beijing. The rest of the villagers, Tseyang says, returned to the village, and as a result are all very poor today. Looking back at the 1950s in 2002 she observed, "They really missed their chance. Even if they didn't get as lucky as me, even if they didn't become officials, at least they would have been a lot better off than they are now. I go back sometimes, and can't believe how poor they all are."

Unlike Tseyang, Yangchen never had the chance to go to China to study, though that was her reason for joining a farm. She was from a servant family of the Kathog Labrang in Ramoche, in Lhasa.[47] One day in 1954, a Tibetan woman who came to the neighborhood selling shrubs for fuel told her about the August First State Farm in the Nordölingka. The Tibetan woman, she said, described it as "a happy wonderful place" that sent its workers to school in China. Though she was quite young, she and three other girls decided to go to the farm. She recalled that upon arriving, "actually there was nothing there," meaning that it was not what she had envisioned from the woman's description. There were only a few houses constructed of packed earth, and other shelter walls made with tin boxes cut in half and filled with mud. However, because "the food was pretty good" she decided to stay. She shared a story about her early days on the farm, when two technical personnel from Beijing taught them how to grow vegetables and watermelons. She recalled wondering about the watermelons:

> For a long time, I had no idea what they were. I stared and stared at them, thinking, "they look like some sort of squash, but then again, they don't look exactly like squash. What could they be?" We never got any—they were always just shipped off to the Military District. I wanted to know what they were. Once I cradled one in my arm wondering what it was. Finally I smashed the thing to see what it looked like inside. The technician came running up, very upset, "why did you smash it? Oh, you shouldn't have done that!"

She married a Han soldier from Shanxi who also worked on the farm and was promoted to deputy team leader in 1962 and team leader the next year. When volunteer youth from eastern China came in 1965 and 1966, twenty-three were assigned to the team that she managed. She divided the fields into small sections and gave each team member responsibility for his or her own section. She complained that the Han youth did not do their work properly because they engaged in political struggle sessions at night rather than sleeping, and that they called her "Liu Shaoqi" and a "capitalist roader" for dividing up their work tasks rather than doing everything completely collectively.[48] Nonetheless, her position at the time as a leader who oversaw volunteer Han youth was one of significant status in the new society compared to both her youth as a servant and the experiences of most poor Tibetans who stayed in villages that were reorganized into communes.

Among the early workers were also women from Kham. Tsegyi was from Jomda County in Chamdo. Her family arrived in Lhasa in 1954 and stayed at Lubu Pangtsang, where a community of beggars lived in tents. She found work in construction, first on the new Kuru Zampa Bridge, and then in the Military District, before joining the July First State Farm in 1957. She worked at different times hauling night soil from Lhasa's latrines, on the farm's vegetable and grain cultivation teams, and in the farm's apple orchard. Tsegyi was especially proud of her role in caring for the apple trees, recalling that she built a special enclosure around them and always gave them extra fertilizer and special attention. She was attached to the trees because of what she viewed as their great historical value on account of Chen Yi's visit to plant them. After her retirement in the 1990s, she was shocked and saddened to learn that they had been cut down, and went to ask the new director of the farm why he had allowed this to happen. "These days the people are new people, and they have new brains. I don't understand how they think. They told me that you shouldn't try to wear old shoes to walk down a new road," she said, referring to the lack of fit between her collective-era subjectivity, forged in the 1950s, and the new road of market reform and development that became dominant several decades later.

Tsegyi also had very fond memories of the rice porridge and steamed bread served for breakfast at the farm, and the generous portions of what she remembered as delicious food. Because her parents were in Lhasa without income, she tried to be frugal, and always saved some food to bring to them. Tsegyi joined the Party in 1962. She recalled that when she was young, she had no interest or belief in religion at all. She was firmly against it. Then, as her six siblings passed away one by one, she gradually started to find comfort in Buddhism. After she retired, she found that she felt better when she invited monks to her house for prayers and services, and started to go on pilgrimages and circumambulate the Lingkor every morning. In her own words, she had become a "very typical religious person." She is not the only one. She told me about Yudron, another retired woman from Kham who had joined the farm very early and was now never home because she was always on pilgrimage. Tsegyi sometimes reminded Yudron that during the Cultural Revolution, she had been very vehemently opposed to religion. But Yudron simply replies that she is old and near death, and therefore "it wouldn't do" not to go on religious pilgrimages. Others like Lhamo, who also joined the July First State Farm early on, never joined the Party despite many attempts to persuade her to join, and despite her great love for the farm and fondness for the old days, because she and her husband Nyima had maintained throughout what they called "a propensity for the Dharma."

Tsegyi's simultaneous renewed faith in Tibetan Buddhism and Party membership clearly ate at her. She frequently wished to discuss the issue. Indeed, such examples of early Tibetan Party members who once fervently criticized religion and persecuted others but now in old age seek out spiritual guidance and take actions to accumulate merit, are common across Tibet. Their presence speaks to what Charlene Makley calls an ongoing quandary of agency in Tibetan communities as they continue to grapple with the nature of morality and Tibetan agency during the violence of the Maoist years.[49] At the same time as Tsegyi is now committed to precisely what was deemed most objectionable by the apparatuses of the state that workers like her helped support, however, she remains nostalgic for her participation in building state power and the legitimacy of the new regime in the 1950s. "Without the Communist Party," she often told me in 2001–2 when we were discussing vegetable production, "we'd have nothing at all now in Tibet. These young people who talk about independence have no idea what things were like before. They have no idea."

Interests and desires are not cleanly mapped onto or readable from singular subject positions, as both sides in the Tibet Question would have it. Tsegyi in many ways encapsulates the official Chinese narrative of liberation: a poor Tibetan woman who labored to transform herself into a new socialist subject and a proper citizen of the PRC, who helped consolidate the power of the Chinese state over Tibetan territory, and benefited personally from it. Yet this did not erase the sedimented traces of her faith and the efficacy for her of its embodied rituals of circumambulation and pilgrimage. She embraces the narrative of gratitude—that Tibetans would "have nothing at all" were it not for the Chinese state's liberation and development—but belies the idea that anyone who believes this would also willingly give up their religious identity, faith, and practices.

The stories of Tsegyi and other early state farm workers like her are also invisible in exile histories, in which they can only be explained as "traitors" or dupes, in a narrative in which an ethnic-national subject position, a loyalty to the imagined Tibetan nation, is the only one that matters. This fails to account for the fraught intersections of nationalism and race with class and especially gender, as well as the construction of a fragile state hegemony in the early 1950s. Though state apparatuses became increasingly coercive, the establishment of state power and the process of state territorialization began with elements of consent forged in part through the promise of gender mobility. The experiences of the early state farm workers show that in the 1950s the CCP was quite successful at convincing at least some Tibetans that Chinese presence was a positive improvement.

The young women who joined the farm, in particular, left conditions of impoverishment as well as their traditional subordinate roles in the household. Though Tibetan women are generally accepted to have enjoyed higher status and greater personal freedom than those in neighboring China and India, they nevertheless had lower status and power in society than men, and were typically relegated to the domestic sphere, responsible for a disproportionate share of the labor burden.[50] Since the eleventh century, the term *kyemen* (Wylie: *skye dman*) meaning "low birth" has been commonly used for "woman." The gendered hierarchy of Tibetan society considered women sites of impurity, justifying their exclusion from powerful sacred spaces but simultaneously responsible for the burden of accumulating merit.[51]

The strategy of allying with poor Tibetan women with the promise (if not the delivery) of liberation from traditional gender roles paralleled, on a smaller scale, the Soviet attempt to recruit Muslim women in Central Asia as a "surrogate proletariat" to spark the revolutionary process where no real proletariat existed.[52] The Soviet Union tried to exploit gender and generational tensions within Central Asian Muslim societies in order to break down the traditional patriarchal household and clan structures, thus allowing for society to be subsequently reconstituted into a socialist system. Women who participated by unveiling or running away from home suffered a severe backlash and were sometimes murdered. In Tibet, too, women were mobilized to break male monastic as well as secular authority. In her study of Labrang in Amdo, Charlene Makley argues that the figure of the Tibetan woman cadre "embodied the culmination of national incorporation as emasculation," and that such women were thus "disproportionately metonymic of a particularly cataclysmic and emasculating regime of value shift for Tibetans" which was key to their state incorporation.[53] The backlash was not nearly as strong in Lhasa as in Central Asia, though women who joined the farms were taunted and harassed during the early 1950s. While many of the early farm workers became loyal to the new state, both through the great improvements in their own conditions as well as through the embodied labor in which they participated, they did not fully accept the terms of their new roles as Chinese socialist subjects, as indicated by their continuing Tibetan Buddhist practice.

Land and Labor on the Communes

The July First and August First State Farms were key sites of state territorialization and the establishment of hegemony in the early 1950s. Throughout the Maoist period, the system of state farms was key to the maintenance of the military and thus of territorial control. At the same time, state farms were envisioned as the highest form of socialist agricultural production, meant to demonstrate the effectiveness of new socialist agriculture to the masses who were organized not on state farms, but in collectives, and later communes. Communes, rather than state farms, were how the overwhelming majority of Tibetans experienced the collective period.

Following the failed March 1959 uprising, the terms of the Seventeen Point Agreement were tossed aside and by February 1960, the government announced the completion of two stages of the first phase of "democratic reform," including the abolition of corvée labor, rent reduction, and land distribution. In the village of Kyichuling, which in the first half of the twentieth century had been home to nine taxpayer households under the jurisdiction of a college of Sera Monastery, as well as of a number of servants of the personal estate of Bragri Rinpoche, the year 1959 was associated with the policy "whoever sows shall reap." Because the old estates were no longer in place to claim the already-planted crops, they belonged that year to whoever planted them. Shortly thereafter, land reform was implemented. Land was seized from the two estates and divided among the peasantry. Each of the sixty-three residents of Kyichuling received five *khal,* or roughly one-third of a hectare of farmland.[54] About a quarter of village land was allocated to a smaller neighboring village. Mutual aid teams were formed, but disbanded again the next year in favor of a cooperative, which villagers called the "big wind cooperative" because it came so quickly, altering the fabric of social organization, like a large and sudden gust of wind. This cooperative lasted for less than a year before mutual aid teams were re-formed.

However, villagers remember 1960 most vividly not for the formation of the short-lived "big wind cooperative," but rather as "the year dogs were eaten." In marked contrast to early state farm workers' fond recollections of plentiful food during the 1950s, the early 1960s on the communes was a time of great hunger, as it was throughout China during the Great Leap Forward famine that killed more than thirty million. In central Tibet, hunger was produced by a confluence of bad weather, poor leadership, and heavy grain extraction. In Kyichuling, new leaders forced villagers to harvest while it was still raining, resulting in rotten crops. In addition, grain stores from previous years were confiscated.

Tibetans regularly consumed yak, cow, sheep and goat, but avoided, and to a large extent still avoid fish and most other meats.[55] The consumption of dogs was unthinkable, alien to past and present Tibetan practice and identity. The killing, boiling, and especially eating of dogs in 1960 marked a particularly traumatic event, the assignment of class labels, as well as a time that the entire social world radically changed. Elderly villages frequently exclaimed conspiratorially, "some people ate dogs!" but were very quick to insist, "of course, *I* wasn't a dog eater." "We have a saying," added one, "only crows eat dogs." Villagers said that leaders ordered them to kill dogs for the purpose of boiling the carcasses and using them as fertilizer. They consistently denied their own participation in this alien consumption practice, which accompanied the alienating forms of labor and social organization that were introduced at the time.

In 1960, landless peasants received a new identity, the class label "the poor" (*ul-pong)*, and former servants were identified as having been *tren yog* (Wylie: *bran g.yog*—lifetime servants).[56] Taxpayer households of Kyichuling who had not had servants were classified as middle peasants whereas those who did were given the classification "representatives of feudal lords." Houses, food, and other possessions of the latter were confiscated and distributed to the poor. Even the possessions of middle peasants were subject to confiscation and redistribution. Dickey, from a middle peasant household, recalled that in 1960 all of her family's *tsampa* was confiscated. However, she had hidden a little bit of *tsampa* by spreading it out in a thin layer under a carpet on her bed. As a result, she claimed, her family was not forced to eat dog meat. The family dared not eat *tsampa* during the day, fearing a "struggle session" against them if they were discovered. Instead, they ate secretly at night. As Dickey told this story, she repeated several times that "no one in this family ever ate dog meat. I never ate dog meat." On the other hand, she claimed that the leader "saved the best parts of the dog for himself and higher leaders. He smeared dog fat on his face. All of the cadres ate dog during that time." The social upheaval of the period is inflected through memories of both hunger and the consumption of what would in ordinary times not be considered food. This was true not only of dogs in Kyichuling but also of horses on the Phenpo State Farm, where conditions of labor and remuneration were much more similar to those on the communes than to the August First and July First farms. Phenpo farm workers remembered: "There wasn't enough to eat on the farm so the government killed a lot of horses and donkeys, put spices on them, and sold them to people to eat. . . . Some people ate them."

The following year, villagers were once again divided into mutual aid teams of seven to ten members each. Team members were required to help each other out with labor on each household's fields. At the end of the year, families who had accumulated fewer hours paid those who had worked more in cash. Those classified as "representatives of feudal lords" were not allowed to join the mutual aid teams, and those who had been classified as "middle peasants" were specifically required to assist the poor members.

The first communes in Tibet were formed in 1963, but most were created between 1966 and 1970, more than a decade after the peak of commune formation across China in 1958.[57] In 1966, Kyichuling was reorganized as a production brigade of Red Star Commune. All means of production, such as livestock and farming tools, were turned over to the brigade, which provided a small amount of compensation to their owners over the next eight years, after which they were owned by the brigade. The commune also purchased tractors. Excluded from the mutual aid teams, those labeled "representatives of feudal lords" were now required to join the commune.

All villagers in Kyichuling between the ages of sixteen and sixty were required to join the production brigades. Although most villagers did farmwork, some were assigned to a sideline work brigade whose members were sent to quarry outside of the village.[58] The agricultural production brigade had a seven-person management team: a senior brigade leader, a junior brigade leader, an accountant, a treasurer, a storeroom keeper in charge of all nonmonetary goods, a political leader, and a women's leader.[59] The team met to decide what kind of work should be done every day. At the end of each day, every worker received a certain number of work points. These work points were assigned after lengthy discussions among the brigade members over how much each person labored and how much that labor should be worth. This was quite different from the situation in the July First and August First State Farms, where workers were paid fixed monthly salaries. Because of their position as state workers rather than commune members, employees of state farms were privileged and sheltered from much of the hunger and deprivation that other Tibetans suffered. This was particularly true of the military August First State Farm, whose workers recalled eating rice and wheat in their mess halls even in 1960, whereas workers on the civilian July First State Farm remember the early 1960s as a time of eating weeds and flowers because of food shortage.[60]

Commune households retained very small private plots for potatoes and radishes. Mess halls and communal dining were for the most part not found in the TAR as they were in many other regions of China.[61] Villagers were allowed to sell potatoes and radishes in Lhasa, but in practice they were too busy with other work assigned by their brigades.[62] There were very few days off during the year—often only three days, beginning on October 1, for PRC National Day, and a few for the New Year. There was also little free time during the workday, which often started before sunrise and continued until after dark.

Around the same time that communes were formed, the state also began to disseminate Green Revolution inputs and winter varieties of wheat and barley. Winter wheat was first cultivated in Tibet on the July First State Farm in 1952, and was grown on a number of state farms through the early

1960s. It was disseminated on a larger scale starting in the late 1960s, together with urea fertilizer, herbicides, and pesticides. Winter barley was introduced around 1970, as was diammonium phosphate. Chemical fertilizers were first distributed for free, and then remained very heavily subsidized for decades.

As was the case throughout China, households were allowed to retain a set amount of grain for seeds, stalks for fodder, and a basic grain ration for consumption; some grain was also set aside in local grain reserves.[63] The rest was extracted by the state through two different mechanisms. One was a set state share of the grain produced, that is, an agricultural tax which in Tibet was called the "patriotic grain" or "patriotic government grain" provision.[64] The remainder was declared "surplus grain" and sold to the state at below-market prices. This surplus was arbitrarily defined, and often increased when international relations went sour and China became isolated. In Tibet, the amount defined as "surplus" increased during the border war with India in 1962.

At the end of each year, communes balanced their total income and expenditures and calculated their net profits.[65] This amount was then divided by the total number of work points accumulated by all members of the commune to determine how much money each work point would be worth. Out of the amount that workers received for their work points, the basic grain ration was subtracted based on the government set price for grain. Monetary equivalents of allocated meat, wool, yarn and other supplies were also deducted. If this sum was more than the amount of money workers had earned, they owed money to the commune. Otherwise, the excess work points were usually given back in kind or cash.

Recalling their experience of the communes, villagers in Kyichuling routinely described it as "the time when we worked twenty out of the twenty-four hours of the day." Even the elderly villagers who framed their recollections of the "old society" in the form of bitter narratives about the harshness of life before the 1950s still described 1960 and the years of the commune to me as the absolute worst times, when they suffered the most from too much labor and not enough food. Like state farm workers, their labor to transform nature through the growing of new crops, digging new fields, building irrigation canals, hauling night soil, harvesting, threshing, plowing, and so forth produced both crops and new forms of subjectivity. However, unlike the early state farm workers, those on the communes did not have the same sense of their labor contributing to a historic, noble cause. Though the liberation of women continued to be an important component of Maoist rhetoric, no surrogate proletariat was needed or specifically sought by the time Tibetan communes were established, and the promise of gender equality was tied to state discourses that repudiated local gendered discursive practices while nevertheless reinforcing male privilege.[66] Looking back, the socialist period under Mao was not a "dream time," as it is for an older cohort of Chinese workers who came of age in factories in the 1950s or for many of the earliest Tibetan farm workers on the July First and August First State Farms, but rather a nightmare of dog eating and endless toil.[67]

DECOLLECTIVIZATION

In Kyichuling, the Household Responsibility System was implemented in May 1984, allocating farmland use rights to individual households, while ownership rights remained with the collective. Other collective assets were also divided, or in some cases such as tractors and collective buildings, sold to individual households. Each of the 302 villagers at the time received roughly three *mu* (one-fifth of a hectare) of farmland.[68] The plots were divided into three grades, and all households given land in each category, resulting in a pattern of numerous small and dispersed plots of land for each household.[69] Villagers were at first unwilling to completely decollectivize, out of fear that this was yet another policy change that would not last for long. Instead they divided into eight groups of households who continued to work together for one or two years before completely decollectivizing to the household level. Even after complete decollectivization, households continued to exchange labor with their relatives and friends.

Unpaid collective labor, including participation in planting and trimming trees, maintaining irrigation canals, and road maintenance also remained mandatory in the village after decollectivization. These tasks also included farming on collective land, land that reverts to village collective use after the holder of its use rights transfers her or his household registration out of the village, whether because of marriage or employment.[70] For the first few years after decollectivization, village leaders continued to dictate cropping decisions, but soon left them solely up to the households. Most families in Kyichuling preferred barley to wheat until the late 1990s, when they began to sublease their land use rights to Han migrant vegetable farmers.

By the late 1990s, Han migrants dominated vegetable farming on the decollectivized July First and August First State Farms as well. After the Agricultural Reclamation Bureau was disbanded as a separate bureaucracy and made a department of the Agriculture and Animal Husbandry Bureau in 1986, management of the August First State Farm was transferred to Lhasa Municipality. By that point, Tibetan workers dominated the work force on the farm. Most Han workers had returned home, leaving only a few retired soldiers, like Dr. Zhang, who had married Tibetan women and stayed on in Lhasa. Land and the greenhouses that were built starting in the early 1980s were decollectivized, and the Tibetan workers on the farm were given use rights to two *mu* of land per person, but were responsible for paying an annual rent. This rent was quite low during the first years after decollectivization. However, as more Sichuanese migrants arrived in Lhasa to rent land for greenhouse vegetable cultivation, the farm management soon realized that much more income could be brought in by renting land to them.

This was necessary as the farm had officially become a business enterprise, the August First Company, which had to stop "eating from the iron rice bowl" and struggled to meet its pension obligations to retired workers. It sought to generate income by renting its former administrative buildings to Han migrants to run dumpling and noodle shops, as well as by renting land to the migrants.[71] Retired workers on the farm suffered a drastic reversal of fortunes, from being members of a high-profile, well-funded and much-celebrated farm who prided themselves on their transformative historical role, to being neglected and underpaid retirees of a struggling enterprise. They received only about half of the monthly pension of retirees on the July First State Farm. Not surprisingly, they—unlike those who experienced the communes—are particularly nostalgic for the 1950s.

With the introduction of economic reforms in the early 1980s, the environmental imaginary that stressed the militant conquering of nature through correct political thought and the force of socialist labor was eclipsed by the privileging of economic growth through "scientific development." This shift was reflected in the differing fortunes of the July First and August First State Farms. Unlike the economically struggling August First State Farm, the July First State Farm continued to receive considerable state support after it was split into different units, including the TAR Academy of Agricultural and Animal Sciences and the Vegetable Research Institute. In 1992, it also began to rent out its land and greenhouses to Han migrant farmers who produced a new Tibetan landscape, wrapping the earth in plastic greenhouses to grow vegetables and simultaneously furthering state territorialization.

Created out of the same piece of "wasteland full of bumps and hollows," the July First and August First State Farms were key sites of state incorporation at a crucial juncture in Sino-Tibetan history. They encapsulated several different modes of state control: provision of nourishment for soldiers, establishing consent and participation of subaltern groups, the creation of new subjectivities, and the enrollment of nature in state formation. First, the products of the farms not only fed and physically nourished the invading army, but also provided a diet of vegetables that was newly introduced to the Tibetan soil but familiar and comforting to the soldiers. Second, the farms were very successful at recruiting young Tibetans from impoverished, landless families to work on them. Many of these Tibetans went on to become powerful cadres within the new government. Even those who did not do so experienced personal mobility that was simultaneously a process of incorporation into the new political structure. This was particularly true for Tibetan women.

Gender played a crucial role in early PRC state territorialization in central Tibet. In 1950s Lhasa, the state farms offered young women from landless families both a way to think of themselves as oppressed through categories of class and gender, and a way to transcend those obstacles. The farms succeeded in giving them a sense of purpose in their labor, so that nearly half a century later they spoke nostalgically of their labor on the farm in those years, even as they disagreed with contemporary policies against religious practice and the direction they saw society taking. Their simultaneous recollections of pride in their labor and stories, told without animus toward those involved, of being accused by other Tibetans of capitulating to the Chinese and doing their dirty work, point to the complexity of subjectivities and unresolved tensions among Tibetans about agency during the Maoist period.

A third mode of control was enacted through the labor of these workers in producing the material landscape. Their "victory" over nature visibly displayed the power of the Chinese state. By hauling soil, reshaping the land through backbreaking labor, and planting vegetables for Han soldiers to consume, Tibetan men and women helped to sustain those soldiers in their task of "constructing the frontier." From the 1950s to the 1980s, labor for the production of a new socialist landscape was mobilized through spectacular state campaigns such as Learn from Dazhai that sought to reproduce the spatial and agricultural patterns of eastern China in the TAR. These transformations of nature and spatial relations contributed to the naturalization of the PRC as a spatial container for Tibetans. At the same time, the labor of Tibetans recruited to transform the landscape was sedimented into their memories and subjectivities, whether nostalgia for their historic participation in constructing the country, or memories of endless toil.

The following chapters turn to the introduction of market reforms in the 1980s, which marked a second major landscape transformation and a new form of state territorialization. The vegetable fields created out of "wasteland" in the 1950s were enclosed in plastic, as Han migrant cultivators, rather than state campaigns, introduced and cultivated new types of vegetables. No longer involved, Tibetans declared themselves "too lazy" to take part in this new type of agriculture. These declarations of indolence are inflected by both the memories of collective period toil and labor discussed here, as well as a new hegemonic state project that construes Tibetans as being in need of development.

II

Plastic

Figure 3. Plastic greenhouses in Lhasa's peri-urban landscape, 2001. Photo by author.

Lhasa Humor

I spent a lot of time in Lhasa laughing, at everything from the slapstick comedy of watching strangers douse each other in buckets of water in the Barkor to pointed and ironic commentaries on state memory work. The latter often referenced the familiar obligation from everyday life in the Maoist era, still revived in official media around important anniversaries, to "speak bitterness" about life in "old society" Tibet. The production of testimonies about the harshness of class-based oppression in pre-"liberation" Tibet was mandatory during the Maoist period as a demonstration of class consciousness and a performance of gratitude. Though sometimes angry and bitter, the counternarratives to these required testimonies were at other times quite funny. A middle-aged cadre offered the following alternative account:

> When [the government] interviewed old people, trying to get them to tell stories about how terrible their former masters were, there were sometimes funny situations when things did not go as they intended. They interviewed a ninety-year old woman in Chushur. They asked her about her life, hoping she would talk about the hardships of her life as a serf on the estate. When asked about her childhood, she said that she remembered the Gorkha army [of Nepal]: "The Gorkha army came to Tibet when they came, and then they left when they left. Later on the English also came. The English army came when they came, and then they left when they left. And then another one came, but this one just stays and stays and doesn't leave." They asked another old lady about the estate where she had worked, and the old woman started crying. The interviewers thought that this time, finally, they were really going to get some good results, some statements about the horrors of life before 1959. But the old woman said through her tears, "there was no one better than my estate master," she said, using an honorific term. "I've never met anyone better than him at all," she added, crying because she missed him.

More frequently, though, I was told jokes, often mockeries of the purportedly sorry state of contemporary Tibetan culture and character, or jests about the feelings of being overwhelmed by Han migrants.

President Jiang Zemin asks TAR Party Secretary Chen Kuiyuan how and what the Tibetans in the TAR are doing these days. Chen replies, "They're not doing anything at all. They're all drunk." When Jiang hears this, he is very happy and orders many more truckloads of Yellow River Beer to be sent to Tibet.

A foreigner visits Lhasa and, standing under the front side of the magnificent Potala, says to himself in amazement, "the nationality that built this palace must have been mighty indeed." Then the same foreigner walks around to the Lukhang, the small park in back of the Potala, and sees all of the destitute Tibetan drunkards, shakes his head, and says to himself, "this nationality is finished. There's no hope for these people."

In the morning, Tibetans listen to Voice of America on the radio and are very happy. Their *tsampa* tastes very good. At night Tibetans watch Chinese Central Television news, and they are unhappy. They comfort themselves by drinking lots of beer.

One day, fifty years from now, two Tibetans run into each other by chance in the Barkor, in front of the Jokhang. They are so surprised and moved that, though total strangers, they embrace and begin to cry, exclaiming "it's been so many years since I've seen another Tibetan!"

One day, a Japanese guy, an American guy, a Tibetan guy, and a Chinese guy find themselves together in the same compartment of a train. They are on a long trip. After a while, they start to chat and get to know each other. Suddenly, the Japanese guy opens the window and throws his Walkman out of the moving train. The other three think to themselves, "My goodness! He's just thrown his Walkman out of the window!" Seeing their surprise, the Japanese man says causally, "Well, you know, in Japan, Walkmen are a dime a dozen. There're so many of them; what's another Walkman? I can always get another one." The four men sit for a while longer and then suddenly the American man opens the window, opens his wallet, and throws some cash out. He says, "You know, in America there's so much money. You can always get more money. What's the big deal?" After this the Tibetan man thinks to himself, "well, now what should I do?" He thinks for a minute or two, gets up, opens the window, and throws the Chinese guy out.

3 Vectors of Development

Migrants and the Making of "Little Sichuan"

> The focal point of the policy of opening the door wider in Tibet should be towards the inner part of the country. . . . We should encourage traders, investment, economic units, and individuals to enter our region to run different sorts of enterprises.
>
> —Ragdi, TAR deputy party secretary, 1995

The trip from Chengdu, the capital of Sichuan province, to Lhasa encapsulates the rapid transformations of Tibet since economic reform. Until the late 1980s, Han cadres who went home for the Spring Festival holiday returned to Lhasa loaded down with large sacks of vegetables. Though the July First State Farm and urban cooperatives grew vegetables for the urban market, and though many government work units had their own plots of land on which cadres grew vegetables for work unit consumption, supply was far from sufficient to satisfy the urban demand, particularly by Han cadres.[1] Over the next decade, the scarcity turned into a glut of vegetables grown by Han migrants, largely in greenhouses built on land subleased from Tibetan peasants in peri-urban villages. Much of the arable land around the edges of urban expansion was covered in plastic. In many villages, every single local household had subleased land to one or more Han migrant families for vegetable cultivation. As a result, the passengers on the plane to Lhasa that I boarded early one morning in June 2005 no longer had any reason to think about the availability of fresh vegetables or restaurants serving familiar cuisine. Instead of vegetables, most were loaded down with cameras and crowded around the window seats trying to get snapshots of the snow-capped peaks below.

On the bus ride from Gongkar Airport to Lhasa, a gregarious Sichuanese construction contractor explained to me that he had begun to do business in Lhasa the previous year. He finds it quite convenient, he said, because "Lhasa is very close for us—only two hours by plane," and while he mostly hires construction workers back at home, he finds it easy enough to hire them once he arrives in Lhasa too. All of his employees are from Sichuan, and his contracts exclusively come from state funding, including infrastructure projects related to the Open Up the West campaign because, he explained, the private sector in Tibet does not offer nearly the same opportunities.

Behind me another Sichuanese man, who had been living in Linzhi County for the past decade, was explaining Tibet to a Sichuanese tourist seated next to him. He extolled the beauty of the landscape and added that life was hard ten or twenty years ago, but no longer: "There are lots of vegetables on the market. Too many! Everything you can get in *neidi* (inland, or Han China), you can get here."[2] In fact, he said, "being here is just like being in Sichuan—there's really no difference at all." As the bus rolled into the western part of town, my fellow passengers cheerfully pulled out their cellphones and loudly began to make appointments in Sichuan-accented conversations to meet their friends for lunch at various hotpot and dumpling restaurants.

Sichuan has more out-migration than any other Chinese province; each year, eight to ten million of its residents are estimated to be working outside of the province, with remittances in 2000 reaching 202 billion RMB, equivalent to its total government revenue.[3] In the TAR as well, Sichuanese migrants far outnumber migrants from other provinces.[4] Vegetable farmers also come from provinces including Henan, Hebei, Shandong, Anhui, Gansu, and even Liaoning, but by far the most come from Sichuan. As a result, many Sichuanese vegetable farmers, shopkeepers, and construction workers feel that Lhasa is a home away from home. As a successful Sichuanese construction contractor informed me, "Our Lhasa is called 'little Sichuan.'" On another occasion, a group of vegetable farmers from Sichuan's Mianyang County scoffed when I discussed with them official population statistics for Lhasa. One man laughed at my apparent obtuseness, scolding me to "use your own eyes and look around yourself!" and his friend, recently discharged from three years of military service in Lhasa, added, "Don't you know that our Lhasa is called 'little Sichuan'?" While this new sense of place is a source of comfort and familiarity to many, it is also a source of nostalgia for others. Indeed, while a great deal of discursive labor is performed by state authorities to rebut the very possibility of Tibetan nostalgia for the past, distant or recent, a growing number of Han visitors and residents are openly nostalgic for the Tibet they once knew, or at least imagined. Tourists in search of an exotic, different Tibet are disappointed by what they feel is a lack of authenticity and by Lhasa's surprising resemblance to other Chinese cities. A young sociologist working in Sichuan opined about her first visit to Lhasa in 2004, "I felt like it was just like any other city in *neidi*. Going to Lhasa, it feels like you haven't even left Sichuan. Everywhere you go, you can hear Sichuanese dialect. Lhasa is also known as 'little Sichuan.'"

Lhasa is experienced as "little Sichuan" not only because of the sheer number of Han migrants from Sichuan in Lhasa, but also because of their very visible domination of economic activities. The process by which Sichuanese migrants came to monopolize vegetable production, as a case study of one of the many economic niches taken over by Han migrants, offers a lens onto the role of state policies in setting the conditions for both migration and the establishment of markets. This state-market nexus in Han migration belies the neoliberal ideology of a placeless, asocial invisible hand, and demonstrates the close intertwining of development as a deliberate project of improvement on the one hand and the expansion of capitalist social relations and value production on the other.

Greatly increased Han migration into Tibet coincided with the replacement of "liberation" by development as the primary official *raison d'être* of state control over Tibet. The naturalization of Han migrant presence in the TAR as agents of development works as a new form of territorialization. State discursive practice welcomes the migrants as bearers of the gift of development who bring needed skills to Tibetans, and through their higher "quality," raise the overall standard of living and the GDP of the region. This chapter explores how the migrants come to see themselves as vectors of development to whom Tibetans should be grateful, when ironically it is actually the migrants who are its most prominent beneficiaries.

The Chinese Presence: Cadres and Migrants

Chinese migration is undoubtedly one of the most contentious aspects of contemporary PRC rule in Tibet. Activists and exiles have long charged that the Han presence in Tibet is a deliberate policy of "cultural genocide" that has resulted in making Tibetans "a minority in their own land."[5] In rebuttal, the PRC government points out that ethnic Tibetans accounted for 93 percent of the population in the TAR in the 2000 census, and furthermore, that Han migration is good for the development of the Tibetan economy.[6] Likewise, Chinese intellectuals have countered that complaints about migration are invalid and contradictory because restrictions on migration across China were long criticized as a violation of human rights; thus, the free and natural flow of migrants to different parts of PRC territory, including Tibet, cannot be reversed without becoming a violation of migrants' human rights.[7] Narratives of migrants as part of a deliberate plan of "population swamping" and destruction of local culture collide with narratives of migrants as voluntary bearers of economic development who bring skills and technology while responding freely to market signals.

To clarify these issues it is necessary to distinguish between temporary migrants and those who transfer their household registrations. For three decades starting in the 1950s, China's *hukou* or household registration system controlled population movement more strictly than in any other state in the modern world, and instituted the agricultural and nonagricultural registrations that became the fundamental social divide throughout the collective period. Because only those with nonagricultural registrations were allowed access to grain coupons, the system enforced a rigid delineation of rural and urban residences that allowed the extraction of surplus from agricultural areas to develop urban industries.[8] The system began to relax in 1984, and in 1988 the State Council recommended that provinces with impoverished populations export their labor to other provinces.[9] Following the abolition of the food ration coupon system in 1992, large numbers of migrants began to move, mostly to the eastern coastal areas where they provided low-cost labor in export-oriented factories that made China "the world's factory floor." Many rural areas across China have emptied out of all but children and the elderly, as working adults leave for employment in towns and cities. Despite the magnitude of the migration and various reforms, the *hukou* system remains in place as of 2012.[10] Migrants are officially classified as "floating population" because they maintain their permanent residence registration in their place of origin.

Until the 2000 census, official statistical data did not count the floating population. Moreover, official statistics have never counted military personnel. Among those that have been counted are cadres, who began to be transferred to Tibet in the 1950s on fixed-term assignments, as part of a larger program of sending teachers and cadres to minority border areas to carry out national policy, lead the "backward" minority nationalities, and integrate them into the Motherland.[11] This policy was suspended during the Cultural Revolution and resumed in 1979, but following CCP Party Secretary Hu Yaobang's landmark visit to Lhasa in 1980, there were five major withdrawals of cadres through the 1980s.[12] In fact, for all but three years between 1981 and 1992, the officially registered net migration to the TAR was negative.[13] This was part of a more general set of culturally and politically liberal policies that followed Hu Yaobang's 1980 declaration that the Communist Party had "let the Tibetan people down," and which included the exemption of farmers and nomads from taxes, a reduction in the number of Chinese cadres, and the revitalization of Tibetan culture, language, and education.[14]

However, these policies were reversed after the nationalist demonstrations that erupted in Lhasa from 1987 to 1989 and ended with then TAR Party Secretary Hu Jintao imposing martial law on the region for more than a year.[15] State authorities responded in part by tightening political control and shifting toward increased use of surveillance technologies, an expanded role for the State Security Bureau, and substantial funding for an informer network.[16] At the same time, in conjunction with Deng Xiaoping's celebrated Southern Tour in 1992 that called for the deepening of economic reforms across China, marketization intensified while state subsidies for infrastructure projects were also increased. TAR leaders debated these changes when they were proposed. Some opposed certain aspects of the reforms in the hopes of creating a more Tibetan-centered development, with preferential economic concessions for ethnic Tibetans. The winners of the debate were those who argued that "water does not flow uphill in Tibet," to indicate that no special policies for Tibet should be enacted with regard to opening up the economy.[17]

The proponents of this position selectively adopted tenets of neoliberal ideology, which calls for free, frictionless flows of people, goods, and money, and assumes that in the interest of allowing the "invisible hand" of the market to work to achieve greatest efficiency, special privileges should not be given to any group of people regardless of differences in the playing field. This set of ideas was mobilized to relax restrictions for outsiders seeking to establish businesses in the TAR and to render unproblematic the removal of barriers to, and thus the increased flow of migrants into Tibet. In April 1992, instructions were issued to government offices in the TAR to convert the ground floor areas of any roadside properties to small shops that could be rented out to retailers.[18] In November, the TAR government relaxed and simplified the acquisition of business licenses, and in December, it removed interprovincial checkpoints on roads between the TAR and neighboring provinces.[19] In the following year, a reported fifty-three hundred new individually run enterprises opened in Lhasa, an increase of 56 percent over 1992.[20] Thus, once controls on movement into the TAR were lifted, the number of private enterprises in the TAR increased quickly and dramatically.

Further policies affecting the Han and Hui (Chinese Muslim) presence in Tibet were implemented following the Third National Work Forum on Tibet in 1994, the third of five National Work Forums on Tibet held in Beijing between 1980 and 2010, and attended by China's most senior leaders. The forum established a new "Aid-Tibet" (Ch: *yuanzang*) program in which eighteen provinces and provincial-level municipalities were asked to provide aid to specifically designated "counterpart" cities, counties, and prefectures in the TAR. It also launched a related program, to send "Aid-Tibet cadres" from these eighteen provinces, as well as sixty ministries and commissions at the central level, to work at all levels of government in the TAR for three-year terms. The Fourth Work Forum, which was held in 2001 and largely confirmed and continued the policies of the Third, extended the commitment of the Aid-Tibet program to 2014. Between 1994 and 2009, 3,747 Aid-Tibet cadres went to Tibet in five batches. The sixth group, sent after the Fifth National Work Forum was held in 2010, included more personnel dedicated to political, religious, and ethnic affairs, and "united front work."[21]

Aid-Tibet cadres who do well—that is, those who serve their terms without being held responsible for any "political problems" under their watch—can often look forward to promotions when they return home. The desire both to have something to show for their brief work stints in Tibet so as to better the case for advancement at home, combined with strong pressure to avoid responsibility for political incidents, creates incentives for cadres to construct buildings rather than invest in projects with less tangible outputs, as politically safe, visible monuments to their achievements. Such buildings, in the words frequently used by Tibetan villagers and urban residents to describe various development projects, are forms of "image engineering" (*xingxiang gongcheng*) or "appearancism" (*nampa ringlug*), their deliberate visibility spectacles of state investment in Tibet's development. The Aid-Tibet cadres are widely disliked by Lhasa residents, who view them unfavorably compared to the earlier generation of cadres who came in the 1950s and who, unlike the newer waves of cadres, often made efforts to learn the Tibetan language.

In addition to Aid-Tibet cadres, other Aid-Tibet programs have also brought official groups of Han to work in Tibet. From 2003 to 2005, one hundred tour guides from across China arrived annually to help Tibet develop its tourism industry, ostensibly because of a shortage of tour guides during the peak season and a lack of qualified English speakers.[22] Tibetan residents of Lhasa tell a different story. One Tibetan Communist Party member described the program as "the thing I hate the most." Her reasons included not only the very high salaries and living expenses provided to the tour guides, who knew little about Tibet and spent the first few months being trained while on salary, but also the priority they were given in employment over local tour guides. As a result, the latter sat idle while the ill-informed Han guides were given opportunities to work. "Not only can they of course not speak any Tibetan, but some of them don't speak English very well, and some of them have almost no experience as guides."

Though the official transfer of cadres creates a significant amount of resentment, their absolute numbers are small, far outweighed by members of the floating population, who began to migrate to Tibet in the early 1980s with the relaxation of the *hukou* system. The flow of migrants was facilitated by the Second Work Forum of 1984, which called for the freeing of restrictions on Chinese opening businesses in Tibet, and established a pattern of development in the years to come with funding for forty-three infrastructure projects including hotels, gymnasiums, and hospitals.[23] Costing 480 million RMB, these were turnkey projects, in which provinces responsible for their implementation brought in all construction needs, from equipment to raw materials to workers. Altogether the projects brought a total of nineteen thousand personnel to Tibet, but created very few backward and forward linkages.[24]

These trends were reinforced and accelerated after Deng Xiaoping's 1992 Southern Tour and the 1994 Third Work Forum, which consolidated the critique of earlier concessions to a special "Tibetanized" form of development, again based on the argument that a restriction on movement would work against the inexorable logic of the market. TAR Party Secretary

Chen Kuiyuan declared in November 1994, "All localities . . . should welcome the opening of various restaurants and stores by people from *neidi* . . . [Tibetans] should not be afraid that people from *neidi* are taking their money or jobs away. Under a socialist market economy, Tibet develops its economy and the Tibetan people learn the skills to earn money when a person from *neidi* makes money."[25] Prior to this time, officials felt pressured to insist that Han migrants were specialized technicians, but this marked a turning point for the encouragement of non-Tibetan entrepreneurialism without any need for justification other than that migrants were naturally good for Tibet's development.

The Third Work Forum also brought with it an additional sixty-two large-scale infrastructural projects funded with 4.86 billion RMB of direct investment from the central government.[26] These were again turnkey projects, which not only thwarted the creation of backward and forward linkages but also brought large numbers of Han Chinese laborers to Tibet, many of whom stayed on or returned later as petty entrepreneurs. These migrants come to Tibet not through an organized program of permanent settlement, but rather with the intention of staying for a few years to make money and then return home, or perhaps to move on to other migration destinations in China. It is the sheer number of migrants who come and go over a period of several years—a few as long as twenty or more, but most in the range of two or three years[27]—rather than their permanent settlement that leads to the feeling of Tibetans becoming a minority in their own land, and to the migrants experiencing Lhasa as "little Sichuan."

Unlike data collected for statistical yearbooks and previous censuses, the 2000 census did attempt to count temporary migrants if they had been away from their places of residence for more than six months; it reported a total of 158,570 Han in the entire Tibet Autonomous Region, of whom 76,581 were reported as residing in the Lhasa Chengguanqu (see table 1).[28] However, because much of the Han migration to Lhasa is seasonal—construction work, dominated by migrants, ceases between October and March—the November timing of the 2000 census would have underestimated the "floating population" which spends at least part of the year there.[29] The summer Han population, by contrast, includes not only a much larger number of migrants, but also tourists, whose numbers in the TAR reached over four million in 2007.[30] Another survey by the Lhasa government estimated 70–80,000 temporary migrants in Lhasa in the winter and 170,000 in the summer, while the Lhasa Public Security Bureau, responsible since 2000 for issuing temporary residence certificates to migrants, estimated the population of migrants as varying between 100,000 and 200,000.[31]

Since the beginning of the Open Up the West campaign in 2000 and the completion of the Qinghai-Tibet Railway in 2006, migrant numbers

Table 1. Population by *minzu*, areas closest to urban Lhasa, 2000 Census

Place	Total	Han	Hui	Tibetan
TAR	2,616,329	158,570 (6.06%)	9,031	2,427,168 (92.77%)
Lhasa Municipality (Shi)	474,499	80,584 (16.98%)	4,741	387,124 (81.59%)
Lhasa Chengguanqu	223,001	76,581 (34.34%)	4,429	140,387 (62.95%)
Lhundrub County	50,895	419 (0.82%)	49	50,335
Tolung Dechen County	40,453	1,868 (4.62%)		38,455
Tagtse County	24,906	212 (0.85%)		24,662

Source: PRC 2000 Census, table A1-6.

have visibly increased. Even the March 2008 protests in Lhasa appear to have led only to a temporary dip in the number of migrants, according to Lhasa residents. However, even with the increase since the 2000 census, and the fact that the large military presence is not reflected in official numbers, there is little evidence to suggest that in the TAR as a whole, Tibetans are a "minority in their own land." Instead, the Han and Hui migrants are largely concentrated in urban and peri-urban areas. Again according to the 2000 census (see table 2), across Lhasa Municipality, the population of residents living under the jurisdiction of city street offices (*jiedao banshichu*) was more than 30 percent Han.[32] If the Public Security Bureau estimate of 200,000 migrants is correct and if these are largely in the urban area of the *Chengguanqu*, then they could very well outnumber Tibetan residents in the same areas (see table 2).

Despite the numbers, Tibetan residents clearly feel overwhelmed by the migrant presence, just as the migrants feel the significance of their own presence. As an elderly woman living in a peri-urban village asked, after she learned that I had previously lived in Beijing, "Tell me. Are there any *gyami* (Chinese) left there? I think there must not be, because they've all come to Lhasa. Lhasa is full of *gyami*. Full, I tell you, full!" Though migrants are largely concentrated in urban and peri-urban areas and in service industries along major highways, a driver who lives in a village near Lhasa expressed the sentiments of many when he claimed that "there isn't a single place in Tibet without *gyami* . . . life is very easy and pleasant for them. No matter what, they can always find work to do. . . . But if a Tibetan wanted to go to inland China to work, no way . . . no one would hire them."

While claims that Chinese migrants now outnumber Tibetans across Tibet are inaccurate, the perception of being overwhelmed by migrants is central

Table 2. Population by *minzu* and by type of township-level unit in Lhasa Municipality, 2000

	Total population	Han population	Tibetan population
City street offices (jiedao)	171,719	62,226	104,203
Urban towns (zhen)	60,117	3,083	56,614
Rural townships (xiang)	242,663	15,275	226,307
Total	474,499	80,584	387,124

Source: PRC 2000 Census, table A1-6.

to the way in which development is experienced and negotiated, particularly because of the role of migrants as vectors of development in official discourse. At stake in claims about migrants such as the ones above is not only the sheer number of migrants but also different conceptions about rights to territory and space, as well as the economic and political marginalization of Tibetans within the broader context of development.[33]

The Political Economy of Development

After economic reforms were launched in 1978, the economy of the coastal areas of China grew quickly while the central and western parts of the country remained relatively stagnant. The coastal region was assigned the task of being China's industrial engine of growth, while the central and western areas would provide natural resources. Deng Xiaoping's maxim of letting some people get rich first, and the theory that the coast would pull the entire country along while wealth trickled west, meant that regional inequality was to be tolerated. In the TAR, real per capita GDP was in recession in the 1980s through mid-1990s, falling to the second lowest in China in 1996.[34] In 1994, investments poured in from the Third Work Forum, including not only the sixty-two infrastructural projects funded by the central government at 4.86 billion RMB, but also 576 construction projects funded with 2.24 billion RMB from fifteen counterpart provinces and municipalities.[35]

Nationally, concerns about economic stagnation in the west were addressed with the Open Up the West campaign announced by CCP Party Secretary Jiang Zemin in 1999 and launched in 2000 with the intent of closing the gap between the newly redefined "western region" and the eastern and coastal provinces, through investment in infrastructure projects to establish the conditions necessary to attract private and foreign investment.[36] However, the campaign was less of a single policy than a set of diverse and fragmented agendas, and a name that was attached to a number of large-scale infrastructural projects that were already planned. Among these was the 2006 completion of the Qinghai-Tibet Railway, which had been planned since the 1950s but was thwarted by immense technical difficulties. It became a key infrastructure project of Open Up the West in 2001, began to run in 2006 after expenditures of more than 4.1 billion USD, and was said by CCP Party Secretary Hu Jintao to be "of great significance in implementing the strategy of great development of the western region, accelerating economic and social development in Qinghai and Tibet . . . strengthening national unity, and jointly realizing the grand goal of building a well-off society."[37] The inclusion of the Qinghai-Tibet Railway supports the argument that, notwithstanding its stated intention of closing the gap between east and west, the Open Up the West campaign is most accurately conceptualized as a program of state and nation building, a renewed "civilizing mission" to more closely incorporate minority ethnic groups, and a reconsolidation of central state control after two decades of decentralization and localism.[38]

With massive state investments pouring in, the GDP of the TAR quadrupled between 1997 and 2007, outdoing even the astonishing growth of the Chinese economy as a whole over the same period.[39] By 2009, the TAR's GDP was nearly 1.7 times that of 2000, and had maintained a double-digit growth rate for seventeen consecutive years.[40] However, this was accompanied by a restructuring of the economy away from productive activities and toward the tertiary sector, of which government and Party agencies became the largest component by 2001. The rapid growth in GDP since the mid-1990s has come almost entirely from this growth in the tertiary sector, primarily administrative expansion, along with periodic construction booms during the building of projects such as the Qinghai-Tibet Railway.[41] In addition to the unusually high proportion of GDP from government administration, the TAR economy is also atypical in that four times more is spent on capital construction than on education—nationally, in comparison, education accounts for more of public expenditure than capital construction.[42]

The rapid growth of the TAR's GDP since the 1990s has come largely from subsidies in one form or another. In 2001, 94 percent of government expenditure was covered by direct fiscal support, mostly from Beijing, and in 2002, direct budgetary subsidies reached 81 percent of GDP. In 2006, the combination of direct subsidies and indirect subsidies (subsidized investment) reached 123 percent of GDP; thus, the TAR rivals some of the worst cases of aid dependency in Africa.[43] These dynamics intensified further after 2008, so that by 2010 direct budgetary subsidies from the central government exceeded 100% of the TAR's GDP for the first time.[44] The negative multiplier effect that has long characterized the dependent economy has gotten steadily worse since the mid-1990s.[45] In 2001, 1 RMB of central government aid to the TAR increased GDP by only 0.47 RMB. This stems from the turnkey nature of most investment, in which subsidies are spent on imports from other provinces rather than on local production.[46] Out-of-province construction companies receive most contracts for subsidized construction and large-scale infrastructure projects. Furthermore, when migrant workers from other provinces are hired on state-subsidized projects, they send home as much as they can of their wages, further reducing the amount of subsidies into the TAR that actually stay there.

Another important structural feature of the TAR economy is the significant gap between urban and rural incomes, the largest disparity in China. Real purchasing power of rural incomes in the TAR dropped in the 1990s while urban incomes skyrocketed, surpassing even those of Shanghai and Beijing to become China's highest in 2002 and again in 2004.[47] The raising of administrative wages for cadres, which happened again after the completion of the Qinghai-Tibet Railway, was explicitly designed as a means of securing loyalty and political stability after the protests of 1987–89.[48] Disproportionately high urban salaries have given rise to a small but highly visible class of wealthy Tibetans and considerable conspicuous consumption of largely imported goods. Lhasa's per capita car ownership is almost equal to Beijing's.[49] At the same time, however, there is considerable urban poverty in Lhasa, with intra-urban inequality that has increased more sharply in the TAR than other parts of China.[50] The combination of a state-supported urban middle class and a system of dependent development creates a key structuring mechanism that has allowed Han migrants to benefit from development support to Tibet.

The migrants do not compete with the privileged class of urban residents, whose consumption, fueled by inflated state salaries, instead creates the demand for services and products such as greenhouse vegetables that the migrants provide. Migrants do, however, dominate in virtually all market niches, in positions that might otherwise be occupied by urban Tibetan poor, and by peri-urban and rural Tibetans. The migrants' experience of their ability to capture the development subsidies poured into Tibet, in the form of consumption for services and goods by highly paid urban cadres and wages of workers on infrastructure projects, is encapsulated by the common statements that "it's easier to find money in Lhasa than at home," "it's easier to find money in Lhasa than anywhere else," or even that "Lhasa is the best place in the country to make money."

The Seeds of the Vegetable Market

Cultivating vegetables is one key way in which Han migrants have been able to earn more money in Lhasa than at home. The origins of Han domination of the market lie in part in government efforts in the mid-1980s to develop Lhasa's vegetable industry, which helped bring the earliest Han vegetable farmers to Lhasa. From there, networks of kinship and native place, together with opportunities provided by decollectivization in the villages around Lhasa, enabled the accelerated flow of vegetable cultivators from other provinces, particularly Sichuan.

In 1984, controls on Lhasa's market prices were lifted and the city government began to give preferential treatment to those who transported and sold vegetables there. However, the Lhasa government also implemented numerous measures to try to increase local vegetable production, including efforts to involve local producers. Referred to as "Tibet's vegetable basket construction," this included the introduction of plastic greenhouses on the state farms between 1980 and 1982, and the building of greenhouses in several urban farming cooperatives and peri-urban villages between 1984 and 1988. Various government departments built steel-frame greenhouses and offered them at a 50 percent subsidy to Tibetan villagers who were willing to sign contracts to take out five-year interest-free loans for the other 50 percent of the cost. However, these programs were all quite small in scale and relatively unsuccessful. Few families participated, and of those who did, few cultivated vegetables for more than two years before renting their greenhouses to Han farmers, who began to migrate to Lhasa around the same time.

Much more influential in shaping the contours of the industry was a 1985 visit by the director of the Lhasa *Chengguanqu*'s Agriculture and Animal Husbandry Department (AAHD) to Shuangliu County, near Chengdu. Impressed by vegetable production he saw there, he asked for Shuangliu County's assistance in developing Lhasa's vegetable industry base, resulting in a cooperative agreement to send three men from Shuangliu to work in Lhasa as technical advisers for vegetable production. On June 20, 1985, Guo Kaizhong, a vocational school graduate who was employed by the Sanxing Township agricultural extension station; Liu Shuquan, from Peng Town and also of the agricultural extension station; and Wang Longkang, a part-time teacher at a school in Shuangliu known for having a green thumb, arrived in Lhasa accompanied by an official from the Shuangliu County Agriculture and Animal Husbandry Department. During the term of their two-year contracts, they worked as technical advisers for the Ramoche, Meru, and Barkor neighborhood vegetable cooperatives as well as in the production brigades of Red Star Administrative Village in Najin Township.

The three were treated well for their work in developing Lhasa's vegetable production. Each was paid 250 RMB per month, more than four times their salaries at home, and they recalled being frequent dinner guests of Lhasa's deputy mayor. Originally attracted to the work by the salary, they soon came to see their work as contributing to the larger project of the development of Tibet. "To speak honestly," recounted Guo in 2001, "we people of Shuangliu have made a tremendous contribution to Tibet."

The arrival of these three Sichuanese technicians also coincided with decollectivization of the urban cooperatives and the peri-urban villages of Lhasa. Cooperative leaders offered the Han men the opportunity to sublease their land for vegetable cultivation. The three recruited their wives and others to come to Lhasa to work on this land. Because travel restrictions to the TAR were still in place at the time, Shuangliu County AAHD officials helped the family members with the necessary paperwork to purchase their plane tickets. Once they arrived in Lhasa, the wives of the three men began to lease newly decollectivized land for vegetable production, while the men were still being paid salaries as technical advisers. Mr. Guo used his wife's name to lease twenty *mu* (1.3 ha), from which he reported a net profit of ten thousand RMB in the first year alone. As the families began to make money growing and selling vegetables, they brought more relatives and friends from their hometowns to Tibet, again with the help of government offices. None of the men renewed their contracts after the first two years. Indeed, the expected transfer of skills between these three men and local Tibetan farmers had little effect on Tibetan vegetable production. In fact, another early Han farmer described the designation of these first three farmers as technical advisers as "a misunderstanding" because growing vegetables in greenhouses in Tibet was so different from the conditions they were accustomed to at home that they had to spend several seasons experimenting with new methods, rather than focus on teaching Tibetans relevant skills. Moreover, their trainees in the Ramoche vegetable cooperative gradually began to lose their collective farmland to urbanization around this time.

Within the first few months of arriving in Lhasa, Guo Kaizhong also sent word back to his home agricultural extension unit that a vegetable production team would be welcomed in Lhasa. Cheng Huaigen and Chong Huaicong arrived in September and December of 1985, respectively, renting ten *mu* of newly decollectivized land that Guo arranged for them. Unlike the first three men, this second group was not paid a salary. Instead, they signed a contract with the Lhasa Municipality AAHD to be solely responsible for their own profits and losses. Besides the land that had been arranged for them, the two approached village leaders in Najin Township to rent additional newly decollectivized land. Discovering that he could not cultivate all of the land he had rented, Cheng recruited eight more relatives and friends to Lhasa to grow vegetables, again facilitated by the Shuangliu AAHD. By the spring of 1986, fourteen migrants from Shuangliu were working together as a vegetable team in the Ramoche vegetable cooperative and in a village of Najin Township.

The second year, Cheng recruited twelve more people from his hometown to go to Lhasa. These Han farmers received substantial government assistance in Lhasa. When they lacked irrigation water, Cheng and the local Party secretary wrote a report together asking the *Chengguanqu* AAHD for assistance with a well and an electric pump, which they received. While the others stayed in Najin, the Party secretary of the AAHD in nearby Tolung Dechen County invited Cheng in 1988 to take over the management of four greenhouses that four Tibetan families had signed contracts for but were unable to successfully manage because of inadequate labor. Cheng did this from 1988 to 1991, bringing more friends and relatives. He returned to his work unit in 1991 to care for his ill elderly mother while his relatives and friends stayed in Tibet. However, the agricultural extension station assigned him to work at a beverage plant that suffered from financial troubles and was unable to pay his salary. He quit in 1996 to return to Lhasa to continue vegetable production, staying until 2005 when he returned home because of health problems.

A third group of four Han migrants from Shuangliu County signed a contract to grow vegetables in Tolung Dechen County in 1986. This group was facilitated by the fact that one was a close relative of the vice director of the Lhasa Municipality Public Security Bureau. They too worked on the basis of being responsible for their own profits and losses, while their travel to and presence in Tibet were facilitated by agreements between government units. The Tolung Dechen County AAHD further assisted these farmers by providing them with free chemical fertilizers, medical services, electricity, and even bicycles.

Thus, within one year, the initial model of sending technical advisers for skill transfer to local Tibetan producers was quickly abandoned and replaced by the idea that it was enough to simply send Han farmers to Tibet to grow vegetables, and that their private profits constituted development. These farmers were nevertheless assisted by travel and work permits, and various forms of aid for irrigation and transportation. Lhasa's vegetable market did not emerge and develop miraculously through the power of the invisible hand, but rather through a process that was shaped by regulatory regimes and government actions.

These three earliest groups of migrant farmers debated amongst themselves about whether it was a good idea to continue to bring their friends and relatives to Lhasa. Some felt that they were only creating their own competition, while others felt that expanding the scope of production would be a positive development. The latter view prevailed and kinship and native place networks fostered the continued growth of the Shuangliu presence in Lhasa. By 1987, some fifty relatives and friends of the initial groups of migrants were in Lhasa growing vegetables, and a few years later, half of the fifty households in Cheng's village in Shuangliu's Sanxing Township were growing vegetables in Lhasa. A survey by the Sichuanese director of the Lhasa Municipality Non-staple Foods Office in the mid-1990s found migrant farmers from Shuangliu leasing some two hundred hectares of farmland around Lhasa, roughly two-thirds of the total area under vegetable cultivation at the time.

By the late 1990s, however, vegetable farmers from Youxian District of Mianyang Municipality, Sichuan's second largest city, began to outnumber those from Shuangliu. Mianyang soon became the most important sending area for migrant vegetable farmers, as well as a key sending area for Han migration to Tibet more generally. Chains of migration from Mianyang can be traced back largely to men who were stationed in Lhasa through military service or who worked there in early government-funded infrastructure construction projects. Whereas farmers from Shuangliu rented recently decollectivized land from urban cooperatives and peri-urban villages in the *Chengguanqu* and Tolung Dechen, Mianyang migrants' connections came from the July First and August First State Farms. The earliest Mianyang migrants started growing vegetables on these farms, and although later migrants rented decollectivized village land, the state farms remained important destinations for Mianyang migrants through the following two decades.

The catalyst of Tibet migration from Mianyang's Yutai village, where in 2005 fully one-third of the out-migrants were in Tibet, was Yan Shishuang, who joined the military at the age of fifteen and was stationed first in Xining and then in Lhasa. He stayed on in Tibet after finishing his service, and was hired to help build greenhouses on the August First State Farm. In 1985, he sent word home of moneymaking opportunities in Tibet, and introduced his nephew and two others to the state farm, where they were initially paid a salary for vegetable cultivation, but soon began to simply rent land from the farm. Mr. Yan stayed in Lhasa for the next twenty years, working as a labor contractor hiring Sichuanese workers for construction projects in Tibet. A second group of eighteen people from the same village arrived the following year, and they too soon brought more friends and relatives.

Another early migrant farmer from Mianyang, Mr. Li, arrived in Lhasa in 1984 as part of a construction team. The leader of his team, also from Mianyang, suggested to him that the two of them should plant vegetables together. The team leader was well connected and thus able to secure a loan from a high-level Lhasa official. They rented a plot of land from a work unit in 1986, and soon after, Mr. Li brought a dozen relatives and friends from his hometown in Mianyang to cultivate vegetables in Lhasa. A third early farmer had an uncle who had arrived in Lhasa with the PLA in 1957, married a Tibetan woman, and settled down there. It was this uncle's presence that had first attracted this farmer to travel to Lhasa, where he had planned to sell pork, but switched to vegetables when he saw how profitable vegetable cultivation was.

Chain migration characterizes the trajectories of virtually all vegetable farmers in Lhasa today; they trace their migration paths to friends and relatives from the same hometown, and back ultimately to one of the early Shuangliu farmers, to soldiers and government officials stationed in Tibet, or to members of construction labor teams sent there that were often associated with the state's turnkey infrastructural projects. Mianyang and Shuangliu are still the largest sending areas from Sichuan. Other sending areas that help make Lhasa "little Sichuan" include Qionglai, Renshou, Nanchong, Daxian, Guangyuan, Luzhou, and Xuning.

The Sending Areas: Migration to Tibet as Development Strategy

Since the gradual loosening of the household registration system, the export of excess labor, generally to the economically prosperous eastern parts of the country, has been a major poverty alleviation strategy of Sichuan Province. Indeed the Party secretary of Sichuan remarked that "we consider migrant labor to be a kind of cooperation between eastern and western parts of the country. . . . They leave empty-handed and return rich—it's like making money from nothing."[51] In migration to the TAR, though, the direction is reversed as the Sichuan farmers travel even further west to a less-developed area, where they capture income not from wage labor in export processing zones but from state subsidies for the development of Tibet. Indeed, in 2000, Lhasa ranked twelfth among cities in China with the lowest ratio of de jure to de facto population—and thus the highest ratio of migrants to local residents—but was one of the few such cities that were not coastal centers fueled by an export processing economy.[52]

The key sending areas from Sichuan to Tibet are neither the poorest nor the wealthiest of villages, but rather those in between.[53] Shuangliu, the richest county in Sichuan, is an industrially oriented area, with significant pharmaceuticals and foodstuffs industries. Mianyang is near the top in terms of GDP among Sichuan's municipalities, with significant revenue produced by its high tech, electronics manufacturing, and aerospace industries, as well as by the military and by multiple branches of the Chinese Academy of Sciences located there. Within the two county-level units, however, the major sending areas are the townships and villages that are most remote from the seat of the county or county-level municipality, the poorest locations within relatively wealthy areas. Despite their average or above-average socioeconomic status within Sichuan as a whole, local leaders and villagers see their hometowns as defined by their lack of development, industry, and information. This motivates town and village leaders to encourage and actively facilitate out-migration, in hopes that villagers will return home with capital to invest in enterprises there.

Yuhe Town, Mianyang

Located in the southeast corner of Youxian District of Mianyang Municipality, Yuhe Town had, in 2005, a population of 20,015, and average farmland holdings of 1.22 *mu* per person. It was once a primarily agricultural town, and continues to have little industry. Migration to other provinces began soon after the implementation of the Household Responsibility System to absorb excess labor. In 2003, in effect formalizing and facilitating what had long since become the major development strategy for the town, the Party committee and government of Mianyang Municipality officially recognized Yuhe Town as a "rural labor development base." Indeed, according to the government, "in accordance with the view of scientific development, and in order to solve the 'three rural problems' (*sannong wenti*) . . . labor out-migration has become one of [the town's] pillar industries."[54] The town established quotas for labor out-migration from each village, as well as numerous services for actual and potential out-migrants, including job skills training, employment information, legal services, and services to make paperwork easier. For example, the town government offers special services during Spring Festival through which migrants who have returned for the holidays can complete and renew paperwork related to birth control and arrange plane and bus tickets, all in one place. There are also village and town services to coordinate the management of the farmland that migrants leave behind, turning it over to families with adequate labor power, while guaranteeing its return to the original households should they come home.

According to the town Party secretary, it is because of labor migration remittances that 70 percent of the houses are now multistory. In 2005, the out-migrant labor force had reached 7,300 people (more than one-third of the population), with an estimated total income of 40 million RMB. Among the 7,300 migrants who were away from the town in 2005, 490 (305 men, 185 women) were in Tibet. These 490 migrants in Tibet ranged in age from sixteen to sixty-one, with an average age of thirty-five and a reported average annual income of 14,400 RMB. Among them, 18 were working in Tibet in construction, 19 in business, 1 in a factory, 2 in services, 2 in road construction, 4 as drivers, and the remaining 444 in vegetable growing. The town government sees migration to Tibet as an important source of income and deliberately tries to foster and encourage these migrants. According to a government work report, "in order for them to even better perform their work leading and motivating other migrants, and in order for Tibet to be a stable out-migration destination for this town, every year during Spring Festival we especially invite a representative [from among the successful Tibet out-migrants] to have discussions with the government, and give them prizes."

Within Yuhe Town, nearly half of the out-migrants to Tibet in 2005 were from Yutai village, indicating the geographical specificity and path dependency of migration trajectories. For out-migrants from Yutai village, Tibet is the location with highest earning potential, followed by Zhejiang Province, where villagers work in the garment industry, and then Jiangsu Province. Economically, Yutai is a fairly typical village in Sichuan, with an average per capita income of 2,900 RMB a year, slightly over the provincial average of 2,700 RMB a year but under Youxian District's average of 3,000 RMB a year. Average per capita income among migrants is reported at 5,000 RMB a year, though is likely to be higher. Of the 2,567 residents (in 708 households), the labor force is estimated at 1,400, of whom 716 were out-migrants. Out of those, in 2005, 208, or just under one-third, were in Tibet. Landholdings in the village are 0.8 *mu* per capita, on which the primary crops are rice, sold to a local seed factory, silk, vegetables, and rapeseed. A small local silk factory was once a township and village enterprise, but was sold to a private entrepreneur after years of operating at a loss.

The Yuhe Town government tries to encourage successful migrants to return home to invest their accumulated capital in the local economy, and boasts of more than thirty returned migrants who have established local industries such as a rice flour processing plant, pig farming, and food processing. In the hope of encouraging others to do the same, the town government advertises the accomplishments of its returned migrants, such as Song Dechao, one among the second group of migrants to go to Lhasa in 1986 through the introduction of Yan Shishuang. In Tibet, Song started out growing vegetables, but also sold vegetables, opened restaurants, and worked in transportation. A member of the Communist Party, he carefully cultivated the trust of the Lhasa Municipality government and profited from his various ventures. The Yuhe Town government claims him as a successful example of their strategy of out-migration, writing that "through ten years of hard work in Tibet, he is now worth more than one million RMB. He also brought more than five hundred people from his village to go to Tibet to plant vegetables, and all of them became well-known ten-thousand-yuan and hundred-thousand-yuan families. Local people in Tibet fondly refer to them as the 'Yuhe community people.'" Today Song lives in Mianyang while his son and daughter remain in Tibet working in the chemical fertilizer business.

The town government also holds up another member of this second group of migrants to Lhasa as a model to emulate. Zheng Zhongwen also started out growing vegetables on the August First State Farm in 1986, but moved on to other businesses, including import of agricultural inputs such as chemical fertilizers, pesticides, and plastics from Sichuan to Tibet. While many migrant farmers from this area have accumulated some 100,000–200,000 RMB over their years working in Tibet, the town government boasts that Zheng accumulated assets exceeding 2 million RMB, and that because of his business in air transport of agricultural supplies, "he even got tired of sitting on an airplane so many times." His success in achieving prosperity in Tibet is further indicated by his ownership of a house in Mianyang City as well as another house in Yutai village built at a cost of over 200,000 RMB.

The fact that migration to Tibet is seen as contributing to the economic development of the sending areas in Sichuan means both that migrants eventually return home rather than staying in Tibet for the long term, and that many migrants are quite successful in earning a significant income there, often more than the same migrants make in coastal areas such as Zhejiang. In this way, state subsidies for the development of Tibet end up contributing to the development of sending villages in Sichuan province.

SUZHI *AND THE* VALUE *OF* PEOPLE *AND* PLACES

Mr. Li was only fifteen years old when he first left his hometown in Qionglai, part of Chengdu Municipality, for Lhasa in 1988. A distant relative in the People's Liberation Army had marched into Lhasa in 1951, stayed on to be a cadre there, and brought Mr. Li's father in 1971 to help with the construction of schools and work unit dormitories. The father returned home in 1983, but went again with Mr. Li in 1988 where they worked together buying vegetables from other Sichuanese farmers and selling them to military bases. From 1993 until 2000, Li worked in Lhasa's "entertainment industry," in gambling and "things that are difficult to talk about." Starting in 2000 he became a labor contractor for the construction of the Qinghai-Tibet Railway, organizing labor crews for various work units including the Xinjiang Construction and Production Corps.[55]

In his capacity as a labor contractor for the railroad, he claimed incorrectly that "the government has a policy against allowing Tibetans to work on the railway." This reflects the general valuation of Tibetan labor, rather than actual policy; Tibetans were employed in railroad construction, though mostly only in low-wage, unskilled labor. "They have no skill," he opined about Tibetans, "They are muddle-headed and can only use their brute strength. They never use brains to figure out how to complete a task well, how to do it better. They're too simple-minded for that." Lhasa had, in his estimation, quadrupled in development status since he arrived, as had the quality (*suzhi*) of the local people. Nevertheless, neither could come anywhere close to being comparable with the development in Sichuan, or the quality of people, like himself, from Sichuan's farming areas.

Members of the floating population who head east are often treated as second-class citizens, denigrated for being a "rural rabble" of "low quality." The *hukou* system means the state does not have to guarantee provision of urban services such as housing, education, or health care to migrants. They are frequently bullied, looked down on by locals, habitually blamed for crime, and paid less than locals.[56] The coding of the migrant body as being of low quality (*suzhi*) "justifies the extraction of surplus value while it also serves to legitimate new regimes of social differentiation and governmentality. The migrant body and its productivity are therefore derogated, producing a surplus value."[57] In postsocialist China, a national value-coding of *suzhi* plays an important role in capital accumulation.

Discussing Han migrants in Lhasa, Hu and Salazar argue that the rural-urban divide produced by the persistent institution of *hukou* predominates over ethnic discrimination. They write, "Urban Tibetans do not perceive rural Han as a status threat or as unfair competitors. Similarly rural Han migrants in Lhasa do not perceive themselves to be in any way part of a dominant ethnic supra-stratum. Because the state provides positive discrimination for ethnic minorities . . . the individual ethnic prejudice on the part of the Han can be easily ignored."[58] Thus, in their view, the most salient factor in social stratification in contemporary Tibet is an institutionalized system that favors urban residents. Individualized ethnic prejudice may exist, but is easily ignorable. Class is largely related to certain occupations, with lower-class traits held by the Han migrants. Nothing else matters.

While it is certainly the case, as Hu and Salazar state, that rural Tibetans are doubly marginalized by their ethnic and rural status, I argue that Han migrants are not slotted into second-class citizen status in the way that Hu and Salazar suggest. Even privileged urban Tibetan cadres, who do not compete with the Han migrants, feel swamped by the Han presence. Moreover, the urban Tibetan poor are not positioned above rural Han migrants by their *hukou* status. Hu and Salazar's analysis is based implicitly on conventional conceptions of space as a passive backdrop or container within which events unfold. In this common view, places are isolated, bounded enclosures within which social actions happen. As space, then, Lhasa is simply a backdrop against which rural/urban and ethnic hierarchies play out. Because space is simply a container for social action, the social position of migrants matters little whether their destination point is Guangdong or Lhasa. If instead we recognize (social) space as a (social) product, as Henri Lefebvre has argued, then it becomes essential to see status and value as determined not only by ethnicity and the rural/urban spatial divide, but also by the *suzhi* coding of the territory of the nation-state in relation to development.[59] Geographical imaginaries matter in both shaping and modifying the effects of the institution of *hukou* status.

Suzhi first emerged as a key concept in discourses around stringent population planning and a post-Mao discourse of "superior birth and nurture," in which the rural population, seen as lacking a consciousness of development, "appeared as a tumorous mass—large in quantity, low in quality—encumbering the national body that strove to join the world of global capital."[60] By the late 1990s a new developmentalism with *suzhi* at its core had become hegemonic across China. As Yan Hairong has argued, the tautological association of *suzhi* and development, wherein low quality is the result of a low level of development, and a low level of development is an indicator of low quality, produces a national value-coding that posits the eastern seaboard as the vanguard, the site of modernity, science, and progress, and the western periphery as backward and lacking in these traits. A national conference on "quality" in 1987 produced a report stating, "*suzhi* [however defined] is for the most part higher in the city than in the countryside, higher in Han areas than in minority areas, higher in the economically advanced areas than in the backward areas."[61] In this national value-coding, there is a dialectical relationship between the quality of peoples and places, in which the characteristics of place are seen to inhere in the persons associated with them. Thus, the migration destination point becomes a place where the migrant accumulates *suzhi*, which can then be brought back to the rural household and become both a demonstration of *suzhi* improvement and a foundation for raising the quality of the local population.[62] Migration is a kind of *suzhi* education that is not only brought back home to the sending village but also passed on by women to their children, raising the quality of the sending population.[63]

Migrant Han in Lhasa, though, accumulate no *suzhi*. Ms. Yang and her husband, who were among the very first group of vegetable farmers to arrive in Lhasa in 1985 and who have lived there for over twenty years, are from Peng Town near the Shuangliu airport in Sichuan, a place they describe as having "excellent conditions." In fact, Ms. Yang reported in 2005 about a recent visit home:

> Some of our relatives said "Ai-yo! You must suffer a lot in Tibet." When we went home, everyone looked down on us. They said "you are pitch black." In our hometown, they wear classy clothes. They dress and eat well. When we go back some people look down on us . . . "pitch black—so scary!" they say, looking at us. In *neidi*, everyone has very white, light skin. "My goodness, what are you doing in Lhasa?" they say.

Far from accumulating quality, Ms. Yang and her husband, who have stayed in Lhasa for an unusually long time, are seen by their relatives and friends to have soaked in the undesirable characteristics of Tibet, lowering rather than raising their status in the national *suzhi* value-coding. Migration to Tibet, even to urban Lhasa, does not qualify as a *suzhi* education.

Tibet's coding as being underdeveloped and a place lacking in *suzhi* is entangled with Han migrants' view of it as being underurbanized. This is another reason that the administrative rural/urban divide is not the only structuring mechanism of status and value determination. Indeed, Lhasa hardly qualifies as urban in the eyes of many Han migrants. Consider a couple from Mianyang who arrived in Lhasa in 1997. The husband had already been away from home for more than ten years, with experience working in the steel industry and as a member of piecework contract construction teams in Ningbo and Hangzhou, as well as in Jiangsu, Henan, and Shanghai. His wife remarked, "Those places are all much better than this place. They're all cities. Lhasa is like one of our little county seats at home." He added:

> In Ningbo, one town is much larger than all of Lhasa city. Just one town! One town [we lived in] had more than three hundred factories, four conglomerates, seven or eight foreign joint ventures. That town was really big!. . . There is a factory there that is one and a half times the size of Lhasa. . . . I worked there for two years. The conditions were excellent, not like those in Lhasa.

Another young Sichuanese woman had this to say in 2001:

> Lhasa is as small as a little county seat back in *neidi*. And the construction is terrible—it's not developed at all! The buildings here are all so short. There are no high-rises. Even the highest building is probably only ten stories tall, but most of them are only one-story. I don't know why. Some people say it must be because of the lack of oxygen here. They can't build any higher because there's not enough oxygen. I can't see any other reason why they wouldn't build taller buildings.

Indeed, one sixty-seven-year-old farmer from Mianyang, two of whose sons were cultivating vegetables in Lhasa, stated very explicitly, "The development of Mianyang is better than that of Lhasa. The most important indicator of development is the expansion of the scale of the city."

By 2005, many returned migrants in the Mianyang countryside felt that Lhasa's development had been fast in recent years, as evidenced by its urban expansion, but also stated that it "still cannot compare to Mianyang's" or "is still far distant from Mianyang." "Tibet is developing quickly, but it can't catch up with Mianyang," evaluated one returned migrant. "The environment is far worse than Mianyang's, sanitation conditions are bad. In the past, there were no buildings and it was full of wasteland, and did not have the appearance of a city at all." Others also judge development in Tibet to be lagging far behind that of their hometowns, based on criteria other than its degree of urbanization. "After going to Lhasa, I discovered that it is far worse than Mianyang. It's hard to describe," and "I'm not exactly sure what is so-called development but Mianyang's development is much better than Tibet's," are typical of how Han migrant farmers view Tibet.

As a result of this value-coding, the very same migrants who are deemed to be of low quality in the factories of the large eastern cities are evaluated as, and often consider themselves to be, superior in quality to Tibetans. "The *suzhi* of the farmers from Mianyang is higher than the local people's, but the *suzhi* of people from Shandong and Henan is even higher." In comparison with people from their hometowns, Tibetans "cannot measure up," "are stupid," and are "simple-minded and not at all clever." When asked what aspect exactly it is about the quality of the Tibetan people that is low, one migrant was unable to clarify, saying only "it's not a matter of what aspect, it's all aspects." A returned migrant who had spent 1996–98 growing vegetables explained, echoing official state discourse, that Tibetans as a whole were unable to catch up with the higher *suzhi* of those from *neidi* because "they've jumped straight from feudal society to socialism, so it was a bigger leap to make."

Representations of Tibetans from the 1950s through the early 1990s as barbaric, dirty, superstitious, and violent contribute to the evaluation of Tibet as a spatial container of low *suzhi* and its inhabitants as suffering from a lack of development. Even as new representations of Tibetans as simple and exotic emerged with the boom in tourism, older conceptions have had a lasting effect. The proprietor of a Sichuanese restaurant in Lhasa, from Chongqing, remarked to me in 2000 that she wanted to go home soon because "I've never thought that Lhasa was a good place. If it weren't for making money who would want to come this place? Nobody . . . A lot of the local people are very barbaric. Sometimes they eat and then don't pay for their food. . . . In reality they are very pitiful, but they are also very barbaric."

Not all Han migrants are negative about the Tibetans they encounter. Some are quite sympathetic, saying that Tibetans are "honest," "warm," "enthusiastic," "straightforward," and "loyal to their friends." Others have mixed views, saying for example: "In relationships, I feel Tibetans are very unpretentious. However they learn very slowly," or "Tibetans are very honest, as long as you don't bother them, they won't trouble you. Tibetans are very enthusiastic. . . . In comparison, Han people are trickier." Regardless, they do not frame Tibetans—rural or urban—as having the potential to embody higher *suzhi* than themselves, while they frankly stated that their own *suzhi* was lower than that of residents of eastern coastal cities such as Shenzhen. The positive qualities they attribute to Tibetans are not those that constitute more developed, or higher-*suzhi*, status. In other words, *suzhi* expresses a relational spatiality. The unevenness of development across China produced by its market reforms inheres through *suzhi* to the quality of the people who are seen to be from particular places. In this way, political-economic processes producing uneven development reinforce a set of status indicators based on that development level. Thus it is not only ethnicity, rural/urban status, and class, but also the qualities and identities of place, space, and territory that matter in the evaluations that Han migrants and Tibetans make of each other in Lhasa. Furthermore, these qualities and identities, produced partially by the political economy of uneven development, also lead to further wealth differentiation by structuring access to opportunity and income. The cultural politics of identity vis-à-vis quality is thus structured by political-economic forces, and also contributes further to labor market differentiation.

In contrast to the typical devaluation of migrant labor based on the low *suzhi* of the migrant body, which not only allows for the accumulation of surplus value but also frequently justifies paying migrants poorly, Han migrant farmers who work in Lhasa are routinely paid more than Tibetans. Often, they do what is classified as higher-skilled labor, but a number of Han migrants told me plainly that they were paid more than local Tibetans even when they did the same kind of work. This did not seem strange to them. Several explained that the income differential was due to the fact that, as migrants, they should be compensated for their travel costs. "We spent a lot of money to get to Tibet, so of course they should pay us more," though this logic does not apply to migrant labor to eastern coastal cities. Another said that the difference between twenty-five RMB a day for unskilled labor for Han migrants and twenty RMB a day for unskilled labor for Tibetans made sense because "the Han learn things very quickly. We can remember how to do the work by just watching once. Some Tibetans need to be taught for a long time." Mr. Li, the Qionglai labor contractor, reported in 2005 that he paid Han migrants sixty to seventy RMB a day and Tibetans at most twenty RMB a day. The difference was more than justified, he explained, because "The *suzhi* of the local people is just too low. They don't understand anything. They don't know how to do anything." He insisted that local people did not mind the lower wages. "They don't care about the money, you see. They're just happy because this way they can learn some skills."

The material force and consequence of the national discourse of quality and development means that the "marginal and precarious legal status" of migrants does not have the same effect in Lhasa as in other provinces. This is true despite the fact that Han migrants in Tibet do not have housing and subsidized education in Lhasa. Indeed, as one key component of quality, education is a good illustration of how political economy and cultural politics are mutually constitutive, and why these intertwined forces position Han migrants in Lhasa in a different way than these migrants are positioned elsewhere.

The lack of access to education in migration destination cities is a tremendous problem for the migrant population, as their children are either denied education altogether or are forced to pay very high fees. Moreover, they are often targets of prejudice because of their dress and regional accents. Schools established specifically for migrant children in cities such as Beijing and Shanghai have been shut down by authorities, leaving the children without access to educational services. In Lhasa, there have been no reports of Han migrant children being denied access to urban state-run schools. However, Han migrants are not enthusiastic about educating their children in Lhasa, because they see its schools as far inferior to those in their hometowns, even if the former is urban and the latter are rural. Indeed, we have seen that education spending in Tibet is unusually low relative to construction spending, and the TAR illiteracy rate is the highest in the country.[64] Sichuanese vegetable farmers often stated that they leave their children at home with parents because of the poor state of the educational system in Tibet.

At the same time, some also note that because the passing score on college entrance exams is lower for those with a TAR household registration than for those registered in other parts of the country, children of migrant Han farmers who managed to procure a TAR *hukou* at the time of the college entrance examination could enter at the lower score. This strategy is well known among migrant farmers, some of whom told me of their plans to purchase a *hukou* for their children for the exams. "To do this is nothing at all—it's a small matter. All you've got to do is pull some *guanxi*. You ask someone and they say 'we have to study the problem.' Then you give them a bit of money and it's no problem at all."[65] Stories about corruption surrounding not only the temporary transfer of household registrations, but also the "selling" of college entrance positions rightfully earned by Tibetan students are rife in urban Lhasa as well as among the vegetable-farming villages on its periphery. Household registration is in these cases not a trap but a tool used by migrant farmers for their own advantage. Their position is enabled in part by the ideology of the quality of people and places. Place imaginaries of quality not only have real material effects, but as we will see in the next two chapters, are also inseparable from the cultural politics of land rental transactions and thus the production of Lhasa's postreform landscape.

Who Benefits from Development?

The fact that Han migrant farmers are able to position themselves vis-à-vis the market to be the beneficiaries of large flows of development money that the central government and other wealthier provinces pour into the TAR is subject to a further irony. Even while migrants see their hometowns as far more developed than Lhasa, and consider themselves to be of higher *suzhi* than Tibetans, they simultaneously fail to connect the source of their remittances home with state funding of the development of Tibet. Instead, many comment resentfully about this funding, seeing the state as too generous to Tibetans and not generous enough to their homes in Sichuan or other provinces.

Indeed, many migrants paint themselves as victims, as against what they interpret as state favoritism toward developing Tibet. Many Han farmers emphatically (and incorrectly) explained to me, "Tibetans have *never* had to pay taxes."[66] Others resented the fact that Tibetans have more arable land per person than they do in their home villages, and that at least until the elimination of agricultural taxes in these areas of Sichuan in 2004, they had heavy tax and fee burdens at home, while Tibetans did not. One greenhouse farmer from Mianyang asked rhetorically, "We're also farmers, aren't we? We're just the same as them. Each year, we have to pay 300 RMB to the government. We have to pay for the officials—pay their salaries. But people here in Tibet don't have to do that."

Like many migrant farmers, Ms. Mu, a woman in her early forties who grew vegetables in Lhasa from 1990 to 1996, described government policy as "extreme care for Tibetans" and stated bluntly that the state simply gave too much aid to Tibet. Further, she said, during the years she was in Lhasa, "it was as if one Tibetan life was worth two Han lives." Others frequently commented, "the central authorities give a lot more support to Tibet than to Sichuan." Indeed, despite the fact that Han migrants' profits from growing vegetables were facilitated by the state through its early programs encouraging vegetable cultivation as well as by the placement of cadres, officials, and soldiers in Lhasa, Han migrants do not recognize the ways in which state policies have lined up with and facilitated their economic interests. Instead, from their perspective, the state has offered too many gifts to Tibet and Tibetans, and none to them. According to another migrant from Mianyang,

> This state gives so much support to Tibet! We never get anything from the state. All that Aid-Tibet money—we never get a cent of it. . . . People like us are completely on our own. If we lose money, we lose money . . . we can only rely on ourselves. The state is always giving Tibetans money—this year they received money for snow disaster relief again. We have plenty of drought and other disasters at home but we don't get anything.

Other Han migrants refer to the Tibetans as their "landlords" and insist that the Tibetans are actually richer than themselves because "There are too many resources going to Tibet. Actually, there are more poor places in *neidi* than there are here in Tibet. The villagers around here are richer than we are in *neidi*." The facts that Tibetan urban salaries were raised to some of the highest in China, and that villagers around Lhasa received more land at decollectivization than villagers in sending areas in Sichuan—typically 3 *mu*, compared to 0.6 to 1 *mu* in the latter province,[67] both contribute to migrant perceptions that Tibetans are wealthy and unfairly receiving state aid, some of which should instead be directed at developing their home villages in Sichuan. This perception of local wealth and disproportionate aid does not, however, alter the migrants' perception that Tibet is less developed than Sichuan.

Along with their simultaneous convictions that the state's gift of development investment to Tibet is disproportionately large and that Tibet is significantly lacking in development, migrants also echo government pronouncements in their understandings of themselves as agents of development. "What we did there was a huge benefit for Tibet" and "we helped to develop Tibet" are common sentiments among migrants, but they see their contribution as being the very fact of growing vegetables for an expanding market, rather than the passing of their skills to Tibetans, which few claim to have done.

***

Among the jagged plots of corn stalks, neat rows of paddy rice, and scattered fish ponds in the quiet sending villages of Yuhe Town, clusters of squat earthen and brick houses are hidden in the shade of lush groves of trees and bamboo stands. Concrete extensions, surfaced with pink, white, and yellow tile, protrude out of some of the earth-hued homes. Entire new tile and concrete houses, with metal pull-up gates, stand apart from the landscape of terraces and water buffalo, mulberry trees and drying corn kernels, as testaments to the remittances their owners have sent home from Tibet. These multistory houses in the Sichuan countryside are one fruit of the gift of development to Tibet.

Were development reducible to GDP growth alone, as the persistent fantasies of economism suggest, then Tibetans have much reason to be grateful given the quadrupling of the regional GDP in just one decade. But the region's GDP is exceeded by the unproductive state subsidies that pour into it; growth comes almost entirely from these subsidies that leave again through imports, creating few linkages to the local economy. Moreover, migrants capture a significant share of the wages and profits from local productive activities; they send as much as possible of their earnings home to pay school fees, as investment capital for new enterprises, and to build houses in the Sichuan countryside. This outcome is enabled by the match between key income-generating strategies of Sichuan Province—the export of migrant labor—and of the TAR—welcoming migrants and reliance on subsidies. Although the general idea behind the strategy of exporting outmigrant labor is to send laborers east, where migrants earn wages while value is extracted from their (devalued) labor to generate surplus capital in export-oriented industries, westward migrants sometimes claim that "the best place in China to make money is Lhasa." Among them are those who have traveled or returned to Lhasa to grow vegetables after stints working in eastern coastal cities.

Just as important as the distorted and dependent economic structure of the TAR is the fact that development is not a singular end point but rather a complex, historically and geographically specific and situated set of social relations, at once material and discursive. With development as the new cornerstone of state legitimacy beginning in the 1980s state officials began to welcome Han migrants as bearers of the gift of development. They became coded as agents of development who were making Tibet a better place, thus strengthening state legitimacy. Tibetans' experience of development is thus intertwined with the experience of an increased migrant presence. The cultural politics of development in Tibet is also the cultural politics of migration into Tibet.

Through their re-creation of Lhasa as "little Sichuan," migrants have been recruited into the task of state incorporation, of binding Tibet more closely into PRC territory, and of naturalizing the boundaries of the PRC as a spatial container for Tibet. Their presence creates spatial relations in Lhasa that make the current spatial-social assemblage hegemonic. The production of Lhasa as "little Sichuan" does far more to illuminate the structures of feeling that undergirded the March 2008 protests than do analyses that flatten out questions of space, geography, and territory in favor of individualized notions of "prejudice." It is necessary to see and understand Lhasa not as a place apart, but rather as a place constituted by and intertwined with other places, particularly the sending villages in Sichuan that view sending migrants to Lhasa as a promising strategy for their own development.

Yet the production of Lhasa into "little Sichuan" and the domination of Lhasa's vegetable industry by Sichuanese farmers were not the result of a single deliberate plan. Government attempts in the 1980s to get local Tibetans to cultivate vegetables were unsuccessful. Plans to invite technicians to teach this skill to locals also failed to have the intended effect. Instead, Han migrants were positioned by the interplay of state and market to take advantage of the opportunity to rent land and become vegetable growers. The migration from Sichuan was not an invisible-hand, market-driven phenomenon free from social relations and government policies, as a neoliberal capitalist ideology would have it. It was deeply embedded in and facilitated by the social relations of kinship and native place networks. It was also structured and enabled by state policies and programs, including not only the invitation and facilitation of early Sichuanese farmers' movement to Lhasa, but also by the flow of state funding in infrastructural projects, which resulted in many Sichuanese farmers being recruited as construction workers in Tibet; by the stationing of soldiers from Sichuan in Lhasa; and by the fact that local governments in Sichuan see out-migration, including to Tibet, as their own preferred policy for poverty alleviation. Ultimately, then, government policies indirectly structured and maintained the contours of Lhasa's current vegetable economy, though not in the way originally intended by policymakers who tried to develop the local vegetable industry by encouraging Tibetan farmers. James Ferguson's statement about the "cardinal principle" of development in his study of development in Lesotho is relevant here: "Intentional plans interact with unacknowledged structures and chance events to produce unintended outcomes which turn out to be intelligible not only as the unforeseen effects of an unintended intervention, but also as the unlikely instruments of an unplotted strategy."[68]

Han migrants see themselves as they are presented in official development discourses, as agents or vectors of development, arriving from a more-developed area to a less-developed one. At the same time, the migrants do not see their interests as being aligned with those of the state. Even though they benefit from central government development funding to Tibet, they are resentful at what they see as the overly generous attention to development there, and the lack of investment in their own hometowns. Even though they are beneficiaries of Tibet's development, they do not like it.

At the same time, their perception of Tibetans as having become unfairly wealthy as a result of state largesse does not translate into an evaluation of Tibet as being more developed than Sichuan; a stay in Tibet can allow migrants to accumulate significant income, but it is not a place of *suzhi* accumulation. Though migrants in Lhasa may be positioned in structurally similar ways to migrants in other cities in China, the power of *suzhi* makes their experience, and the experience of them by local residents, quite different. In sum, migrants to Lhasa were not deliberately transferred but were nevertheless facilitated in their sojourn in and production of little Sichuan. But this does not tell the full story of how they dominate economic activities such as peri-urban vegetable growing. After all, vegetable farming requires local residents to rent out their land to the migrants. The next chapter turns to the micropolitics of Tibetan marginalization in these transactions.

Signs of Lhasa

Slogans are a defining feature of the Lhasa cityscape. Emblazoned on red cloth banners hung between streetlamps across streets and on the sides of buildings, imprinted on city buses, pasted on billboards of all shapes and sizes, and featured as part of product advertisements, they are quite simply everywhere, making Lhasa a space with an extraordinarily high "quotient of ideological density." Some residents claimed not to even notice them anymore. Just as they read novels or aimed sunflower seed shells at each other during meetings, they had simply stopped seeing the signs, opening the gap between the performative and the constative, producing new meanings in a nonoppositional way.[1]

For me as an outsider, though, it was impossible to ignore the slogans that shouted at me from all directions. Some marked specific events, such as the opening of the Qinghai-Tibet Railway, while others sought to perform territorialization by reinforcing more general authoritative discourses about development, gratitude, urbanization, harmony, and unity. Below is a selection from the decade.

2000

Long Live the Great Unity of the Nationalities!
The Han and Tibetans Are Members of One Family
The Dalai Is the Greatest Obstacle Obstructing the Normal Functioning Order of Tibetan Buddhism
Be a Civilized Citizen, Build a Civilized City

2001

An Open Lhasa Welcomes You
Enthusiastically Celebrate the Fiftieth Anniversary of the Peaceful Liberation of Tibet!
Be Grateful for the Warm Concern of the Party and the Central Government
The Chinese Communist Party Is the Choice of History and the People
Resolutely Oppose and Struggle Against Splittists and Construct a Civilized Campus
Deepen Reform, Expand Opening Up, Accelerate Development, Protect Stability
Nationality Culture Also Belongs to the World
Raise the Quality of the People, Contribute to the Development of Lhasa's Tourism Business

Rely on Scientific and Technological Advances to Realize Leap-over Development
It Is Everyone's Responsibility to Maintain the Security of Society
Completely Expose and Criticize the Dalai's Splittist Crime. Take the Splittist Struggle to Its Root
Gratitude to the Central Government for Their Warm Care of the Tibetan People
Without the Communist Party, There Would Be No New Socialist Tibet

2004

Development Is the Only Hard Truth
Support Tibet's Economic Development, Comprehensively Construct a Well-off Society
[On a Petro China ad:] Let Us Have Together a Piece of Blue Sky

2005

[On a Budweiser ad:] Enthusiastically Celebrate the Fortieth Anniversary of the Founding of the TAR
The Han and Tibetans Are One Family, Joining Hands to Reach New Heights
Keep Up with the Times and Move Forward, Blaze New Trails, Use Outstanding Achievements to Greet the Fortieth Anniversary of the Founding of the TAR
Tomorrow's Tibet Will Be Even Brighter
Advance Boldly in a Unified Way, Reform and Innovate in Order to Work Hard and Struggle for an Even More Unified, Democratic, Prosperous, and Civilized Socialist New Tibet
Be Steadfast in Ideal Conviction, Be Steadfast in Political Standpoint, Be Steadfast in the Most Important Tasks, Be Steadfast in Aims for the People, Steadfastly Implement a Flourishing Tibet

2006

With the Qinghai-Tibet Railway Achieving a Strong Sound, Lhasa Emerges as a New Musical Score
Enthusiastic Congratulations on the Smooth Opening of the Qinghai-Tibet Railway—China Mobile's Network Covers the Entire Line
Many Thanks for the Help and Support of the Central Government and the People of the Whole Country!
The Development Zone Is Very Promising
Enthusiastically Celebrate the Opening of the Qinghai-Tibet Railway
Accelerate the Opening Up of New Districts, Construct a Harmonious Lhasa
With the Opening of the Qinghai-Tibet Railway, Lhasa Will Enjoy a Better Future
Establish a Peaceful Lhasa, Construct a Harmonious Society

2007

Construct a Complete System of Management Regulations for City Planning
Welcome to the New Special Economic Zone, Check in at the New Sunshine City

2008

Construct a National-level Civilized City. Promote Leap-Forward Social and Economic Development
Thoroughly Practice Scientific Development Ideology, Energetically Tamp Down Grass-roots Foundational Work
[Four billboards one next to the other on the road from the airport to Lhasa, beginning and ending with SUV ads:]
Tibet Himalaya Auto Industry Limited: Qishi SUV
Long Live the Mighty Chinese Communist Party
Lhasa Welcomes You
Long Live the Grand Unity of the Entire Country's Nationalities: Luba SUV

2009

Security Is Effectiveness. Civilization Is the Image. Stability Overpowers Everything. Unity Is Strength. Establish a Harmonious Lhasa. Construct a Glorious Home. Bring Benefit to the People of Tibet.

4 The Micropolitics of Marginalization

> The concept of "overdetermination" is an attempt to avoid the isolation of autonomous categories but at the same time to emphasize relatively autonomous yet of course interactive practices. In its most positive forms—that is, in its recognition of multiple forces, rather than the isolated forces of modes or techniques of production, and in its further recognition of these forces as structured, in particular historical situations, rather than elements of an ideal totality or, worse, merely adjacent—the concept of "overdetermination" is more useful than any other as a way of understanding historically lived situations and the authentic complexities of practice.
>
> —Raymond Williams, *Marxism and Literature*, 1977

The official discourse of development in Tibet posits Han migrants as agents of technology and skill transfer, bearers of development and science, and vectors of progress. Even though early Sichuanese farmers were much more successful at bringing their own friends and family to Tibet as petty entrepreneurs than at fostering vegetable cultivation among Tibetans, officials continue to insist that "experienced vegetable growers from other provinces have been invited to pass on new know-how to local vegetable growers and this has helped raise . . . output."[1] When I described my research plans to a Tibetan scientist at the beginning of my fieldwork, he suggested that he already knew what the outcomes would be: I would find that Han greenhouse farming benefits Tibet through technology transfer to the less–scientifically inclined and less-innovative local villagers. "The Han have a greater ability to adopt new technologies than Tibetans do. Without them, Tibetan farmers would be stuck forever with the old way of doing things." Or as a social scientist in Beijing informed me in 2000, "the Tibetans learn from the Han and greatly improve themselves." He suggested that once Tibetans learned from the migrants how to grow vegetables in greenhouses, they would take over and the Han would move on to other forms of labor or commodity production.

In fact the proportion of Han vegetable farmers has only increased over time. In 1994, Tibetan vegetable farmers told a visiting researcher in Lhasa that there were as many Tibetans as Han migrants growing vegetables, but by 2000, Han migrants completely dominated vegetable production.[2] Up until the mid-1990s, Tibetan vegetable farmers included employees of the July First and August First State Farms, members of urban neighborhood cooperatives that had cultivated vegetables during the collective period, and a handful of Tibetan villagers who had volunteered to participate in the 1985–86 program that offered subsidized greenhouses. However, these Tibetans left vegetable farming from the mid-1980s to mid-1990s, in many cases renting their greenhouses or plots to the growing number of Han migrants arriving in Lhasa.

The percentage of Tibetans involved in vegetable production began to decline in the mid-1980s on the August First State Farm, and 1992 on the July First State Farm. Though former Tibetan workers on both farms were initially given the option of renting greenhouses at a significantly lower price than were charged to Han migrants, many began to drop out of vegetable cultivation. The July First State Farm implemented a system whereby the farm paid for production inputs, and workers were required to sell the vegetables they produced to the farm and to turn over a certain amount of money to the farm each year. Instead, most workers began to rent out their greenhouses to migrants. Rather than renew contracts with these Tibetan families, the farm instead rented land and greenhouses to Han migrants at a higher price. By 2001, only a handful of Tibetan vegetable farmers remained on the state farms. These were all families who had worked on the state farms during the collective period rather than new entrants to vegetable production, all of whom were Han migrants.

In the early 1980s, urban vegetable cooperative members such as those of the Barkor, Meru, and Ramoche neighborhoods, received subsidized or free greenhouses as part of the "vegetable basket program," which also introduced greenhouses to the July First and August First State Farms between 1980 and 1982. They were the original targets of the technical training project that brought the earliest Sichuanese farmers to Lhasa in 1985, but as we have seen, little skill transfer occurred, and the idea of bringing technical personnel was quickly abandoned in favor of enabling migrants to come grow vegetables on farmland that was being decollectivized around that time.[3] Urban cooperative members were initially required to cultivate vegetables themselves rather than renting out their land, but as competition from Han migrants increased, the cooperatives' profits decreased and they began to allow rentals. By 2000, most cooperative members stated that their inability to compete left them with no choice but to rent out at least some of their greenhouses. By 2005, furthermore, these plots, once on the edge of urban Lhasa, were squarely within its downtown area and had largely been paved over by urban construction.

A similar dynamic took place in peri-urban villages where a few families had chosen in the mid-1980s to participate in local government programs that offered subsidized greenhouses to village households. Those that so chose quickly abandoned their greenhouses or leased them out to Han migrants within a few years. While Tibetans were abandoning vegetable farming, the number of Han migrants cultivating vegetables increased rapidly. By 2000, there were only a handful of Tibetans entering, and usually quickly exiting, greenhouse vegetable production through various government and nongovernmental development projects. The putative transfer of technology, skills, and science from the Han migrants did not occur. Instead, the migrants took over from Tibetans leaving production on the state farms and urban cooperatives, and more important, began to sublease land previously used for barley and winter wheat from Tibetan peasants in peri-urban villages. In most of the more than twenty villages around the urban center where Han migrants were renting land, all local households had subleased at least one of their Household Responsibility System plots to Han migrants. As a typical example, in 2000, the eighty-nine Tibetan households of Kyichuling village were subleasing land to ninety-six migrant Han households.

Despite the general resentment toward Han migrants and the state policies that bring them to Tibet—as demonstrated in the protests in spring 2008 and in everyday speech acts against authoritative discourses—and in contrast to what might be expected from the transnational Tibet Movement's narrative about Chinese migration, Tibetan households who sublease their land to Han migrants do so willingly. Although a boycott of migrant goods or an organized movement to refuse to rent land would be impossible within the political context, individual households have the ability to decide not to rent to migrants. Indeed, where government programs built greenhouses for Tibetan villagers, local officials often specifically exhorted villagers *not* to rent out their greenhouses and instead to grow vegetables themselves. One former township leader remarked in 2001: "The township leaders . . . used to scold them. . . . We told them: if you grow the vegetables yourselves, you will make twice as much money as you do by renting the land," but no matter how many times he tried, "it was impossible to get them to grow vegetables."

Tibetan villagers earn roughly twice as much from renting out their land to the migrants as they do by growing grain crops. The low market price for grain, combined with a reversal of the policy of mandatory sales of "surplus grain" to the state beginning in the mid-1990s, meant that in terms of income, crop agriculture became for Tibetan farmers "just a way of passing the time."[4] This is the reason given by Tibetan villagers for being quite eager to lease their land to Han migrants. At the same time that an economic logic seems to prevail, however, the Tibetan villagers earn far less on rentals than the Han migrants do by growing vegetables. Moreover, few have turned the increased labor time made available by having fewer crops to plant into a significant additional source of income. Instead, Tibetan farmers in those villages where greenhouse vegetable production dominates have mostly turned to living on an economy of rents.

Vegetable cultivation is not the only way in which Tibetans have turned to rents for a living. After their farmland had all been expropriated by the early 2000s, residents of once-agricultural but now urban neighborhoods such as Lhalu made a living primarily by converting their spacious courtyards into dozens of small rooms that they rented out to Han migrants. Even as they earn an income from rentals, however, Tibetans have also been pushed out of participation in most labor market niches and productive economic activities. Furthermore, their situation is made more precarious by the fact that migrant vegetable farmers who do not earn profits frequently disappear without paying their rents, leaving Tibetan renters with no recourse to collect their lost income.

Why, then, do Tibetan villagers rent out their farmland rather than growing vegetables themselves? Why does an economic logic seem to hold in explaining the decision to rent out their land rather than grow grain, but not in the decision to rent out their land rather than grow vegetables themselves, which could both reduce incentives for at least some Han migrants to stay in Lhasa, and help Tibetans keep a foothold in one of many economic sectors in which they are being marginalized? This chapter addresses these questions by examining the micropolitics of the process through which Tibetans have left, and appear to continually choose not to participate in, this sector of the economy, from the perspectives of ethnographic political economy, cultural politics, and the analytics of space and place. My discussion demonstrates that each perspective is incomplete without the others, and further that political economy, cultural politics, and the production of space mutually constitute each other. In doing so, I argue that Tibetan nonparticipation in vegetable farming is overdetermined.

The analytic of overdetermination rejects interpretations of Marxism as necessarily reductive, deterministic, and economistic, making space for cultural activity to be significant, rather than merely a reflection of economic factors. As Raymond Williams suggests, the concept of overdetermination refers not to laws that govern an entire process, but rather to the setting of limits and exerting of pressures, taking into account "historically lived situations and the authentic complexities of practice."[5] Bringing the concept of overdetermination to bear on greenhouse farming in Lhasa means seeing political, economic, and cultural pressures as intertwined but not reducible to one another. As anthropologist Donald Moore puts it, "productive inequalities infuse but do not determine cultural politics."[6] Mine is an argument about Tibetan nonparticipation in vegetable farming not as a straightforward product of a reified and unchanging "Tibetan culture," but rather as the overdetermined outcome of economic pressures, power-laden cultural meanings, and dynamics of space and place that are constantly being struggled over and reshaped.

THE POLITICAL ECONOMY OF VEGETABLE PRODUCTION

Income

Informal income is notoriously difficult to determine with any accuracy, and that of migrant vegetable farmers is certainly no exception. Many migrant farmers claim at first that they "barely make any money," though they also say that they come to Lhasa because "it is easier to find money here than at home." One of them estimated, based on a decade of experience in vegetable farming, that 30 percent of growers make a significant profit, 40 percent earn enough to get by, and the rest lose money. Others, however, claimed that "everyone who doesn't squander their money gambling definitely makes a profit." Whereas migrants I interviewed in Lhasa frequently downplayed their earnings, forty returned migrants in Mianyang and Shuangliu uniformly reported having earned enough to send remittances home and to save for house construction. According to the government of Yuhe Town in Mianyang, the average annual income for vegetable farming migrants in Lhasa in 2005 was 14,400 RMB, compared to the average per capita income in Sichuan that year of 2,900 RMB.[7]

Migrants' own estimates of their net incomes varied widely, ranging from allegedly nothing, to between 2,000 RMB and 50,000 RMB per year, or between 1,200 RMB and 15,000 RMB per *mu* of land rented.[8] Some migrant vegetable farmers do indeed become very wealthy, as those advertised as success stories by the Yuhe Town government in Mianyang, discussed in chapter 3, suggest. A small number of farmers run away without paying their rent, suggesting an inability to recover their costs. More typically, though, migrant farmers report net incomes between three and ten times what they pay in rent to Tibetan farmers.

Some of the variation in reported income is also due to changes in incomes over time. Vegetable farmers reported that the highest prices for vegetables and the most profitable years for cultivation were between 1994–96, with a decline after 1997–98 as the number of migrant vegetable farmers increased rapidly. As one who came later put it, the earlier cultivators "came to eat the rice; we just went to drink rice soup."[9]

Inputs: Land, Labor and Capital

Rents and Contracts

Migrants who come to Lhasa for vegetable farming typically select villages (or state farms) where their relatives and others from their hometowns (*laoxiang*) are already settled. They then survey the remaining grain fields for the best plots, and ask Tibetan households for permission to rent the land—or more precisely, to sublease the use rights that Tibetans hold through the Household Responsibility System. In virtually all cases, the Tibetan households agree and the two parties sign a one- to three-year contract, often under the auspices of the village leader.[10] Three years is usually the maximum contract term because the intensive production conditions in the greenhouses are conducive to the development of root diseases that affect vegetable growth. Han farmers say that if they only use chemical fertilizers (as is often the case), diseases may develop after two to three years. However, if they also apply organic fertilizers, they can stay for five to six years. Although many Han farmers move every two to three years, a few have stayed for nearly a decade on the same piece of land.

When Han migrants first began to cultivate vegetables in Lhasa in the mid-1980s, they rented extensive plots of land (often 10 to 15 *mu* or more). Greenhouse construction was rare at the time; working on outdoor plots is less labor intensive but also less productive. Rents doubled from 250 RMB/*mu* in 1985, to about 500 RMB/*mu* in 1991, and then rose to between 800 and 1,000 RMB/*mu*/year by 2000–2001. The full range of prices in 2001 was between 650 and 1,400 RMB/*mu*/year, with villages closest to the urban center charging the highest rents. Prices stayed around 1,000 RMB with the same level of variability through the next eight years, though the actual villages in which rentals were occurring moved out from the city center as urban expansion paved over many villages that were previously sites of extensive vegetable cultivation. Within villages, rental prices vary slightly by the quality of the land, judged not only by soil fertility, but also by proximity to irrigation canals and by presence of trees blocking sunlight.

When asked about how rental prices are set, both Tibetans and the Han migrants claim to be powerless vis-à-vis the other. Tibetans claim that they rent their plots at whatever price the Han are willing to pay, whereas the Han insist that they pay whatever the Tibetans ask. In fact, prices are set through a process of bargaining in which the Han migrants have an advantage. This differs from the classical understanding, based on the labor theory of value, in which ground rent reflects the power of landed property over capital. The classical view, from Ricardo and Marx, distinguishes between two forms of rent: absolute rent, the level of which is independent of the fertility of the land; and differential rent, which depends on the surplus originating from competition between different sources of capital, including differences in the natural conditions of production, as well as the unequal application of capital to improve land quality and spatial factors such as cost of transportation.[11] Differential rent is limited by existing market prices, whereas absolute rents are determined by landed property's use of extramarket means to increase price. In other words, "in one case, rent is determined by price; in the other, price is determined by rent."[12]

There is differential rent in greenhouse vegetable production, reflecting quality of land (shade, proximity to irrigation), and especially distance from market. Tibetan villagers explained that they couldn't just raise their rents, because if they did, the Han would refuse the land and move to villages further from Lhasa, where rents were lower. Indeed, this frequently happened. In 2001, the typical rental price in Kyichuling was 1,000 RMB. A number of Han renters decided this was too expensive and moved to the next village, forcing Kyichuling residents to lower their rental price to 900 RMB the following year. While neighboring villages regularly undercut each other to compete for Han renters, Tibetans within a single village do not usually do so. In some villages, village leaders set a unified price for lowest allowable rents.

From a Marxian perspective, rents are deductions from capitalist profits that are captured through the ownership of land as a factor of production. Thus, absolute rent is the expression of the social power of landed property over capital, manifested in the struggle over control of surplus value.[13] In Tibet, however, local farmers are not landowners but rather only hold use rights to the land. Moreover, the social position of migrants above locals as expressed through *suzhi* enhances their social power in bargaining. While Tibetans are by no means powerless in the transaction, the process of ground rent setting does not reflect the power of landed property over capital to increase the price through extramarket means. During the years of peak vegetable profitability in the mid-1990s in particular, when the ratio of vegetable profits to rental prices was highest—often a factor of ten—a different balance of social power between migrants and local villagers could have resulted in higher rental prices for villagers.

This power relationship, different from that assumed in the classical understanding of absolute rent, is also manifested in the unenforceability of contracts between migrants and villagers. These contracts vary widely in terms of standardization within a village, as well as of village leaders' involvement.[14] Usually the village household keeps one copy in Tibetan and the migrant household one copy in Chinese; sometimes the village committee has a third copy. Village leaders can assist villagers to remeasure the land when they rent it out, especially if migrants insist on this being done, but the main rationale for signing the contract under supervision is for the village head to be able to intervene if the Chinese farmers "cause trouble." However, Han farmers whose vegetable production is not going well—who barely break even or worse, can't recover their input costs—sometimes run away without paying rent. For example, in 2000 and 2001, three Han families ran away from Kyichuling village without paying more than 11,000 RMB of rent owed to Tibetan families. In the summer of 2002, another Han family ran away without paying 7,000 RMB owed to three Tibetan households. Cases of Tibetan families who lose expected rent of 5,000–6,000 RMB, not to mention the opportunity cost of not producing grain that year, are common in peri-urban villages.

When Han farmers do run away without fulfilling the terms of their contracts, Tibetan households and village leaders can do nothing about it. Neither villagers nor village leaders have the resources or means to pursue compensation. The cost of traveling to Sichuan or other provinces to search for the migrants would greatly exceed the original land rental price. More important, the contracts have no real legal standing. Villagers cannot sue greenhouse farmers for not abiding by their contracts, and township and village leaders are unable to truly enforce them, as they sometimes explicitly remind Tibetan villagers during meetings. Instead, they admonish villagers to have unity with the Han farmers. Indeed, given the contracts' lack of enforceability, one of their main purposes seems precisely to be providing leaders an opportunity to regulate political unity between Tibetans and Han.

Han migrants are fully aware that the contracts are not enforceable. One explained:

> There is nothing definite. You can sign a contract, or not sign a contract. It's flexible. For example, if I have money in July or August, I can pay early. But if I don't have money, then I can pay late. Contracts are not very useful. For these things you can't really talk about the law. . . . After all, if I sign a contract with you, and I lose money and then leave, it is impossible for you to come and find me. For such a small amount of money, it's impossible that you would come all the way to *neidi* to track me down. You'd spend more money on the road searching than the amount I owe you! Where would you look for me?

Another farmer from Mianyang explained, "The contracts don't mean anything to us. They are only for the Tibetans." Migrant farmers do not deny that some among them run away without paying when they lose money—or even simply to keep more profit. However, other Han migrants complained that Tibetan villagers "don't understand legal matters" and sometimes demand payment earlier than the contracts specify, or ask for a higher price after the contract has already been signed. One woman fumed, "It makes me so angry! We Han—if we sign a contract, then we'll pay the money on time according to whatever the contract has specified. We Han are generally trustworthy. . . Those people really piss me off! They come today to ask you for money, and you tell them to wait until such and such a day. Then they come back tomorrow." She suspected that a Tibetan in the village had put a curse on one of the Han farmers after he refused to pay the rent owed by a relative who had run away without paying:

> the woman of the household from whom they rented the land told the [Han] family, "if you can't pay that rental fee then you go and die!"

> And then—he died! He really died. On Nyangre Road, in front of the vegetable market. A car hit him and killed him. . . . She cursed him to death.

These complaints notwithstanding, Tibetan villagers' demands for early payments or other changes to contracts go mostly unmet by the migrants.

The looseness of the contracts was on display one day in 2004, when I was sitting in a friend's house in Kyichuling village on the day the family was supposed to receive rent payments from the two Han families to whom they had leased their land. Their contracts were on two scraps of paper, with the area of land, the price per *mu*, and the date the payment was due handwritten in cursive Tibetan, but nothing else—no names or citizen identification numbers of the Han renters, no deposits, and no red seals that mark official documents in China. A Han woman to whom they had rented out their land showed up at their house with a male migrant, to whom she had subcontracted the land she had subleased. Because the woman had signed the contract, she should have been responsible for the payment, but she claimed that she needed to remeasure the fields to distinguish between the land she was using from the land that she had subcontracted out, and further that she had gotten confused about the date of the contract when subleasing the land. The Han man came to ask for a month-long extension on his share of the rent. The woman told the Tibetan family, "You have to let him pay later; if you do, he won't want to run away, but otherwise he might run away." The woman also refused to pay, and no money changed hands that day.

Tibetan village leaders have tried to devise methods of inducing Han farmers to make their payments, or at least to minimize possible losses. Some require that the contracts record the migrants' citizen identification numbers, but this is of little use insofar as it does not help with tracking down those who have run away, and false identification cards and numbers can be easily used. Some villages require the Han to pay their year's worth of rent in two installments. Where, as is typically the case, payment is due only once a year, leaders try to choose a date when vegetables are still in the ground, so that the Han are less likely to abandon the fields.

The most obvious way to lower the risk of losing money is to require a deposit, but this is uncommon. A minority of households takes deposits in the range of 10 to 40 percent of the rent, but most households do not take any at all, because the migrants refuse to pay. Migrants claim they simply cannot afford to pay a deposit before they begin to earn money each year. According to many Tibetan villagers, if they ask for a deposit, the Han will simply go to the next Tibetan family—who won't require a deposit. In other words, a lack of collective action increases these risks of loss for

Tibetans who rent out their land, yet village or township rules about taking deposits have not been considered. At the same time, some attribute the willingness of Tibetans to engage in these transactions without a deposit to be exemplary of the difference between Tibetans and Han migrants. When I asked one Tibetan villager why her family does not get a deposit, she replied:

> Why? Because they're Chinese. The Chinese rent our land and then they say, "Bring soil, bring wood, bring electricity" and we do, and we don't even collect a deposit. Really, it'd be better to get a deposit. But we don't. Tibetans have good hearts. If one [migrant] signs a contract with a Tibetan, and then can't pay on time, Tibetans don't count it at all. They tell us about their hardship, and we just say "okay, don't worry about it." Tibetans have compassion.

Intravillage Rents and the Spatial Distribution of Land

The interaction between the spatial distribution of the Household Responsibility land rented by Han migrants and intravillage rental price norms also significantly shapes Han domination in vegetable production. At decollectivization in Tibet, as across China, farmland was categorized into different quality grades, and households were given an equitable share of each grade of land. This has led to a spatial pattern in which each family has use rights to many small plots of land, dispersed around the village. In the peri-urban villages around Lhasa, households typically have six or more plots, some barely large enough to fit a greenhouse (100–500 square meters). As a result, Han vegetable farmers usually rent land from multiple Tibetan families who have contiguous household plots.

This spatially dispersed pattern of plots gives Han farmers a subtle advantage over Tibetans. Although Tibetan families without sufficient land can sublease land from other villagers, such transactions are quite uncommon, and usually occur only in cases where households who had few members at decollectivization and thus received little land now have much larger families than their fields can support. The rent is usually paid in grain rather than in cash. A typical example would be one peri-urban household renting land from three other village families and paying them one-tenth of the harvest in a form of sharecropping. If cash is involved (usually in rentals from the village committee, rather than directly from other households), rents are very low; norms are less than a quarter of what Han farmers pay. One Tibetan villager, who farmed vegetables in greenhouses for several years before quitting, suggested that the small size and the spatial dispersion of his plots were the main barriers to greater success in vegetable cultivation. When I asked him why he could not consolidate land closer to his home by renting land from other villagers, he replied simply, "That would never happen!"

Tibetan villagers' reluctance to rent out land to their neighbors at the same prices as they charge Han migrants is a manifestation of a form of moral economy, an unwillingness to fully commodify social relations within the village. By contrast, Han farmers have no previous social ties within the village, and Tibetan farmers expect to establish no relations with them other than purely economic ones. Because they are outside of village and kinship politics, it is much more straightforward for Han farmers to lease land from several Tibetan families at once. They can more effectively consolidate land to take advantage of economies of scale in greenhouse building. They usually do this by renting adjacent plots from willing villagers, though occasionally local Tibetans comment that they did not want to rent out certain plots but had no choice. By this, they mean that all of the other families with land nearby rented their land to the Han, leaving only their small plots sandwiched between many greenhouses and making irrigation and plowing very inconvenient on that plot. One villager complained that because Han greenhouses surrounded his plot, there was no easy path on which he could carry his harvested grain home. Still others stated that the intensive chemical use in greenhouses affected grain production on their nearby fields, again giving them no choice but to rent out their plots, and making it easier for Han migrants to consolidate larger fields for their greenhouses.

A slightly different example clarifies the logic of disembedded social relations. A former monk from Phenpo, now a Lhasa businessman, planned to remodel his new private house in order to transform the ground floor into a row of small shops that he could rent out. Despite his dissatisfaction with policies that he felt were leading toward a loss of Tibetan culture, he planned to hire Han rather than Tibetan construction workers because, as he put it, "the Chinese are less troublesome."[15] If he hired Tibetans, he would feel obligated to serve them tea and good food, whereas with Han migrant workers, the transaction is much more straightforward: all he has to do is pay them a salary. In addition, he said, he finds it embarrassing to repeat instructions to Tibetan workers because of his concern about offending them. However, he is not embarrassed at all about giving the same repeated instructions to Chinese workers. Like greenhouse vegetable farmers who rent land at high prices to the Han but to their neighbors only in kind, he hired Han migrants rather than Tibetans as laborers out of a reluctance to engage in marketized economic transactions with those with whom he had social relations shaped by strong cultural norms. He and the villagers are willing to engage in these marketized transactions with the Han, who as both cultural and literal strangers are already disembedded from social relations. Paradoxically, then, the Han farmers' outsider status enables rather than restricts their access to Tibetan land for greenhouse vegetable farming. This demonstrates both the mutual constitution of cultural politics and political economy and the ironic ways in which culturally constructed notions of proper behavior can contribute to marginalization within the changing economy and ultimately to greater pressure on cultural continuity through the influx of migrants.

Capital: Inputs and Startup Costs

In addition to rental payments, other inputs for peri-urban greenhouse vegetable farming include plastic sheets, bamboo poles, chemical fertilizers, organic fertilizers, agricultural chemicals, and seeds.[16] The plastic sheets used to cover the greenhouses must be changed every eighteen months to two years, and the bamboo poles used as frames every two to three years. Prices on the latter, obtained mostly from the forested region of Nyingtri, rose by almost a factor of seven between 1996 and 2000.[17] Migrant farmers typically spend 3,000–4,000 RMB a year on chemical fertilizers, including diammonium phosphate, urea, and carbamide, and sometimes supplement these with sheep manure purchased by the truckload. They also make extensive use of pesticides and fungicides. Many migrants report receiving advice from Han sellers of agricultural chemicals on how to use them. Some also state that they get them for free from Tibetans, who receive free or subsidized chemicals but often do not want to use them for religious reasons. The Han purchase seeds from Sichuanese migrants working in Lhasa, or sometimes bring them from home. In addition to these input costs, some migrant farmers also pay a transfer fee to other migrants as a startup cost. Migrants wishing to leave Tibet, move on to other economic activities, or simply move to other plots of land often turn their greenhouses or plots over to other migrants for a fee. This is most common on the state farms, but is occasionally also practiced in peri-urban villages on land seen as highly desirable; fees depend on whether what is being transferred includes the greenhouses and the vegetables inside of them.

With all of these inputs, the initial capital costs of greenhouse farming can be high. Han migrants estimated spending anywhere between 2,000 and 8,000 RMB per *mu* of greenhouse land as a startup cost. Several said that it is impossible to make a profit without an initial 10,000 RMB to invest, while others reported bringing initial investments ranging between 2,000 and 30,000 RMB. Most borrow at least some of this initial investment not from banks, but rather interest-free from their friends, family members, and others from the same hometown, with reported loans ranging from 1,000 to 10,000 RMB, usually paid back within a few months to a year. Migrants who do not bring any capital with them usually start out working for others or working with relatives to save money, which they then use to invest in their own greenhouses.

Han migrants generally do not have easier access to formal credit than do Tibetan villagers. Investment in houses, tractors, and cars, together with the fact that government programs have given subsidies for greenhouses for Tibetans, suggest that while access to startup capital is certainly a limitation for some Tibetan peri-urban villagers, it is not as important as other factors in shaping Tibetan nonparticipation in vegetable agriculture.

Labor

Greenhouse vegetable farming is a time-intensive activity. On a typical day, a Han migrant farmer gets up at 3 or 4 a.m. if vegetables need to be brought to the crowded wholesale market, or at daybreak when growing vegetables; comes back to rest around noon; then works again from 3 p.m. until 8 or 9 p.m. Migrants complain about the bitterness and difficulty of the labor, calling their income "blood-sweat money." However, others describe enjoying the relatively straightforward and simple lifestyle of vegetable farming in Lhasa. At home, they explain, they have to raise chickens and pigs, grow various crops, and fulfill many social obligations, whereas in Tibet, life revolves around growing vegetables and preparing meals in pressure cookers, without other things to worry about.

Migrant couples often leave their young children, along of course with their grain fields and livestock, at home. Thus the Han farmers have fewer demands on their time than local Tibetan villagers, demands on whose labor include care for children and livestock. In addition, Tibetan vegetable-cultivating villagers generally retain some part of their land for grain cultivation, either because they have inconveniently located plots that the Han migrants are unwilling to rent or because they want to keep some grain production for livestock fodder, which is useful for producing milk. Keeping part of the family's land also provides some insurance in case Han migrant families run away without paying. In the initial years after the surplus grain policy shifted, many also wanted to keep their grain supplies plentiful in case the mandatory sale of grain to the state was reinstated.

Furthermore, even when a household has rented out all, or nearly all, of its land to Han farmers, its members usually still have informal labor obligations to work on the land of family and close friends during the harvest. Tibetan families stay in these informal mutual aid relationships in part because Han greenhouse farming is not viewed as permanent—most Tibetan villagers believe that the Han migrants will move away after several years, as has indeed been the case (though often because of urban expansion). Thus, they maintain these relationships in anticipation of needing future mutual assistance. In addition, some Tibetan villages have continued to impose compulsory labor obligations to plant trees and maintain irrigation canals with fines for those who do not participate, whereas Han migrants are excluded from such obligations. While not terribly onerous in terms of total amount of work time per year, collective labor obligations are another reason that Tibetan villagers are able to mobilize less labor for greenhouse vegetable farming than Han migrants. The differential availability of labor for greenhouse farming is a result of the fact of migration; the structural difference is that Tibetans do not have nearly the same opportunities to out-migrate and position themselves in other labor markets across China to capture benefits provided by either government investments or growing private opportunities, the way Han migrants are able to in Tibet.

The retention of some farmland helps explain why Tibetan peri-urban villagers' participation in off-farm labor, which they refer to as "side work," has not increased as much as might be expected given the large-scale leasing of land to migrants. Some villagers have managed to use savings from rentals to purchase items such as tractors, which they use to exploit off-farm labor opportunities in construction or transportation. Most, however, stick to more common forms of off-farm labor such as selling radishes and potatoes, both home grown and bought from other farmers, raising pigs, operating bicycle rickshaws, and working in construction and quarrying. These activities are often not very profitable. Villagers often refer to construction simply as "Chinese work" because so much of it is handled by Chinese labor contractors. Because of their preferences for hiring their own *laoxiang*, and because they consider Tibetans less skilled and of lower *suzhi*, they routinely pay Tibetans significantly less than Han migrants. Furthermore, construction is seasonal, generally coming to a halt in the winter, precisely when farmers have the most time on their hands. Indeed, during my frequent visits to Kyichuling village in the winter months, I almost always found a dozen young and middle-aged village men gathered in the teahouse, smoking, singing karaoke, and playing mahjong. These men did some construction work and petty business in the summer, but were idle all winter.

The lightened labor load that does result from renting out land is not shared evenly between Tibetan men and women. Women, who do more of the farmwork, including harvesting, threshing, and winnowing, generally continue to have farm labor obligations even after land rentals. Men, on the other hand, often slack off in their attempts to find off-farm labor. At a year-end meeting, one peri-urban village leader commented extensively on the gendered shift in labor patterns:

> These days mothers and daughters are doing most of the farmwork. Most boys drive tractors and do other types of side work. Some boys leave the house in the morning to go to work, but at noon they're sitting in the pub and drinking *chang* for the rest of the day. Some boys leave home to drive tractors or look for side work, but then they aren't seen for half a year. They do a bit of work in the morning but spend the rest of the day drinking beer. When they come home they have no income to show. . . . If you drive a tractor, don't stay in the city all year. Come back and help your family.

Economic reform has not only benefited the Han relative to Tibetans, but also Tibetan men relative to Tibetan women.

Most Han vegetable cultivators do not pay for labor power. Instead, they work the greenhouses themselves, often as couples or with relatives, with additional support from friends and family during busy times. However, some Han farmers do hire Tibetan villagers, usually on a daily wage, to work in their greenhouses. These are often the very same Tibetans whose land use rights the Han farmers have subleased, resulting in a curious situation in which Tibetan "landlords," as the Han migrants sometimes call the Tibetans, labor for a wage on their own land. This was more common in the 1980s, when the early Han farmers had closer relationships with village heads, making it easier to hire Tibetans for 3–5 RMB a day. Standard daily rates rose to 10 RMB a day in 2000, and to 20 RMB a day five years after that, equal to the lowest daily rates paid for construction labor, and much lower than the standard wage rate paid to Han migrants.

One Han farmer explained that she and her husband rarely hire help, but when they do, they always hire Tibetans because they are willing to work for so little. On the other hand, using Tibetan hired labor sometimes only confirms to Han migrants their disdain for Tibetans. One migrant stated, "I once tried to hire a Tibetan to work, but it was impossible. These Tibetans just won't do what you tell them to. Even if they know what you want them to do, they just won't do it correctly." Another said that he had tried to hire Tibetans because they are cheaper than Han workers, but "they're no good . . . the Tibetans don't do high-quality work. They're a bit stupid. They don't learn very quickly." Others complained that Tibetans they hired pulled out vegetables by mistake, thinking they were weeds.

The tasks for which Tibetan laborers are hired—weeding and tilling the soil—do not prepare them to become vegetable growers themselves. When asked whether his hired help might try to grow his own vegetables in a few years, one Han migrant laughed, saying, "I only hire him to till . . . not to grow vegetables or apply chemicals." Even where Han migrants hire Tibetans as laborers in vegetable production, technology transfer does not occur.

Market Networks

Han migrants dominate not only vegetable production but also vegetable sales in both the wholesale and the retail markets. This also discourages Tibetan participation in vegetable farming because of the need to sell their vegetables almost exclusively to Han wholesalers and retailers. They have a more difficult time establishing relationships with middlemen, or finding sympathetic buyers to give them a better price on their produce, than do Han migrants selling to people from their hometowns.

As with vegetable production, the percentage of Tibetans involved in vegetable sales has decreased since the early 1980s. Until 1985, vegetable marketing was done exclusively by Tibetans, in the Tromsikhang market near the Barkor, and at a market near the Potala Palace. That year, a man from Chongqing, reportedly the first Han vegetable seller in Lhasa, began transporting vegetables by truck from Sichuan to sell in Lhasa. By 1994, more than three hundred Han peddlers transported vegetables from the cities of Chengdu, Lanzhou, and Xining for sale in Lhasa, and sellers from Sichuan dominated the city's seven vegetable markets.[18] Of the remaining Tibetan sellers, accounting for less than a quarter of the total, few had stall space, and most instead paid a small daily fee to sit on the floor outside markets.[19] By 2000, there were virtually no Tibetan sellers in any market other than the Barkor market, and even there, Tibetans accounted for fewer than 20 percent of the sellers. After the wholesale market on Nyangre Road was established in the early 1990s, vegetable farmers began to take their produce there. As with the retail markets, Tibetans are barely present in this market; of the more than a thousand sellers there in 2001, no more than a handful were Tibetans, selling potatoes in one small corner.

Han vegetable producers state that vegetable sellers make more profit than they do, but that social connections and capital are more necessary for selling than growing vegetables. In particular, relationships (*guanxi*) are necessary in order to get a stall. In addition to the official rental fees, it has become the norm for sellers to charge a transfer fee of several thousand yuan, or demand a gift from those who might want to take over their stalls. Without relationships, it is difficult to find someone willing to transfer their stall at all, and certainly not for a lower price. One Han farmer reported that in 2002, it was still fairly easy to get a stall and a transfer fee was not necessary, but that by 2005, stalls were difficult to obtain and transfer fees had become the norm. On the other hand, several Han vegetable sellers reported that they gave stalls to their friends rather than selling them, sometimes in order to keep open their own options for returning to vegetable selling.

The rentals and transfer fees pose problems for potential Tibetan sellers in several ways. First, many of the markets offer stalls on an annual rather than monthly basis. This makes them less feasible for village farmers who still have land and thus labor obligations during certain times of the year. Even those who have time to sit in the market year-round do not have close relationships with the Han sellers who now dominate there, and thus they are unable to buy the right to rent a stall. Though there were initially Tibetans involved in vegetable sales, their profits began to decline as competition from Han migrants intensified, pushing many of the early sellers out of the markets. As the scale of vegetable production and thus also of vegetable markets began to expand rapidly, the new entrants were almost entirely Han migrants. Once Han migrants dominated the markets, it became very difficult for other Tibetans to break in, because of their lack of social networks with those Han migrants already in the market, and because of the villagers' alternative labor obligations. This in turn contributes to the marginalization of Tibetans in vegetable production.

CULTURAL POLITICS OF VEGETABLE CULTIVATION LABOR

In his study of development and the Patel caste in central Gujarat, India, geographer Vinay Gidwani argues that neither new institutional economics nor Marxian political economy can adequately explain the rise of piecework employment in the area. Inattention to culture and power in these approaches leads to a failure to take into account the way in which a preference for piecework by the Patels, who do the hiring, helps consolidate markers of social distinction and a collective identity in which they see some forms of work as superior to others. For the Patels, the pursuit of "leisured work" through hiring on piecework rather than supervising labor risks productivity losses, thus upsetting the original class basis on which distinction can be practiced. In other words, "the sense of distinction that their class position demands seems to hinge precisely on what it is not, on the face of it, economically rational."[20] At the same time, because the working-class men of the region consider supervised wage labor degrading, they prefer piecework that allows for working at one's own pace and without supervision over the possibility of higher earnings. This helps explain Gidwani's observations during fieldwork of not only young, affluent Patel men, but also less well-to-do young men spending their days even in the busy agricultural season lounging around, gossiping, and playing cards rather than engaging in daily wage labor. The apparent idleness of the latter cannot be explained by conventional economic theory, but neither does it simply conform to elite stereotypes about the poor.

Instead, understanding these embodied preferences for certain types of work over others requires attention to power, cultural logics of practice, and the relational and regulative fields of meanings within which labor and leisure decisions are made—but these are missing in conventional economic and political-economic accounts.[21] Changing material conditions of work over time change the multiple social and cultural meanings of work, which in turn shape work practices.[22] "Cultural" here does not refer to a domain separate from "economic" or "political," nor to something that exists only on the plane of consciousness.[23] Instead, following Bourdieu, culturally shaped forms of conduct and cultural logics are embodied dispositions that show up as regularities in practice.

I use the term "cultural politics of work" to refer to power-laden, shifting meanings, as well as to what Gidwani calls the cultural logics of practice that govern embodied dispositions that shape preferences and conduct toward work. Tibetan dispositions to avoid vegetable cultivation, like the preference for piecework by both Patels and those they employ, do not seem economically rational. Specific logics of distinction and embodied cultural meanings make nonparticipation more attractive for Tibetans than the possibility of earning greater incomes by engaging in vegetable cultivation.

Multiple dimensions and layers of the cultural politics of work shape dispositions around Tibetan nonparticipation in vegetable farming. These simultaneously maintain an ethnic distinction and contribute to Tibetan economic marginalization. One of the most important aspects of the cultural politics of work is the pervasive explanation by Tibetans that they do not grow vegetables because of their own indolence and aversion to hard work; this is the subject of the next chapter. Here, I turn to meanings and dispositions around greenhouse vegetable cultivation specifically rather than "hard work" in general.

The use of night soil as fertilizer by Han greenhouse farmers stigmatizes vegetable farming as "dirty" work for some Tibetan villagers. One of the few Tibetan farmers who volunteered to take part in a state-subsidized greenhouse program reported that very few other families volunteered, because they "look down on greenhouse farming as dirty work."[24] Han farmers also occasionally complain that vegetable farming is dirty work, but associate it with being low-class or lowly (*xiajie*) labor. For Tibetan peri-urban households, the connotations of filth are associated with ethnicity rather than class. One resident of Tolung Dechen remarked that villagers have to dig wells now because the irrigation water from which they used to drink has been polluted by Han migrants: "There are many Chinese around growing vegetables. Their customs are not the same as ours. They do things to pollute the water—we don't do these things."

Forms of distinction include not only the meanings of filth or dirt associated with particular forms of work, but also embodied dispositions or habitus, Bourdieu's term for systems of dispositions that enable practices to be "objectively harmonized" among a class or group "without any intentional calculation or conscious reference to a norm."[25] One of the most commonly cited reasons Tibetans gave for not participating in government-subsidized greenhouse programs in the 1980s was that, unlike the Han, they were unable to labor inside greenhouses because the heat makes them dizzy and sick, gives them headaches, and can induce high blood pressure. Some talk about themselves as being physiologically distinct from Han migrants in their inability to withstand the heat of greenhouses. Indeed, local Tibetan leaders in a village where a government-subsidized greenhouse program had failed attributed the failure in part to the villagers' health problems and the headaches they experienced from the unaccustomed heat. One Tibetan who worked briefly in a greenhouse commented, "The Han work very hard. We can't stay in the greenhouses for very long. If we go pick weeds in the greenhouses, we can't stay inside for more than a few minutes at a time. Our heads hurt. When the water drops [from condensation inside the greenhouses] fall onto our heads, it hurts." Wearing fewer or thinner layers of clothing, as the Han farmers do, to mitigate the effects of the humid heat did not seem to present itself as an option to Tibetan peri-urban villagers, who instead understand and invoke their bodily dispositions with regard to the heat as a marker of fundamental difference from Han migrants.

Skills and Science

In addition to the heat of the greenhouses and the association of Han vegetable farming with filth, Tibetans cite their lack of skill, experience, and knowledge of science as a key reason that they do not grow vegetables for sale. They assume not only that Han migrants have a great deal of experience growing vegetables, but also that their skills come from reading books and their more extensive formal education: "We Tibetans have no skills. But the Han know how to read [Chinese] and they learn how to apply chemicals. They have more expertise. They've gone to school." Others stated:

> We Tibetans can't grow vegetables like the Chinese can. It's just not possible. Most of them have good educational levels, they have all gone to school, and so they all have science. They know how to read. . . . These days growing vegetables requires science. Tibetans don't know how to do this.

> We don't have the skills, like the Chinese do. . . . They use all sorts of chemicals. . . . If one buys chemicals from the store, all the instructions are in Chinese.

> The Chinese are more expert than Tibetans. They use a lot of chemicals. They use more science.

Here, the discursive invocation of skills and science as a part of the cultural politics of identity vis-à-vis greenhouse vegetable farming is interwoven with structural barriers of language discrimination and educational opportunity. Middle-aged and older Tibetan villagers cannot, for the most part, read Chinese. Thus, they cannot read the instructions to use agricultural chemicals even if they wanted to. (Most do not want to use agricultural chemicals, however, for religious reasons and out of concerns about health and food taste.) Most manuals and booklets about vegetable cultivation are available only in Chinese and therefore are not useful for older Tibetan farmers. The younger generation does, however, learn Chinese in schools and should be capable of reading instruction manuals. If the purported technology transfer between Han migrants and Tibetan peri-urban villagers did in fact take place, the lack of skills and knowledge about inputs would no longer be a barrier to Tibetan vegetable farming, but it is.

Although Tibetans attribute a great deal of experience and skill to the migrants, most Han vegetable growers do not view themselves as possessing much of either. While many Han migrant farmers do grow a variety of vegetables at home for their own consumption, few have experience either with greenhouses or with producing vegetables for sale. When asked about their vegetable cultivation skills, about half of the migrant farmers I interviewed said that they did consult books to learn how to grow vegetables, while others said that they had neither prior knowledge or skills, but simply learned to grow vegetables by experimenting on their own, or by watching and asking friends and family who had been in Lhasa longer than they. Although literacy and education are important, some Han farmers succeed with neither. One illiterate fifty-year-old farmer from Henan told me that he relies on other more experienced Han farmers for assistance. Advice from private (Han) merchants of seeds and agricultural chemicals is also important, again putting Tibetans without social relationships with these vendors at a disadvantage.

However, the invocation of a lack of skills and scientific knowledge is not just a reference to a set of structural barriers but also an identity claim, a marker of difference between Tibetans, who lack science, and Han who possess it. The self-identification of Tibetans as nonscientific is particularly significant in the context of a state discourse that labels Tibetans as superstitious and lacking in understanding of science because of their unwillingness to use chemical fertilizers and other agricultural chemicals, particularly pesticides, out of religious concerns about killing insects. Though not as politicized as other practices such as the recitation of mantras by ritual specialists to control the weather and prevent hail, which is firmly considered superstitious and thus antistate, the refusal to kill insects with pesticides is frowned on by government officials. The conflation in official discourse of science with these agricultural inputs also shapes the way science is understood by Tibetan villagers. As one peri-urban villager, a nephew of a former ritual specialist in preventing hailstorms, stated:

> In the past we didn't have pesticides, but these days. . .what do they call it? Science. In reality "science" just means "for killing." In the past there were no pesticides or chemical fertilizers but the crops grew well. . . . These days after they apply the chemicals the heads of the grain turn completely yellow.

By claiming a lack of science and skills, Tibetans are also claiming an inability to use pesticides, the use of which goes against Buddhist precepts not to take life. By pleading ignorance, they can more effectively refuse to use pesticides and thereby adhere to Buddhist principles, which in turn is both a marker of Tibetanness and a form of distinction between themselves and Han migrants. This ignorance at times seems quite willful, as when a woman from a peri-urban village remarked, "Oh yes, at the meetings they are always telling us to use science, but no one listens to them really. They tell us about chemicals to use. We really don't know what they say at the meetings, and no one really does anything." Or as another remarked succinctly about new government agricultural plans, "All this science—it's no good!"

Gendered Work: A Tibetan Women's Vegetable Farm

As we have seen, Tibetan men have disproportionately taken advantage of the reduction of labor demands resulting from the rental of land to migrants. Peri-urban village men are far more likely to lounge in teahouses and karaoke bars than women; this holds for urban Lhasa as well, where the visibly unemployed and underemployed are disproportionately male. Social status plays an important role in gendered outcomes in the labor market, as many of the income-earning opportunities now available in the urban service sector are considered menial, low-status, and inappropriate for men, but less so for women. The gendered meanings of work play a role in structuring outcomes in vegetable farming as well, as seen through the experience of one exceptional, successful Tibetan vegetable farming cooperative—composed almost entirely of women.

In 1997, a Tibetan lama living in England decided to fund several poverty alleviation projects near Lhasa, including vegetable cultivation for income generation. The quasi-governmental Tibet Development Fund administered the funding in two villages in Tolung Dechen County, one of which was successful while the other failed after three years. Here I discuss only the successful village, where the fund spent a total of about 30,000 USD between 1997 and 2001, and which operated until the village was urbanized in the mid-2000s. Initially 50 *mu* (3.3 ha) of village land were set aside for vegetable cultivation, though after a year, the manager decided that the team could not handle production at this scale, and returned 20 *mu* to the individual families, who rented the land to Han migrant farmers. In contrast to various government projects that have been implemented to encourage Tibetans to grow greenhouse vegetables, which only minimally compensate villagers for their household plots if they are used for vegetable farming, money from this project was used to pay households 700 RMB/*mu*/year. The fact that this rent is on a par with the amount villagers would receive from Han farmers reduced the initial incentive to rent the land out to Han migrants, as happened with government-run projects.

Because the goal of the project was to generate income, anyone who joined the farm was guaranteed an income of 10 RMB a day.[26] Workers received wages only for days worked, but were allowed to take unpaid days off to attend to other tasks at home. Thus, they had the potential to earn 3,500 RMB a year, but the average was closer to 2,000 RMB. Although the daily wage rate was somewhat lower than the 15–20 RMB daily wage rates for construction, the latter were unstable and seasonal while the vegetable project provided families with a stable, year-round income.

At the beginning of the project, forty villagers—one man and thirty-nine women—signed up. However, most of the workers dropped out within the first year. According to the manager, most of them found the labor too tedious and difficult. The sixteen remaining workers as of 2002 were all women from families with very little participation in other off-farm labor opportunities, and women who had elderly parents or children to take care of. The vegetable farm was an attractive option for them because it was located in the village itself and work hours were flexible, allowing them to run home to take care of chores during the day. Work typically began around 8:30 a.m. Most went home for lunch around 11:30 while two stayed on rotating duty at the vegetable compound. After lunch work began anytime between 12:30 and 3p.m., and continued until sunset, or until the tasks for the day had been completed. In addition, two women sold vegetables each day at small nearby markets, or when more vegetables were available for sale, at the Lhasa wholesale market.

When I asked why there were no men, the women workers replied that men were "not able to endure" the painstaking work required in vegetable cultivation, whereas women had the patience to do that kind of work. Village men occasionally joined the farm, but typically quit after a day or two. "The problem with the men in this village," said the manager, a Tibetan man who had learned to cultivate vegetables by working as a temporary laborer at the July First State Farm, and who was paid 1,000 RMB per month by the fund, "is that that they don't like to work. . . . Most of them have no ability whatsoever. They like to play mahjong all day, drink tea, and they say that it's too hot in the greenhouses." The brother of one of the women workers concurred: "men don't like to do work like weeding," and more generally, staying all day in a greenhouse is "too annoying" for men.

When I commented on the absence of men during one visit, an older woman laughed, saying, "Growing vegetables is women's work." I asked why that was the case when Han men grow vegetables. She replied, "Yes, but Tibetan men aren't like that. They don't do this type of work. They can set up steel bars and build the greenhouses, but when it comes to weeding and harrowing—they're no good at it at all. They don't like to do it." She added, "Most of us working here are mothers of children." The women added that within their own households, they were also responsible for grain cultivation. I wondered out loud where their husbands were. After some joking ("We don't have husbands. We're all single!"), several complained, "They sit in the teahouse and drink beer all day. They don't do anything at all."

Tibetans conceive of vegetable farming as a form of labor that requires a great deal of patience and the ability to stay in one place, both gendered traits that Tibetan men are coded as lacking. The association between Han men and vegetable farming also subtly codes Han men as less masculine than Tibetan men. Indeed, vegetable production and consumption are both gendered for Tibetans. Whereas vegetables have long played an important part in Chinese cuisine, diets in central Tibet were until recently not rich in vegetables. Instead, meat played a much larger role both symbolically and materially. To some extent, Tibetans consider Chinese men effeminate because of their vegetable consumption, though this is changing.[27]

A number of different factors came together to cause the relative success of the farm compared to many other attempts at Tibetan vegetable cultivation. Among these were the fact of significant external funding (though this was true of failed government projects as well), the competence of the manager, the decision to pay a daily wage, and the cooperative structure that gave more flexibility for labor requirements than would have been available in an individual household. The farm's decision to reduce the use of chemical fertilizers to a minimum also helped it develop a niche among Tibetan consumers, who reportedly preferred the resulting taste of the vegetables. However, the gender composition of the cooperative also played a significant role. Like Tibetan men, the women claimed that the greenhouse work was harmful to their health, raised their blood pressure, caused headaches, and was generally "very hard work," but unlike men, they were nevertheless willing and able to withstand these conditions.

Space and Place in Vegetable Farming

As the number of Han migrants in Lhasa has increased, Tibetans have become less rather than more likely to be vegetable farmers. The narrative of technology transfer that is supposed to make Tibetans more rather than less able to participate in the market economy assumes that Tibetan villagers and nearby Han migrants will interact and work together, sharing knowledge, skills, and ideas. In fact, this rarely happens. Han farmers' status as outsiders gives them an advantage in terms of consolidating plots for an effective scale of greenhouse production. While a moral economy prevents the full commodification of social relations within the village, Han farmers' persistent status as strangers allows them to more easily rent land at higher prices from Tibetan villagers. Spatial patterns and social relations each produce the other, explaining how Han farmers remain strangers who interact very little with Tibetan villagers, precluding the transfer of skills.

Map 3 depicts the landscape of Kyichuling village, a typical peri-urban vegetable farming village, in 2001. Perhaps the most conspicuous feature is the sheer number of Han-built greenhouses, which are not only numerous

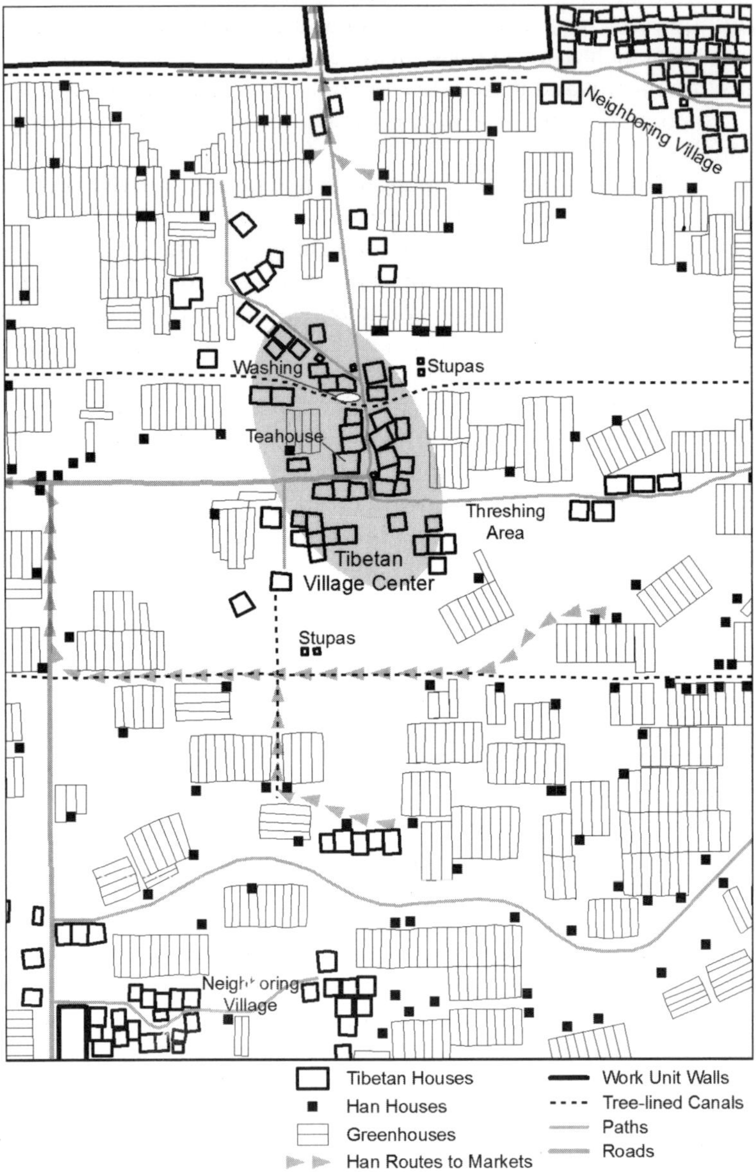

Map 3. Social-spatial relations in a peri-urban village. The map covers an area of approximately 1 km². Digital cartography by Mark Henderson based on a survey map by Jeff Lodas, 2001.

but also quite large (ranging from roughly 5 by 25 meters to 8 by 40 meters in area). The spatial distribution of Han and Tibetan houses is also immediately apparent. The Tibetan households are located in a centralized cluster, an old pattern in this area. Of the eighty-nine households in Kyichuling in 2001, the nine named households of the village's taxpayer families prior to 1959 still had houses standing in the central area of the village, also the site of the former Sera Monastery estate. The Han migrants' temporary houses, by contrast, are located right next to their greenhouses, in the middle of the fields. This gives the migrants easier access to their greenhouses and the ability to keep guard over them at night, but places their dwellings at a significant distance from those of most Tibetan villagers.

The differences between Han and Tibetan dwellings are also visually striking. Han migrants' occasional references to Tibetans as their "landlords" do not describe the actual legal property rights system nor the balance of power between the parties, but the appellation seems to be reflected by the stark visual contrast in housing. Tibetan houses and courtyards are spacious, constructed of whitewashed stone and adobe, with decorative dark red awnings and prayer flags staked on each corner of the roof. A chained dog usually guards the entrance to the courtyard, which almost always has a solar cooker heating a pot of water and rows of flowers bursting with color. Hand pumps and small, neat lawns became popular additions in the late 1990s. Around the courtyard are separate rooms that serve as kitchens, several combination bedroom–sitting room areas, and shrine rooms. In addition, there is usually an area for storage of farm tools and piles of dung for fuel, and sometimes a cowshed in the courtyard as well.

By contrast, the small and makeshift mud brick houses of Han farmers, with their corrugated tin roofs held down by rocks, scream out their impermanence. Han migrants build their dwellings to be cheap, because their goal is to save as much money as possible to send home. The dwellings are temporary in nature not only because their owners do not plan to stay in Lhasa permanently, but also because they often move to new locations within Lhasa every few years to deal with soil fungi and deteriorating soil quality after intensive cultivation. The typical house has a main room that serves as a kitchen and storage chamber for vegetables and farming tools, and perhaps one or two small rooms off to either side, just large enough for a bed. Most are dark, dusty, and threadbare, making the Tibetan houses seem opulent in comparison.

Place Making and Social-spatial Distance

Han migrants and their greenhouses are clustered on blocks of optimal farmland, leaving Tibetan farmers the rest of the fields—far from paths or irrigation, or shaded by trees—for grain cultivation. Due to the rentals, Tibetan villagers have less land to farm and thus less farmwork to do than they did in the past, and spend less time on the fields. Because of the clustering of their houses, Tibetan farmers do not regularly encounter many Han migrants in their daily paths through the village. In Kyichuling in 2001, household and village affairs took place in the village cluster (marked approximately as a shaded oval on map 3), usually revolving around the village committee office, near the former estate building, which doubled as a popular teahouse. Groups of men frequently gathered to play mahjong in the teahouse, whereas women could often be found washing clothes in the main irrigation ditch just north of it. Villagers, young and old, gathered to burn incense at two pairs of village stupas near the village center.[28] Male village youth spent much of their time in Lhasa looking for work or enjoying its karaoke bars and pool tables. Most elderly residents walked to Lhasa each morning to circumambulate the Lingkor, returning to their homes in the late afternoon to rest. In the winter, these residents frequently sat together in a courtyard or just outside a village home, to warm up in the sunshine. During the harvest season, Tibetan men and women spent their days between the fields and the threshing area, then relaxing for a picnic and *chang* in the fields after the day's work was done.

Han farmers, by contrast, stayed in their greenhouses and their houses right next door. When not working, groups of Han families often congregated in one family's small dwelling to play mahjong or eat lunch together. When leaving the village, the Han farmers generally walked from their greenhouses to the paths nearby and traveled directly to the wholesale vegetable market in Lhasa. Several such paths are marked with arrows on the map. They did not usually travel to the places of Tibetan sociality in the village, nor did the Tibetans often come and visit their gathering places.

The result of the different spatial locations of Han and Tibetan houses, their work sites, and gathering places, is that although the Tibetan and Han farmers live in relatively close proximity to each other, within a small village, they live separately and travel along different routes. They effectively create distinct places, through an array of embodied practices, meanings, and social relations. The work of place making includes embodied movement, as well as narratives and discursive practices, the stories that people tell about themselves in relation to a location.[29] For Han migrants, these villages are a temporary home, "little Sichuan," where they work very hard to accumulate money to send and take home. For Tibetans, village land has material and symbolic significance not only as the primary source of livelihood, but also as a link to the past, expressed through named fields and houses, and as common territory linking all those over whom the village's birth deity (*khe lha*) presides.[30]

Embodied practices are also place-making practices; "place, nature, and locality [are] transformed—invented, even—through physical, corporeal action."[31] Tibetan villagers' and Han migrants' embodied practices of eating, sleeping, gathering, cultivating crops, and walking are all ways in which place comes into being. De Certeau writes that walking "is a process of appropriation of the topographical system on the part of the pedestrian . . . it is a spatial acting-out of the place."[32] The walker actualizes certain possibilities in a spatial order, bringing places into existence. This is how, through everyday practice, different paths are actualized as places within the set of all possibilities. Kyichuling village articulates at least two sets of itineraries of its inhabitants, two sets of possibilities in the spatial order.

These places are not static, but rather are always being made and remade, through embodied practices, discursive practices, and spatialized social relations. Conceiving of space as "a moment in the intersection of configured social relations" and place as "a particular set of social relations which interact at a particular location," Doreen Massey asserts that the specificity of place is formed not by a deep-rooted, static identity, but rather by the presence of particular sets of social interrelations, some of which stretch beyond any particular locale.[33] Thus, the social is necessarily spatially constituted, just as the spatial is socially constituted. When Han migrants first arrive in a Tibetan village to grow vegetables, they usually have no prior social relations with Tibetan villagers, though they usually have such relations with other migrants from their hometowns. This social distance is inscribed through the location of their houses and greenhouses, and the paths they walk through the village. Now that most of their fields are rented out to the Han, the Tibetan farmers no longer need to walk to them, and spend their time instead in their homes and courtyards, in the teahouse, in remaining fields, at stupas and incense burners, and on the circumambulation route to Lhasa. The initial social distance between Han migrants and Tibetan villagers is spatialized through their separate places of dwelling and sociality, and repeatedly enacted through the different routes they take in moving through the village. This spatial distance and their separate place-making practices reinforce the initial social distance. This maintains two distinct sets of social relations that interact at the particular location of the village. They are not completely separate from each other, and indeed the separate routes through the village of the Tibetan villagers and Han migrants are produced in relation to each other. Nevertheless, this mutual reinforcement of the socio-spatial arrangement creates a situation in which technology transfer—which requires interaction, sharing, and working together—is very unlikely to happen.

Instead of having close relationships of teaching and learning, Tibetan villagers are surprisingly ignorant about the Han farmers to whom they have rented land. Although there are exceptions, many are not sure about which province their renters have come from. Nor are they aware of how the Han manage the land or conduct daily affairs. They see their relationship with the migrants as a strictly monetary one. I spent the first month after my arrival in Lhasa for fieldwork simply trying to establish which villages around

Lhasa did or did not have rent land rentals to migrants. As I walked down the potholed dirt path toward Kyichuling village, I stopped a middle-aged Tibetan man walking in the other direction to ask whether this might be a research site of interest for me: "Do these villages have any Chinese (*gyami*) in them?" He responded, "The villages have no *gyami* in them. The *gyami* are by themselves. They build their own houses." To him, the village is where the Tibetans—and not the Han—live.

This spatial-social separation was also instantiated during Kyichuling village's celebration of an agricultural festival about a week after Tibetan New Year.[34] After the rituals of the festival in a field, a group of elderly villagers settled into the courtyard of a nearby house. There they sat on the ground while others came and offered them *chang* and *tsampa*. Soon several circles formed, as villagers took out their thermoses of sweet tea and butter tea, and picnic baskets full of New Year's goodies—small fried cookies, chips, and hard candies. After some picnicking, two older women stood up and began a circle dance. Other elderly villagers joined in their singing and dancing. In the middle of all of this, I heard someone say "*gyamo!*"—"Chinese woman!"—and I looked up to see a Chinese vegetable farmer come into the courtyard and quickly and wordlessly lead her little boy away. The boy, no more than five years old, had been playing with the Tibetan children. The woman made no eye contact with anyone present, nor did the gathered villagers acknowledge her presence beyond the announcement that she was in their midst.

The Han farmers, for their part, are similarly ignorant of Tibetan villagers. They are generally aware of who the village leaders are, how much rent they have to pay, but of little else. As one Sichuanese woman responded when I asked what the Tibetans did now that they had rented out their land to her and her relatives, "I don't know about them . . . they're over there, we're over here." Another Han man said about the local villagers, "Well, some Tibetans are really very unreasonable. We Han usually stay together. We research our own things [meaning better methods to cultivate vegetables] and the Tibetans do their own things. They don't come to ask us. We have very few relations with them."

Language, Trust, and Social Relations

The spatial distance between the clustered village and Tibetan gathering places and the houses and greenhouses of the Han migrants make it easier for the latter to depart without paying rent and without being noticed. Those who do so often leave some vegetables in the ground and a few articles of clothes on a line to make it look as if they are still there. This contributes to the Tibetan villagers' perception of the Han migrants as "tricky" and untrustworthy, which further discourages close social relationships. Some say that the social distance is deliberate. One Tibetan whose family in Kyichuling had rented all of its land to Han farmers stated, "We have very few relations with the Han. It's better that way. If the Han farmers try to give our children vegetables as a gift, we always tell them to refuse the gift. Otherwise, later when it comes time for them to pay you, they will call you *laoxiang* and they won't pay on time; they will keep asking for an extension. It's best not to be too close to them."

By contrast, most Han farmers attribute the general lack of communication with the Tibetan villagers to a language barrier. According to one Han woman, "We have no way of having relations with them because we can't understand them and they can't understand us. The language is not the same." Another compared the difficulty of learning Tibetan with the ease with which she had picked up Cantonese while working in Guangdong, "For most of us—if we stay in Guangdong for a year—then we can speak and understand Cantonese. It's not very hard. But Tibetan—there's no way. It's just like trying to learn a foreign language. So there is no way to cooperate with the Tibetans who have no education. We have very few relations with them. We just pay our rent once a year—that's it." When I asked the Han farmers if they had learned Tibetan, or were planning to do so, they usually laughed, or said, "No one wants to learn Tibetan. Nobody learns Tibetan."

One relatively prosperous Han vegetable farmer from Liaoning expressed a very negative view of the Tibetans, but then tempered his anger with an explanation of the language barrier:

> These Tibetans come and steal everything. . . . Not just vegetables—also electric wiring and pipes. I've already had two stolen. Just a little while ago I caught three girls stealing one of them. I called the Public Security Bureau but then I couldn't talk to them. Then they talked in Tibetan to the PSB officer, so who knows what they said? These Tibetans will steal anything. . . . The main problem is that we have no way to communicate with them. They can't understand us and we can't understand them. If we could talk to them then we could understand their intentions more clearly.

Similarly, a Han migrant in Tolung Dechen explained:

> . . . those people over there—they're all speaking Tibetan. We can't understand a word of it. . . . We don't have much contact with Tibetans here. Every day we just plant our vegetables, so we don't have much contact. If we were often together with the ordinary folks for a long time, then we would be able to understand them. But we don't have much relations with them.

Despite this referral to the language barrier by some migrants, younger and middle-aged Tibetan peri-urban villagers generally do speak and understand Chinese, though middle-aged villagers do not read or write it. Language difference is not as much of an obstacle as might be inferred from Han migrants' comments, which seem to refer as much to socio-spatial distance as to Tibetans' actual language ability. The few Han migrants who claimed that they did speak Tibetan often knew only a few phrases, whereas Tibetan villagers who claimed not to speak Chinese often knew more Mandarin than the Han migrants who claimed to speak Tibetan. The reference to the language barrier by Han migrants (but rarely by Tibetan peri-urban villagers) reflects as much the assumptions that come with Chinese language dominance as anything else.

Some migrants do perceive that, even without close relationships, their general presence has changed Tibetan villagers. In a type of imperialist nostalgia, they look back to the better days when Tibetans seemed more innocent and different from themselves.[35] One Sichuanese farmer complained that when he first came to Lhasa in the mid-1980s as a construction worker "the Tibetans didn't even know how to use a scale." Now, however, they've learned from the Han to bargain, which gives him a headache in the market. A Han woman in Tsalgungtang assessed the situation as follows: "These Tibetans are getting sharper and sharper. They've learned how to be sharp from us. When we first came here seven years ago none of them could speak standard Mandarin. Now they can."

In addition to the language barrier invoked by many Han migrants, some also referred more specifically to ethnic and territorial tensions. One farmer from Mianyang claimed, "Tibetans look down upon the Han." When asked to elaborate, he stated in 2005 that the reason their attitude was poor was "because they want independence. Tibetans say that Tibet belongs to Tibetans, they say, 'this territory is ours.'" But, he suggested, the ones who "hold the Han in contempt and say 'this territory is ours'" are the ones who are old and uneducated. "In the future, the young people today won't say such things." Like many others, he had a firm conviction that the attitude he sometimes picked up from Tibetan villagers that "this land is ours and outside people don't belong here" was disappearing. The riots in Lhasa and the targeting of migrant shops in 2008 dramatically proved this conviction to be unfounded. The continually reproduced social-spatial distance between Han migrants and Tibetan villagers precluded the migrants from being able to accurately read Tibetan sentiments and Tibetan interpretations of their ongoing marginalization vis-à-vis the migrants.

All this should not be taken to imply that greenhouse vegetable cultivation is the key to Tibetan economic success, and that if only Tibetans would grow vegetables, they would no longer be marginalized. Instead, greenhouse vegetable farming is exemplary of the much larger pattern of Tibetan marginalization vis-à-vis Han migrants, and illuminates how the hegemonic project of development works on and through the agency of Tibetans and Han in producing the landscape. The gradual takeover of vegetable production by the migrants, whose presence helps accomplish state territorialization, naturalizing the PRC as a spatial container for Tibet, illustrates how territorial control is effected through material practices of landscape production. The transformation from barley and winter wheat cultivation to more input- and technology-intensive vegetable cultivation through the embodied labor of Han migrants and the agency of Tibetan villagers helps consolidate state incorporation.

Tibetan peri-urban villagers invoke an economic calculation when they explain why they would rather rent out their land to Han migrants than continue to grow barley and wheat: changing relative prices of inputs and crops make renting out twice as profitable. The configuration of various different modes of power in Lhasa produces subjects for whom alternatives such as refusing to rent to Han migrants lie outside the realm of common sense or the politics of the possible. Tibetan farmers' participation in a phenomenon that continues to attract Han migrants to Lhasa nevertheless contributes to Tibetan marginalization, fueling anger and resentment that burst through in the extraordinary Lhasa riot of March 2008. This too faded rapidly with the strong assertion of sovereign power, and greenhouse farming and the Han presence soon returned very much as it had before, with Tibetan villagers once again deciding to rent out their land to migrant farmers.

However, an economic rationale of profit maximization does not hold in Tibetan villagers' nonparticipation in greenhouse vegetable farming, which persisted even during the years when Han migrants frequently made ten times in profits what the Tibetan villagers collected in rents. In choosing not to participate, Tibetans appear not only to fail to do what earns more income, but also to reproduce their own marginalization. This is further strengthened by the fact that Han migrants who fail to profit pass on their losses to Tibetans by simply running away, and that most Tibetan farmers do not use their extra labor time to engage in other profitable income-earning opportunities or investments. Tibetans are not *homo economicus*. The state development project to educate them as better market actors, in part by learning from Han migrants imagined as more advanced in market rationality, is interrupted by other rationalities and culturally specific and historically produced understandings of identity, labor, and value.

This phenomenon must be understood as overdetermined, and produced by intertwined political economic and cultural political pressures, as well as by the co-constitution of social and spatial relations. Property rights and the spatial distribution of household plots at decollectivization, together with a moral economy of intravillage land rentals, converge to give Han migrants as outsiders an advantage over local villagers in consolidating scales of land needed for greenhouse cultivation. The gendering of vegetable cultivation labor also contributes to the failure of most efforts to start Tibetan vegetable cultivation, while at the same time serving to reproduce Tibetan men's sense of their own identities. Similarly, the association of Han vegetable farmers with skills and science lacked by Tibetans reflects both structural inequalities in education due to differences in the broader political economy of development in the TAR as against other provinces, as well as a form of identity claim that gives Tibetans a reason to maintain their Tibetan Buddhist practices while deflecting charges of superstition and thus of antistate sentiments.

Embodied preferences for certain kinds of work over others are missing in conventional political-economic accounts, but necessary for understanding the dilemmas and complexities of hegemony, development, and marginalization. Distinction and regulative fields of meaning that shape preferences are real forces that have significant impacts in Tibet. In this way, political-economic processes of marginalization are in part produced by cultural meanings and preferences for certain types of work, and marginalization in turn creates a drive for distinction between Han and Tibetans, resulting in choices that unintentionally help reproduce further marginalization. These Tibetan dispositions to avoid vegetable cultivation are set within a broader cultural politics of work and indolence to which I now turn.

Science and Technology Transfer Day

The transfer of science and technology by the state to Tibetan villagers is intended to be accomplished both directly, through state-sponsored efforts, and indirectly, by way of the villagers' proximity to Han migrants. In February 2001 I had the opportunity to observe the former in action during a day in which science and technology were brought to "the masses." Called "The Three Go Down to the Countryside" (*sange xiaxiang*), this was a mandatory annual event in which Lhasa work units traveled to a rural area to promote (1) science and technology, (2) education, and (3) hygiene, with the overarching goal of alleviating poverty. That year's program, which was with the Tibetan medical hospital and several institutions of agriculture and animal husbandry, was held in a township seat only a short drive from Lhasa.

We arrived at the township government's courtyard to see a banner hanging across the entrance proclaiming this a day for science and technology. Inside the courtyard was a stage with a long table with microphones, and a row of nine chairs. In front of the stage and spanning its width was a multicolored balloon arch on which "Rely on Technological Progress, Realize a Leap Forward in Development" was emblazoned in Chinese. Two balloons on either side carried a similar slogan in Tibetan. Around the courtyard, work units had set up booths with exhibits. Staff members from the hospital and the animal husbandry bureau were dressed in white lab coats, giving them an air of knowledge and authority. The Vegetable Research Institute displayed poster boards showing a variety of flowers, vegetables, and greenhouses, as well as packets of seeds, potato cultivars, and pamphlets about vegetable cultivation. Another exhibit included small glass display cases holding varieties of barley seeds.

Some young children had come early, wearing their school uniforms and sitting cross-legged in two rows directly in front of the stage. The villagers drifted in, and by the time the program began there were some six or seven hundred audience members. Sometime later, a group of uniformed soldiers marched in and sat to the right of the stage, followed after a few minutes by a truckload of maroon-robed nuns who sat to the left of the stage, directly facing the soldiers. Thus was created a visually striking bifurcation of space.

The event began with speeches by several work unit party secretaries. One spoke about the need to be civilized (*wenmin*), the importance of education, and how modernizations could be achieved only through the use of science and technology. Others spoke of the urgent need to oppose superstition and to use science instead. After the speeches began a program of more than twenty songs and dances by staff members from various Lhasa work units. These "cultural" presentations, presumably designed to make science and technology transfer more palatable to the villagers, had little to do with agriculture, health, science, or technology, but carried with them the presumption that village culture was inferior to what could be brought from the city. Most of the performances were familiar Tibetan songs and dances, with references sprinkled here and there to China and to gratitude to the CCP. There were also a few oddities, including four Tibetan male agronomists dressed in drag and lip-synching to a pop song. The program was interrupted about two-thirds of the way through when TAR deputy party secretary Tenzin arrived to present gifts to the children of a nearby orphanage. A television and a video-CD player were given to the township, and a refrigerator to an impoverished household. Development and poverty relief had arrived in the form of gifts.

At the conclusion of the performances, the audience, who had sat patiently throughout the day, converged on the display booths around the courtyard. The largest crowd, pushing and shoving, formed around the Tibetan hospital's table, where doctors read pulses and gave out medicine. Villagers mobbed the other tables as well. Far too many bodies crowded chaotically around the small spaces for any actual conversation or dissemination of information to take place. Instead, this was an occasion for the sport of free sample collection. At each table were hundreds of pamphlets about greenhouse vegetable production—only a small number of which were in Tibetan and so were useless to most of the villagers—which the visiting technical experts from Lhasa threw to the crowd. The Vegetable Research Institute had brought several cartons of its newly developed brand of spicy fries. Two staff members climbed onto the table and threw their packets of greasy potatoes and Chinese-only pamphlets into the crowd, and the villagers fought over them eagerly. This was "technology transfer" Chinese-Tibetan style: the great science giveaway.

The villagers then sat in circles for the highlight of the day, a picnic of dried meat, vegetables, baskets of bread, and jugs of *chang*. During the feast, the agricultural experts recruited audience members to sing. After two more hours of merriment, the event was over and the villagers returned home with their free samples. Staff members from Lhasa's work units were also free to go, having fulfilled their annual duty to disseminate science and technology to the "ignorant masses." The villagers had fulfilled their duty as well, to attend the day of performance, food, and drink, and to bear witness to the presentation of gifts.

5 Indolence and the Cultural Politics of Development

> Development is the foundation of resolving Tibet's problems. We must build Tibet into a better place through *hard work*, develop new businesses that can help people become affluent, accelerate the pace of development, improve the quality of development, make constant efforts to expand the capacity for self-accumulation and self-development . . . firmly seize the precious opportunities created by the country's strategy of developing western China . . . firmly handle the two important projects—development and stability—ensure Tibet's leaps-and-bounds economic and social development. . .and work hard to build . . . [an] affluent, civilized and harmonious socialist new Tibet.
>
> —Hu Jintao, PRC president and CCP general secretary, 2006 (emphasis added)

> Everywhere else in the world, people have to work all day, every day, all year round, but we Tibetans only work for four months and then spend the other eight months sleeping. . . . Tibetans are hopeless in terms of development. We sit around all day, don't want to work hard.
>
> Tibetans just learn bad things from the Chinese. These days [Tibetans] steal, lie, and cheat. They don't learn any of the good things. Tibetans don't see the bigger picture, [Tibetans] are satisfied with what little they have.
>
> Tibetan businessman, 2004

> Soon we'll be so developed, we won't even need to eat!
>
> Tibetan resident of a peri-urban village near Lhasa, 2002

The grounding of state legitimacy on economic development and the delivery of a comfortable and prosperous society (*xiaokang shehui*) involves a delicate balancing act, in which officials stress the development that has already been achieved while also pointing to the great gaps that can only be addressed through further state intervention and the self-cultivation of Tibetans as desiring subjects of development. This is evident in the statements of many top leaders, such as that of Hu Jintao above, as well as in an article that appeared in the *People's Daily*, the official mouthpiece of the CCP:

> Whenever one mentions Tibet, one usually associates it with backwardness, with being closed and with barrenness. . . . Tibet [has] a very, very long way to go for its economic development. . . . But this is no reason for Tibet to be content with the present situation and not to think of making progress. . . . Backwardness is not terrifying. Being geographically closed is not terrifying. What is terrifying is rigid and conservative thinking and the psychology of idleness.[1]

According to this discursive formation, Tibet's lack of development, its still-pathetic place along the spectrum of China's provinces despite the benevolence and gifts from the state, is the product of Tibetan indolence—Tibetans' "closed and conservative concepts" and "idea of doing nothing" all of which must be urgently overcome in a "great tide of large-scale development," as TAR Party secretary Chen Kuiyuan put it in 2000.[2]

Reminders of development are everywhere in Lhasa. Slogans boldly emblazoned in white characters on red banners admonish citizens to "Deepen Reform, Expand Opening Up, Accelerate Development, Protect Stability," or admonish with Deng Xiaoping's slogan, "Development Is the Only Hard Truth." Development circulates not only in banners, leaders' speeches, meetings, and policy documents, but also finds its way into the intimate social spaces of the home and the teahouse, as the subject of everyday conversation and humor, in redeployments that both reflect state discourse and exceed its boundaries.

Seductive and powerful, development is one of the most influential and defining ideas of our time, profoundly structuring socio-economic transformations around the world.[3] Critiques of development have also proliferated. The "postdevelopment" critiques that emerged in the 1990s analyzed development first and foremost as a regime of knowledge and power, emanating from the West, that enframes and constitutes its objects in particular ways. Development in this view acts likes a machine that creates new targets for development intervention.[4] Though insightful, the postdevelopment approach tended to rely heavily on textual representations, substituting a kind of discursive determinism for neoliberal or Marxist economism.[5] This elides the actual practices, processes, and cultural politics through which development projects are enacted, contested, and altered, including the way in which development transforms identities and subjectivities.[6]

I adopt instead an ethnographic approach to development as a "crucible of cultural politics."[7] In so doing, I argue for the importance of culturally specific idioms through which development is experienced as a project and process that is not everywhere the same around the globe; these idioms are also materially important in shaping political-economic outcomes. In Tibet, the state emphasis on the need for Tibetans to work hard and build their capacity for "self-accumulation and self-development" has incited its opposite, a trope of Tibetan indolence, as a key idiom through which development is experienced and its meaning reworked in Lhasa today.

Peri-urban Tibetan villagers frequently invoked indolence when I spoke with them about why they rented out their land to Han migrants rather than growing vegetables themselves. In a distinct echo of state discourse, they claimed that the reason they don't grow vegetables is that Tibetans are lazy, don't like to work, and can't work as hard as Chinese. As one woman explained:

> We Tibetans really are falling far behind because we're lazy. . . . In Lhasa, we drink *chang* all day. It's "bottoms up" all day. Really! We just make a little bit of money, and are satisfied, and think about having a good time. It's true; that's how it is.

These utterances about natural Tibetan indolence are not confined to conversations about, or spaces around, vegetable farming. A prolific discourse of Tibetan indolence and Han productivity circulates throughout Lhasa. Tibetans, rural and urban, young and old, speak about how Tibetans don't like to work, sit around in teahouses, bars, and at home; do nothing but hang out and "wander around," and are too "spoiled" to work; in short, that they are lazy. The Han Chinese, on the other hand, are said to work hard; to have the ability to "endure" hard work, eat "bitterness" (*chiku*), and get up early and work until late. Tibetans invoked the figure of the lazy Tibetan not just in my interviews about vegetable farming or other economic activities, but also in jokes, spontaneous conversations over dinner, at the bus stop, and in taxis. "Have you noticed," a young Tibetan taxi driver whom I had never met before asked me when I told him that I am from the United States, "that Tibetans in Lhasa are never busy? [We] like to sit around all day. We don't like to work. We can't work as hard as the Chinese. Tibetans are not like the Chinese." "Why?" I asked, surprised by his voluminous thoughts about work. "It's a habit. Tibetans like to drink *chang* all day. The Chinese don't do that." "Has it always been like that?" I asked. "No," he replied, "During the collective period there was no such thing as sitting in one place. There was no rest at all. If we were to go back to the collectives now, no one would be able to work like that anymore, because everyone has become spoiled."

This trope of indolence resonates not only with state development discourse that incites Tibetans to work harder and shed their "psychology of idleness," but also with a common Han view of Tibetans, espoused for example by a Sichuanese migrant cobbler in Lhasa who said, "The Tibetans are lazy. It's only natural that Han people show them how to work,"[8] or a Sichuanese vegetable farmer who told me, "Greenhouse vegetable planting requires a great deal of hard work. Tibetans just don't work that hard." These resemblances might be thought of as mimetic reenactments of external representations. Francesca Merlan writes, for example, that "Fourth World or indigenous peoples are highly susceptible to others' representations of who and what they are, and this susceptibility plays a large role in shaping their conditions of life."[9] Vincanne Adams describes the Tibetan situation in contemporary Lhasa as one of mimesis, a spectacle of scripted simulation in which "Tibetanness is scripted by Chinese and Westerners and is internalized by Tibetans in performances that create and reinforce cultural differences between these groups."[10] While external representations are certainly powerful, such accounts risk confining subaltern agency to a process of mirroring—of following scripts written in advance by others' representations.

Instead, I argue that the trope of indolence is one of two key idioms through which Tibetans, as subjects who are not self-sovereign, autonomous, and fully formed, but who nonetheless exercise agency, engage with a specific project of development, one that is presented as a gift and has territorializing effects. The idiom of indolence, like the idiom of Tibetans being "spoiled" by development, is not epiphenomenal or "merely cultural."[11] Rather, the broader political economy shapes the cultural idioms through which development is understood and negotiated, and these in turn constrain and shape the possibilities for maneuver within the larger trajectory of political-economic change. Furthermore, despite their echoes of official and Han migrants' representations of Tibetans as lazy, these tropes are also historically and culturally constituted, informed by gendered conceptions of what counts as work and of what sorts of work are worth doing. They are not reducible to either mimetic re-enactment or "everyday resistance." Instead, a Gramscian conceptualization of contradictory consciousness shows how these historically inflected idioms are complex and contradictory ways of negotiating development as a hegemonic project.

Common sense, "a conception of the world mechanically imposed by the external environment," is always fragmentary and incoherent.[12] It differs from mimesis in that it never exists by itself but rather is always imbricated with good sense critical conceptions. Rather than being a dead end that forecloses possibilities of change, it is precisely on the terrain of common sense that ideological struggle takes place.[13] At the same time, good sense, which is neither inherited nor uncritically absorbed from the past, folds back into common sense, despite a clear diagnosis of the nature of domination. As a result, "a marked degree of disenchantment with the prevailing system . . . can coexist with a calm acceptance of the system and belief that there is no systematic suppression of personal chances in life."[14] This contradictory condition of both disenchantment and acceptance characterizes different moments in the deployment of the tropes of indolence and of being "spoiled," and thus in the experience of development more broadly.

Elements that can be interpreted as good sense, and those that are common sense, are always co-existing and interconnected.

This analytic, paying attention to the inherent interconnection between "penetrations" and "limitations," in Paul Willis's terms, is useful for considering indolence *both* as speech act (the spoken claim to indolence), *and* as a referent to particular patterns of labor and exertion, shaped by culturally and historically constituted and gendered notions of work. Rather than assume that speech acts about patterns of labor are transparent reflections of embodied habits of work—that is, that Tibetan statements about their own dislike of work simply convey the reality of embodied labor patterns—I take the speech acts and the embodied habits as related but distinct and separable phenomena, both characterized by contradictory consciousness. I examine first the claim of indolence as a locutionary act, and then embodied patterns of labor. Both layers are composed of elements of uncritical adoption of state discourse as well as of critical acts of identity formation and claims of distinction. These elements are themselves shaped by sedimented histories and memories of the past, as well as by contemporary political-economic conditions. I then turn to the idiom of being "spoiled," which connects the experience of development across the social fields of agriculture, urbanization, and labor, all of which affect the production of the landscape.

Indolence as Self-critique

The trope of indolence seems difficult to take seriously. "Aren't they just saying that?" and "Of course Tibetans are no more or less lazy than anyone else, so why does it matter if some people say that?" are two common reactions.[15] Thus, there is a tendency to dismiss statements such as this, by a Tibetan woman from a peri-urban village: "We who are called Tibetans are very strange, as we don't like to work and instead are lazy and stupid compared to the Chinese." One might argue that because such statements don't really reflect reality (because Tibetans are not objectively lazy or stupid), the statement has no analytical value.

However, a performative analysis of speech, in which speaking is not merely a transparent reporting of a real condition or action but a form of action in and of itself, suggests that the very fact of making statements about laziness, "not liking to work," and, in a related manner, about being "stupid," "lacking in skill," and "spoiled," is worthy of attention. To speak is to do, and thus to speak about indolence is an act deserving of analytical engagement, as a separate question from patterns of time allocation in particular forms of labor. A performative understanding of speech allows for speech acts to be both mimetic and the locus of agency, located within the possibility of variation in the regulated process of repetition that is signification.[16]

As Judith Butler suggests, this approach allows for an analysis of "how a subject who is constituted in and by discourse then recites that very same discourse but perhaps to another purpose . . . that's agency, the moment of that recitation or that replay of discourse that is the condition of one's own emergence."[17]

Spoken self-critiques of the Tibetan work ethic are sometimes completely serious and sometimes self-consciously ironic and humorous; the distinction rests upon a vocal inflection, a turn of the head, a mocking note, an exaggerated drawl, or a particular gesture, distinctions that require ethnographic methods to uncover.[18] What appears to be a self-deprecating and mimetic repetition of the hegemonic discourse can simultaneously be a repetition that performatively produces a positively valued distinction or difference between Tibetan and Han.

Among the harsh critics of Tibetan villagers' work habits are Tibetan elites, both village officials and urban intellectuals. Their critiques contain an element of class and status superiority, also mapped onto the urban-rural divide, though their statements often refer simply to "Tibetans" rather than more specifically to "Tibetan villagers" as the locus of the problem. For example, a retired Tibetan CCP official of a county agricultural office explained to me that "Of course, Tibetans *could* plant vegetables themselves. But you see, they do not like to work. Tibetans waste a lot of time sitting around and drinking." Local officials also blame Tibetan laziness not only for their failure to grow vegetables, but also for their reluctance to use agricultural inputs such as chemical fertilizers.

Similarly, a respected Tibetan scholar and Lhasa resident articulated the following analysis of Han domination of greenhouse farming:

> The main reason is that [Tibetan] people these days are *so lazy*. They sit around and drink . . . they don't like to work. Thus, there will never be any improvement [of the economy]. Because there are too many places to hang out in the city, people just sit around all day. . . . These days the farmers come to the city to wander around. . . . They don't work. As a result there is no development.

Tibetan villagers invoke this discourse of indolence with as much regularity and conviction as do urban residents, usually through comparisons with the Han, who they construe as much harder-working. One middle-aged Tibetan from Kyichuling explained, "The Chinese farmers work hard, very hard. They get up early, at 4 a.m., to go to the market. Then they work early in the morning, and until very late at night. . . . Tibetans don't get up early and work until late. It's too much work for Tibetans." A villager who participated in the 1985 state-subsidized greenhouse program explained that the main reason other Tibetans in his village did not take part was that they "cannot endure hard work," and that grain cultivation is easier work in comparison to vegetable farming because "one only has to work hard for a short period of time, not like in a greenhouse."

A Kyichuling resident in his seventies, who rents his own family's farmland to Han migrants, stated that all vegetable cultivators are Han because

> Tibetans don't like to work! This is what we like to do: In the morning, we like to drink our delicious tea, then all day long we like to drink our delicious barley beer, and we like to have very delicious food to eat. All the Chinese need to do is drink water and eat a few vegetables and that's it! We Tibetans don't like to work. We like to sit in the sun all day.

His over-the-top remarks and tone of voice suggested that in saying that Tibetans "don't like to work," he was also mocking the Chinese for not knowing how to enjoy their lives. The injunction to reform one's condition of indolence produces repetitions such as this one, which "exceed and defy the injunction by which they are generated,"[19] turning a critique into a positive assertion of difference.

On some occasions, the question of whether laziness is the root cause of Tibetan nonparticipation in vegetable farming became the object of debate, indicating that it is also taken seriously as self-critique. In one household in Kyichuling, a younger man told me that Tibetans lack the skills that the Han have for vegetable cultivation. However, his father-in-law immediately interjected that the real explanation is not lack of skills but rather dislike of work. Villagers often invoke this theme of lack of skills compared to the Han together with the trope of indolence. For some, what appears as laziness is actually a lack of skills, while others, in a more critical vein, insist that lack of skills is simply an excuse for laziness: "These days Tibetans have nothing because they are lazy. There isn't any such thing as knowing or not knowing how to work. If you want to do it you could learn."

This sometimes self-critical nature of the claim of indolence as a locutionary act also became apparent when Tibetan friends and acquaintances presented a critical view to me, but defended Tibetan work practices in front of Han migrant farmers. One woman in her late thirties, who had lived for much of her life in rural Phenpo, remarked to me in private conversations on numerous occasions, "Tibetans are lazier than the Chinese—isn't that so?" However, when we were together with a group of Han migrants who implied that Tibetans should just work more, she immediately defended Tibetans, saying that the problem was not that Tibetans are lazy, but rather that they search for work but can find none, and further that "we work hard too!" The juxtaposition of her defense of Tibetan industriousness to Han migrant farmers with her private assertions about Tibetan laziness suggests that in addition to working as positive claims of difference, these statements about indolence are also sometimes self-critical. As performative statements, claims of indolence are also often articulated through the idiom of being "spoiled," to which I return below. First, however, I turn to other layers of indolence as expressed in gendered, and historically, culturally, and religiously inflected patterns of labor.

Culturally Constituted Notions of Work

Just as the act of reiterating "we're lazy" establishes an identity claim vis-à-vis the Han, so too do actual embodied labor practices and patterns of time allocation, which are shaped by culturally constituted notions of work. Sir Charles Bell, a British political officer who lived in Tibet for almost two decades in the early twentieth century, implicitly noted the culturally constituted nature of work in his description of Tibetan work habits:

> By Europeans, and occasionally by Japanese also, Tibetans are often described as lazy . . . when there is nothing to do, they can stay doing nothing for a long time without falling into boredom or peevishness. But, if work is to be done, there is no shirking . . . [at harvest] the peasants and their households rose at one or two o'clock at night, partook of a little tea and barley flour and went out immediately to their plots of land . . . while they worked, they sang. . . . No eight-hour day here, but rather eighteen.[20]

When Tibetans in Lhasa claim that they "cannot get out of their beds in the morning to work," they are referring to specific activities, such as vegetable cultivation, and not to others, such as rising long before dawn to circumambulate the Lingkor for several hours. Barley cultivation is a type of work for which Tibetans willingly and regularly rise early and toil long hours without complaint. Sowing and harvesting barley, whether for the household or for other families as part of reciprocal labor obligations, is time-consuming and requires an enormous expenditure of labor power, but this is not what Tibetans refer to when they say that they do not like to work.

Cultural conceptualizations of work adopted uncritically and unquestioningly from the past are, in themselves, what Gramsci would have called common sense, "traces of previous systems of thought that have sedimented into everyday reasoning,"[21] in opposition to good sense. Uncritical historical sedimentations include certain gendered notions of labor; for example, food preparation, child rearing, and cleaning are done by women, but are not usually considered "work." But a conscious embrace of certain types of labor and rejection of others can, even if drawn from traditional conceptions, also work in the context of Han migration and Chinese state hegemony to establish claims to self-worth in the face of assimilating pressures. They are forms of identity making, where identity is not a fixed, underlying attribute of an unchanging self, but rather something that emerges from practice and is always contested and in motion. The association of vegetable farming with filth is one such cultural dimension of work specific to Han greenhouse vegetable cultivation. Across wider fields of work, religious ideals of compassion and avoidance of taking life are frequently invoked, as in the following conversation between Jampa, a monk from a village in Phenpo, and Tsering, from a village near Lhasa. What is important is not the truth or falsehood of compassion as practice, but rather its deployment as an explanation for patterns of choosing (or not) certain forms of profit-making labor.

TSERING: If one is not afraid of sin (*dig pa*) then one can become rich very quickly. As a farmer, if I were not afraid of sin, I would kill animals. For example I'd keep many ducks. . . . Ducks grow quickly—in just three months. I could sell each duck for twenty-six yuan and save up a thousand yuan in no time. But we Tibetans don't want to take any lives. We work, but as long as our stomachs are full then that's good enough. . . . No matter how much I'm able to do, no matter how many tens of thousands of yuan I make, when I die, I can't take even one cent with me. . . . Because of society's development, one has no choice but to work these days. But we fall behind. We Tibetans think first about one job, then think that work causes a lot of sin, so we switch to another.

JAMPA: Tibetans think about having compassion and are afraid of accumulating demerits.

TSERING: Yes, because of compassion, we fall behind. Tibetans think, as they are about to kill an animal: I should have compassion. This is the main reason that there is a big gap between Tibetans and Chinese.

JAMPA: They don't recognize compassion.

TSERING: Right, they don't have compassion. They'll do any kind of work at all.

JAMPA: Tibetans have a lot of forbearance, as well as compassion and fear of sin. As a result, Tibetans lose all of the work to the Chinese . . . the [Tibetan] farmers think "this is enough for my livelihood," and then do religious activities, but the Chinese are not like this. They just close their eyes and do anything at all.

A Tibetan Buddhist Work Ethic?

More generally, reminiscent of Max Weber's attribution of capitalist economic success to Calvinist doctrines in Protestantism, Tibetans in Lhasa invoke a religious explanation—Buddhist principles and practices—for their work ethic and hence economic status. The characteristics that Tibetans ascribe to their work ethic are, however, strikingly opposed to those identified by Weber as the three overriding imperatives of the "spirit of capitalism": amassing wealth and profit beyond individual needs, toil and self-denial, and avoiding the use of wealth for personal enjoyment; to make, save, and keep money is the proper use of one's time and hard work, and accumulation of wealth is an end in itself.[22] By contrast, many Tibetans in Lhasa claim that their religious beliefs and practices explain why they are "easily satisfied" with what they have, and do not feel driven to toil to amass wealth and profit beyond their needs. A Tibetan farmer in her forties explained it in this typical way: "Tibetans don't like to work because [we] think, 'even if I work today, I might die tomorrow anyway.'" An urban resident explained this ethic as follows:

> We have a saying that a human life is as long as a cat's yawn—that is, very short! Tibetans think: if my life is so short, there is no reason to work so hard. After all, when a very rich person dies and when a beggar dies, they are exactly the same. Neither of them can take anything with them when they die. . . . This kind of thinking—that I should work just hard enough to get by—is very popular among Tibetans. . . . I myself have frequently thought this: I have enough, so I don't need to keep feeling dissatisfied or strive for more.

In another statement of the same ethic, a Tibetan doctor said to me,

> If I have ten yuan and someone else has twenty, nobody thinks "I should try to make twenty yuan." I just sit and relax. This is related to religion. People think, "I'm going to die anyway, what's the point of working so hard?"

Related to this are the ideas that Tibetans "can't save money" but also that they *don't* save money, because wealth accumulation and labor beyond the fulfillment of basic needs are not valued.

Scholars of Tibetan Buddhism, both Western and Tibetan, sometimes dismiss these ideas as merely the misconceptions of those who do not truly understand Buddhism. One Tibetan scholar laughed at these ideas:

> No, no, no. These people don't really understand Buddhism. . . . If [Tibetans] don't work hard, they are just plain lazy. It's not because of religion. One should work as hard as one can, just not be attached to one's work. Ninety percent of people don't understand the essentials of Buddhism. The essence is to control your mind (*sem*).

Indeed, it is possible to find Buddhist sutras that support both sides of the argument; some suggest that one should give up one's wealth and meditate, while others discuss the importance of gaining and protecting wealth.[23]

Here, however, my concern is not with the correct textual interpretation of Buddhist doctrine, but rather with the social fact of the mobilization of religious rationales by lay Tibetans in Lhasa, and with how they use their interpretations to make sense of their day-to-day lives in the context of state development as a territorializing project.

From their practical understanding, to be easily satisfied is a positive quality that sets Tibetans apart from Han migrants, whose purpose in coming to Tibet is precisely to accumulate wealth to take home. A Lhasa resident explicitly criticized what he sees as the Han drive for accumulation, made worse by development:

> On the one hand being easily satisfied is not good, but on the other hand I think this is a very good way of thinking. In [inland, Han] China, people do not have religion, and people's minds have big problems these days. People are always saying: economic development, economic development, economic development. Now I get a headache whenever someone starts to talk about economic development . . .
>
> For Tibetans, the number one priority is for their *sem* to be happy. If their *sem* are happy, then, as for everything else, if they have just enough, then that is good enough. The Chinese, however, just think about money. They get more and more money, but their *sem* are unhappy. We say that wanting more and more is the source of all suffering . . . Buddhism says not to have too much desire. These days, in China, people are really in psychological danger. With everyone only thinking about economic development, it's easy to have a lot of jealousy. . . . I'm so bored of hearing about economic development.

This statement encapsulates a way in which Tibetan statements about themselves ("easily satisfied") and the Han (who want to make money) give Tibetans the moral upper hand in an active production of ethnic difference. It posits a very different regime of value in relation to labor than does the dominant national value-coding of *suzhi,* which positions Tibetans at the bottom of a hierarchy of worthiness because of their purported inability to cultivate in themselves the desire and capacity for greater productivity and accumulation.

Another difference between Weber's spirit of capitalism and this Tibetan Buddhist work ethic turns on the Protestant commitment to self-denial and the avoidance of using wealth for personal enjoyment. Tibetans in and around Lhasa, by contrast, pride themselves on their ability to have a good time: "If Tibetans make a little money, then [we] go on picnics and enjoy ourselves." Indeed, time spent on unhurried leisure has a long and significant history in Lhasa, as Heinrich Harrer and Sir Charles Bell both noted with regard to the pervasive practice of picnicking, which Bell called Tibetan townspeople's "national pastime."[24] This was particularly true of the nobility in pre-1950s Lhasa, but today picnicking is common among not just wealthy urban families, but also rural and poor households. Indeed, most occasions—whether village meetings, circumambulation, mountain deity propitiation rituals, festivals, or visits to monasteries—call for a picnic and a good time. A woman in her fifties joked to me about this Tibetan penchant for having fun: "Americans would be shocked. In America, if you go to a party you don't even stay for two hours. In Tibet, at New Year's, we party for fifteen days straight." Tibetans in Lhasa explain this difference as a logical outcome of the religious principles outlined above: that "you can't take it with you" and therefore you might as well enjoy.

Though powerful, this invocation of a Tibetan Buddhist work ethic does not explain all situated practices and patterns of work, as the following three examples of lacunae show. First, given that donation to monasteries as well as sponsorship of individual monks is a widely accepted practice for accumulating religious merit, it would seem equally logical for Tibetans to argue that they should labor more, in order to be able to donate larger accumulated profits to religious institutions. Indeed, since the revival of Tibetan Buddhism in the 1980s, monasteries and individual reincarnate lamas have amassed considerable wealth from lay offerings that they have used in some cases for grants, loans, and alternative development projects such as the building of schools and orphanages.[25]

Second, there is a noticeable pattern in Lhasa of Tibetan businesspeople being much more likely to be involved in large-scale business with significant profit potential (such as antiques, medicinal herbs, and carpets) than in petty daily sales with slow but steady earnings. A third significant aspect of Tibetan work and accumulation in Lhasa that cannot be accounted for by appeals to a religiously based work ethic is the gendered nature of labor and the public performativity of leisure. As we have seen, the few successful cases of Tibetan vegetable cultivation have been the work of women, who are thought to be better able to cope with the "annoying" and patience-requiring labor of vegetable farming. Tibetan men are much more likely than women to be found idle since economic reform. When Tibetans discuss the fact that "Tibetans don't like to work," they often refer implicitly to Tibetan men. Women do a large share of the farm work, whereas Tibetan men spend much more time than women in teahouses and bars, both public, gendered spaces of leisure. Taken together, these social phenomena suggest that patterns of work are shaped by, but not reducible to, understandings of religion; they are also structured by the project of development and its assumptions about Tibetans as perpetually lacking in qualities of self-cultivation and hard work, and thus always in need of gifts of development.

Interrupting Development/Capital

The opposition between the spirit of capitalism and the articulations of a Tibetan Buddhist work ethic, along with the way in which the latter is thought of as opposed to economic development—as with the Lhasa resident who claimed, "I get a headache whenever someone starts to talk about economic development"—suggests that the refusal to "work hard" in activities such as greenhouse cultivation reflects more than the recognition of ethnic subordination and the marginalization of Tibetans in the broader political economy. It also expresses a limited refusal of a more general nature, of development's association in China today with market rationality and capitalist relations of production. Vinay Gidwani, discussing a farmer he meets who is unapologetic about his bad habits of drinking and disliking work, and who replies that he simply works when he wants and rests when he wants, observes that the farmer's behavior "frustrate[s] the recuperative desires of capital":

> He arranges to use his labor and his activities of consumption in time and space at *his* pleasure. Of course this is not always possible because he is *not* outside the gravitational pull of capital. But he seems to be trying to put together a mode of existence that is not readily conducive for the circulation of value . . . he is producing a crisis in one molecular point through which capital as value must pass. Call it a counterforce. It is resistance in *that* sense.[26]

Gidwani uses this ethnographic evidence to argue that though capitalism is hegemonic, it cannot "assimilate all forms of life that oppose its aspirations."[27] Instead, it has a "para-sitic" existence, simultaneously feeding on the energies of what is outside itself but always confronting multiple forms of value that are "not-capital." The farmer resists not in the sense of direct opposition but rather by being unintelligible to capital, a potential blockage point for the circulation of value.[28]

In Tibet, development became a key legitimizing narrative for state power with the shift away from state socialism and toward the contemporary authoritarian capitalist system. Tibetan celebrations of their ability to have a good time and not work as hard as the Han are a way of confronting their marginalized place, but also an expression of a form of being based on cultural logics with systems of value not fully captured within the sphere of capitalism. That is, they are not fully subjectified by development, which requires aspirations for self-improvement, self-development, and self-accumulation that they have not completely adopted. Though theirs is by no means an outright or wholesale refusal of either development or capitalism, the easy satisfaction ethos of "you can't take it with you" and the patterns of labor subsequently engendered form a partial blockage point for both.

The Bountiful Land

In addition to Tibetan Buddhism, Lhasa residents also ascribe their laid-back work style to the bountifulness of the Tibetan environment, which historically provided them with all that they needed and, unlike crowded eastern China, necessitated very little sense of urgency. According to a professor at Tibet University, one source of Tibetan "laziness" is the fact that "Tibet is a vast land," with plenty of space and little need for competition over resources. In this view, Tibetans were blessed by a giving landscape that did not require them to struggle, and thus allowed them to be satisfied with what they had. This condition of satisfaction rather than competition contributes to Tibetans' lack of engagement in new economic activities such as greenhouse vegetable cultivation.

This view of the Tibetan landscape as life-giving and nurturing contrasts sharply with both the Han migrant view and state representations of the Tibetan environment as harsh, barren, and unforgiving. Sichuanese migrants stated, "In my hometown, the scenery is better in the winter than it is here in the summer in Tibet," and "the mountains here are ugly and barren. At home they are covered with trees and very green." One young Sichuanese woman, talking about what she had heard about Tibet before joining her relatives, and what she found once she arrived, commented:

> I knew that Tibet is not the same as *neidi*. . . . But I had no idea it would be so desolate here. The feeling I get when I look at these barren mountains without a single tree is one of desperation. It's not at all like our *neidi*, where everything is green and good. As soon as I got here I had a feeling I shouldn't have come. . . . In *neidi* there are many more parks, which are beautiful. The land itself is like a park. And there are many famous mountains in Sichuan, all of which are very beautiful.

For this migrant, the mountains of Tibet were neither famous nor beautiful, a view that is diametrically opposed to the importance of these mountains in Tibetan conceptions of the landscape, through the propitiation of mountain deities and ritual mountain circumambulation. Her view of the landscape as the opposite of "park-like" is antithetical to the Tibetan view, in which the English words "park," "grove," and "picnic" are all captured by the common term *lingka*. There were more than forty named parks in Lhasa in the early twentieth century.

These two very different environmental imaginaries are invoked in very different views and explanations of Tibetan patterns of work. One migrant farmer from Sichuan commented, "Tibetans only think about today. They take one day at a time. If they have enough for today, then that is good enough, they are satisfied with just enough. They're not like the Han, who are always thinking about tomorrow." This echoes very closely Tibetans' descriptions of themselves, but the migrant's explanation was very different: "Life in Tibet in the past was very difficult. Tibetans were lucky just to have enough to eat." He argued that because life was so tough in the past, because it was a struggle just to fill one's belly, Tibetans are now complacent. Contrast this with Tibetans' own explanation of the same work ethic: life on the Tibetan plateau was in fact rather easy. Land was plentiful and there was no fear of starvation. Without competition, Tibetans did not develop a sense of struggling to survive in the way that the Chinese did, with many people and few resources. Tibetans and Han migrants marshal dramatically different views of the same landscape in their attempts to explain real differences in patterns of work and accumulation under development. Sedimented histories and ways of being in the landscape are linked in this way to contemporary patterns of labor.

Laziness as Antinostalgia

Contemporary constructions of work are inflected not just by understandings of the relationship between humans and the environment over the *longue durée*, but also by much more recent memories of the Maoist period and collectivized labor. In the 1990s, anthropologists found many Han villagers and factory workers in China to be deeply nostalgic for the collective period and angered by the dominant devaluation of the Maoist past in comparison to the marketized present.[29] Indeed, nostalgia for the collective era appeared to be a constitutive feature of the postreform experience, with villagers in some communities "nostalgic, often passionately so, den[ying] that the present had any merit. They claimed that they loved the years of the Maoist revolution. . . . The virtue of the past seems to grow out of fear of the present."[30] No time seems as good as the Maoist past for those left behind by economic reform. Yet even among villagers who were benefiting from reform in the economically prosperous eastern parts of China, there persisted a "sadness and anger at the devaluation of the past at the hands of the present," and a recurrent nostalgia for the early years of socialism.[31]

By contrast, when older Tibetan villagers speak about the commune period, they frequently describe it as the time that "we worked twenty out of twenty-four hours a day." As one woman in her late fifties explained about life on the commune thirty years ago: "We really suffered. In the daytime, we had to work. At night, we had to work. In twenty-four hours we only rested two or maybe four hours every day. The rest of the time we had to work." The present, she said, is much better in comparison because nobody tells you what you must do. Similarly, Dickey, a sixty-eight-year-old resident of Kyichuling at the time of my interview, recalled that villagers had had very little time to sleep at night under the commune:

> There were all sorts of work. The leaders came to find us at any time. Cadres came from Lhasa to inspect our work at night as well as during

> the day. There were meetings all the time. . . . We had so much work that we slept in the fields. We just left our houses standing there. We ignored our houses the whole time and slept in the fields. You never knew when [the leaders] might give you some work to do, even in the middle of the night.

A third woman from Kyichuling, nicknamed "Granny Brigade Leader" for her role during the collective period, commented:

> These days are the best. Compared with the brigade, things are much better now. You don't have to work if you don't want to. . . . During the brigade there was so much work to do. During the harvest we had to work at night. These days who works at night? If you want to work, you work. If you don't want to, you stay home and sleep.

The present, she said, was much better in comparison: there is plenty of time to relax, and nobody tells you what you have to do. Tibetan residents of Kyichuling in their sixties and seventies often made a thumbs-up gesture when describing the present to make sure I understood how they felt about today as compared to the collective past. When I spoke with them about their lives, the recent history of their village, or changes in agriculture and land use, villagers consistently described the collective past as a period of endless toil. Another Tibetan villager recalled about the 1960s and 1970s, "We had to work from very early in the morning until very late at night. Nobody would have been sitting around like we are right now."

One woman exclaimed, in a rejection of *suku*, the "speaking bitterness" narratives of the 1950s about the oppressive conditions of the "old society," "the present time is good, just like the old society," because both times were characterized by relatively lower workloads compared to the drudgery of the collective period.[32] Similarly, a former worker on the Phenpo State Farm, which resembled a commune much more than the July First or August First State Farms in the way labor was organized and remunerated, bitterly condemned the collective past while rejecting the narrative of liberation from the old society:

> None of the work we did was of any benefit at all to the people. It was all for the state. The people got to keep nothing. If we were sick, we were given nothing. We were just like animals. . . . The grain wasn't for us . . . many people committed suicide. They worked so hard all the time and had nothing to take home, nothing to eat, so they became desperate . . . Servants in the old society were not servants like you think. They were given food and clothing and were paid twelve *khal* of grain every year.[33] Of course it is true that there were some servants who

> were not paid. Of course some people had it better than others . . . but compare that to us when we were servants of the state farm! We didn't get clothing and we had to pay for our own food.

Others remember both the "old society" and the collective period as being times of excessive work and bitter hardship. Dickey stated that during the "old society," "small households" sometimes brought blankets to sleep outside when there was "too much" work to do. However even as these statements echo the 1950s "speaking bitterness" practice, which interpellated Tibetan subjects as citizens of the new PRC, they are not contrasted with nostalgia for the Maoist period.

Hard work and long hours were common across China in the collective period. Lisa Rofel quotes one urban factory woman as remembering that because workers were so excited about socialist construction and the need to defend China against America, "For seven days we didn't sleep. We just kept working." But these memories are nostalgic, "paean[s] to themselves."[34] In contrast, Tibetan memories of collective labor on the communes (as opposed to the earliest labor on the July First and August First State Farms) are anything but nostalgic. The act of telling stories of a collective past filled with endless hours of meaningless labor speaks both to the past from the perspective of the present, and to the present from the experience and memory of the past.[35] Remembering the collective as a time of endless toil and hunger, as well as of aberrant and alien consumption experiences, Tibetans say, "these days are the best." Their distinctly un-nostalgic memories of labor and life during the collective period give declarations of indolence in the current postreform period a decidedly celebratory element. Work patterns in the present are thus shaped by memory practices of the collective past and the particularities of the Tibetan experience of collectivization coming shortly after the initial violence of "liberation." Both declarations of indolence and embodied patterns of choices made in work hours and forms of labor express a sense of relieved distance from the Maoist past.

Spoiled Tibetans

As a hegemonic state project, development in Tibet encounters a landscape of historically sedimented memories that animate the situated practices and idioms through which it is received, negotiated, and contested in complex and contradictory ways. Among the most powerful of these are the trope of indolence, and the idiom of being "spoiled," a closely related and powerful way of negotiating and domesticating the project of development, and of contesting its meanings.

Against the state discourse of a Tibetan "psychology of idleness" that must be overcome through development, is a contrary deployment of indolence as something that is not inherent, but rather a condition that results after one becomes "spoiled" (*kyag lang shor*) by development and thereby rendered dependent or incapable. This idiom is used not only with regard to patterns of Tibetan labor within the larger political economy, but also by older Tibetan villagers to describe how younger ones are influenced by the city, and by farmers to describe the effect of state-mandated overuse of chemical fertilizers on their soil. As a pervasive idiom, to be spoiled is much more than just a way of describing individual behavior, or a particular patch of soil. It is about personal experience as well as a collective condition; it is about a relationship with the past, and—with its suggestion of permanent ruin—it expresses a deep pessimism about the future.

Tibetan peri-urban villagers frequently invoke this idiom, like that of indolence, to explain why they rent out their land to migrants rather than trying to earn more money by cultivating vegetables themselves. A Tibetan resident of Kyichuling in his seventies explained why in his village in 2001, there were more Han migrant families renting and working the land than local Tibetan households: "These days many Tibetans lie and many steal. Many do nothing but hang out. These days Tibetans are very spoiled. It is bad to spend all day not doing any work."

At a year-end meeting in another peri-urban village in 2000, the Tibetan township leader admonished villagers about the need to work hard and not sit around, play mahjong, and drink beer and hard liquor all day. If they did, he warned, they would become spoiled and "lose their foundations," at which point it would be too late for them to recover. A Tibetan Party secretary of another peri-urban village complained that village youth who had attended middle school in Lhasa had enough skills to grow greenhouse vegetables, but didn't because they were spoiled by city schools. As a result, they were not diligent and did not want to learn. They didn't put their minds into work, she said, but rather wanted to hang out all day in teahouses or playing mahjong. Soon, she said despondently, the whole village might become a village of beggars. She and many others blamed this turn for the worse on the fact that the village was too close to urban Lhasa, where there were too many places to lounge around and while away time. This spoiled young people, and drained their willingness to work.

The idiom of being spoiled critiques both state-sponsored education and the political economy of reform, under which Tibetans have had a very difficult time competing with Han migrants for employment. Peri-urban Tibetans complain that their village youth are lured by the prospects of urban employment, which, after years of school, seems more appealing than returning to the village. However, as the same Party secretary quoted above noted, "Our Tibetans' work [products] are not as high quality as those of the Chinese. Young people can't find work even when they look for jobs. As a result, they have no goals." This spoils young people.

Nor is this problem limited to youth. Instead, as one middle-aged farmer put it, "everyone is the same, the younger ones learning from the older ones, and everyone learning from their friends. Everybody here is spoiled." The Tibetan idiom of being spoiled expresses the experience of what David Germano calls a "deep, abiding cultural depression among Tibetans, from the educated youth and religious elite to nomads and villagers."[36] Germano focuses on the alienation and feeling of inadequacy he found among religious communities in the eastern Tibetan region of Kham where he argues that migrants' racism and material superiority create inferiority complexes among local residents. In Lhasa, despondency about not being able to find salaried employment is translated into the idioms of being too lazy and spoiled to work.

Nonetheless, a Tibetan woman from the Lhalu neighborhood, where most families have lost all of their farmland to urban construction and where unemployment and underemployment are now rampant, remarked that "*because* there are no more places to work, the people of Lhalu have become lazy and the men sit all day in the restaurants and do nothing." Here, we see the lack of economic opportunity framed not as the effect, but rather as the cause of laziness. Thus, despite the negative connotation of spoiling, the idiom also contains a critical diagnosis of Tibetan marginalization as a result of structural factors: Tibetans are spoiled by economic marginalization, rather than being marginalized because they are spoiled.

Spoiled by the City

In all of these deployments, we see a reversal of the contemporary valorization of the urban, which has become increasingly identified across China as the primary site of development and of political, economic, and cultural interest. The imperatives of reform produced an ideological shift across China; whereas the Maoist period saw severe restrictions on urbanization and considerable ambivalence about the urban, cities are now understood as the embodiments of progress and modernity.

Many Han migrants to Lhasa echo this view of the city as metonym for development. As we saw earlier, for the migrants, Lhasa is defined by what it lacks in terms of adequate size and degree of urbanization, level of *suzhi*, and degree of development. Lhasa's relatively small population contributes to the migrants' perception of it as backward and undeveloped. Only large cities have the potential to be civilized, developed, and desirable. By contrast, many Tibetan peri-urban villagers express a deep ambivalence about the effects of the rapidly expanding city of Lhasa. They attribute their indolence to the city's excessive number of "places to hang out." Some maintain that the penchant against work is particularly pronounced among those who live too close to the city and its many temptations, while those who live in remote rural areas work harder because they are less distracted. In a generational argument, peri-urban villagers also claim that Lhasa, with its bars, karaoke lounges, and pool tables, spoils children by luring them away from agriculture. After children spend time in the city, at school or searching for employment, they are unable and unwilling to adapt back to village life. Rather than disciplining Tibetans with clock and calendar, making them more industrious and diligent, the city makes Tibetans lazy.

The city's excessive number of places to loiter include those associated with alcohol, gambling, and prostitution, making the city also a morally ambivalent place. Tibetans, old and young, often commented on excessive alcohol consumption in city karaoke bars and *nangmas* (Tibetan-style karaoke lounges) as another indicator of how spoiled and unwilling to work Tibetans have become. Even more pervasive, though, is the association of Lhasa with prostitution, which Tibetan men and women of different ages frequently brought up in conversation. A teacher in his thirties shared his views:

> The main reason that [Tibetan peri-urban farmers] don't like to work is that they live very close to Lhasa. Lhasa is very strange. We learn all the bad things from inland China, and none of the good things. Inland China gets karaoke bars, and immediately Lhasa has karaoke bars. Inland China gets bars, and right away Lhasa has bars. Inland China has prostitutes, and then right away Lhasa has prostitutes . . . in Lhasa, the "flowers bloom everywhere"—there is prostitution everywhere you turn. . . . I think this is exceedingly dangerous. . . . Look, as a result, there are so many divorces now! The main reason is prostitution.

Women, too, joked and complained about rampant prostitution, sometimes blaming Tibetan men for visiting sex workers but other times blaming the government and the (predominantly Han) prostitutes. A Tibetan woman in her fifties described indignantly how the latter "block [Tibetan men] in the streets and try to pull them into their shops." She also charged that the government purposefully does nothing to stop prostitution despite its illegality, before placing her index finger over her pursed lips to indicate that such things should not be said out loud. In 2000, two young female Tibetan middle-school teachers averred that the persistence of the problem was due to government corruption. They joked that Jiang Zemin's national "three stresses" (*sanjiang*) campaign, in which the CCP and government were to stress study, stress politics, and stress righteousness, had taken a peculiar form in Lhasa, where the "three stresses" had become "stress mahjong," "stress corruption," and "stress prostitution."

Lhasa's disproportionately high numbers of sex workers are kept employed in part by a large military presence and the influx of money associated with state development projects. Many Tibetans also believe that the very noticeable phenomenon is an effort to distract Tibetan men from more political concerns, keeping them off the streets and away from protest. Others suggest that it is a deliberate government strategy to "pollute" Tibetan culture.[37] Though there are a rising number of Tibetan sex workers, often young girls from rural areas, the focus of complaints is for the most part on the larger number of Chinese prostitutes.[38]

This pervasive concern about prostitution (which is not new in Tibetan society) is animated partly by discontent about Han migration and repression of public dissent. In addition, prostitution is also coded as a distinctly urban phenomenon; Han migrants to Tibet move to urban areas, not rural villages, and conversely where Han migrants go, further urbanization follows. The voluble discourse about the problem comes to stand in for the more general and pervasive spoiling effects of the Chinese city landscape, equated in state discourse with economic development. It forges a link between development as spoiling Tibetans through overindulgence, leading to an inability to work hard, and development as leading to an adulterated condition of moral laxity. As such it encapsulates the uncertainty experienced by many rural and peri-urban Tibetans. As increasing numbers either move voluntarily to the city in search of work and cash income, or are forced to become urban through land expropriation, many have come to accept the premise of state discourse that the city is the site of development and of the future. As the idiom of "becoming spoiled" indicates, however, many are also deeply ambivalent about just what kind of urban future it will be.

Spoiled by Chemical Fertilizer

The condition of being spoiled is not unique to humans. One of the most common complaints I heard in Lhasa from Tibetan farmers was that chemical fertilizers had spoiled the soil in their fields. Farmers in many TAR villages were still required as late as 2000 to purchase a set quota of chemical fertilizers, whether they wanted to use them or not. Typically, local officials provided chemical fertilizers at the beginning of the growing season and collected payment after the harvest, or deducted the cost of fertilizers from mandatory grain sales. These distinct policies were implemented because of both the conflation of chemical fertilizer use with "scientific" agriculture, and the official view of Tibetans as particularly lacking in science. The coding of Tibetans as unscientific motivated the imposition of development through the provision of subsidized fertilizers, long after such measures were no longer considered necessary in other provinces.

For example, a retired Tibetan agricultural official from Tolung Dechen County told me in 2001:

> Agriculture is very strong here in Tolung because we use many chemical fertilizers. In the beginning, the ordinary people did not like to use chemical fertilizers. They did not know the benefits even when higher levels of government gave them for free. . . . But now that local farmers recognize the benefits of science, some use a hundred or more *jin* per *mu* (750 kg/ha). . . . In the valleys, the farmers use agricultural chemicals. The thought level of the masses there is not a problem. They understand the benefits. But in some upland places that have many monasteries nearby, the farmers use too few agricultural chemicals. They are superstitious and don't want to kill insects. The difference in productivity is very high.

He went on to claim that agriculture in villages with a "high level of science" is as much as forty times more productive than in upland villages. The problem with the latter, he said, was not so much their topographical location as the fact that they tended to be closer to monasteries (which are often located in high, remote places), and thus subject to greater religious influence while also being simultaneously further from the scrutiny of officials and scientists in Lhasa. These remarks refer to the fact that villagers often refuse to use pesticides for religious reasons, and that such refusal is more common in remote villages than in those near the city. In practice, the rain-fed agriculture and less fertile soil of higher-altitude villages can account for productivity differences. However, this official downplayed ecological factors, and instead emphasized the conflation of rural locations with religious and therefore "unscientific" Tibetans, thus reinforcing the valorization of the urban as the site of more scientific and developed citizens.

Tibetan villagers, including village leaders, bemoan not only the high cost of unwanted fertilizers, but also the way that fertilizers have spoiled the soil, much the same way as proximity to the urban center of Lhasa has spoiled their children. To be spoiled is to have a bad habit; applying too much chemical fertilizer to the soil gives it a bad habit, one that is very hard, if not impossible, to break. Once spoiled by chemical fertilizers, the soil loses strength and is ruined. According to many farmers, crops grew well during the "old society" even though chemical fertilizers and pesticides were not used. Now, however, like a person who has taken so much medicine that it loses its effect, the soil barely responds to chemical fertilizers, making it necessary to apply ever-increasing amounts. Tibetans often explained the spoiling of the soil to me by comparing it with the effect of alcohol:

> It's like this. If someone drinks beer and liquor all day long, you can tell them all you want not to drink, or to drink less, but it does no good at all.

> They can't stop, because they're spoiled on the beer and liquor. It's the same way with chemical fertilizers.

In peri-urban villages, rationales about the spoiling effects of chemical fertilizers are based not only on observations of how chemical fertilizers affect grain cultivation, but also on observations of Han vegetable farming practices. Chinese migrant farmers often move every two to three years to a new location because plant diseases and fungi take hold after a few years of the intensive production conditions—high rates of pesticide, herbicide, and fertilizer application—in the humid greenhouses. According to Tibetan farmers, these inputs cause sickness in the soil. Or, as one explained, "the soil dies" after a few years of vegetable production. Han migrant farmers are aware of these negative effects of chemical inputs, but claim that market competition leaves them with no choice but to use large quantities. They acknowledge using fewer inputs at home when growing vegetables for their own consumption. Indeed, one Sichuanese farmer exclaimed that the amount of chemical fertilizer he uses in Lhasa is "truly frightening!" and another reported, "really, it's not good to use too much."

Even so, Han farmers' idioms for talking about their use of lesser amounts of inputs at home and their belief that overuse of chemical fertilizers is detrimental to long-term productivity differ significantly from those offered by Tibetans. For Tibetans, the spoiling of the soil is also connected to their concerns about the health effects and the taste of food grown with such fertilizers. They often said that vegetables, particularly potatoes, grown with chemical fertilizers were tasteless, or tasted bad. Too much fertilizer also caused potatoes to become too large, overripe on the outside while still hard and unripened on the inside. While they are not nostalgic for the collective era, Tibetans around Lhasa do feel nostalgia for the taste of food before chemical fertilizer use became the norm, as a woman in her forties explained:

> These days vegetables have no taste at all. In the past we only used natural fertilizers. The radishes were so delicious! Very tasty. These days they don't taste good. They call it science and say it's better. There are more vegetables now but they have no nutrition and no taste.

"Although science is good, as for chemical fertilizers—well, they're pretty bad, aren't they?" remarked a peri-urban villager, "You can see this clearly from potatoes. They grow very large but they taste terrible. They make your mouth numb." Still others say that the vegetables "don't taste quite right" and that fertilizers cause a loss of their medicinal qualities. Many Tibetans avoid using chemical fertilizers when growing potatoes for their own consumption, out of concern for their health. Chemical fertilizers, they believe, spoil not only the soil, but also the taste and nutritional qualities of food.

The term "to spoil" is used to make sense of agriculture, urbanization, economic marginalization, and the relationship between education and employment under conditions of a rapid influx of migrants coded as bearers of the state's gift of development. It is in this sense that spoiling is not only an explanation for the observed effects of new chemical inputs on soil and food, but also a more general idiom through which Tibetans experience development.

Tibetans understand and negotiate the Chinese state project of development through tropes of indolence and of the condition of being spoiled. These idioms, which help organize memories of the past, experiences of the present, and expectations for the future, are both familiar and specific. The trope of indolence as the image of the "lazy native" draws easy comparisons with other historical and contemporary situations, especially in the contexts of colonialism and development. Simply noting that stereotypes of lazy indigenous or impoverished peoples are rampant, however, does not complete the analytical task of understanding how these patterns are produced. As Stuart Hall explains with reference to racism, "It is often little more than a gestural stance which persuades us to the misleading view that, because racism is everywhere a deeply anti-human and anti-social practice, that therefore it is everywhere the same."[39] Indeed it is precisely the familiarity of the lazy native as a figure in development discourses that makes it all the more imperative to analyze its production in particular places, within specific political landscapes.

The terrain on which development is negotiated is shaped by written and unwritten policies that have made the TAR a political and economic zone of exception. The extreme urban-rural income gap, the subsidy-dependent and distorted economy, the turnkey nature of Aid-Tibet projects, the poor educational system, the concentration of investment on infrastructure and on raising cadre salaries, the lifting of restrictions on migration, and the abandonment of efforts at a "Tibetan-first" development strategy are all political-economic structures and policies that have made it easier for Han migrants than Tibetan villagers to benefit from state investment through the purported freedom of the market. National development produces not only spatial inequalities between eastern and western China, but also differentiation within Tibet itself, between Tibetan residents and Han migrants. These political-economic conditions shape the cultural idioms through which development is experienced, and these idioms in turn constrain and reshape the possibilities for maneuvering within the larger political economy, through situated practices such as the refusal to engage in greenhouse farming.

The particularities of the trope of Tibetan indolence can be emphasized through a brief comparison with Syed Alatas's study, *The Myth of the Lazy Native*. Examining the image of Malays, Filipinos, and Javanese from the sixteenth through twentieth centuries, Alatas argues that because they were unwilling to become tools for colonial capitalism, and because they did not measure labor by the clock, they developed a durable reputation as being lazy. As Alatas notes, this image was deeply interwoven in the political-economic history of the region. It functioned first as moral justification for systems of forced delivery and forced labor under colonial capitalism, and later as capitalist justification for maintaining low wages. In Tibet, by contrast, the "laziness" of Tibetan farmers refers to their work on land to which they themselves have long-term use rights. Rather than functioning to justify forced cultivation, it produces a common sense understanding of Tibetan marginalization under economic reform and development. Furthermore, whereas Alatas presents the image as being wielded exclusively by colonialists, in Lhasa today, Tibetans themselves participate actively in the everyday circulation and reproduction of this discourse.

Common sense enactments of the trope of indolence, both as speech act and as embodied patterns of labor and time allocation, help naturalize Tibetan failure to benefit from the massive amounts of money that the central state pours into the economic development of the TAR. At the same time, however, the trope of indolence is also a good sense claim that refuses hegemonic imperatives of self-cultivation in the service of state territorialization. It gives Tibetans the moral high ground vis-à-vis Han migrants in a different system of value than the one championed by the state under capitalist reforms, and sometimes becomes a way of expressing a critical insight into the structural underpinnings of economic marginalization. Appeals to culturally constituted notions of labor, with their roots in history but deployed under different conditions today, work as both common sense and good sense.

As with the trope of indolence, the idiom of being spoiled also links together ambivalence about the urban with ambivalence about the agricultural landscapes being produced by development. To be spoiled is to be drawn pleasurably but negatively into a relationship of dependency. It is to develop a range of bad habits, which Tibetans attribute to development. Chemical fertilizers, brought by efforts to produce a new "scientific" agrarian landscape, spoil the soil in much the same way as urbanizing Lhasa spoils Tibetan children, and development spoils Tibetans in general, making them unable and unwilling to work hard. Food grown by the "hardworking" migrants is often said by Tibetans to taste bad, but is coded by state discourse as being more scientific and developed because of the higher levels of agricultural inputs used in its production, their effects on the soil notwithstanding. These idioms are not only performances that enact and reproduce Tibetan cultural identity but also commentaries on larger political-economic forces. They reveal the contradictory and contingent ways in which Chinese development in Tibet, as a historically and geographically specific project presented as a gift that cannot be refused, is both present and poison, both desired and resisted.

III

Concrete

Figure 4. The new urban landscape. *Xiaokang* ("prosperous") model houses in Red Star Village, 2009. Photo by author.

Michael Jackson as Lhasa

Figure 5 Michael Jackson as Lhasa. Installation art piece titled *Transplantation* (*Yi Zhi*), 2004. Both art piece and photo by Benpa Chungdak (Benchung).

How have Lhasa's rapid development and urbanization been experienced by its residents?

Transplantation, an installation piece by artist Benpa Chungdak (see figure 5), speaks to this question. He set up the piece in January 2004, to the south of the Potala Palace, the backdrop to the photo. Unlike artwork that merely acts as a "report" of the surface of society, this piece was a deliberate attempt by the artist to dig into layers of meaning, to enter society and get involved with it.

The piece of earth on which the installation was placed had recently been the home of the TAR Song and Dance Troupe, which like so many other long-established landmarks, had been moved to a new location in the name of urban development. The ground had been torn up and it was not yet clear what—good, bad, ugly—might replace it. Thus the foundation on which the installation was laid was itself in a state of transition, an embodiment of uncertainty: What would become of it? What shape would it take?

The piece connotes hybridity and borderlands. It does not celebrate them. Transplantation, says the artist, is when you take a stem of one kind of fruit tree and graft it onto another, producing a fruit that is the same as neither the first nor the second. The Tibetan term is *ra ma lug*, "neither goat nor sheep," neither fish nor fowl.

Michael Jackson is *ra ma lug*. Lhasa as Michael Jackson.

The artist explains:

> It was the first day of Spring Festival (Chinese New Year). The Chinese were celebrating, and there were lots of Chinese in Tibet, so it was an interesting time. That's why I put the New Year's figurines there. They're usually pasted on doors at Spring Festival, to beckon wealth for the New Year.
>
> I first saw a poster of Michael Jackson around 1982. Someone must have brought the posters in from Nepal. He was very popular. I was really into him when I was around fifteen or so, when I was in high school. People would look at his posters and remark, "What a beautiful girl!" He had long hair and such, and so everyone thought he was a girl. That's one of the reasons I picked Michael Jackson—because it was hard to tell if he was a girl or boy. And then also, he used to be black but then he became white. This is very much like Lhasa culture. It's very much like Tibet. This kind of mixture and confusion is very prevalent. To be not-this and not-that is very much akin to our culture, to our experience, here in Tibet.
>
> Before the installation, I had watched a TV program about Michael Jackson. They showed him as a young black boy—really very good-looking—and then what he would have looked like at his current age, had he never done anything to alter his appearance. Then they showed what he really does look like now, after all of the alterations he has made to his appearance. The shape-changing has had very bad results; his new appearance is very much like our society here. He wanted to be beautiful, so he made some changes, then after a little while, some more alterations, then some more changes, and now look at the results. Our society is like this, making changes here and there. Even the people's ideology is like this, thinking only about now, making changes for short-term benefit. Do we really need a square in front of the Potala Palace? Someone thought it would be

beautiful to have one and made the change right away. It's the same with urbanization and the uprooting of the Song and Dance Troupe. It might be good-looking for now, but it will have bad results in the future. This will be the future of Lhasa: Michael Jackson as what he is now compared to what he could have been.

You'll see that the ground is wet. I watered the piece, as if growing a tree. It represents growth, the growth of the problem of Michael Jackson. What's growing is a new culture, a strange culture, one that is not Tibetan, Chinese, or Western, but rather a strange hybrid.

And the color is also significant. Red is a very important color for the government, on the one hand, the color of politics. But it's also a very important color for Tibetan tradition. The Potala is red, and so is Marpori [the hill on which the Potala stands]. Red symbolizes tradition. But the red that I used for Michael Jackson isn't quite red; it's between red and pink. It's a gaudier color, the type that's used to attract attention for buying. Pink stands for the commercial, the sexual, that which is not stable. So it's a contest, a competition between the pink in the foreground and the red in the background.

The enclosure is symbolic too. It's a cage, a barrier. If you are inside looking out, you have no freedom. It's an obstacle to getting out; you can look but you can't get outside. On the one hand it's like protection, but at the same time you're protected, you're also captured. It has that meaning too. From the outside, it's like a police barricade, a barrier to entry. You can see, but you can't enter. People outside can see what's happening inside, the growth and ongoing change in this sensitive place—in front of the Potala. You can see the growth of the strange hybrid, the problem, but it's difficult to enter, to do anything about it. All you can do is watch it happen.

Its spatial position, with Potala as background, is also significant. The Potala is a very old and important structure for Tibetan culture. Today, however, the government places great importance on the square in front of the Potala, though, even though it is strange. It is a mix of the old and new. It's hybrid. And the results are very odd.

Finally, the piece itself is a border. Temporally, it sat at a point of transition, between the known past of the Song and Dance Troupe's occupation of this symbolic space, and the unknown future of the landscape. Ontologically, the piece is on the border of art and not-art, of art and play. It's not completely play as it's not without meaning, but it's not quite a piece of art, as in a statue or sculpture, either. It's neither this nor that.

Like the idioms of indolence and of being spoiled, the metaphor of Lhasa as Michael Jackson captures the experience of development as state territorialization, with its disorienting urban expansion and the negotiation of a rapidly shifting Tibetan identity through the influence of linguistic and cultural policies as well as Han migration. As "the Negro Caucasian," Jackson embodies the cultural confusion of the Tibetan state of *ra ma lug*, denoting both its conflicted state of identity as well as its rapidly shifting urban landscape, with its mixture of Chinese modern and faux Tibetan architecture. As Patricia Williams[1] noted in *The Nation* on Jackson after his death, "he literally erased himself before our eyes," much as the streets of Lhasa have done with rapid urbanization and the new urban plan. The installation *Transplantation* resonates too with Williams's observation that Jackson's—and Lhasa's—transgressivity was not just theater, but also a narrative of paradox and suffering.

6 "Build a Civilized City"

Making Lhasa Urban

Be a Civilized Citizen, Build a Civilized City.

—Billboard, Lhasa, 2001

When interviewing migrant vegetable farmers and the Tibetans who rented land to them in 2000–2001, I frequently visited the villages of Dongkar Town. One was located at the fork in the road just west of the July First State Farm, where West Liberation Road leads out of Lhasa's continuous built-up area toward the road to the airport on the south, and to the county seat of Tolung Dechen to the north. This village was home to an early Tibetan vegetable farmer who had adopted greenhouse cultivation for a short period of time in the mid-1980s. I sometimes chatted with him, as well as with the son of a local *ngagpa,* a ritual specialist in reciting mantras to control weather and protect crops against hail, who told me about past agricultural practices in the village. The peri-urban landscape of the village was typical, marked by greenhouses, barley and wheat fields, and white adobe houses.

Four years later, the scene was disorienting and almost unrecognizable. Villagers had lost all of their farmland to the building of the national-level Lhasa Economic and Technological Development Zone, approved by the State Council in 2001. The widening of Liberation Road in preparation for the September 2005 celebration of the fortieth anniversary of the founding of the TAR had claimed parts of homes, and the new road was now much higher than the decrepit remaining fragments of houses. Raised sidewalks abutting doorsteps hid dogs chained just outside front doors, making a stroll along the sidewalk a dangerous proposition. Aluminum rods and assorted pieces of plastic and wood jutted out of the roofs of the remaining one-floor structures. The villagers had been told that they would need to move very soon to a new concentrated settlement being built for them, that they would receive no compensation for their old houses, and that their new homes would be generously subsidized but nevertheless would require an additional contribution from each family. There was a pensive air about the soon-to-vanish village. Children rolled tires down the newly widened road, and a few Tibetan women assisted construction crews to build stone pillars on the road, while older folks sat on their doorsteps, counting their prayer beads or staring out into space.

I met a middle-aged man and his wife collecting plastic bottles to sell. "If you have farmland, then every year you will at least have something to eat," they said, but now they had nothing. They had to move because their land "belongs to the Tibet Autonomous Region and Lhasa Municipality and Tolung Dechen County government," and the government wanted their land to remake the landscape, planting flowers and a lawn and building a public square. At first, they thought they had a choice to either build their own houses or take a government-built house, but later they learned that everything must be unified. "If we build our own, then some might be big, and some might be small; some might be good quality, and some might be bad quality." Quality houses of uniform appearance were of utmost importance, and so in the end, the job was given to a construction team all of whose workers came from other provinces. "The only thing left for us to do," the man stated glumly "is to go and pick up the key." He added, summing up their condition, "It's really become city."[1] Down the road, an elderly woman who was about to lose a two-floor granite-brick house built just three years prior said that only one of the four members of her household had been able to find occasional work since their farmland was expropriated. "Now she goes to do construction when there's work to be found, and when there's not, she just sits around." "[It's] really become the city," she said, by way of explaining their lack of employment.

Across town, on the east side of Lhasa where the new campus of Tibet University was about to be built, I visited Granny Lhamo, a woman in her seventies whose dry wit I enjoyed. She'd always been rather sarcastic, but now her humor darkened considerably. "You've returned," she observed, when I showed up at her house this time. "Did you come to see if I was dead yet?" Her house was typical, enclosing a spacious courtyard with a row of cheerful potted flowers and a neatly trimmed green lawn. Large south-facing windows warmed the rooms inside, which were ornately decorated with wooden beams painted in bright yellow and blue hues.

As I sat in her living room drinking tea, she explained, "They say that these houses we have are no good, and that we all have to live in a new way, all clumped together. In tiny little houses where there'll be no room, no space at all for us to turn this way or that." Her son earned a decent salary at a work unit in Lhasa, so fear of the possible costs of the new house and the family's future livelihood was not at the heart of her claustrophobic reaction. "I was really hoping to die before I have to move. You see, there's lots of space here, it'd be easy to move my corpse. There, in that narrow little space, it'll be very crowded. No place to move." Asked why they had to move into apartment blocks, her daughter and granddaughter both replied that their village had been drawn inside "the red line," referring to the new urban plan for Lhasa. Granny Lhamo speculated in greater detail about the design of their new houses: "They want to build it that way so they can use less space and fit more people. This is so they can create more empty space. The city is going to stretch all the way to here. . . . There are going to be a lot more people. A lot more people are coming to Lhasa, you know. And they need a place to stay."

Her bleak ruminations linking the problems she foresaw in carrying away her own corpse, hemmed in by narrow walls, to the clearing of space for the inexorable spread of the city, evoke a strong sense of disorientation, and of socio-spatial rupture. They also suggest the need to understand the radical urban transformation of Lhasa, a process that has seen the paving and building over of many former sites of greenhouse vegetable farming, sending its Tibetan residents into apartment blocks and its Han migrant farmers to sublease land in villages further out from the urban center.

The scale and pace of China's urbanization in the past three decades has been remarkable, fueled by accumulation by dispossession and displacement, with new growth coalitions of developers and local governments building luxury homes for the middle class on land expropriated from peri-urban farmers. Land expropriation, resettlement, and a rash of new house building driven by local governments' capital accumulation are also producing Lhasa's new urban landscape. At the same time, though, the urbanization of the TAR and particularly Lhasa has its own specific imperatives and cultural valences as a form of state territorialization that is experienced as a profoundly disorienting rearrangement of the socio-spatial contours of everyday Tibetan life.

Cultural Histories of the Urban

Understanding the full implications of the argument, made by many PRC government officials, that "the only way out for Tibet is urbanization," requires an examination not only of increases in the population and extent of built-up area over time, but also of culturally specific experiences and conceptualizations of the city and of urban/rural dichotomies. As historically the largest and basically the only urban lay settlement in the Tibetan cultural world, Lhasa is key to understanding the urban as a category of thought. Founded in the seventh century after Songtsen Gampo unified Tibet and moved his capital there, the appellation "Lhasa" appears to have referred originally only to the Jokhang Temple itself. Though the Jokhang and Ramoche Temples made Lhasa an important pilgrimage site from the moment of their construction, only after the Fifth Dalai Lama rose to power as sovereign of Tibet in 1642 did Lhasa become a true seat of government administration and a political center.[2]

Detailed information about Lhasa's population up until the twentieth century is scarce. In 1904, British members of the invading Younghusband expedition estimated it at 30,000, including 20,000 monks. Estimates in the 1950s are usually around 30,000, although some suggest that the total population was 50,000–60,000, including 20,000 lay residents.[3] At that time Lhasa consisted primarily of densely packed clusters of alleyways and side streets branching off from the three-kilometer Barkor circumambulation route. Nested within the Barkor was the Nangkor, in the Jokhang Temple, and encircling it was the larger Lingkor circumambulation path; together these three routes defined the spatial imaginary of Lhasa. Despite its minuscule size, Lhasa's residents viewed it as expansive and large, as suggested by the saying, "Lhasa is already large, and on top of that there is the Ramoche."[4] Although market towns existed along trade routes, no other settlement approached Lhasa's population. The second largest settlement in central Tibet, Shigatse, had a population of 9,000 in the middle of the twentieth century.[5]

To what extent, though, did residents of Lhasa or other smaller market towns along trade routes think of themselves as city or urban residents? The Tibetan term today commonly translated as "city," *grong khyer* (Wylie; pronounced *trong kyer*) has a long history.[6] However, it was originally used primarily in the abstract and for translations of Sanskrit texts; it is classically defined as a place with "all of the eighteen crafts such as blacksmithing."[7] It does not, however, appear to have been used regularly as a designator of Lhasa or other actual Tibetan settlements; the appellation *lha sa grong khyer* is associated more strongly with the PRC administrative category of Lhasa Municipality than with historical Lhasa as a pilgrimage site or cultural, religious, and political center. Indeed, in Dungdkar Rinpoche's comprehensive encyclopedia of places and names in Tibetan cultural history, the term *grong khyer* appears in a number of entries, but none refer to places in Tibet. Instead, it appears in *grong khyer kho khom*, one of "three capitals" in Nepal; *grong khyer na la da*, the birthplace of one of the Shakyamuni Buddha's main disciples; *grong khyer gnas bcas*, the city of Ayodhya; *grong khyer pa tha na,* the city of Patna in India, and so on.[8] Neither *grong khyer lha sa* nor *lha sa grong khyer* appear as entries, nor does the entry on "Lhasa" highlight its status as an urban population center.[9]

Tibetan has a number of terms that share the root *grong*, all of which indicate a place of settlement. Some terms can today be used to refer to both city and village. For example, *grong khul* can be translated as either "village area" or "urban area," *grong skor* is "going around a town *or* village," *grong khyim* is either "a household in the city" or "a household in the village," *grong sne* is "the edge of a town/city/village," and even *grong tsho*, used today for the administrative category of village, can refer to both village and town.[10] The malleability of the term *grong khyer* as "settlement" rather than the more specific "large and densely populated settlement" can also be seen in texts such as *The Mirror Illuminating the Royal Genealogies*, a fourteenth-century chronicle of the royal line and the history of Buddhism in Tibet. In it, a *bodhisattva*-ape pleads with Avalokitesvara, wondering how he will feed his offspring, saying, "da lta yi dags grong khyer lta bur 'dug,"

"Now [the country of Tibet] resembles a town[/city] of hungry ghosts."[11] It is clear that *grong khyer* refers here not to an actual city but to a broader realm. More generally, the fluidity of the various *grong* terms reflects a conceptualization of a spectrum of settlement sizes and population, rather than a strictly binary opposition between the rural and the urban, or between the city and the countryside.[12]

This spectrum contrasts significantly with English, where "country" and "city" have distinct etymologies and meanings. "City" is derived from the Latin *civitas*, "community" (in turn derived from *civis*, "citizen"), which eventually came to be used to refer to the urban as opposed to the rural part of a community. "Country" on the other hand, comes from *contra*, "against," and had the original sense of "land spread out over against the observer."[13] The widespread use of "country" to mean "rural," in opposition to "city" in the sense of "urban," began in England in the sixteenth century; over time "city" began to imply not only a distinctive order of settlement but also a whole different way of life.[14] "Country" became associated with a natural way of life, with peace, innocence, and purity, but also with backwardness, ignorance, and limitation. The city, by contrast, became associated with learning and communication; it was also a place of noise, ambition, worldliness, and corruption, and of adulthood and the future. The dichotomous categories of city and country each work to imply the absence of the qualities of the other. Each is the other's constitutive outside.

This mapping of opposing meanings onto "city" and "country" as fundamentally dichotomous modes of life is quite different from Tibetan uses of the terms *grong khyer, grong rdal*, and *grong tsho*, which did not spatialize binary moral qualities. In particular, *grong khyer* is used as a neutral descriptor of settlement, as in the Tibetan origin story in which "all the plains were transformed into fields, many towns were built,"[15] and does not come to stand in for qualities such as corruption, decay, civilization, or learning. Indeed, much of what is interpreted as "urban" in secondary accounts of Tibetan history refers specifically to large monasteries such as Drepung and Sera, which were not considered by local residents to be part of Lhasa. The qualities of learning and civilization, associated in English tradition with cities, were in Tibet associated specifically with monasteries and other religious institutions—rather than with the urban as a particular social form. Lay/monastic was a far more important categorization of social life and structure than village/city.[16]

The Chinese historical conceptualization of city and country is again different from both the English and Tibetan cultural traditions. The contemporary term for "city" (*chengshi*) combines the characters for defensive walls (*cheng*) and market (*shi*), two ubiquitous features of Chinese urban form, while the terms for village or countryside (*cun, nong cun, xiang xia*) are unrelated. The character for market, *shi*, also came to mean "city" beginning in the 1920s, and is widely, but loosely used today.[17] In imperial times, the city wall was emblematic of a sharp distinction between urban and rural, as well as between "civilized" and "barbaric." In contrast to Tibet, the urban form and the spread and extension of walled urban centers were seen as having been central to the development of Chinese civilization up to the end of the imperial era.[18] Walled cities were landmarks of traditional China, symbols of authority that linked to other walled units up and down the administrative hierarchy.[19]

Although the sociological separation of urban and rural was arguably not as sharp in China as in the West, the Chinese conceptualization of the city as a special form of civilization has been present since at least the Taoist writings that theorized about utopian cities in the second century AD.[20] By late imperial times, cities were seen as centers of vice and corruption while rural life was seen to foster virtue. Imperial bureaucrats and officials often maintained country homes even while they spent their entire lives in cities, which they used as bases of wealth and power.[21] Chinese intellectuals in the early twentieth century debated urbanism, with some yearning for a return to China's past glory, which they identified with a rural ideal. Others argued for the revitalization of urban-rural ties and reintegration of cities with the countryside, while others still welcomed Westernized cities as symbols of modernity and progress.[22] Though quite different, these positions all accepted a conceptual urban-rural dichotomy, and associated urbanization with some form of modernity.

This city/country binary in imperial Chinese cultural history, together with its absence in culturally Tibetan categories of thought and practice before PRC incorporation, suggests that urbanization in Tibet must be interpreted not only as a technical matter of construction and increased density of people and buildings, but also as the laying down of a new grid of legibility and state territorialization of space. Thus, my argument here is not that Lhasa was not a cultural, political, and economic center like cities in China and Europe. It was. In all three historical traditions, cultural, political, and economic centers have developed interdependently (Mumford 1961). My argument is instead about the types of meanings that are mapped onto the city as a cultural, conceptual category. Insofar as subjects are produced by, rather than existing autonomously prior to discourse, the creation of administrative scales of city and village together with the dichotomous moral ordering of those scales, as discursive practices of the state, also significantly shapes the practice and experience of everyday life, beyond the merely technical aspects of urbanization.

Valorizing the Urban Scale

Turn-of-the-twentieth-century debates among Chinese intellectuals played out in a different form several decades later in the "two-line struggle" within the Mao-era Chinese Communist Party: leaders such as Liu Shaoqi and Deng Xiaoping supported an urban-led development strategy while Mao Zedong, who saw cities as centers of corruption, espoused an anti-urban bias. The result was a system that prevailed until economic reform, which transferred agricultural surplus to the urban manufacturing sector, and privileged urban workers compared to rural commune members, but which treated cities as a necessary cost of industrialization rather than valuable in their own right. State-owned industries were not well integrated into local urban economies, and the government generally neglected urban infrastructure. The imposition of the *hukou* household registration system prevented substantial rural-urban migration for more than three decades, and rural villages and townships were by and large not allowed to expand their built-up areas until the reform period was well underway. As a result, before 1978 the level of urbanization across China remained below 20 percent.[23]

New political-economic imperatives of economic reform and globalization then produced an ideological shift valorizing the urban scale, and leading to extraordinarily rapid urbanization.[24] Between 1978 and 2003, the number of Chinese cities with a population greater than a million increased from thirteen to forty-nine, more than doubling again by 2012. Similarly, between 1980 and 2002, the urban proportion of China's population grew from 20 percent to 40 percent, an increase that took forty years in the United States, and by the end of 2011 over half of the Chinese population was urbanized.[25] With urbanization now a major goal of China's development strategy, the rate of urbanization itself is seen as an index of the degree of provincial development.[26] This view of the city as a metonym for development is clearly articulated by Han migrants to Lhasa in their evaluations of Lhasa's development status and the *suzhi* level of its local residents, as we saw in chapter 3. It is also reflected in the ambivalence of Tibetan peri-urban residents about the "spoiling" effects of the city and the qualities of development it embodies.

Cities are now privileged through policies that give preferential treatment to designated urban jurisdictions. Cities at higher administrative ranks have greater decision-making powers and economic planning authority over their surrounding rural areas.[27] Scaling up to the urban is a way to make a place more attractive to investors, and to eliminate land use conflicts between cities and adjacent counties, thus enabling urban areas to more easily access land and water supplies and spurring faster growth. Across China, including Tibet, this has led to a wave of "administrative urbanization," conversions of counties to cities and townships to towns as deliberate efforts to increase the power of administrative units through promotion to an urban rank.[28] Although rural townships and urban towns are technically on the same rank in the national administrative hierarchy, the valorization of the urban means that the conversion from township to town is a shift to a more prestigious scale and greater power in political-economic relations with other places.

Of course, the rapid urban transformation across China has not only been administrative. The massive investment into the built environment that underlies China's spectacle of urban expansion has been both a fix to absorb capital and thus prevent a crisis of over-accumulation, as well as a territorial process of establishing legitimacy through increasing property values.[29] Several legal and policy changes, including the 1988 formal establishment of a market for land leases, enabled the real estate industry to emerge as a growth machine and urbanization to become a key site of state building and legitimacy. Collectives are forbidden from leasing out their land for nonagricultural construction, but county, municipal, and district governments, or the primary development companies they establish, can requisition the land, transform it into state-owned urban land, and auction it off to secondary commercial developers.

The result has been the expropriation of more than 13 percent of China's total arable land from some 60 million peasants by 2003, in a phenomenon of accumulation by dispossession that Chinese scholars have dubbed the "new land enclosure movement."[30] Farmers' compensation for their expropriated land is capped at less than thirty times average annual crop production of the land over the previous three years, whereas no cap is set on the conveyance fee paid by developers who acquire the land from the expropriators. Local governments, which often do not remit the required percentage of this fee to higher levels of government, have turned to land conversion to meet the needs of financial growth and intensified place competition created by fiscal decentralization.[31]

A key driver of the commercial real estate market that now provides revenue for local governments was urban housing reform, which began in the 1980s in response to the severe urban living space shortage created by decades of work unit welfare housing. The 1990s witnessed a boom in completely private middle-class housing, often built in prime locations in the urban core on land formerly occupied by lower-class urban residents who, like their peri-urban counterparts, were resettled and displaced in a wave of accumulation by dispossession.[32] The result has been a spatialization of class in Chinese cities, with distinct types of residences and neighborhoods occupied by people of different economic strata.[33]

Urbanization as Development

The valorization of the urban, the equation of cities with development and modernization, and the ideological importance of urbanization are if anything even more pronounced in China's ethnic minority areas, which tend to be less urbanized and have smaller local populations. State authorities see urbanization not only as a shortcut to development and modernity, but also as a way to overcome ethnic autonomy. Within China's Law of Regional National Autonomy, regions, prefectures, and counties can be "autonomous" and associated with particular *minzu*, but cities cannot. Instead cities are "customarily associated with things 'Chinese.' " Writing about this process in Inner Mongolia, anthropologist Uradyn Bulag argues that the benefit of an administrative promotion from county to city, particularly for local leaders, "checkmates ethnic sensitivity" about loss of ethnic autonomous status.[34]

Urbanization in Tibet is associated with an increased Han presence, as well as the acquisition of Chinese language and Han food and clothing preferences. One Chinese scholarly account of Tolung Dechen County suggests that rural urbanization there led to "watching TV and videos . . . and playing mahjong," which signal a departure from the "backward and confining nature of their past [rural] life."[35] Furthermore, the account describes traditional Tibet as having been "lacking [in] urbanization motivation." Since economic reform, however, peri-urban villagers have become "keen on urbanization" and as a result, villagers have become more "rational" in their dealings with religion, treating the recitation of scriptures as "a commodity" to be purchased.[36] This portrayal of peri-urban villagers as keen on urbanization contrasts with villagers' own common idiom of urban influence as having "spoiled" them, eliding the ambivalence they experience about urban-associated changes from mahjong to the commodification of religious services.

Along these lines, officials portray urbanization as both the result of the inevitable juggernaut of progress, "the inevitable outcome of the world economic development and an unavoidable stage,"[37] and as a deliberate gift for which Tibetans are and should be very grateful. Officials and scholars recommend the acceleration of Tibet's urbanization as both a tool and a sign of economic development that will close the gap between Tibet and the prosperous eastern regions. The staking of government legitimacy on gratitude for development-as-urbanization is illustrated by the following segment from a widely distributed DVD, *Celebrating the 50th Anniversary of the Peaceful Liberation of Tibet*, produced by Chinese Central Television:[38]

> In today's Tibet . . . houses are nicer and communication is easier. Tibetans call the present era the age of bliss and happiness, long dreamt of by their ancestors.
>
> Shortly after the peaceful liberation, Lhasa only covered an area of 3 square kilometers and had almost no modern facilities. After several major expansions, Lhasa now has an urban area of more than 50 square kilometers. Modern city functions have been enhanced and the living standards of its residents have improved.

> Lhasa is a symbol of Tibet's great changes. The urbanization process in the whole region has been accelerated. Now within the jurisdiction of Tibet there are two cities, 71 county capitals, and 112 towns. The total township area is 147 square kilometers with an urban population of 420,000. Massive changes have taken place not only in ancient towns like Lhasa, Rikaze, Zedang, Changdo, and Jiangze but also in newly built towns like Bayi, Ningzhi, Shiquanhe, Ali, Nangchu, Langxian and Zhamu. These towns are like glittering pearls, scattered on the snow-capped plateau.

Not surprisingly with this privileging of the urban scale, administrative urbanization has been practiced in the TAR through the promotion and consolidation of rural townships into urban towns. Across the TAR the number of towns (*zhen*) increased from zero in 1986 to 140 in 2006, while the number of rural townships (*xiang*) declined from 2,069 in 1987 to 543 in 2006.[39] Here, promotion to the urban scale declares less the presence of urban conditions and more the intention or desire for urbanization and its accompanying capital accumulation and prosperity, parallel to the process of municipalization in Inner Mongolia which, Bulag writes, in moving away from "the nationality form and content of autonomy" is useful for "exorcis[ing] the haunted failure of modernization in minority regions."[40]

In Tibet, the consolidation of towns provides a new opportunity to reshuffle officials and post Han cadres as town-level leaders. Given that the town/township is the lowest level of government within the official hierarchy, and that the leaders of townships have historically been Tibetan, this administrative level has been seen as a weak link in Party control.[41] In 2003, 280 Han officials were sent to be leaders of rural townships and urban towns for the first time.[42] Administrative urbanization thus contributes to the project of weakening ethnic autonomy.

Administrative urbanization also accounted for some of the reported 30 percent increase in Lhasa Municipality's urban population between 1990 and 2000.[43] Administrative urbanization does not necessarily entail an increased population density or enlarged built-up area, though it does bring with it a desire and promise of these transformations in the future. Furthermore, it instantiates the rural/urban dichotomy, and enables reconfiguration and consolidation of state territorial power. At stake are the effects and experiences of this new socio-spatial conceptualization and practice.

PRIVATE HOUSING IN LHASA

As part of the production of Lhasa's expanding urban landscape, the building of private "retirement homes" (*tuixiu fang*) began in the late 1980s and picked up to a frenzied momentum over the next two decades. During my trips to Lhasa from 1998 through 2009, it seemed as if all of my urban resident friends and acquaintances were preoccupied with their house loans and with *zhuangxiu*—modeling and remodeling. Because new houses in China do not come finished with tile, flooring, light fixtures, or other such necessities, *zhuangxiu* must be completed after house purchase, a process that can take several months and add an additional one-third to total housing cost.[44] Retired or soon-to-be-retired cadres were the first to build and occupy retirement homes, though as time went on, younger Tibetans who were employed by work units but were not anywhere near even the very young retirement age in Lhasa also began buying, modeling, and moving into their "retirement homes." In the early years, rank, status, and number of years served in a work unit qualified employees for a certain amount of land on which to build. Work units typically subsidized the houses, provided loans, or both, depending on the unit's financial strength. In some cases they deducted housing costs from the cadres' monthly salaries. The specific property rights situation with respect to full ownership and ability to sell the house varies with the amount paid.

A large proportion of private commodity housing across China is obtained in an organized fashion through work units, which negotiate with real estate developers. However, the term "retirement home" to denote work unit involvement in the process of buying a private house appears much more prevalent in the TAR than elsewhere. The likely origin of this is the government policy of building homes for retired Han cadres who had served in Tibet in retirement communities in Chengdu, Sichuan. Tibetan cadres asked for houses as well, leading to the introduction of the retirement home concept in the TAR. Increasingly, cadres from other parts of Tibet also flock to Lhasa on retirement, favoring its greater amenities and lower altitude. They too live in retirement homes, in residential communities in Lhasa organized by their work units.

In the summer of 2002, the government announced a plan to give out a cash subsidy to retired cadres who had previously built retirement homes but not received any assistance, or who had not received the full amount of the subsidy. Cadres felt entitled to their retirement homes, including in residential areas built on expropriated farmland, and complained that subsidies were not as high as promised. Ordinary urban residents also complained about the subsidies, saying, "they get rich, while we get poor," and dubbing retirement communities "waiting-to-die villages." Retirement communities spatialize not only class but also other forms of status and identity, as in one neighborhood of county-level and higher cadres nicknamed "Tiger and Leopard Village." Retirement homes tend to be built in the "new *Simsha* (nobility) style," Tibetan in appearance but with many modern amenities; usually they are two-story houses built around a courtyard with a small lawn in the center and kitchen and bathroom in separate rooms in the courtyard rather than connected to the larger main living space.[45]

Prior to 1959, Lhasa's population was clustered in the Barkor, though in the first half of the twentieth century some nobility had started to move into new houses in what was then the outskirts of town. After the uprising, the government confiscated the large Barkor courtyard homes of Lhasa's wealthy residents and redistributed them to poor urban residents (and used others for offices or staff dormitories). As these buildings deteriorated, they began to be demolished. Many Lhasa residents became cadres and thus lived in cadre housing; today about half of the city's indigenous population is employed by the government.[46] In the mid-1990s, as the government raised their salaries, many more cadres moved into retirement home villages further from the center of town. One family of formerly wealthy merchants of my acquaintance, for example, had their Barkor house confiscated in 1959. In the 1990s they took early retirement and moved to New Unity Village, north beyond the Lingkor circumambulation route, where they built a heavily subsidized "new nobility" home. The house had a comfortable sunroom and yard, and around the courtyard were not only the living quarters for the family and the maid, a Tibetan girl from an impoverished village family in Shigatse, but also a separate kitchen and bathroom as well as three single rooms that the family, who frequently complained about the Han presence in Lhasa, had rented out to Han sex workers from Sichuan.

In addition to separate, single family housing, new private housing in Lhasa also includes what is widely referred to as *anju* or "comfortable housing," a term that has come to be used for any private row housing. The term was first used to refer to units built by real estate companies but purchased by work units as retirement houses. Among the earliest in the late 1990s was a settlement occupied by Tibet University instructors on farmland expropriated from Najin Township. This form of *anju* is thus distinct from the identically named national Comfortable Housing Project implemented in 1995–98, which aimed to provide housing for middle- and lower-middle-income households, and which was subsequently replaced by the Affordable Housing (*jingji shiyong fang*) Project. It is also distinct from the TAR rural house-building program, also called the Comfortable Housing Project, which began in 2006 and is discussed in the next chapter.

As a result of the construction of these various types of retirement housing complexes, an increasing number of former Lhasa residents have moved out of the Barkor, the traditional heart of Lhasa, to larger private housing further from the center. Tibetan, and to some extent Han migrants now occupy many of the small apartments carved out of the large Barkor courtyard complexes in the 1950s, leaving the remaining original residents of the Barkor to opine that "you can hardly find any real Lhasa people anymore. They've all moved to retirement homes far away. It's all outsiders here now." This inverts the more typical Chinese urban pattern, in which the newly rich take over the prime urban core while lower income families are pushed to the periphery.[47]

By the mid-2000s, completely private, commercially built houses (*shangping fang*) developed by real estate companies and divorced from work unit involvement became common. While villagers lost their land and livelihoods to urban expansion, some cadres were able to take advantage of the system to acquire two, three, or even five houses. For example, taking advantage of back door social connections, a husband and a wife might manage to each secure a retirement home through their respective work units, and another house through a parent or parent-in-law, and perhaps another commercially built house purchased on the private market. The process of urbanization-as-development has thus exacerbated the gap between the haves and have-nots: a small number of urban cadres with high salaries and social connections that enable them to profit from accumulation by dispossession in the production of the urban landscape, and the much larger number of urban poor and rural peasants who lose out but who are nonetheless expected to be grateful for development in the form of urbanization.

One typical community of private houses in Lhasa is the Sacred City Flower Garden, construction of which began in 2001. Built on a large block along Sera Road, on what was then urban Lhasa's northern edge, its 8.7-hectare area includes 158 houses and a condominium complex. The front half of the community consists of detached single-family "villas." With their beige-pink brick exteriors, white balconies and pillars, and Western-style wooden front and garage doors, these villas bear no resemblance to locally familiar architectural styles. The developer evidently held their imported design as a closely guarded secret, as when I visited in 2004, I was quickly chased out by a Tibetan security guard after snapping a couple of photographs of the houses' exteriors, an activity which the guard informed me was strictly prohibited.

Behind the villa section, with its super-deluxe 485-square-meter houses (including courtyards) and its 283.5- and 245-square-meter variants, is a section of what is called "Tibetan style" or *anju* houses, rows of adjoined single-family houses built with Tibetan façades of simulated stone masonry and striped awnings above the windows, but without the traditional internal pillars or wooden ceilings.[48] When I first visited in 2002, the real estate office displayed a 1:150 model of the entire complex along with a graphic on the wall that indicated which houses had already been sold, and which were still available. Many of the less-expensive Tibetan style houses had already been sold to work units that had purchased them for their employees, while the villas in front were mostly being purchased directly by private individuals.

The state-owned real estate company advertised these houses with a glossy brochure featuring digitally generated images highlighting ideas of greenery (*lühua*) and ecology or eco-living (*shengtai*).[49] Its sixteen pages depicted sophisticated urbanites strolling near a fountain surrounded by banana and palm trees (figure 6); a smiling little girl holding up a goldfish in a plastic bag; a tropical beachfront; sunset over a snowy field; a composite image of a telephone, several laptops, an Enter key, stock market indicators, and a globe; and a toddler in a bright red, yellow, and blue plastic playground. Not a single person depicted is even vaguely identifiable as Tibetan in features or dress (nor are pet goldfish culturally acceptable in Tibet), and the landscapes are also completely alien there.

The lush and decidedly un-Tibetan landscapes portrayed in the brochure instead evoke an image of the green oasis that became prevalent across China in the 1990s for advertising luxury housing.[50] Appearing opposite improbable scenes of temperate rainforests are claims that Sacred City Flower Garden is "the green ecological community of the capital," "the ecological small zone with the highest greenery rate in all of Lhasa," and "Lhasa's first ecological small zone that introduces water scenery." Greenness and ideas of ecology are commodified and appropriated for a specific mode of middle-class living that tries to be "closer to nature" by reconstructing nature and imposing a new environmental imaginary quite different from the local landscape. At the same time as selling a politics of urban exclusivity through greenness, the company, which boasts of being the largest real estate development firm in the TAR, also thanks Chinese Communist Party policies and guiding principles, including the Open Up the West campaign and the construction of the Qinghai-Tibet Railway for providing favorable

Figure 6 Selling villas and ecological living in a decidedly un-Tibetan landscape. A page from the Sacred City Flower Garden brochure.

development opportunities. State and market come together to create new forms of urban, "developed" living for a small, privileged stratum of Tibetans, predicated on the erasure of older places and landscapes. Urbanization and urban living are sold not only as markers of civility and development, but also as a form of being in the world that bears few if any markers of Tibetanness.

The Lhasa Master Urban Plan

The construction of these middle-class, eco-living "gardens" is part of a program of rapid urban expansion built on the backs of peasants whose farmland is expropriated and houses relocated. Lhasa's revised "Master Urban Plan (2007–2010)" designates a new Central Urban District in which all remaining farmland will be expropriated in the ongoing "new land enclosure movement." Issued by the Lhasa Municipality Land Management Bureau for public comment in 2008 and approved by the State Council in 2009, the Urban Plan is a central element of Lhasa's urbanization, acting as a tool for territorial control and encoding a vision of how spatial reorganization can lead to development.[51] A legally binding document that enables the expropriation of rural farmland either for immediate urban construction or to be held in reserve, it calls for the urban conversion and zoning into the new Lhasa Central Urban District of parts of Tolung Dechen County's Dongkar, Nechung, Yamda, and Ne'u Towns/Townships; as well as parts of the *Chengguanqu*'s Ngachen (Najin), Dogde, Tsalgungtang, and Nyangre Townships.

The stated goal of the plan is to "promote Tibet's socioeconomic development by leaps and bounds, speed up Lhasa's achievement of a comfortable and prosperous *(xiaokang)* society and its process of modernization, and effectively guide the scientific development of the Lhasa central city," as well as to "enhance the capacity of self-development" in Tibet. It emphasizes not only Lhasa's sense of lateness in terms of its "weak foundation" for and its lag in achievement of modernization, but also the city's need for "harmonious development" and stability and its ecological and cultural advantages, particularly for the tourism industry. It promises urbanization as a way to achieve a longed-for state of development that is nonetheless always out of reach.

The strong association of urbanization with development is reflected in the indicators offered for the goal of transforming the entire planning area into a well-off society by 2017; these include raising the urbanization rate from the 2006 level of 40 percent to 75 percent, and reducing the population of farmers and nomads from 257,000 to 175,000.[52] This transformation is envisioned to take place through both migration to urban areas and the conversion of rural to urban land uses, including a built-up area of 78.5

square kilometers out of the total 286 square kilometers of the newly defined Central Urban District, and the zoning of the current seats of Chushur and Tagtse Counties as core industrial areas. Zoning is a newly favored technology of spatial governance in the plan, which divides the new Central Urban District into eight smaller zones, including Dongkar District for a new city center, and East City District for administrative offices, residents, and education. Zoning is significant in that it attempts to redesign the city by creating a new correspondence between function and form, imposing a modernist rationality to transform a more organic and less legible landscape.[53]

When the urban plan was opened for public input, wealthy, informed, and relatively elite urban residents of new private homes on Footprint of the Gods Island (*Xianzu Dao*) saw that it included a plan to convert their new community to a tourism resort area, and were able to successfully petition to change the plan.[54] This was in marked contrast to the plight of peri-urban villagers. In Dongkar, farmers' attempt at a petition was met with intimidation, while in Najin, villagers stated that nothing could be done to change their zoning into the "red line" of urban construction. Other urban residents, too, expressed both apprehension and fatalism when it came to the urban plan, particularly in relation to its projected population numbers. The plan calls for the population of the newly defined Central Urban District, which does not correspond to any previous administrative unit, to rise to 450,000 by 2020, but several urban residents told me with great conviction that the increase would be to 1.5 million people. They speculated that over-crowding in inland China was behind government plans to expand the city, as a place for the excess Han population to settle. Their reactions suggest that while the plan was open to comment, the process and ability to influence it were not open to a wide public; the reactions also reflect a sense of being overwhelmed by both migration and urbanization.

Just as important for residents as the projected population numbers for the expanded city is the spatial restructuring of their everyday lives through the building of apartment complexes and row houses to replace previously scattered single-family houses. This is true not only for the new resettlement communities built for farmers who have lost their farmland but also of *chengzhongcun*, or "villages in the city." This term is used across China to refer to former villages on the urban edge that become surrounded by the city as land is expropriated for urban uses. You-tien Hsing notes that "villages in the city" differ from urban neighborhoods in that they retain their collective rights to land and their collective governance structures, limiting the control of metropolitan governments.[55] In Lhasa, however, designated "villages in the city" such as Lhalu do not retain collective land or have much bargaining power vis-à-vis the *Chengguanqu* government.

Moreover, the very first "village in the city" to be renovated, Karma Kunsang, was never a village collective at all but rather an urban neighborhood that began to be developed in the 1980s. The designation "village in the city" does not correspond to a legal classification but is rather a policy model, which in this case is being used to justify plans for certain forms of "development" in an area that was never actually a "village." A 2009 newspaper article about the impending renovation claims that "in Lhasa, if you mention Karma Kunsang, the image that arises in the mind is one that is dirty, chaotic, and bad: no sewers, no street lamps, no level roads," and that as a result, the two-to-three-year reconstruction process to begin in 2010 is "undoubtedly a piece of news that excites the residents of Karma Kunsang."[56] While the residents would indeed welcome sewers, lights, and functional roads, they are less excited about the part of the plan that calls for the development of retail strips, or the complete relocation of themselves for the duration of the reconstruction, and then resettlement into new four-floor apartment blocks, of which they will occupy units on the first two floors to replace their current single family houses. One resident stated that the masses have no choice in this or in cases of land grabs by local officials because "this is what socialism is, right? It means we have to do whatever the leaders tell us to do."

The process of urbanization—here the conversion of already-urban "villages in the city" into what is deemed a more proper form of urban—is one that through concentration and spatial rearrangement reshapes the embodied experiences and social-spatial practices of everyday life. The production of the urban landscape involves not only the physical creation and extension of built-up areas, but also other ways of producing orderly forms of spatial and architectural organization seen as hitherto lacking but necessary preconditions or signs of development. The visual orderliness of the planned new homes lays down a new grid of legibility and discipline. Indeed, Lhasa residents frequently remark that they believe they are being concentrated in a unified fashion in these apartment complexes not only to "make space for the Chinese" but also "because people gathered together like that are easier to manage."

Finally, at the same time as urbanization according to the urban plan works to define the embodied spatial experience of a "developed" life, it also serves as a source of accumulation by dispossession and displacement. The Lhasa Municipality Development and Reform Commission states that the government will meet the cost of constructing three main roads within the new Karma Kunsang neighborhood, but that the rest, particularly demolition of existing houses and compensation to the residents, will be left to real estate development companies. Moreover, "in order to create a new kind of residential community with a graceful environment and rational housing" the government has decided to look for business among "national large-scale real estate development companies and associated investment companies."[57] Lhasa is thus undergoing massive demolition not only of the old, but also of the not so old, in an effort to become developed and modern through the reordering of both the visual appearance and the experience of space. The demolition of recently built single-family houses in favor of uniform row houses and apartment blocks conjures the appearance of development, producing a developed urban landscape through a process of "creative destruction" that fuels capital accumulation for coalitions of real estate development companies and local governments.

Land Expropriation and Relocation

Under the Master Urban Plan, Dongkar Town in Tolung Dechen County, just west of the edge of the Lhasa *Chengguanqu*, is to become a new city center. To turn this vision into a reality, Tolung Dechen County expropriated the land of three of Dongkar's six villages for urban development, as well as for the widening of a major road and other commercial and government buildings. The other three villages lost their land later on to the national-level Lhasa Economic and Technological Development Zone. Residents of the first three villages were settled together in one newly built housing area, and residents of the remaining villages in another.

Though residents of the three Tolung Dechen villages who were relocated and their farmland expropriated by the county government see this very much as a land grab, the local government has portrayed it not as an income-generating activity for themselves, but rather as an example of state generosity in giving development to local residents. In fact, government officials have described the land enclosure as part of the New Socialist Countryside program, which does not involve expropriation of farmland.[58] In 2007, *China Tibet Magazine* ran a feature about these three villages entitled "Comfortable Housing and Happy Lives of Tibetan Farmers and Herders":[59]

> It is obvious that the new houses of farmers in Tolung Dechen County are more beautiful than some in Lhasa City. . . . The village leader explained to us that the changes were brought about by the housing project. In the past, village residences were scattered and the structure of their houses was poorly designed. Nowadays, the old-fashioned village has gone and a new one has emerged which is bright, comfortable and modern.
>
> Drolkar, the governor of Tolung Dechen County, told the author that this village has undergone a comprehensive change: renovations or rebuilding of houses, upgrades to water supply, electricity and telephone, improved roads and access to solar energy. All of this is the face of the new village socialism.

> The old Changpa in Dungkar Village moved to this village in July 2006. It costs 160 thousand Yuan to build his house of 200 square meters; 80% donated by the government and 20% from his own funds.
>
> Governor Drolkar said that having a comfortable house like that of Changpa closely relates to the increased development of cities. . . . The old house of Changpa has been brought into the system as one part of Dungkar in Lhasa City. His old house was therefore withdrawn by the County Government from future marketing development and preserved as second grade land. Thus, the County Government input funds Changpa and others to exchange their houses . . . within three to five years, all the rest of the farmers and herders in this county [will] be living in comfortable, modern houses.

The article fails to mention that it is not only houses that have been "withdrawn," but also all of the villagers' farmland, which they had no choice but to sell to the county government at the government-determined price of 30,000 RMB/*mu*, of which 2000 RMB/*mu* was retained by the village in a fund meant to support the development of means for villagers' future livelihoods.[60] Far from being "withdrawn from future marketing development," the land appears to have been "withdrawn" precisely for the purpose of marketing development—by the county government. In fact, rumors about land speculation were rife among villagers and nearby Tolung Dechen County residents about this and other land deals, with some reporting that the county government was planning to sell the land for up to twenty times what the villagers received in compensation. As a land grab disguised as part of the creation of a "new socialist countryside," this is a case of what critics in other parts of China have dubbed "fake urbanization leap forward."[61]

The villagers moved to their new compact settlement area, built on former farmland, in July 2006. A year later, in the summer of 2007, the former location of Village No. 1, just up the road from the new settlement area, had not yet been occupied by any new construction. Instead, below the ruins of Dongkar Fort perched on the nearby hill was a sad jumble of half-demolished houses with mud bricks strewn about and the remnants of kitchens and living rooms still recognizable amidst the rubble. The white walls enclosing the land on both sides of the road were stenciled in red characters: "This land has been reserved by the Tolung Dechen County government." While some villagers believed that the county government had already made a decision about which enterprise to sell this land to, others believed that the county was still searching for the highest bidder. Like many county governments across China, Tolung Dechen's would have an incentive to keep some expropriated land in reserve, as it appeared to be doing in 2007, to use as collateral for other projects to be financed by bank loans.[62]

The new two-floor semidetached townhouses came in three standard sizes and models, each of which was presented as selling at an "insider's" price at which residents of Dongkar were eligible to purchase, versus a market price double the amount (though the recipients did not receive house deeds and were not supposed to sell their houses).[63] Villagers had two payment options. Those who felt confident about the value of their existing houses could request compensation for these, and then pay the full insider's cost of their new house. Few families picked this option because they did not know how the government would determine the value of their houses, in part because no real market for rural (as opposed to urban) housing exists. The far more commonly chosen option was for the villagers to pay 20 percent of the insider's price, while the government paid 80 percent, referred to as a "donation," though in this scheme villagers received no compensation for their existing homes.

The new houses are very much urban dwellings, with electricity, which the residents also had in their previous locations, and running water, which they did not. The houses are equipped with more amenities than the residents' previous village homes, alluded to in *China Tibet Magazine's* gushing mention of "TV sets with big screens, audio equipment and computers."[64] A village leader, nervous about saying anything negative about the resettlement, emphasized to me that the new houses were much better than old ones: less dusty and thus easier to clean, and equipped with running water. Yet his family, like most others in the settlement, had installed a pump in their courtyard so that they would not have to pay for water, an unfamiliar and unwelcome prospect for most of the villagers. In addition, while proclaiming the excellence of the houses, he was having his house remodeled in a more Tibetan style.

Designed by a Chinese contractor, the houses are in the hybrid "New Tibetan" style, what local residents sometimes refer to as "Tibetan on the outside, but Chinese on the inside." The outer wall layer of granite bricks, the style of courtyard doors, and the painted wooden trim around windows and doors distinguish the houses from typical construction in other parts of China. Nevertheless the houses are what most Lhasa residents call *gya khang* ("Chinese house"), rather than *pö khang* ("Tibetan house"), the latter being characterized by internal pillars, round timber roofing beams, and mud brick or stone walls. Temperature in *pö khang* is much more uniform—warm in the winter, cool in the summer—than in the new houses, which residents said are so hot on the second floor during the summer that they can barely stand to be upstairs. This is due largely to the concrete plank ceilings, as well as to the inner wall layers of concrete bricks.

Though little could be done about the basic construction material, the resettled residents still had to paint and install all the fixtures before moving in, and took this as an opportunity to remodel. The contractor had designed the buildings in a very popular contemporary open style, which did not appeal at all to Tibetan villagers, many of whom added one or more internal walls. The houses were also designed with kitchens tucked in the inside corners, which families found too small and awkward because they lacked chimneys, designed as they were for gas stoves rather than the locally preferred wood- and dung-burning stoves which importantly also provide heat. Many families converted these kitchens to storage areas and built new Tibetan-style kitchens in their courtyards. Many also kept their inside bathrooms for showers, but built new bathrooms with toilets in the courtyards, considered less awkward than having them inside the houses. All of these expenses, viewed as important for turning a house into a home, together with the additional expenditures for basic installation of floors, painting, and fixtures, typically cost an additional 30,000 RMB, though wealthier families were said to have spent upward of 80,000 RMB remodeling and redesigning the houses.

These villagers thus experienced urbanization through their personal home spaces as a process of adapting to and modifying an imposed style of living, one they thought of as more Chinese than Tibetan. The only option presented to them in the course of losing their farmland and being moved to urban-style communities was to take a Chinese-style house, elements of which were modifiable at personal expense while others, such as the thermal properties of "modern" construction material, were not. The project of making Lhasa urban and making peri-urban villagers urban citizens, presented as the only path toward development and the inevitable way of the future, is thus experienced in ways deeply entangled with the cultural politics of identity. As both the Urban Plan and the *China Tibet Magazine* article make clear, the resettlement of Dongkar residents is central to the process of incorporating Dongkar into the planned expansion of Lhasa's urban built-up area. The higher-density settlement and the tighter spacing between the houses lead some resettled residents to express a feeling of claustrophobia. Others described disliking the suffocating feeling of the new construction material that produced houses that breathed less, or circulated less air. For most families, the resettlement has resulted in a significantly smaller living area, and for all, the new hundred-square-meter courtyards are much less spacious than their former rural courtyards, which makes it impossible for them to continue to keep livestock, a principal source of dissatisfaction.

At the same time as resettlement has led to a profound transformation of the embodied experience of space and spatial relations, it has also caused villagers to face the immediate material problem of how to earn a livelihood without farmland. The village leader suggested that the conversion to urban living also required a change in the thought patterns or subjectivities of the residents, saying, "the government says that the farmers' thinking must be changed to city residents' way of thinking—everyone must be encouraged to go out and find wage labor ["side work"] now." According to residents, many families had to draw from their farmland compensation to pay for their housing costs, leading to considerable anxiety. "We have no choice now but to work under the Chinese," said one resident, explaining that there was occasionally construction work available, but not nearly enough for all of the unemployed.

As a result, the resettlement has reinforced the Tibetan reliance in Lhasa on an economy of rents, reinstantiating the apparent contradiction of Tibetan residents unhappy about the extent of Han migration nevertheless subleasing their intimate household spaces to migrants. Some families have constructed extra rooms in their courtyards that they then rent out to Han entrepreneurs, who use them as small dumpling or bread shops. Some families who have sought to take advantage of the resettlement program by legally splitting into multiple household registrations (*hukou*), thereby becoming entitled to more than one house, have also rented out entire houses to migrants. One village leader, for example, received a separate house for his son, which he then rented out to a migrant to save up, he said, for his children's tuition.

In addition to these individual rental strategies, the local government also invested in construction of three large buildings along the edge of the road in front of the new neighborhood. These were planned to generate even more income for the 304 households in the settlement than they had previously earned from renting their land out to migrant greenhouse vegetable farmers.[65] Leaders planned to rent these buildings out to a single businessman, who would then lease the individual spaces to smaller-scale entrepreneurs to develop into stores, restaurants, and a hotel. The income from the rent would then be redistributed to the villagers. More than a year after construction was complete, however, the buildings still stood completely empty, located as they were in a relatively inconvenient site vis-à-vis downtown Lhasa. Continued urban expansion may very well turn it into a desirable location, attractive to the big investor the village leaders are counting on to maintain village livelihoods through rentals. In the meantime, however, villagers were instead trying to make their living doing petty business such as selling bread in Lhasa, driving vehicles, or working as security guards.

The widespread process of peasant relocation following land expropriation in China's rapid urbanization frequently not only leads to economic deterioration but also "disconnects them from their historically formed sense of place and place-based collective memory."[66] This process of deterritorialization is profound for Tibetans as it is tied to their separation from the local deities that preside over their territory and community fortunes, suggesting ultimately the "loss of long-term, social vitality on Tibetan terms."[67] One village in Dongkar was the site of a stupa that had been destroyed during the Cultural Revolution but subsequently rebuilt.[68] When the village was relocated, elderly villagers wanted the stupa to be moved. They were required to ask permission from both the local government and the United Front, an agency under the CCP in charge of managing relations with non-Party elites, and which plays an active role in managing minority and religious affairs. After providing evidence of the stupa's long history, the villagers were eventually allowed to move it to a piece of land at the very back of the new neighborhood, though they were not provided with any assistance to do so. They collected money, invited monks to perform the requisite prayers and rituals, and then dismantled and reassembled the stupa. While this represented a partial reterritorialization, the villagers stated that the local territorial and birth deities unfortunately could not, by their very nature, be invited to move, making the resettlement a significant break from a long history and set of relations between the villagers and the land that is the basis for their common fortunes.

Like residents of these three villages, residents of Dongkar Town's other three villages were informed in 2004 that they would be moving soon. However, their move took much more time, and even in 2007, red circles around the character *chai*, meaning "demolish" or "raze," could be seen all over the still-standing white walls of the traditional village houses. Throughout urbanizing China, *chai* has become the ubiquitous harbinger of destruction, appearing mysteriously overnight and without warning to inform nervous residents of their impending dislocation.

These villagers had already lost their farmland in 2003–4 to the first phase, or Zone A, of the Lhasa Economic and Technological Development Zone. Marked at one end by a large billboard of Deng Xiaoping benevolently proclaiming "The Developing [sic] Zone is Very Promising," (*kaifa qu da you xiwang*), the zone was approved by the State Council in 2001 to encompass 5.46 square kilometers of land of both the Lhasa *Chengguanqu* and the western part of Tolung Dechen County, including Dongkar Town. This marked the arrival in Tibet of the second wave of the "zone fever" that had swept across China first throughout the 1990s, and again in the early 2000s. As they turned from an experiment by Deng Xiaoping into a development regime with few if any controls, Special Economic Zones fueled the real estate boom.[69] However, they did not prove terribly effective at generating growth, and one report found that 85 percent of the designated development zone areas across the country were actually sitting empty and undeveloped.[70] The intensification of rural unrest over land grabs, compounded by the need for macroeconomic adjustment, motivated the Ministry of Land and Resources to launch a campaign in 2004 that led to the return to state land reserves of more than 60 percent of land marked for development zones, and that linked development zones with local cadre corruption.[71]

However, this nationwide trend toward a less rosy view of special economic zones has not affected Lhasa, where the Economic and Technological Development Zone was in 2010 very much touted as a sign of progress, development, and success, even though much of it still stood empty. This was despite a package of preferential policies aimed at attracting investors, including a 90 percent reduction in the income tax rate, lower interest rates on loans, and a 50 percent reduction in land use costs, among other incentives. As of 2009 the land that had been cleared of farmers was being used to house a handful of enterprises: traditional Tibetan medicine, yak meat processing, *chang*, mineral water, handicrafts, railway maintenance, mining equipment, and a few car dealerships and supermarkets.[72]

The compensation scheme for houses here was different from what had been offered to the first three Dongkar villages. In this case, each household received a 44,000 RMB subsidy toward the cost of the new house. In addition, the villagers were compensated for their old homes at the rate of 700 RMB/m^2 for more expensive granite brick–clad houses, and 300 RMB/m^2 for mud brick houses. Though the rate was based on the relative price of the materials, many villagers argued that it was unfair because granite bricks could be resold once a house was demolished, whereas mud bricks had no resale value. This compensation was also provided toward the purchase of the new houses, which cost 145,000 RMB for a 179-square-meter house and 126,000 RMB for a smaller house of just over 150 square meters. Some villagers who had recently invested considerably in building large granite brick–clad houses received enough in compensation to have money left over after the transaction, but many had to draw on the compensation they received for farmland that was lost to the Special Economic and Technological Development Zone to pay for their new houses.

When these villagers learned about the impending expropriation of their farmland for the zone, along with residents of Nechung Town, slated to lose land to Zone B, and residents of Yamda and Ne'u Townships, soon to lose land to a large wholesale market and the Lhasa train station, they petitioned the regional government for higher compensation.[73] They were unsuccessful, and were deterred from attempting any further action by the threat that their petition would be represented as a "political problem"—a splittist threat to state territorial sovereignty. The villagers were severely reprimanded for not "climbing up the ladder"—for going straight to the TAR government without first going to their lower-level leaders, and were threatened with jail time if they did not desist from their petition immediately. Villagers also claimed that the county leaders threatened to ensure that children of the petitioners would not receive jobs in the future even if they managed to pass civil service examinations. Thus in Tibet, the threat of splittism has become an exceedingly effective tool for primitive accumulation and the production of the urban landscape.

These villagers also fared much worse than the other half of Dongkar Town in the location and type of resettlement housing they received. Unlike the townhouses of the first resettlement area, theirs were long apartment-like blocks with up to twenty units in one structure. Some of the long rows of houses are spaced only about four meters apart (figure 7). The units were also built very close to the Qinghai-Tibet Railway, with the front row virtually abutting the elevated tracks. Villagers who in 2007 were waiting to be moved were unhappy with the quality of the construction and particularly averse to the rearrangement of space—the small size of the courtyards, the density of the settlement, and the fact that the spacing of housing rows would make it very difficult for them to get sunlight in the winter, an important consideration in Lhasa's climate. Some referred to the new houses as "places to raise pigeons" because the size of the courtyards would make raising livestock impossible. Their current homes, even though one story high, were, they felt, spacious rather than narrow and cramped. One older woman remarked sarcastically, "It seems they don't want us to raise our livestock anymore. Oh yes, they say it's so nice, so clean. So nice and clean without livestock. So nice and clean without grass. So nice and clean and poor!"

Another woman remarked about the land expropriation, "In the past the Chinese Communist Party was good. They said to give land to the people without land—the servants. Now our land is being taken away from us."

Figure 7 Resettlement houses of those relocated from the national-level Lhasa Economic and Technological Development Zone, 2007. Photo by author.

The implication that the CCP was returning these villagers to the state of landlessness and poverty that they were supposed to have been liberated from was a striking appropriation of the CCP's own rhetoric to comment on contemporary processes of the new enclosure movement. These former peasants understand urbanization, presented as a gift of new houses and modern living, both as expropriation and as a restructuring of embodied spatial experience from living in a Tibetan-style spacious house to a Chinese-style cramped and narrow one.

Xiaokang Living

On the opposite side of Lhasa, Najin Township's Red Star Village has been designated in Lhasa's Master Urban Plan as the new East City District, zoned primarily for municipal administrative offices, education, and cultural and exhibition functions. Red Star Village's urbanization has been more gradual than that of Dongkar, and has followed a somewhat different trajectory but toward a similar result in terms of land expropriation and local residents' experience of development as urbanization.

In the late 1990s and early 2000s, the landscape along the bumpy cobbled road from the built-up area of Lhasa east through the five "natural villages" of Red Star Administrative Village was one of whitewashed mud brick and stone houses and courtyards, wheat and barley fields, one-room mud brick huts built by migrants, and greenhouses filled with vegetables.[74] By 2004, residents of Tangchen and Kyichuling natural villages had already learned that their farmland would be taken over for the construction of a new campus of Tibet University and that they would eventually have to move into *anju,* concentrated "comfortable" row houses, because the whole area had been designated for urbanization. Not knowing when this would happen, however, residents in all five villages continued to rent out their land to migrants, including new migrants from Gansu Province who specialized in growing flowers rather than vegetables.

Over the next five years, Red Star changed from a quiet agrarian landscape to a dusty, noisy construction zone. Han migrants who manufactured concrete bricks and Hui carpenters producing Tibetan-style furniture for the Tibetan consumer market replaced the vegetable-cultivating Han. As these migrants moved in, local Tibetans rented out their farmland at 2,000 to 3,000 RMB/*mu*, two to three times the rent they had received for vegetable cultivation. Whereas they had previously been concerned that concrete brick manufacturing would be harmful to the soil, villagers no longer worried about this as they resigned themselves to losing their land and given that the construction had cut off irrigation sources anyway. As the sound of saws and the smell of sawdust and paint from the migrant carpenters' labor filled the air, Tibetan villagers sat idle. Local residents stated that the migrants, with their power tools, could make Tibetan furniture much more quickly and cheaply than Tibetans themselves, thus capturing another economic niche from Tibetans. Stacks of timber, and painted tables and cabinets in various states of completion, filled makeshift yards, cluttering the previously open villages. As the density of the villages increased with concrete brick manufacture and furniture construction, so too did the piles of trash. Some lots abutting the few remaining vegetable greenhouses were taken over for plastic recycling or simply became garbage dumps. Tibetan villagers complained about the Chinese migrants and their garbage, but did little as they waited resignedly for relocation.

Local residents expanded their courtyards and divided them up into small rooms that they rented out as living space to the migrant brick makers and carpenters. By 2007, residents of all five natural villages had been notified that they would sooner or later be moved into four-floor apartment blocks, which they would have to purchase using compensation for their farmland and current houses. Expropriated farmland was to be compensated at 100,000 RMB/*mu* (roughly 224,000 USD/ha), of which the households would retain 40 percent while the village committees would keep 60 percent to invest both in the building of resettlement houses and in enterprises for residents' future employment. According to villagers' understandings, their current houses would be compensated at 850 RMB/m^2—for any area enclosed by a roof, but not for the spacious courtyards that characterized local homes. One resident of Red Star explained his understanding of the logic for compensation: "because they say that the land belongs to the Communist Party, we only get compensation for land on which there is actually a house. This is because they say that the land belongs to the Chinese Communist Party. It is not ours; we are just borrowing it."

Unlike the relatively wealthy and well-connected residents of Footprint of the Gods Island who successfully fought the slated destruction of their neighborhood in the Urban Plan, Red Star Village residents expressed full conviction that they had no choice about whether or not they could stay in their village houses. "We have no freedom to say we will stay. They tell us we can't say no," said one. "We are not allowed to say we don't want to move. The ordinary people don't know anything. The leaders don't tell us anything," said another. They did not know which work units would be taking over their land "because we have not seen the plan. They don't let us look at the plan." Indeed, residents of other villages claimed that when Tangchen villagers tried to complain that their compensation was inadequate, they were warned, "this is for building a school and thus complaints are not allowed. If you complain, it will be a political problem," again demonstrating the way in which "politics" becomes a management tool in the TAR not only to secure state territorialization but also to enable primitive accumulation.

Nevertheless, villagers sought as best they could to take advantage of the situation. A frenzy of building ensued after the compensation packages were announced: houses sprouted multiple additions with concrete brick walls, cheaper than the favored granite bricks, competing for space with a flurry of brand-new house construction. Villagers paved over large portions of their courtyards in concrete and covered them with corrugated tin roofs, so that they would count as a covered part of the house, and thus be included in the calculation of total area for compensation. They also planted new poplars, in anticipation of the 30 RMB per tree promised when moving time came. Many families created new separate household registrations for adult children and built new houses for them so that they would be entitled to separate resettlement houses, while others built big extensions in order to receive larger compensation packages. The mad rush to build finally ended in 2009 when each house in each village was spray-painted with a red number, indicating that the house had been measured for compensation and that any further building or enclosure would not be compensated. In the process, the number of houses in Kyichuling village grew from 70 to more than 150.

In 2006, a Chinese construction company was hired to build the new four-floor housing complexes. Kyichuling and Tangchen residents were apprehensive about moving into the apartments, which were designed as first-and-second-floor units below separate third-and-fourth-floor units. The lower apartments had only very small courtyards, leaving residents frustrated at the inability to keep their livestock. The upper-level apartments, with no courtyards at all, were to be sold to outsiders at a higher price but stood empty as of 2009.

Like villagers in Tolung Dechen, residents of Red Star expressed a preference for their single-family houses, which were more spacious, had larger courtyards, and allowed for a greater distance between families. Asked why they had to move into the apartment buildings when this was clearly not a preference for any of them, one resident replied that the edict had come from the former head of the *Chengguanqu*:

> The villagers said many times: thanks, but we don't want to move into four-floor apartments. We want two-floor single-family houses. We don't want them. . . . But the head of the *Chengguanqu* said at a meeting, "Have any of you ever been on an airplane and looked down? Have any of you ever been to the top of the Potala Palace and looked down? Well, there's a certain way the city is supposed to look. It's supposed to have high buildings.". . . After this, no one dared to say anything anymore. Everyone had no choice but to pretend to agree.

State officials and planners regard the visual spectacle of the urban—with its neat, orderly rows of multistory construction contrasting with the scattered, squat single-family homes of the village—as necessary for both creating an image of development and prosperity that can attract investment and also shaping residents' visions and subjectivities as properly civilized city dwellers.

Indeed, the resettlement of these households is part of a government project, with funding from Aid-Tibet counterparts Beijing and Jiangsu Provinces, named the Model *Xiaokang* (Well-off) Village. According to one official description,

> walking into . . . the village's residential district, row upon row of the residents' new four-floor apartments leap into view . . . the greenery on both sides of the path and in front of the buildings makes one's heart carefree and happy. . . . The former village . . . was both dirty and chaotic . . . there is now water, electricity, roads, communication, and radio and television . . . and the greenery rate has reached 30 percent. . . . A local villager told this reporter, "In the past our houses were constructed of wood and earth, so that water frequently leaked when it rained. Now with our new houses . . . we have reached a prosperous livelihood."[75]

The highlighting of the attractions of "green" living is ironic given that much greater levels of greenery—agricultural land—previously surrounded the houses. Electricity, radio, and television were already part of the existing village infrastructure. Running water was new, but many preferred digging wells in order to avoid paying for water. As was the case in Dongkar, the Chinese labor contractor who determined the floor plan constructed the houses in what local villagers called "Sichuanese style." Residents found it awkward to have kitchens and bathrooms inside, and spent an additional 20,000 RMB on average adding internal walls within the apartment units and building new kitchens and bathrooms in the courtyard spaces. Villagers were also skeptical of the quality of the brick building material, preferring their long-lasting mud brick wall construction. "Look at the Potala Palace!" exclaimed one Kyichuling resident, "It's more than a thousand years old and still standing, so of course our houses last for at least fifty or sixty years if not more." Unlike mud bricks, they explained, concrete bricks "expire" after thirty years and fall apart. As a result, the villagers asked for their new houses to be made of granite, another material that in their experience does not expire. Instead, their apartments were constructed of red clay bricks, which "they told us is good—warm in the winter and cool in the summer [unlike concrete], but we don't know."

The new apartments were built in two standard sizes, one 209 square meters in area, and the other of 149 square meters. Villagers were charged 650 RMB/m^2, receiving 50 square meters for each person in a household with a local household registration. For the remaining area, if any, the villagers were charged 850 RMB/m^2, compared to the 2,400 RMB/m^2 that was assessed as the market price and which anyone without a local household registration would be charged. A few households in Tangchen had enough savings to purchase two apartments, one at the subsidized price and another, smaller unit at the market price. Villagers claimed that the original plan was for the villagers to sell the empty upper-level units and keep the profits for future investments and livelihood options, but that instead, the apartments were to be sold en masse to a managing agency, which would then sell the third- and fourth-floor units at a greater profit.

As was also the case in Dongkar, villagers were very concerned about the loss of their farmland. Their new houses were less dusty than their old village homes, but this came at the price of having no work to do and no means of sustaining a future livelihood. Nevertheless, because it was the first *Xiaokang* model village to be finished, it became a frequent object of both newspaper and television reporting (figure 4). Residents explained, "We are told at meetings that we must say, 'This is thanks to the Communist Party.' We must say life is very happy and full of fortune now." TAR Party Secretary Zhang Qingli himself came for a visit, in advance of which every household was given a national flag to hang in the courtyards and reminded to speak about their gratitude for their new houses and new lives. "The leaders say the new houses are very, very good," commented a resident of another village, "We can't say anything else about them except in our own homes." Failure to perform gratitude for the gift of *Xiaokang* houses, a biopolitical project aimed at improving the conditions of living of Tibetans, would be tantamount to a rejection of the state's territorial sovereignty.

Though construction in Tangchen started later than in Kyichuling, it was finished sooner, thanks to Tangchen's larger fields and fewer households. In fact, after the brick basic structures were complete, Kyichuling's apartments stood empty for several years. Water and electricity had not been installed, nor courtyards built, when construction came to a standstill. "The buildings are becoming old just sitting there. The wind slams the doors shut, blowing everything here and there and everything is starting to fall apart though we haven't even moved in yet," villagers complained, saying that the construction had ground to a halt because the labor contractor ran out of money. Some villagers speculated that the contractor, who received the work because he was from the same hometown as their township leader, made money by undertaking construction projects, half-finishing them, and then moving onto the next in order to grab as much land as possible in anticipation of rising prices.

The village committee of Kyichuling was itself required to raise much of the capital needed to pay the contractor to build the resettlement houses that would then be sold to the villagers. The village committee's money, in turn, was to come from the 60,000 RMB/*mu* per household retained by the village as part of the compensation package offered to villagers for their expropriated farmland. Because Kyichuling lost less land than Tangchen and had more families, many of which had split up into new households entitled to compensation, the original investment from the village resulted in the building of too few apartment blocks, especially because villagers were offered only the first-and-second-floor apartments. This left the villagers in limbo. Nearby construction had cut off all sources of irrigation and thus prevented them from working on their remaining farmland, and yet the village committee did not have enough capital from farmland compensation to complete construction. Villagers were thus left to wait for other work units to come and expropriate their remaining farmland so that the village could finish building their resettlement homes. Ironically, then, villagers waited idly to lose farmland so that they could use the compensation to pay to move into resettlement apartments built on their expropriated farmland.

The loss of farm work and the scarcity of other labor options for the villagers of both Tangchen and Kyichuling have reshaped the contours of everyday life and the idioms through which they experience and negotiate development. Some provision has been made for alternative income sources. A handful of young village men are employed as security guards, and twenty-nine one-room stores were built for residents of the two villages, directly across from the gates of the new university campus. Those who drew straws for the stores paid 400 RMB/month rent to sell snacks and provide pool tables for students. Official reports also discuss plans to build a five-star hotel on remaining village land by bringing in outside investors. For the most part, though, the villagers are idle—much more idle than they have ever been.

One middle-aged woman stated that while their new houses are indeed very pretty, their *sem*—their minds—are unhappy because there is nothing to do and there will be no way to make a living once their compensation packages are used up. When I visited in the middle of the day, her husband and her friend were drinking shots of Lhasa Beer, joking that this is what life was like now that they had become "retired farmers." Commenting on the widespread consumption of alcohol in the village since land expropriation, a young security guard stated glumly, "Those who are called Tibetans are so stupid!" adding that once they had run out of money they started to drink home-brewed hard liquor. "That's better," said his cousin, "that way at least you die faster and get everything over with." Her father, a former village accountant, now spends his mornings circumambulating the Lingkor, and then gathering with other villagers in the late afternoon to drink into the evening. While the others drink home-brewed *chang*, he insists on purchasing beer, to the chagrin of his family. Sitting in front of a pile of empty Lhasa Beer bottles while watching his wife play cards, he told me sheepishly that these days he tries to drink quickly because he can no longer sleep if he does not drink. "I'm spoiled now," he explained.

While these former farmers frequently spoke of being spoiled by alcohol consumption now that they had become urbanized, the idiom of being too spoiled to work hard, so prevalent a few years prior, had vanished from their vernacular because there was simply no work to do. Even small-scale potato and radish selling was very difficult now despite their remaining parcels of land, because the irrigation water supply had been cut off. They claimed that Han labor bosses did not hire them when they went for construction jobs. Thus while a decade prior they declared a celebratory indolence that indexed the absence in the reform period of the excessive labor obligations of the Maoist era, the urbanized ex-peasants now had no work to do even when they wanted it. Apprehension about the future, when land compensation would run out leaving former villagers vulnerable to becoming the urban underclass, helped drive them to their new condition of being spoiled by alcohol. However, this was not just a result of fear of having no income; it was acutely present even in those families who could rely on household members receiving regular salaries. This new idiom of being spoiled also very much expressed a lost sense of purpose, and an experience of spatial rupture and social dislocation that, for them, accompanied urbanization.

In the spectrum of cities across China, Lhasa is small in both population and area, a fact that fuels migrant images of Lhasa as lacking in development and of its residents as having low *suzhi*. In the dominant spatial practices of China after reform, the higher a city's position in the administrative hierarchy, the more urbanized and developed, and the larger and more populous it is supposed to be. The disjuncture between Lhasa's administrative status as regional capital city and its size confirms to Han migrants the low quality and undeveloped status of its residents. At the same time, viewed in relation to other urban areas in the TAR, Lhasa's rapid and disproportionate urbanization makes more sense if it is thought of as an outpost of an emerging, colonizing western Chinese regional economy with its hub in Chengdu, that is, in terms of a westward-expanding Han China, rather than in terms of Tibet as a cultural region.[76]

This resonates with a historical analysis that suggests that not only the valorization of the urban, but also the very conceptual framework of the urban/rural dichotomy, constitute a significant break from the traditional way of organizing and experiencing the arrangement of space along a continuum of settlement sizes. The production of the urban landscape involves the introduction of new representations of space—the Urban Plan and its embedded ideology of urbanization as prerequisite for and sign of development—that bring with them dialectical changes in perceived and lived space, the two other elements of the conceptual triad Lefebvre poses for understanding social space.[77] Thus Lhasa's rapidly changing aesthetics and spatial form cannot be treated as natural or neutral, despite the way in which urban planning is deployed as if it were nothing more than a technical act of development. Urbanization necessarily involves the introduction of new socio-spatial practices, such as living in smaller spaces and in closer proximity to neighbors, and the abandonment of older ones, such as raising livestock and growing crops. In Tibet, these processes are compounded by the introduction of the category of the urban itself as a way of ordering and controlling space. Furthermore, the living spaces provided in the course of resettlement for urbanization, such as kitchens inside houses rather than in courtyards, are perceived by Tibetans as alien forms. While rearranging these living spaces to the extent possible, newly urbanized residents cannot change construction materials or expand courtyards. For them, urbanization is thus inextricably intertwined with the deepening influence of Han culture on their lives, making urbanization as a form of development part of a larger trajectory of state territorialization.

Middle-class Tibetans have been able to purchase houses in new "retirement home" and commercial residential districts, made desirable through representations of green oases and images of sophisticated living that have little to do with Tibet's material or cultural landscapes. In working to acquire sometimes multiple homes in the form of new residential "villas" that spatialize class and status, urban Tibetan elites actively participate in the power-laden production of the new urban landscape. This is accomplished through the expropriation of farmland from peasants, who are subsequently concentrated in neighborhoods of row houses and four-floor apartment buildings, labeled models of the New Socialist Countryside or new *Xiaokang* living, and celebrated in official publications for lifting their residents out of "dirty and chaotic" conditions, and bringing them modernity and prosperity. In return, their recipients must perform gratitude for these gifts from the state.

Local government attempts to address issues of future livelihood of those whose land has been expropriated have ironically reinforced Lhasa's economy of rents, whereby Lhasa residents who find it difficult to break into labor markets or other economic niches come to rely on renting out their intimate household spaces to outside migrants—the very ones for whom they feel their concentration in urban space is designed to make more room. Thus, they reproduce the contradiction found earlier in greenhouse vegetable farming, in which they feel at once marginalized by Han migrants while at the same time contributing to the continual reproduction of that very marginalization.

The Aftermath of 2008 (II)

Winter

A light dusting of snow has settled on the barren brown mountains to Lhasa's north and south. They form a majestic backdrop to the growing city, now expanding across the river. The air is frigid. Women in *chupas* covered by heavy winter aprons, woolen hats, and face masks obscuring all but their eyes walk past the young Chinese soldiers standing at attention at every intersection.

Golden plaques have sprouted throughout the city exhorting Tibetans to build a harmonious society.

The Barkor is a sea of masked faces and varied accents. On the rooftops next to the Makye Ame Restaurant and across from the Jokhang, armed soldiers stand guard, rifles in hand, ready to fire. Security cameras look out onto the crowds from their rooftop perches. Life tries to go on as normal, with wizened old women in Lhasa on pilgrimage, wrapped in scarves and layers of sheepskin, brushing shoulders with young Han soldiers with their riot shields and walkie-talkies. What do they think about as they brush past each other?

Travel has been restricted for months, but for a brief period, pilgrims have been let in once again. A crowd of hundreds appears in front of the Jokhang, from morning to night, each participant with his or her own blanket-wrapped prostration board. Others prostrate themselves around the Barkor, with wooden blocks on each hand and padded knees, which allow them to take three steps and then a running jump toward the ground, sliding the wooden blocks against smooth granite blocks of the newly paved path, sliding several feet before coming to a stop. Prostration is not monopolized by those clad in heavy sheepskin. Ripped jeans and Barbie backpacks are also perfectly good accoutrements for the pious act.

Deep in the maze of alleyways behind Tsomonling the military presence is more intense. Around 5 p.m. a brigade of fifteen soldiers clad in green, sporting rifles, riot shields, and protective helmets with face guards, march past me in single file.

I receive a text message from a friend, with whom I am to meet to catch up on life:

> I am very sorry to tell you that I cannot meet you. It is not a good time for me. Hope you will understand. Wish you well and sorry again for this.

And a phone call from another:

> It's me. I'm sorry. We had a meeting this morning. They say we cannot go out randomly. They said it's no good, we cannot go out. I'm really sorry. . . . I'll explain this to you sometime when we meet in person. I'm really sorry.

The conflation of any foreign or international connection with the "political" selectively denies Tibetans full membership in the global community, even in this era of intensified globalization.

Summer

Helicopters. There they were, the first morning I returned in June, fifteen months after the unrest: two helicopters flying low, circling the city, heading north. A few hours later they appeared again, flying south. A new part of the cityscape, every morning and evening and sometimes in between, two or three helicopters circled slowly, almost grazing the rooftops. How much must it cost, I wondered, to fly so low above such high ground? Did the expenses incurred count as part of the central government's generous investment in the development of Tibet? And why was it necessary, given all the new surveillance cameras that had appeared in the last year? It's no longer possible to walk ten meters in the Barkor without another camera capturing and recording you, so the helicopters seemed an expensive redundancy at best.

It was especially surprising to see them in the summer, the peak of the tourist season, when normalcy would, I thought, be key to marketability. There were still many Chinese tourists, and a few clusters of foreign tourists here and there, but the streets seemed strangely empty, nothing like the throngs of tourists and sold-out hotels of 2005, 2006, 2007. Despite high tourist season, the People's Armed Police were still out in full force, groups of four or five in their army fatigues standing at attention with their riot shields and guns. The only thing that had changed since December was that some of the groups were now posted inside police barricade tapes. Looking down from my hotel window, I saw a group of five armed and riot shield–bearing Han soldiers, young and fresh-faced but wearing stern visages, marching in formation down Beijing Road. The two in front walked in lockstep with a little Tibetan *mo-la*, an elderly woman stooped over, carrying a bucket, sandwiched between them. She turned her head to look at one soldier and then back at the ground, trying as best she could to scurry along, but couldn't quite muster the strength to pass them, nor did they try to walk around her, but simply surrounded her as part of their rigid, moving formation.

The evidence accumulates that guilt is fate, that the zone of indistinction between law and violence is wide and dismal. "Afterwards, people were arrested for no reason." No questions were asked, no attempt to determine innocence or guilt of participating in the unrest, or of committing a crime. Just arrest.

> Once my husband was outside of the apartment complex when he saw some police who looked like they might come after him. He turned very slowly and very calmly started to walk away. A young couple also saw the police, were frightened, and started to run. The police saw they were running and so grabbed them, yanked them by their hair, and threw them into the police car and hauled them away. There was no evidence they had done anything wrong. They were guilty of being frightened of the police. For two or three months afterwards, young men dared not step outside of their houses. Going outside meant exposing oneself to the likelihood of arrest. No reason needed. They arrested thousands. Sometimes they arrest people in groups at night. These days everyone is frightened. Even in your own home you're frightened. Whenever there's a knock on the door, even if it turns out just to be a friend, it's terrifying. It might be the police coming to take you away. They don't need a reason these days. You don't need to have done anything at all. They went to the big courtyards and ordered all the young men out. They pointed a gun at each one and asked, "Did you participate in Three-One-Four [The demonstrations of March 14, 2008]?" Anyone who appeared nervous was arrested and thrown in jail. Of course many people were nervous, even if they hadn't participated. It's too frightening to live here.

7 Engineering Indebtedness and Image

Comfortable Housing and the New Socialist Countryside

> Hence, giving becomes a means of acquiring a power. Gift-giving has the virtue of a surpassing of the subject who gives, but in exchange for the object given, the subject appropriates the surpassing: He regards his virtue, that which he had the capacity for, as an asset, a power that he now possesses.
>
> —Georges Bataille, *The Accursed Share*, 1989

> The society which carries the spectacle does not dominate the underdeveloped regions by its economic hegemony alone. It dominates them as the society of the spectacle. Even where the material base is still absent, modern society has already invaded the social surface . . . by means of the spectacle.
>
> —Guy Debord, *Society of the Spectacle*, 1967

Since the 1980s, and particularly after the deepening of market reforms after 1992, the Chinese state has staked the legitimization of its sovereignty over Tibet on Tibetan gratitude for the gift of development. In 1985, the Central Committee of the CCP and the State Council announced that the Yangzhuoyong Lake Power Station would be constructed "as a gift to Tibetan people."[1] The sixty-two large-scale Aid-Tibet projects launched in the TAR with the Third Work Forum on Tibet in 1994, which marked a turning point ending culturally liberal policies and ushering in large-scale Han migration to Tibet, were presented as a "gift to the Tibetan people."[2] The fortieth anniversary of the founding of the TAR in 2005 provided another occasion for the prominent presentation of development "gifts," including an electric power control system, the expansion of West Liberation Road leading into Lhasa, and new houses on Highway 318 between Lhasa and Gongkar Airport.[3] In the late 2000s, a new gift became common: houses. The State Council released a White Paper in March 2009 stating:

> Thanks to the care of the central authorities and the support of the whole nation, Tibet has witnessed remarkable progress in economic

> and social development. . . . Before the democratic reform, more than 90 percent of Tibet's residents had no private housing, the peasants and herdsmen had very poor living conditions. . . . Today, with the construction of a new countryside and the Comfortable Housing Project underway, 200,000 households, comprising nearly one million peasants and herdsmen, have moved into modern houses.[4]

The Comfortable Housing Project, as part of the construction of the New Socialist Countryside, is a program of large-scale investment in rural housing across the TAR that began in 2006. By January 2010, the TAR government announced that through a total investment of 13.3 billion yuan (1.95 billion USD) the program had "solved housing problems for 1.2 million farmers and herdsmen from 230,000 farming and herding families, which accounts for 80 percent of the demographic with relatively poor housing conditions" in the entire TAR a year ahead of schedule, and that by the end of 2010, the "housing problems for the remaining 20 percent of farmers and herdsmen" would also be solved.[5] Of the total investment, some 500 million USD came from direct government subsidies.[6]

This spectacular wave of rural and peri-urban house building has generated substantial controversy. In a newspaper article published shortly after the launching of the program, reporter Tim Johnson claimed that "In a massive campaign that recalls the socialist engineering of an earlier era, the Chinese government has relocated some 250,000 Tibetans—nearly one-tenth of the population—from scattered rural hamlets to new 'socialist villages,' ordering them to build new housing largely at their own expense and without their consent."[7] In response to being misquoted by Johnson in the same article, anthropologist Melvyn Goldstein responded with this assessment of the Comfortable Housing project in Shigatse, in the western TAR:

> The general housing program is part of the CCP's attempt to raise the standard of living of rural Tibetans . . . The housing program now underway is meant to encourage and financially assist villagers to build new houses. . .This is a popular program in the areas where we work and is voluntary. . . this is a relatively benign program aimed at improving the quality of life and goes along with government interest in speeding up rural electrification, running water programs, etc.[8]

According to Goldstein, Childs, and Wangdui, the program represents a shift in Chinese development strategy nationally as well as in Tibet toward one of "people first" (*yi ren wei ben*) development, which turns away from a strict emphasis on GDP growth toward social improvement and people's livelihoods. In contrast, drawing on James Scott's notion of "seeing like a state" and the reordering of society from above for legibility, Françoise

Robin describes the program as one of "reshaping the rural landscape and controlling its inhabitants," leading to "the total disruption of the social network of the countryside."[9]

This chapter speaks to the substantial controversy that has surrounded different interpretations of this house-building program by taking seriously the official narrative of the houses, a synecdoche of development, as a gift—a form of indebtedness engineering.[10] As anthropologist Charlene Makley writes of her work on gendered development encounters in Rebgong, an Amdo Tibetan area of Qinghai Province, recent state development campaigns have offered the "Chinese state and private investors the powerful moral high ground of the generous (obligation-free) gift . . . any gift publicly taken as 'generous' must be seen as the outcome of a politics of conversion."[11] Accepting the official narrative of housing by conceptualizing it as a gift productively illuminates the contradictions of development and Tibetan agency in producing the landscape, providing a way to steer between the antinomies of the interpretive debate over new housing in Tibet. The gift relationship calls into question the very meaningfulness of the question of "voluntary" participation in such development programs. At the same time the logic of the generous gift also elucidates the importance of visual prominence, of being seen and thus acknowledged. Spectacle, that is, is integral to Comfortable Housing, and more generally to development and state territorialization in Tibet.

The Grammar of the Gift

Mary Douglas comments in her introduction to Marcel Mauss's *The Gift* that "the idea of a pure gift is a contradiction."[12] Indeed, the central theme of the voluminous anthropological scholarship on the subject is that there is no such thing as a free gift. Instead, the gift is always double-edged, containing elements of both present and poison, generosity and violence, sharing and debt. The question of reciprocity therefore looms large. Mauss was particularly occupied with the question of what creates the obligation to reciprocate in "archaic" societies. Though his answer about the entanglement of the giver's soul (the *hau*) in the gift was widely rejected, his question motivated a long-standing concern with the question of reciprocity.[13]

Marshall Sahlins's typology of gift exchanges classifies gifts by three types of reciprocity: generalized, balanced, and negative. In generalized reciprocity, often illustrated by the parent-child relationship, the obligation to reciprocate is repressed or not overt, but it is not absent.[14] However, it is generalized reciprocity, rather than balanced or negative reciprocity, that reaffirms the social hierarchy and differential power relations over time.[15] The trope of Tibetans as children of the patriarchal parent-state is pervasive in Tibet, with Han and Tibetans portrayed both as "daughters of one mother—China" as well as elder and younger brothers of the broader Chinese (*Zhonghua*) nation.[16] The widespread deployment of the family metaphor, including some Tibetans' anthropomorphization of "Father State," giving a singular agency to the state and casting it as a patriarchal father figure,[17] suggests the relevance of generalized reciprocity for the state development gift.

However, this raises a number of questions: What are the implications of Mauss's work on "archaic" societies for modern states? What are its implications for relations not between social actors, but between a state and its citizens? Modern, centralized state societies with an advanced division of labor and a significant commercial sector enable the ideology, though not the reality, of a "pure" gift—one that is given completely without reciprocity, obligation, and recognition, by placing gifts and commodities in two separate social systems.[18] Within this modern ideology, "commodity exchange establishes objective quantitative relationships between the objects transacted, while gift exchange establishes personal qualitative relationships between the subjects transacting," a highly abstracted simplification of what is often the blurring or overlap of these transactional orders.[19]

Nevertheless, the ideology of the pure gift is significant in that it fosters economism. The argument that a gift originates from a pure impulse of generosity and truly entails no obligation assumes, in a sense, the same autonomous individuals found in economic models.[20] Thus, the conviction of a free, pure gift, unentangled by social ties and obligations of any kind, actually entrenches "the ideological elaboration of a domain in which self-interest rules supreme."[21] Indeed, this is why Mauss came to his moral conclusion that the combination of interest and disinterest is preferable to their separation.

The ideology of development as a pure, free gift is belied by the prevalence of conditionality of all kinds.[22] Development aid is highly asymmetric and an effective practice of symbolic domination, in its transformation of the donor's status from dominant to generous. The international development aid system pervades state building and sets it in motion, configuring recipient countries as spaces for the cultivation of donors' values.[23] As discussed in the introduction, however, literature that considers development from the lens of the gift has for the most part considered the relationship between international donors and recipients, or interstate relationships, rather than the relationship between a nation-state and its own citizens.[24]

In considering this latter relationship, as I have argued, we cannot reify the state, assuming it is a discrete, coherent, ontologically real object. Yet this is precisely what the grammar of the gift creates: a recognition and consolidation of a reified giver, or as Derrida suggests, "a subject and a verb, a constituted subject . . . seeking . . . to constitute its own identity."[25] This grammar of the gift is crucial to understanding how development-as-gift works to deepen state territorialization. The Tibetan receipt of housing as gift is not the outcome of a rational strategy by a unified actor called the state, which can be clearly bounded and definitively delineated from the nonstate. Individual state authorities, government officials such as TAR Party Secretary Zhang Qingli, propose specific policies, implemented by others. The larger effect of such development projects, however, is to consolidate recognition of the state by asserting a separation between the state, which does the developing through giving, and its populace, the object and recipient of the development-gift.[26] In contrast to disciplinary power and its meticulous ordering of space and movement, development uses the "gentler" violence of gratitude to reinforce the effect of a state that lacks ontological presence in and of itself.

By positioning the Tibetan populace as recipients of the development gift, the grammar of the gift naturalizes the PRC as a spatial container for Tibetans and makes a claim that the Chinese state is the legitimate caregiver for this contentious space within the broader Chinese nation. As such, the gift becomes an alibi that at once claims the TAR as Chinese territory and structures a specific response to the lack of appreciation of the gift by its unruly residents. In particular, when the gift fails, when recipients refuse to act properly loyal, rejecting recognition of belonging to the nation-state, sovereign power exercises its presence by relegating these recipients to a zone of indistinction associated with the state of exception, as was graphically demonstrated in the aftermath of 2008.

Gifts as Spectacles

In his work on the gift, Mauss made frequent use of the example of the potlatch, in which material goods as well as rituals, military services, women, and children are exchanged. Failure to participate in the seemingly voluntary giving and receipt of presents leads to warfare. Mauss describes this competitive giving in these terms:

> The purely sumptuary form of consumption . . . in which considerable amounts of goods that have taken a long time to amass are suddenly given away or even destroyed, particularly in the case of the potlatch, give such institutions the appearance of representing lavish expenditure and childish prodigality. In effect, and in reality, . . . useful things are given away. . . . But the reason for these gifts . . . [is that it is] through such gifts [that] a hierarchy is established.[27]

For such hierarchies to be established, the gifts must not only be lavish, but just as important, visibly lavish for all to see. The social relations reproduced by the potlatch work through a process of bearing witness.[28] The sumptuary destruction of accumulated wealth produces hierarchy, recognition, and power only if the wealth is dramatically displayed before it is destroyed or given away; it must, in other words, be a spectacle.

The gift character of the gargantuan wave of house building, resembling a potlatch in its scale and grandeur, points to the role of spectacle in development in the TAR. By using the term spectacle here, I mean to emphasize the rule of appearances, and the elevation of the realm of the image as a technique of power. I draw on Guy Debord's notion of domination of underdeveloped areas through the "surface" of spectacle and image, rather than through economic hegemony alone.[29] This surface of the spectacle works not only in a negative, repressive, controlling sense, but also as a positive form of power, one that produces.[30]

In contrast to the concentrated spectacle of bureaucratic dictatorship that dominated the Maoist era's parades and campaigns, the diffuse spectacle of capitalism that characterizes the development gift is one of commodity fetishism. For Debord, both forms of spectacle are united as "different forms of a single alienation," which is the "existing order's uninterrupted discourse about itself, its laudatory monologue."[31] In postreform Tibet, the diffuse spectacle of development works both as what Debord describes as a "permanent opium war which aims to make people identify goods with commodities,"[32] and as a means of communication of the state with its citizenry. In the provision of houses on a massive scale, the spectacle of development appears not in the form of rituals or parades but through the materiality of the built landscape itself. The solid, persistent spectacle of new concrete and other structures communicates not only with Tibetan recipient participants, for whom the houses reinforce the presence of the state, but also with Chinese citizens, for whom they reinstantiate the logic of the state as generous gift giver. Indeed, the spectacle is more convincing for the latter, while Tibetan participants comment on the duplicity of the newly built landscape by calling their new houses examples of "image engineering."

The New Socialist Countryside and Comfortable Housing

First announced in October 2005 at the Fifth Plenum of the Sixteenth Party Congress, the "Construction of the New Socialist Countryside" (*shehuizhuyi xinnongcun jianshe*) was declared the top priority for China's modernization, and the most important national goal in the Eleventh Five Year Plan period (2006–10). More of an overarching strategy than a concrete plan, it clearly indicated an intention, in the face of CCP concern about increasing rural unrest, to focus on rural development and to redistribute resources and income toward rural areas. Specific measures associated nationally with the New Socialist Countryside included the complete elimination of agricultural taxes, extension of the rural cooperative medical system, and elimination of fees for compulsory education in rural areas. Other plans and goals included the installation of more rural water conservancy facilities for both drinking water and irrigation, road construction, provision of more affordable hospitals, expanded use of biogas and solar energy, and completion of the rural power network and electrification for all citizens by 2015. In terms of the New Socialist Countryside's priority areas such as education, labor productivity, living standards, and access to medical personnel, the most progress has been made in China's wealthy eastern provinces, while the TAR ranks at the very bottom of the list.[33]

The New Socialist Countryside has been partly influenced by the New Rural Reconstruction Movement, an intellectual, student, and peasant movement that has called for attention to rural livelihoods and for "industry helping agriculture" rather than agriculture continuing its long role of supporting industry. However, whereas the New Rural Reconstruction Movement calls for cooperatives and the revival of culture as a Polanyian "double movement" response to the rural crisis engendered by China's insertion into global capitalism, the state campaign is ultimately aimed at deepening capitalist relations by building a greater internal market for consumer goods. Unlike the New Rural Reconstruction Movement, the state New Socialist Countryside project does not call for a revalorization of traditional culture or champion a value system opposed to an overriding emphasis on economics; indeed in Tibet, the New Socialist Countryside very much promotes the opposite.[34]

In both means and ends, the New Socialist Countryside also resonates with Mao-era campaigns. In fact, the very same phrase, "new socialist countryside," was frequently used from the 1950s to the 1970s, such as in 1956 when the National People's Congress embraced as its "struggle target" the goal of "constructing a new socialist countryside."[35] Like the past campaigns, the current New Socialist Countryside also calls for improving rural infrastructure and rural cooperative medical services, and free compulsory education; it has been organized through propaganda and lecture teams, and has at times been coercively implemented.[36] In one case in Henan Province, officials and teachers were required to return to their home villages to pull out crops planted in front of peasant homes and along roads in the name of "village beautification," and poor villagers who objected were threatened with having their welfare subsidies discontinued.[37] Critics have dubbed illegal land grabs for conversion to lucrative real estate development in the name of the New Socialist Countryside, as in the case of Dongkar in Lhasa, "fake urbanization leap forward."[38]

Implementation of the New Socialist Countryside in the TAR differs significantly from the national program in one key respect: the key focus of government spending on providing new houses for basically all of the TAR's rural residents. The TAR is the only provincial-level entity with such a project. In contrast, the provision of housing is not mentioned as a component of the New Socialist Countryside nationally, where the emphasis has been on improving rural infrastructure, education, and medical services. Once again, the TAR is a zone of exception.

The TAR house-building program is managed by the Comfortable Housing Project (*anju gongcheng*) Office, under the Finance Bureau.[39] Like "New Socialist Countryside," the term "Comfortable Housing Project" has been used nationwide, but refers to something different than in the TAR. The national program targeted urban areas in the 1990s as part of housing and real estate reform, and aimed to rapidly increase the total stock of urban housing. It involved mortgage loans and was designed to enable a transition to a more market-based housing system, as well as to solve structural housing shortage problems created over several decades by the work unit housing allocation system. The identically named TAR program is directed at rural housing, does not generally increase the total stock of housing, and involves outright subsidies and three- to five-year bank loans, rather than market-based, longer-term mortgage loans.[40]

At its launching in 2006, the TAR government announced that within five years the Comfortable Housing Project would provide housing for 80 percent of the 70 percent of all rural TAR households in need of new housing, with the remaining 20 percent to be built soon after. The figure of 70 percent was determined by excluding the 117,800 rural households deemed to have already "enjoyed government policies" to receive "safe and appropriate" housing, that is, which had already been targets of programs including settlement of herders, resettlement for poverty alleviation, and housing for farmers in Tolung Dechen County who had lost their land. Lhasa Municipality's implementation of these programs in 2004–5, together with a 2005 project to build new houses along the Lhasa–Gongkar Airport highway, were cited as valuable experience for the implementation of the region-wide Comfortable Housing Project.[41] In 2008, Lhasa Municipality and Nyingtri and Ngari Prefectures declared that they had met their 80 percent targets two years ahead of schedule, and the following year, the regional government announced that the TAR as a whole had completed the plan of 80 percent, or a total of 219,840 households, one year ahead of schedule. By the end of 2010, the TAR declared that it had brought new housing to all rural households in one form or another.[42]

The Comfortable Housing Project thus became an umbrella term to integrate a number of previously fragmented rural housing projects in place before the Eleventh Five Year Plan: "pastoral sedentarization" (*mumin dingju*); resettlement from endemic disease areas; resettlement for poverty alleviation; the "prosperous borders and wealthy households" (*xinbian gongcheng*) project for border areas; and "house renovation" (*minfang gaizhao*). Pastoral sedentarization aimed at providing housing for

40,396 pastoral families, many along the sides of roads, throughout the TAR. This was a continuation of a long-standing effort to help pastoralists "strive toward modern, civilized, new lives," but is not to be confused with ecological migration, a pastoral resettlement effort, implemented primarily in Qinghai Province, meant to move herders and their livestock entirely off the land.[43] Resettlement from endemic disease areas has largely been for villages where Kashin-Beck disease, a bone disorder associated with iodine insufficiency and fungal contamination of barley grains, is prevalent. Poverty relief includes both resettlement from disaster areas and additional subsidies for house construction. The "prosperous borders and wealthy households" project is designed to "enrich the border inhabitants, consolidate frontier defense, and enhance the border inhabitants' patriotism," and includes the heavily subsidized construction of houses, as well as building of roads, communications infrastructure, and towns.[44]

However, by far the largest component of Comfortable Housing Project, and the only one relevant to peri-urban Lhasa, is house renovation, a term that encompasses both the remodeling and the reconstruction of existing houses as well as the building of completely new houses, and which applies to all rural households that are not already targets of the other specialized projects.[45] Direct subsidies from the TAR government varied for each of these different types of housing, with house renovation set at 10,000 RMB per household.[46] Local governments also contributed in some areas; Lhasa Municipality contributed 4000 RMB per household, making the standard subsidy in the municipality 14,000 RMB per household.[47]

Some media reports about Comfortable Housing suggested that government investment in the first year alone was more than 2.8 billion yuan, and that the government investment over five years was 13.3 billion or even 15 billion yuan.[48] However, these figures actually represent the total investment, not that from government subsidies alone; the latter is in the range of 500 million USD, or some 3.2 billion yuan.[49] The basic funding principle of Comfortable Housing from the beginning has been that the primary source would be funds raised by farmers and herders themselves, with auxiliary funding from financial subsidies, and investment from Aid-Tibet counterparts and credit funds, as summarized in the saying "The state gives a bit, financial administration subsidizes a bit, the bank borrows a bit, the masses prepare a bit, and society helps a bit."[50] Overall, government subsidies account for one-sixth to one-third of house building costs.[51] Averaged across Lhasa Municipality, government subsidies accounted for 33 percent of total home investment, 21 percent came from bank loans, 23 percent was contributed through rural labor, and the remaining 23 percent was farmers' own cash investment from their savings or through private loans. Closer to the city of Lhasa, subsidies generally account for 20–33 percent of the total cost of the houses.[52] While official figures suggest that farmers' own investment, including private lending, existing savings, and value contributed through local labor account for around 46 percent, Goldstein, Childs, and Wangdui found in Shigatse that farmers themselves contributed roughly 60 percent of actual expenditures.[53]

The program came with conditions. Across the TAR, the government required houses to be built with separate accommodations for people and livestock, changing a long tradition in many areas in which the ground floor of a house is a barn. In Lhasa Municipality, the new houses were also supposed to separate kitchens from bedrooms, and to have at least 20 square meters per household member. Households were provided with a collection of blueprints from the TAR Construction Bureau, all of which met these biopolitical requirements, implemented with the intention of improving hygiene and health.

Aside from these conditions, however, there were no region-wide mandates for the building of houses. The regional government's building principle was encapsulated as "resettlement where it is appropriate to resettle; build new where it is appropriate to build new; renovate where it is appropriate to renovate."[54] County governments were supposed to decide in consultation with village committees, on a voluntary basis, to resettle "if appropriate," and if so, to move near township headquarters, roads, villages, and streams. The choice of whether to build or renovate was supposed to be voluntarily decided by the individual household, and building materials were to be those that were locally available.

However, local governments sometimes imposed additional requirements. Tolung Dechen County mandated that houses could not be built with traditional mud bricks and instead must be constructed of concrete or stone bricks. Other local governments mandated that all construction be completed in one year, that houses must have concrete floors and stairs, or that new houses must be concentrated and built alongside roads, a favored approach for making the provision of various social services easier and less costly. The closer to major roads and to Lhasa, the more likely villagers were required to rebuild in new locations. The TAR government claims that overall 80 percent of new houses were built in their original locations and the remaining 20 percent were shifted within their villages and townships, though Chinese scholars have pointed out an overemphasis on concentration in the implementation of the program.[55]

The choice of whether to renovate an existing house or rebuild a new one was also supposed to be up to the individual household, though much more rebuilding appears to have taken place than renovation. The Lhasa Municipality Comfortable Housing Project Office estimated that 80 percent of households built new houses. In an evaluation midway through the program, Chinese scholars pointed out that the emphasis on new construction and relative neglect of rebuilding and expansion were a problem, as was local governments' additions "to the basic requirements laid down by the regional government, arranging construction responsibilities that exceed the plan and are not appropriate . . . adding to the herders' and farmers' burden."[56] Despite these and other criticisms, however, new construction has been emphasized, contrary to the stated principles but perhaps not to the overall spirit of the Comfortable Housing Project as key to the achievement of the New Socialist Countryside in the TAR.

Why Housing? Cultivating Self-development, Securing Sovereignty

Given the national focus of the New Socialist Countryside Program on rural development through provision of rural infrastructure, medical services, and education, why is the construction of private houses the overwhelming thrust of the program in the TAR? The focus on the need to improve and civilize housing of segments of the population deemed particularly backward and in need of improvement can be seen in the history of development and nation making around the world. Timothy Mitchell describes plans and attempts to destroy old houses and construct new model villages for peasants in Egypt in the 1940s and again in a 1990s development project. He argues that peasants are framed as the constitutive outside of the modern nation, declared to be "uncivilized and unhygienic so that in rendering them civilized and clean, the nation could be made." They can enter into the nation only by submitting to an act of violence: eviction from and reconstruction of their intimate spaces of dwelling.[57] Even more so than peasants, Tibetans are the constitutive outside of the Chinese nation, both excluded and included through development and the urge to remake their backward ways of living.

More specifically, the disproportionate spending on housing can be traced to TAR Party Secretary Zhang Qingli, who is credited in policy documents and media reports for developing a theory of Comfortable Housing as both the "incision point" (*tupuo kou*) and "breakthrough point" (*qieru dian*) for the achievement of the New Socialist Countryside in Tibet. Official reports said that he was motivated by his travels in rural areas shortly after being appointed to his post in May 2006, during which, "of all of the things he saw, the poor state of the houses of local farmers and herdsmen moved him the most." He therefore decided to help improve the lives of local people by improving their houses, saying, "This is the Tibetan way of building the New Socialist Countryside."[58] His utterances suggest the othering of Tibetans as outside the properly developed Chinese nation because of their unhygienic and uncivilized ways of life, which must be changed for them to be included in the nation, while simultaneously suggesting Tibetan desire to be included through these transformations—for example: "In the construction of the New Socialist Countryside, the thing that ordinary people most long for is to be able to live in safe and suitable houses, to be able to drink clean and hygienic water . . . and to be able to hear the sound of the Party and the central government."

The official justification for Comfortable Housing as the breakthrough point is grounded in the assertion that Tibet's form of the New Socialist Countryside must be unique compared to other parts of China, because of the "constraints of Tibet's special natural geographic environment and its society and history" and its "special geographic location," which result in Tibet's rural economic development having "weighty and fundamental social contradictions."[59] Yang, An, and Zhou note that because of the TAR's atypical secondary sector, the TAR cannot simply copy the *neidi* model of industry leading agriculture, but instead should prioritize investment in agricultural production in order to increase rural income. However, they go on to suggest that the key to reaching the goals of the construction of the New Socialist Countryside, which they define as being to "develop production, a comfortable livelihood, civilized local customs, neat and tidy villages, and democratic governance," is not to invest in agricultural production but rather to raise the quality (*suzhi*) of the farmers and herders, and to improve the relatively weak "self-development capacity" of Tibetans.[60]

An official at the Lhasa Municipality Comfortable Housing Project Office explained the logic of the self-cultivation of development subjects in more detail:

> The changes in the living conditions of the nomads and farmers brought about by Comfortable Housing will spur the construction of basic infrastructure and drive changes in their basic way of thinking. This can drive a whole series of things; it is the starting point. First the very basic thing is the living conditions, with many generations squeezed in one house–father, brides, and grooms. This is very common among Tibetans. So the idea is to change their way of living. . . . Comfortable Housing is the breakthrough point, the most basic foundation for the New Socialist Countryside. A foundation: first I need to have a good place to live and then I can think about other things. Now that my house is built, I need furniture. I need to buy that, so I need money for it, so then I need to make money. It's a way of changing people's mindsets.

Government leaders claim that through participation in the Comfortable Housing Project, rural residents' "wait, depend, and request" mentality has changed to one that is more proactive and market-oriented.[61] By receiving the gift of development, they become more rational economic actors. This posits the provision of new and improved housing for the rural residents of the TAR as a mechanism for Tibet to finally leave behind its "blood transfusion" economy through yet another massive subsidy that will finally transform Tibetans into higher *suzhi* subjects who improve themselves toward greater productivity. Living in higher-quality houses should cultivate a greater desire for material goods as well as the will to work hard as market actors to achieve the newly desired level of consumption. New modern houses will transform Tibetans into subjects who desire development, providing the "structural adjustment in the sphere of human subjectivity" needed to raise their *suzhi*, transform their consciousness, and thus begin to solve the problem of development.[62] This is, fundamentally, the theory of why Comfortable Housing will work as the entry point and catalyst for achieving the broader goals of the New Socialist Countryside, of improved rural livelihoods in Tibet.

However, closely intertwined is another logic, of housing as a form of development for which Tibetans cannot but be grateful, which in turn binds Tibetans ever closer to the state space of the PRC, securing state territorialization. Officials claim that the project has

> made rural residents firmly believe that only the CCP can help them live in houses that they never dared dream about and strengthened their confidence and determination to follow the Party wholeheartedly. It is effective political education for rural residents. It promotes Lhasa's harmony and stability and the relationship between the cadres and the masses. . . . It has helped establish a good image for Lhasa domestically and internationally and has become a window for socio-economic development that the city has achieved.[63]

Thus, the project is to bring not just development, but also its inseparable twin, stability—the disappearance of challenges to state sovereignty. Gratitude for housing is expected to bring Tibetans closer to the CCP and its cadres, and push them further from the Dalai Lama. The director of the Lhasa Municipal Comfortable Housing Project Office extolled the virtues of the program:

> The Dalai repeats over and over again whatever about "human rights," but despite his decades of shouting, he has not contributed one single brick, one cow, or one penny to the rural masses of Tibet. No matter how pleasantly he speaks, there is no way for him to let the rural people live in safe and usable housing.[64]

To bolster such arguments, scholars and officials draw on the State Council's statement that improving the livelihoods of the rural masses is not only the number one requisite for Tibet's socio-economic development, but also "the basic condition and foundation for grasping the initiative in our struggle against the Dalai clique."[65]

Furthermore, intertwined with the role of housing in securing territory and achieving development is its design to also achieve the image of development, for both local residents and Chinese and international observers. Officials repeatedly stress its status as a "window for socio-economic development" and its utility in establishing "a good image." As a place saddled with place imaginaries of underdevelopment and backwardness, Tibet must perform its development, conjuring it into existence. The image of development is key to its status as gift: gifts must be visible to have an impact. They must be seen to be effective.[66]

Indebtedness Engineering

Expectations of gratitude, recognition of the PRC Party-state, and performances of loyalty belie Comfortable Housing as a free gift. But this is not the only way in which the gift is not free. Because government subsidies cover on average only 25–33 percent of the total cost of houses, the remainder must come from bank loans and farmers' own savings or private loans. According to a regulation enacted by the TAR branch of the Agricultural Bank of China (ABC) in April 2007, households became eligible for 10,000 to 30,000 RMB loans, with loans for multistory houses not to exceed 30,000 RMB and for single-floor houses not to exceed 10,000 RMB. These were three-year loans on which local governments paid the interest, making the loans effectively interest-free for their recipients for three years.[67]

In conjunction with local branches of the ABC, county governments determine households' eligibility for and the amounts of these loans based on assets and perceived ability to repay. Officially designated poverty households are eligible for larger subsidies, but not loans. The 2007 ABC regulation officially separated the Comfortable Housing loan program from an existing TAR loan program that had been initiated in 2001 and made certain households eligible for three levels of loans (referred to as gold, silver, and copper cards) for productive investments such as tractors and trucks.[68] Nevertheless, local officials in many places continued to tie house construction or renovation to this three-card system, allowing only those who qualified for a card to borrow for a house, and limiting households' ability to borrow for other investments.

Like borrowers across China, households around Lhasa are deeply uncomfortable with being in debt for housing, frequently citing their bank and private debts as being of great concern.[69] Worries about indebtedness are more pronounced in villages closest to Lhasa and along major roads, where specific requirements about house size and construction material have been strictly enforced and where houses therefore cost more on average than in other areas, or where local officials have applied pressure on households that are reluctant to build. In some villages close to Lhasa, residents also expressed resentment against locally imposed rules requiring the demolition, or banning the rental or sale, of old houses.[70] Renting and selling are technically forbidden, though sometimes practiced informally, because rural households do not have house deeds. Comfortable Housing Project houses do not come with formal house deeds, though some township governments and administrative villages are issuing "township house deeds" or "small house deeds," for those who pay back their bank loans, while withholding them from those who do not. These unofficial deeds recognize a household's long-term use rights to the house (but not the land), but do not afford the same protections and rights as official deeds.[71]

The Comfortable Housing Project's interest-free loans were originally set to expire in three years. However by 2007 the TAR branch of the ABC had extended the loan period from three to up to ten years; villagers would be required to pay the interest on the loans after three years but time to pay off the principal was lengthened, in order to "reduce the burden" on farmers and pastoralists.[72] This change reflected bank as well as policymakers' concerns about nonpayment of the loans. United Front official Bi Hua argued, for example, that some farmers and pastoralists would not be able to repay, while others were not willing to do so. This would in effect transfer their credit risk onto banks, "likely turning into bad credit for the banks and in the end, the government will have to pay the bill."[73] Similarly, a TAR bank research group suggested that villagers should avoid overinvestment in houses that interfered with investment in productive activities, and proposed the establishment of a government fund to guarantee the loans in order to reduce credit risk for financial institutions.[74]

Ultimately, both because there is no established, legal rural housing market, and given the nature of this housing-as-development program, foreclosure is not a possibility. Though banks try to exert pressure on villagers to repay loans, houses themselves are not taken back. The absence of a rural housing market prevents a rural house from having an exchange value. As noncommodities, these houses are governed instead by the logic of the gift, always retaining an association with the giver and primary owner, namely the state. Debt forgiveness transforms a monetary debt into a larger debt of gratitude. Indeed, a United Front official states this very directly, recommending that for especially impoverished households, "the government should grant special care and completely relieve them of all of their debts, in order to let this 'benevolent project' of Comfortable Housing sit at the bottom of the farmers' and herders' hearts."[75]

In addition to the bank loans, which generally account for one-sixth to one-third of the total cost of building, most households also have to take out private loans. In Shigatse, an average of two-thirds of the households' own investment come from savings while one-third comes from private borrowing.[76] Goldstein, Childs, and Wangdui observe that loans from relatives in Shigatse normally do not come with repayment deadlines or interest.[77] By contrast, private loans around Lhasa, often from those who have salaried positions in the urban area, typically have interest rates around

12 percent, which a bank report suggested could negatively affect the region's financial stability.[78] Regardless of interest rates, it is clear that the Comfortable Housing Project engineered a massive wave of indebtedness, both to banks and private lenders, as well as to the state for its subsidies, over the five-year span of the project. Before returning to a general discussion of housing as gift, I turn next to a closer look at how the project has been implemented, understood, experienced, and negotiated in different locations around Lhasa.

Image Engineering: Houses by the Side of the Road

Both the giving of gifts and the obligatory performance of gratitude marked the 2005 celebration of the fortieth anniversary of the founding of the TAR. A poster distributed to rural residents across the TAR for the occasion (see figure 8) depicts CCP General Secretary Hu Jintao, who advanced to his position by cracking down strongly and enforcing martial law after the Lhasa demonstrations in the late 1980s when he was TAR Party secretary, draped in Tibetan ceremonial scarves and offered *chang* by two Tibetan women wearing elaborate Tibetan headdresses and huge smiles. They gaze adoringly upward toward Hu Jintao, while he looks ahead. Their bodily posture suggests not only that Tibetans were delighted by and welcomed the return of Hu Jintao to the TAR, but also their subordination and gratitude for his presence and all that it signified.

Among the development gifts presented at the fortieth anniversary was the Lhasa-Gongkar Road House Renovation project, which included both remodeling and rebuilding of houses along the new, shorter section of Highway 318 between Lhasa and Gongkar Airport just in time for the celebration of the anniversary. TAR Vice Governor Lobsang Gyaltsen announced that this housing project was implemented "to demonstrate to the outside the vast changes of socio-economic development and reform and opening in the TAR, and to *give a gift* to the fortieth anniversary of the TAR."[79]

Cited as a pilot project for the implementation of Comfortable Housing, the Highway 318 project shared with Comfortable Housing not only the same funding structure but also the goal of serving as a "breakthrough point" and stimulating villagers' desire to achieve a better standard of living and self-development. On its completion, one government report suggested extending the project to other main roads in the TAR so that "*the appearance* of farmers and herders' housing conditions will be improved." Another report suggested that the project had stimulated villagers' awareness of and desire to reach a prosperous (*xiaokang*) standard of living, that it had produced "three new's"—new villages, new houses, and new appearance, and further that the creation of a new village appearance had stimulated the tourism industry.[80] The participants referred to themselves as being part of *namdrang* (Wylie: *rnam grangs*), or "the Project," the general term with which Tibetans refer to Comfortable Housing. Thus I include it here as one of many variations on the Comfortable Housing Project, one that particularly stresses the visual element of the gift—the importance of the *appearance* and the gazing at or witnessing of the generosity of development.

The very first village after the crossing of the Yarlung Tsangpo and Kyichu Rivers on the way from Gongkar to Lhasa is Nub village, one of two administrative villages in the township of Chushur County where the housing project was implemented. The 287 households were informed in 2004 that all families living within two hundred meters of the road were required to demolish their old houses and build new ones by August 2005, regardless of when their current houses had been built. In addition, two of the five teams, or natural villages, were required to completely relocate to the side of the road. Those who did not live within two hundred meters of the road and who were not required to relocate could, if they chose, remodel rather than rebuild their houses; altogether 75 percent of the households rebuilt. Because of the short time frame, households were not able to use their own labor. Instead a Tibetan construction contractor, who hired both Han and Tibetan laborers, handled the job, making the houses more expensive than they would have been had local labor been used. However, painting of the house trims was the responsibility of the individual families. In July 2005 the villagers were in a panic because their houses had only recently been completed and they had only until mid-August to paint their houses or face a fine. Those households who did get their painting done on time received a bonus after the official tours were over. As one villager explained to me, "Hu Jintao said the houses here are no good. Now he's coming back [for the anniversary] and he wants to see how much things have improved."

The ground areas of the new houses, including courtyards, were standardized according to household size.[81] Initially all affected households were told they were required to build two-floor houses, though as the deadline approached, a few who could not afford to build two floors were allowed to build only one. All but a few houses along the road have two floors whereas many of the houses further back, which cannot be seen from the street, have only one story. More strictly enforced was the building of a separate area for livestock, and the ban on traditional mud brick construction. Though granite is preferred, it is also considerably more expensive, leading most households to choose concrete, which makes the houses much hotter in the summer than mud brick construction. Many households chose a mixed design, with some ceilings constructed with traditional wood beams but others of concrete planks, to save money. Despite these slight variations inside, the uniformity of the exteriors gives the village a very orderly appearance from the road (figure 9).

Figure 8 Posters of Chinese leaders adorn a sitting room in a new house by the side of a road, 2007. The posters were given out at the 2005 celebration of the fortieth anniversary of the founding of the TAR. The middle poster features Hu Jintao visiting Tibet for the anniversary. Photo by author.

These households received a subsidy of 3,265 RMB per family member, as well as a 50,000 RMB five-year interest free loan.[82] Though some houses cost as little as 70,000 RMB to build, others that were finely tiled and decorated cost upward of 200,000 RMB. One woman who lived in a new house along the road stated in 2007 that she had only repaid a total of 600 RMB after two years, and had no real plans or ideas for how her family would clear the loan. Instead, she and other villagers hoped that if they did not pay back the loan, their debt would eventually be partially or completely canceled. This suggests that the financial debt, while important in further integrating Tibetan villagers into wider circuits of capital flows, is of relatively little importance for development in comparison with the debt of loyalty. The possibility of loan forgiveness increases the gratitude that villagers must demonstrate, for example through the reception of state visitors and frequent flying of national flags, including for the 2005 TAR anniversary and the 2006 opening of the Qinghai-Tibet Railway.

The same project was also implemented further up the road toward Lhasa, in a nearby administrative village of Tolung Dechen County. Here again the

Figure 9 Image engineering, 2007. Spacious and orderly two-floor houses line a main street; houses in less conspicuous locations are often smaller and have only one floor. Photo by author.

project required all households living within two hundred meters of the road to build new two-floor houses, with less than a year's notice, and did not permit traditional mud brick housing construction.[83] Each family received a subsidy of 25,000 RMB, and everyone who built in the first year—all who lived along the side of the road—was eligible for five-year 50,000 RMB loans, while those who built later claimed that the loans were no longer offered because of neighboring Nub villagers' inability to repay. One villager who had been required to rebuild claimed that they had been told "if you don't dismantle your old house by the Ongkor festival, we will send tractors to level it for you." Because the families wanted to save the small-diameter wood poles used for ceilings to resell, they dismantled their own houses but complained about the fact that they had no ownership rights (*rang dag*), as they would have preferred to keep the houses and rent them out. Keeping the old houses, however, would have defeated the goal of the orderly and uniform appearance of grand new houses by the side of the road. By contrast, many of those households that were hidden from the road, and that claimed not to have received the same deals on loans, were allowed to keep their old houses. Though the practice was not legally sanctioned because of a lack of deeds, many were as of 2007 taking advantage of the village's proximity to urban Lhasa and selling their former houses to retirees or cadres from the city.

The houses in the village closest to Nub are imposing, but not particularly well designed. Many were built without windows on three sides, an outcome of choices made by the Tibetan contractor hired for the job, which villagers seemed unable to explain. "Who knows?" said one woman who lived in such a house. "It must be cheaper for the boss to build it that way. He came around with a floor plan and we looked at it and said okay. We didn't have any experience with it." Here, all of the houses are built with concrete ceiling planks rather than traditional wood construction—"Chinese" houses rather than Tibetan ones in the villagers' perceptions. "It's much better to live in a Tibetan house but now everything is Chinese."

No provision was made for the villagers to continue to keep livestock in the courtyards, which were very small. Instead, like the urbanized farmers discussed earlier, these villagers tried to maintain a few livestock by tying them to electricity poles along the street or building small makeshift shelters

Figure 10 The Chinese national flag and Tibetan prayer flags fly atop this newly built Comfortable House on a main thoroughfare, 2007. Photo by author.

outside of their courtyards. Worse, the contractor did not build the houses with toilets or kitchens, necessitating that the families invest an additional 10,000 RMB to build these facilities in their courtyards.

From the side of the road, these houses are impressive looking (figure 10). Officials traveling from the airport to Lhasa see the neat and orderly two-story houses, with their granite and concrete bricks and national flags flying from rooftops, as impressive testaments to state development and citizen loyalty. Yet the residents state that their new houses are not suitable for the climate, hot in the summer and cold in the winter. When first completed in time for visual consumption by visiting officials during the celebration of the fortieth anniversary of the TAR, they were barely functional as homes, lacking kitchens, toilets, or functional courtyards. They are examples of "image engineering."

Image and appearance are integral to the Comfortable Housing Project, visual proof of the gift of development. Official reports state for example that the Comfortable Housing Project in Sakya, in western Tibet, is intended "to *improve the appearance* of the county seat town" through relocation of households from remote areas to the county seat and near the highway.[84] In villages where some households have chosen to neither rebuild nor remodel their houses, local governments often give a small amount of money to these households to make cosmetic changes to match the Comfortable House appearance, a practice officials call "putting on clothes and a hat." This spectacle of development created by image engineering marks both a "laudatory monologue" and a claim that the Chinese state is the legitimate and benevolent caregiver of this contentious space of the Chinese nation.

Variations in Comfortable Housing

A Model Village

Just beyond the red line of Lhasa's Urban Plan lies Najin Township's Peton village. Located on the new urban edge, Peton was by 2007 home to many Han vegetable farmers displaced outward by urban expansion. It was also designated as a "village of special emphasis" (*zhong dian cun*), or model village, for the New Socialist Countryside in Lhasa's *Chengguanqu*, and thus is frequently visited by reporters, television crews, high officials, and even selected groups of foreign journalists brought to the TAR on official visits.

Among the 62 households in the village, 23 rebuilt their houses and the rest remodeled. Total government subsidies of 25,000 RMB per household for those who rebuilt accounted for roughly 29 percent of total expenditures, while loans averaging 24,000 RMB per household accounted for 26 percent, and the remaining 45 percent of the total house costs, averaging

94,000 RMB, was paid through villagers' savings and private loans. Two designated poverty households built houses entirely from the 50,000 RMB subsidy they received, while other houses reportedly cost as much as 250,000 RMB. Those who renovated received 15,000 RMB subsidies to paint and lay concrete in the courtyards.

Peton's status as a model village makes the appearance of the new houses of paramount importance, as they must convince both officials and other outside observers of the generosity and effectiveness of the development gift, as well as serve as a visual catalyst for other Tibetan villagers to cultivate self-development. Villagers were given only one year to either build a new house or remodel, unlike the three to five year window offered in most villages. In 2008, on the center of the gate of the perimeter wall built around the new housing compound flew a gargantuan Chinese national flag flanked by two Olympic flags, while the houses lined up in orderly rows also displayed national flags.

The footprints of the Comfortable House courtyards are uniform, though the houses inside vary in size according to which house plan the families chose.[85] Some houses have only one story while others have two, but all are built in a hybrid Tibetan style with red roofs, painted trim, and kitchens and bathrooms in the courtyard, but also with concrete plank ceilings rather than timber beams. Villagers here chose to use concrete because it is much less expensive than timber, rather than because of a mandate. Due to their proximity to rapidly expanding Lhasa, villagers felt that given the opportunity, they could informally (though not legally) sell their old houses to Tibetans from Kham, which would help them repay their loans on the new houses. However, the village and township leaders forbade this, on the principle of not giving higher leaders who came to visit any reason to think "there hasn't been any change here" if they saw the old houses still standing. Thus, they required old houses to be demolished.

Because Peton is a model village, its residents are frequently advised on how to prepare their homes for visits as well as about what they should say to visitors. This advice includes not just a prohibition on saying anything negative, but also, according to several villagers, not discussing their loans. One villager complained that visitors were generally taken only to the houses of the rich families, and that others had to borrow televisions and other household amenities in advance of visits. Another villager, a middle-aged woman who had remodeled rather than build a new house, explained that the village is used "to show how rich farmers have become. Shit rich! They show that lives of the farmers have turned around and that they are happy and rich now, but it's all lies." Despite her vociferous dissatisfaction, she noted that if it were not for the loans, the villagers would have been quite happy with the new houses, because "who doesn't like a new house?" But the loans were, from her perspective, a source of tremendous anxiety and concern for the village as a whole, even though she herself had not taken one out.

The visual logic of the development gift pervades the entire bureaucratic structure of governance through the way in which cadres' performance is evaluated. As cadres at each level of government hope for promotions, they devise ways to demonstrate both the spectacle of development and the gratitude of its recipients. "The cadres have to chase points. That's why there's so much lying and showing," explained one village resident. Even those who are quite satisfied with their housing, or who remodeled their houses with subsidies only, recognize this. When I asked one such Peton villager whether Comfortable Housing meant that there had been development, he laughed and said, "There's no real foundation for development. It's just for show." He described the reason for its implementation as "probably appearancism" (*nampa ringlug*), creating a humorous neologism combining "appearance" (*nampa*) and "ism" (*ringlug*). In other words, the houses follow the principle of the spectacle, the presence of the surface form even in absence of a material foundation.

Multiplying Households

Just past the train station in Tolung Dechen where freight headed to Lhasa on the Qinghai-Tibet Railway is unloaded lies the large administrative village of Gatsal, with over four hundred households at the beginning of the Comfortable Housing Project in 2006, and more than six hundred by 2009. This rapid increase resulted not from extraordinary population growth, but from villagers' attempts to make the best of the Comfortable Housing Project as it has been implemented here.

As with other parts of Tolung Dechen County, households were eligible for a 24,000 RMB subsidy and, in some cases, a three-year interest-free loan of up to 20,000 RMB. Many households took private loans to supplement the subsidies and government loans. Though the county forbade mud brick construction, it did not impose regulations on the size or shape of houses. The local government also permitted very poor households to build houses costing only the amount of the subsidy of 24,000 RMB. Wealthy households built homes that cost up to 200,000 RMB. Once the new houses were completed, the year of their construction was painted in red next to their front doors.

Villagers' experience of the program has been one of uncertainty and constantly shifting policies. One resident explained that the project was originally to last only three years, and was to be voluntary. They were at first told that they could build anywhere, including on their farmland, or even on the farmland of neighbors as long as an appropriate exchange took place and both parties agreed. Those who chose to participate eagerly built on farmland in part because these villagers had also been told that the area would eventually be urbanized, and that the seat of Nechung Town would be moved to their village. Thus, they reasoned that they would receive greater compensation for their farmland if there were also houses sitting on it. By the fourth year, however, villagers were told that any remaining households that had not built a new house were required to build, and further that because the village was running out of space, their new houses could not be built on farmland. Instead they would have to be built on the locations of their current houses, or else on threshing grounds or other nonfarmland space.

Residents also said that that were told they could not keep their old houses, but they found a way to get around this rule: a rapid wave of household splitting, where two or more members of an existing household applied for a separate household registration (*hukou*). The old household would then build a new house as part of the Comfortable Housing Project (which the new household, legally formed after the project was initiated, was not required to do). The original household could then live in the newly built house, while the newly formed household could take the old house. Villagers saw this as a way to build new homes for sons and daughters.

While maneuvering adeptly to take the subsidies to build new houses, villagers at the same time suggested that the reason the government was implementing this program was "to demonstrate that the villagers have become rich, but it's just for show. Some houses are empty inside." One resident, who works as a tour company driver and whose family did not build a new house until the very last year of the program, argued that people in the TAR had not yet reached the level of development where they should be building houses. If there were true development, he said, residents would build houses on their own. "Since people are losing farmland [for example, to the railway] anyway, they could be using that money to send their children to school, but instead they are using it to cover the cost of the houses, leaving them with no more money for education." Houses, he said were not really their priority or what they needed the most. His wife, who was often in poor health, added that she believed it would have better for villagers to stay in their old houses and eat better, take better care of themselves, and spend more money educating their children.

Building within One's Means

Much further up the valley past Gatsal, the bumpy, rocky, unpaved road ends at Mo village. The Tolung Dechen County government required Mo villagers, like all residents of the county, to build with either concrete or granite bricks; it forbade mud brick construction and mandated the separation of livestock from houses, though enforcement of the former was stricter than of the latter requirement. Villagers were also informed at first that they were to rebuild in a centralized settlement area with neat rows of houses, and dismantle their old houses, but these rules were not enforced. After the first year, local government officials announced that not moving to the centralized location was acceptable as long as each house was located in a small cluster of two to four houses, to make future infrastructure easier to provide.

Although village leaders initially said that the project would last for only three years, it was later extended to five. They told all families to build houses, but did not specify any penalty for not building. Nevertheless, all families participated. Each family was eligible for a 24,000 RMB subsidy and a loan of up to 20,000 RMB. Houses in the area generally cost between 60,000 and 100,000 RMB to build, depending on both the materials and what sort of labor was hired to work on the house. Tibetan labor contractors charged 95–100 RMB/m^2 if the house owner supplied all of the materials, and 580–650 RMB/m^2 for both labor and materials.

The village leader stated that his 133-square-meter house cost 60,000 RMB to build. Of this 24,000 RMB came from a subsidy, 20,000 RMB from the three-year loan, 4,000 RMB from his own savings, and the remaining 12,000 RMB from private loans with an 18 percent interest rate. In contrast to the image engineering that appears on the side of major roads, in this village there was no emphasis on building large houses. In fact, township officials advised families not to take on larger loans than they could handle, and to build within their means. They were offered the option to build houses that would cost only the 24,000 RMB provided as a subsidy, though villagers pointed out that this was enough only for a 40-square-meter house. Rather, than trying to persuade households to build large, visually stunning houses, township leaders emphasized curbing what some policymakers have called the "competitive spirit" in the hearts of farmers and nomads who are "jealous and competitive and strive to build grandly . . . without taking into consideration that they do not have the ability to pay back their loans . . . wasting resources and increasing the credit risk of the Comfortable Housing Project."[86]

Divided Subsidies

An hour from Lhasa by car, the villages near Phenpo, the county seat of Lhundrup, experienced a very different form of implementation of Comfortable Housing than those closer to the city. Here the government generally enforced no requirements on building materials and allowed new houses to be built anywhere. They were supposed to be built with two stories, but the rule about separating livestock from human dwellings was not enforced. Most families who took part rebuilt their mud brick houses on the same spots as their old houses, so that they could reuse materials. Also unlike villagers closer to Lhasa or in Tolung Dechen County, most did not hire construction crews but rather used more traditional forms of mutual labor support (*mi lag*), making the houses less expensive. Loans were tied to the three-card system, in which the loan amount was determined by what the family had been eligible for in the past, and loans in subsequent years of the program became available only if all village families had made their scheduled loan payments in the previous year.

The biggest concern here was that there were fewer subsidies available than the number of families that wanted them. Villagers speculated that most of the intended subsidies never reached them. In one village, residents claimed that a township official, who died in a car accident after he had been confiscating Dalai Lama photographs, had "eaten" much of the money. When a new township leader took his place, there was no money left to distribute. Instead of the 14,000 RMB promised as a subsidy, they claimed only to have received 4000 RMB, forty-five pieces of timber, and windows, all of which were distributed only after the houses were complete. This forced them, they said, to borrow money up front for construction. Furthermore, timber was useless once the house was completed. They speculated that township officials had good relations with the Chinese labor crew that installed the windows, and that they had purchased a large quantity of timber in the past to resell, but had not done well, and so were now giving it away because they had no cash. Residents of a nearby village claimed that only those who had been chosen for the program in the first year received the full 14,000 RMB subsidy. By the second year the subsidy shrank to 10,000 RMB, and in subsequent years, the original 14,000 RMB was split between two or three families, leaving some with only 5,000 RMB, clearly not enough to build a house. Households were supposed to be chosen each year by drawing straws, but they claimed that relationships and back door connections played an important role as well.

This situation was not unique. Across the TAR there are other documented cases of housing subsidies that did not reach the farmers, leading some policymakers to urge that subsidies be disbursed directly to households rather than that released to county governments.[87] Far from major roads and cities, the imperative to spectacle is less pressing. A development gift is still given to, and on some level greatly desired by residents, but whether because of corruption or inadequate funding, the gift delivered is less than what is promised. The government's claim to have given all rural households in the TAR new housing by the end of 2010 is a considerable exaggeration.[88]

The Ambivalence of the Gift

The interpretive battle over Comfortable Housing as the key component of the New Socialist Countryside has raged on since 2006, largely around three issues: whether forced resettlement is part of the project, whether the project impoverishes its targets or improves their livelihoods, and whether or not participation is voluntary. For example, Human Rights Watch stated that "The Chinese government's latest campaign of forcing Tibetans to reconstruct their homes is deepening poverty rather than boosting economic development. . . . Affected villagers are not able to contest the decision or refuse to participate, even if complying causes them great economic hardship."[89] Drawing on their fieldwork in Shigatse, Goldstein, Childs, and Wangdui strongly rebutted such claims, arguing that in their fieldwork sites, Comfortable Housing has not involved resettlement, has improved the standard of living by providing a stimulus to the rural construction sector, creating more jobs, and has been entirely voluntary. Indeed, as in the case of Phenpo, they find that more households wanted subsidies than could be accommodated, and that villagers "demonstrate[d] a degree of agency, and control over their lives" insofar as they were able to simply ignore several aspects of the program that were not to their liking, such as the plan to build new houses along the road and to build a separate barn for livestock. Thus, they conclude that arguments about the coercive nature of the programs are simply incorrect and that if and when there is coercion, it is an exception rather than the rule.[90]

The experiences of villages around urban Lhasa suggest that implementation varies significantly. The closer a village is to a main road or to Lhasa, the more restrictions on building materials, size, and (re)location of new houses, and the more the houses are a form of image engineering, spectacles of development. In some villages, new houses must be built in orderly rows and old houses must be demolished, while in others, villagers can keep their old houses and build new houses wherever they like. Subsidies vary, as do loans. Whereas in some villages, households feel pressured to build, in others, residents have scrambled for subsidies that are insufficient, whether because of corruption or inadequate budgeting.

The extent to which Comfortable Housing deepens poverty or boosts economic development is not straightforward to determine. The project could be seen as a tool for discouraging high rates of savings and boosting consumption, and thus part of a broad-scale adjustment to the Chinese national economy. Many of the construction crews are Tibetan, or composed of both Tibetans and Han migrant workers. Pastoralists in Nagchu, for example, almost exclusively hire Tibetan farmers from Shigatse to build their houses, and families that have purchased trucks can rent them out to transport construction materials. While these materials, such as concrete bricks, windows, and doorframes, tend to be produced by outside Han- and Hui-dominated companies, there is little doubt that the five-year wave of house building has also benefited Tibetan construction workers. By the end of 2007, the government estimated that the total income generated by rural residents through Comfortable Housing, as builders, transporters, carpenters, and painters, was 230 million RMB, while the total government investment was 2.473 billion RMB. In this way, the project stimulated the rural economy and created jobs and wages, though not very efficiently.[91] Rather than emphasizing the creation of construction jobs, however, official analyses of the program to date have focused on a purported increase in income due to an expansion of tourism attributed to Comfortable Housing, and to the development of markets as a result of a higher overall level of development.[92]

Despite the effect of the subsidies as an economic stimulus, debt is clearly a source of great anxiety. Even families who can afford their houses state, "the problem is that poor households all have huge loans they cannot repay." These comments echo banks' concerns that the loans might affect regional financial stability, and that insufficient levels of subsidy may impoverish some households. Those poor enough to be designated as official poverty households receive larger subsidies, but those just above the official designation are likely to encounter difficulty repaying loans. Though foreclosures do not seem to be a possibility, banks can and do apply pressure by calling debtors out in public meetings and threatening to withhold other loans from the village or to take other assets such as livestock. Anxiety about loans seems to plague even those who objectively should not have problems repaying, suggesting that it stems not only from actual inability to repay, but also from the fact that incurring debts to banks for housing is an unfamiliar practice, one that binds its participants more closely into wider networks of capital.[93]

Villagers' comments about their debts also underscore deeper contradictions of agency and ambivalence about the New Socialist Countryside, calling into question how to interpret the "voluntary" nature of participation. On the one hand, the government has insisted that the program is completely voluntary, but on the other, that by the end of 2010, *all* rural households deemed to need improved housing had in fact built new houses or remodeled their old ones. Government officials also claim that after the first year, when some households were wary of the program until they saw their neighbors take advantage of it, "there are no cases of people not wanting to participate."

How do government targets come to align perfectly with the desires of its residents? This improbably perfect match is explained in part by the fact that, as is almost always the case in China, the extent of project implementation is less than officially claimed; Goldstein, Childs, and Wangdui found that in their project sites, just under 50 percent of the eligible households received housing subsidies, significantly less than the government's 80 percent target.[94] Beyond this, there are also clearly cases where Comfortable Housing is not completely voluntary, as in image engineering projects along Highway 318, and other places where local governments have implemented

Comfortable Housing "as a political responsibility and used hard and rigid measures to fulfill quotas."[95]

For the most part, however, not only is there is no overt coercion, but villagers also strongly desire to take advantage of the gift of free money so long as it is being offered. Social pressure to follow the community in building upgraded houses also plays a role in the decision to borrow and build a house. Yet all of this is simultaneously tinged with dissatisfaction about the hegemonic frame within which one's "voluntary" choices can be made, leading to a tangle of incongruities and quandaries about the housing gift.

For example, one Phenpo resident explained the program in dark terms to me as follows. Using Tibetan alliteration, he argued that "the project," *namdrang* (*rnam grangs*) should be renamed *namdo* (*rnam rtog*) meaning "ill-omened," or even *namkalo* (*gnam kha log*). Given the required loans and the rising prices of construction material since the building of the railway, he said, by the time the house exteriors are finally completed as testaments to the state's ability to bring prosperity to Tibet, the insides of the houses are left completely empty of money, food, and everything else, leaving their owners with their mouths (*kha*) hanging open, staring at the sky (*gnam*), a backward or wrong (*log*) state of affairs. Yet this same man was one of the few in his village who had managed through good relationships with leaders to obtain a project house, in a village where funds were not available to all. Furthermore, when asked whether the project was good or bad his sister replied that it was both. Of course, she said, everyone liked free money from the state—and indeed the limited time opportunity to capture the subsidy, or free money, is precisely the reason many give for participating in the program. The problem, they say, is the loans that are required and the indebtedness that results, or as she put it, "everyone was thinking only of taking the CCP's money but instead everyone ended up accumulating huge loans."

When I asked members of one family in Peton village whether building the houses was voluntary, they laughed, as if I had told a very funny joke. "Voluntary! Haha! No. Not voluntary at all," adding, "Oh there was so much trouble!" with villagers signing up for houses, taking their names off the list, and then signing up again. Yet this was a family that had only remodeled their house with a subsidy, rather than taking out a loan to build a new house. Two neighbors in Mo village, where villagers were encouraged to build only within their means without many conditions, gave different interpretations of the program. One stated both that "The leaders said that everyone must build a house" and also that "there was no one who said they did not want to build a house." He was quite satisfied with his house, saying that he had been very worried about the loan, but now that he had built the house, he believed he could slowly pay off his debt. His relative and neighbor, however, stated simply that the leaders had insisted that everyone must build. He was also less optimistic about his loan, saying, "when I think about the house, I have no regrets, but when I think about the loan I do have some regrets." Another said that if you really didn't want to build, you didn't have to, but then you would be the only person left in the village with a mud brick house, and would seem poor and impoverished.

This type of social pressure, of measuring up to one's neighbors in the quality of one's house and one's development status, is significant. Consider a family of five in Gatsal village, who had just built a home in 2003 and still had loans to repay for it as well as for a car they had recently purchased. They decided when the Comfortable Housing Project was first implemented in 2006 that they would not participate, but in 2009 they built a new Comfortable House after all. They changed their minds in part because leaders stated that everyone should build. "If everyone in the village has done it and you are the only one who hasn't, it looks bad and the government can make your life difficult since you have to live here. They have many opportunities to scold you, and also to scold your neighbors for not making you conform." Another reason, though, was that they were frequently asked by neighbors and friends, "Why haven't you built a new house?" making them feel embarrassed and inadequate.

Like many other families, they had maneuvered to keep both their original and their new house, despite rules against doing so, by splitting their household registration into two. Though their initial reason for not building a house was that they felt it beyond their means given existing debts and the need to pay tuition for three children, they did not opt—as was possible in their village—to simply take the 24,000 RMB subsidy and build a very small house using only that money. Instead, they borrowed extensively on the private market (as they were not eligible for a bank loan because of existing debts) to build an 80,000 RMB house. At the same time, they expressed great distrust of the program by claiming that the hidden agenda of Comfortable Housing lay in the fact that the three main years of the house building, 2006–8, were the three astrological "obstacle years" of the Dalai Lama, during which, according to tradition, nobody should build a house as it would bring him bad luck and ill fortune. They speculated that this was the real reason the government had decided to implement the program. Like many others I encountered, they thus displayed a striking ambivalence toward the program, frequently contradicting themselves about whether or not they had really wanted to build, and whether or not it was, in the end, voluntary.

Indeed, building a Comfortable House, like receiving a gift, is an act framed within a set of meanings and structures in which the very concept of the purely voluntary does not apply. The decision to build a Comfortable House is for the most part not coerced, but it is not voluntaristic either, in the sense that the choice to do so is completely free. There is no completely free-standing, autonomous subject outside of the compulsions of development as a hegemonic project, which cultivates desires in its subjects for material improvement, made more appealing by its appearance as an opportunity to take free money. At the same time the very act of being given the gift already implicates its receiver within a set of relationships and recognitions of state and citizen that constrain as much as they enable. This recognition acknowledges the state and its territory as a container for Tibetans, included through exclusion into state claims over Chinese national space. The gift of a house is simultaneously desired and feared, good sense and common sense, a contradiction of development written in concrete into the Tibetan landscape by Tibetans themselves as they participate actively in the production of the TAR's new peri-urban and rural landscape, altering its appearance.

PRESENT OR POISON?

The ongoing emphasis in the TAR not only on urbanization but also on large-scale investment and construction of rural and peri-urban housing through the New Socialist Countryside suggests that no matter how important urbanization has indeed become across China, the state has not become completely urbanized. The development of rural areas remains significant in state building.

The controversy over Comfortable Housing in the TAR has arisen in part from its very different forms of implementation in different places. However, there is much more at stake in this spectacular housing project. My argument is not that the houses—given as both a symbol of and foundation for further development through the cultivation of Tibetans into rational market actors and high-quality citizens—are sometimes a present and sometimes poison, but rather that taking seriously the logic of the gift means that it is always some combination of both. In building a house as part of the program, regardless of the circumstances, a relationship of recognition is established between the recipient and the Chinese state, entrapping the recipient in that relationship of citizenship and belonging.

The obligation to perform gratitude to the state for development cannot be separated either analytically or in the minds and subjectivities of its targets from the material improvements in livelihoods that the project may or may not bring. Development is never reducible simply to a technical problem of rational improvement. Understanding the New Socialist Countryside housing project as an aporetic development gift enables one to steer between two problematic ways of interpreting it: either as always a coercive scheme foisted on passive victims, or as a technical project of improvement, defined by benevolent intentions and separable from power. As Tania Li suggests, one can "take seriously the proposition that the will to improve can be taken at its word . . . but [it is] not [development's] master term."[96]

In many instances, villagers around Lhasa simultaneously express resentment, anxiety about financial indebtedness, and the desire to take the opportunity to acquire a subsidy, a free gift, from the state. This gift comes from the state's amassed wealth, accumulated and then given away in a lavish, extravagant expenditure, a five-year spectacle of agonistic giving that transforms its recipients as well as the landscape. The enticement of free money is strong. Indeed, many view the taking of the subsidy as an act of agency, of finally having an opportunity to take advantage of the Party-state ("we were thinking only of taking the CCP's money"). But by entering that relationship, villagers become further bound to continue to recognize themselves as belonging to the Chinese nation-state and its territorial claims. Their performance of loyalty is not an option, but an obligation. It is the result of indebtedness engineering.

This indebtedness came into plain sight after the March 2008 unrest. Not only those who had personally participated in the unrest, but also anyone with family members who had been arrested in connection with the events, had their project subsidies canceled and were passed over in the implementation of water, electricity, and other new service provisions. In Gatsal, households that had signed up to build project houses that year but had not yet received their subsides, were reportedly in a state of panic that in retaliation for the March 14 events in Lhasa, their subsidies would be withheld, suggesting a very clear understanding that the gift they had received was contingent on the demonstration of continuing loyalty, of never questioning the ontology of state space as Chinese territory.

Residents in one village reported that after March 2008, the number of projects given increased dramatically: water taps, biogas, and even some very large farm implements such as tractors poured in. The quality of food served to students in school also greatly improved. The following summer, several Tibetan and Han government workers showed up, presenting themselves as checking up on the Comfortable Housing Project. They started by coming into village houses and asking a few questions about each house, before beginning to carefully inspect its entire contents. Whenever a forbidden image of the Dalai Lama was found, they scolded the residents, telling them, "you don't need any more projects. Your projects come from over there [India]," and further that from now on, anyone who kept such an image would be ineligible for all future development projects.

The debt of gratitude, to be repaid through the performance of loyalty on dictated terms such as the clearing of one's house of photos of the Dalai Lama, is a heavy one that many find difficult to bear. Anxieties about their ability to pay this debt of loyalty are partially displaced onto Tibetans' anxieties over the more tangible monetary debt of the loans. This helps explain the frequent expressions of distress about the loans, even among those who have the financial capacity to repay them, and despite the fact that those who truly cannot do so will not have their homes taken away from them.

A forgiven monetary debt transmutes into an even greater debt of loyalty. Monetary debts transmogrify into debts of loyalty, while anxieties about the latter are displaced onto the former, in a politics of fear that makes it difficult if not impossible to speak directly about gratitude as anything other than spontaneous and natural.

The determination that the people of Tibet needed new houses, above all else, in their pursuit of the long sought-after but always elusive goal of becoming developed is more "people-first" than the building of infrastructural projects such as the Qinghai-Tibet Railway, but leaves open the question of why other possible development measures, such as improving the quality and increasing the number of rural schools, are less important components of the New Socialist Countryside. The building of houses for each individual family is a way to both cater to and reinforce the desire for material goods that is a constitutive feature of self-developing subjects. It is also a form of spectacle, a method to effect domination not through economic extraction but rather through economic largesse, massive spending, and the provision of material goods. Spectacle reinforces the hegemony of development even in the absence of residents' material means to build new houses. Long portrayed and imagined as backward, Tibet's development is to be conjured through appearancism, the engineering of images. Its development is based on an economy of appearances.

The hegemony of states around the world has been built on the promise of bringing development to their citizens. This dynamic is intensified in the relationship between the Chinese state and its sometimes unwilling Tibetan citizens, from whom a lack of proper gratitude for the delivery of development is read as evidence of a rejection of state sovereignty. As homes, houses provide the intimate space of dwelling and of everyday reproduction of the family. The gift of a house is thus an exemplar of biopower as the fostering of life, and the improvement of the population associated with development. However, this biopolitical rationality is intertwined with indebtedness, and ultimately to the threat of being relegated to a state of abandonment in the space of exception, producing new articulations of biopolitical and sovereign modes of power in post-2008 Tibet.

Moving away in the analysis of gifts and development from an exclusive focus on foreign aid toward development as a political relation between states and subjects, we can see that development is a process through which the state is ontologized and state territory naturalized. The grammar of the gift, when used to legitimate and frame statist development, entails not only this reification of the state and its space, but also a nationalist claim that the state is the rightful and legitimate caretaker of the TAR as part of a Chinese nation, belonging to which Tibetans can neither fully claim nor disavow. The changing appearance and form of the built landscape of both the rural and urban TAR, produced in part with Tibetan labor and savings, territorializes through the logic of the gift.

Conclusion

Development has most often been told as a singular story: of Western imperialist expansion, of the invention of the Third World after World War II, of being essentially another name for capitalism as an abstract, totalizing, and unitary force. Such narratives too neatly package contradictory and indeterminate assemblages of socio-spatial phenomena shaped by particular geographical processes into a final predetermined outcome in which aspirations and desires for development can never be anything other than an extension of a specifically Western mode of being. They erase the long imperial history of China as a colonizing center engaged in territorial conquest, a sedimented history that shapes the present through official narratives of gratitude, gifts, and Tibet's belonging to China since the Yuan dynasty.

In tracing state territorialization in Tibet through the experience of development as a gift, I have advocated a conception of development as a specific political project between states and subjects. Focusing on contemporary processes of development in Tibet reveals both the difficult and complex realities of being Tibetan in contemporary Lhasa, and the character of development as a Chinese state project. The point is not, of course, that a particular Chinese form of development is exceptional or isolated from those in other places—far from it—but neither is it merely a local reenactment of a privileged Western essence.

The stakes are high because of Tibet's peculiar position vis-à-vis both China and the West. China's history as a semicolony means that it is constituted on a principle of difference, attempting to articulate its own path to development through which it can be modern without becoming Western. The acute awareness of China's position within a global hierarchy of nation-states, of needing to "catch up" with the West, makes development and underdevelopment constitutive of Chinese identities. At the same time, however, within China there is another ordering, which posits the Han ethnicity and the industrialized, urban eastern seaboard as the site of developed, modern, high-*suzhi* citizens, who must lead the way as models for the rural, western, low-quality, backward minorities, of whom Tibetans are the most extreme case. If China is constituted by difference from the West, then Tibet is a difference within that difference. As a periphery in the making, it provides a distinctive and revealing view of the state.

As an internal other, Tibetans are positioned as backward and lagging behind, in need of the guidance and benevolence of the Han and the state. Their backwardness must be ameliorated through a series of gifts, first socialist liberation, then development in the form of market rationality, a spirit of hard work and entrepreneurship, urbanization, and civilized housing. Their constant lack and their permanent failure to measure up, whether in their *suzhi*, scientific knowledge, technical skills, willingness and ability to labor diligently, or desire for capital accumulation, legitimates state development intervention, which enables them to be included in the broader Chinese nation-state. This inclusion is compulsory, as Tibetan belonging to the spatial container of PRC territory is naturalized. Their simultaneous exclusion from the nation-state, as an internal other always in need of improvement, and their compulsory inclusion into the nation-state and its space, marks the topology of the exception that characterizes Tibetan life in the PRC. This exception is again not universal in character, but specifically experienced and negotiated through culturally and historically inflected idioms. Because development does not work in the same way everywhere, understanding development requires knowledge of how places are constituted, and how spaces and landscapes are produced.

In bringing this ethnography to a close, I return to the question of why the Tibetan landscape looks the way it does today. I have argued that the social relations of its production from the 1950s to the present, particularly the contradictory role of variously positioned Tibetans in the material transformation of the landscape, are easily obfuscated. Three specific moments in the trajectory of landscape production over the past half century shed light on the flaws of multiple dominant narratives about Tibetan lives in the PRC, produced for various audiences.

First, in the early 1950s, the conquest of nature framed as separate from society and untouched by history offered impoverished Tibetan women a way to transcend social obstacles through their labor, simultaneously interpellating them as PRC citizens. Their experience and memories make clear that early state territorialization was a gendered, and indeed emasculating process. Its embodied labor created complex subjectivities and tensions about Tibetan agency and participation in state projects that remain unresolved today.

Second, the production in the 1990s of the new peri-urban plastic landscape speaks to Han migration to Tibet, one of the most disputed issues of the Tibet Question. In contrast to claims about deliberate population transfer, ordinary migrants such as vegetable farmers who domesticate Lhasa for themselves by transforming it into "little Sichuan" are not sent through any such program. Instead, the loosening of travel restrictions into the TAR, justified through selective neoliberal notions of "free" flows and by flawed assumptions of an equal playing field; family and kinship networks; and the ability of a class of cadres whose income derives from state subsidies to purchase vegetables and other commodities and services, came together to fuel the influx of migrants. The vegetable market itself did not spring into existence through the force of an invisible hand, but rather was deliberately created at first to feed Chinese soldiers and cadres, and later also Tibetans as vegetables became integrated into the local Tibetan diet. As part of this deliberate creation of a vegetable production industry, local officials also tried to foster Tibetan involvement, subsidizing greenhouses and telling Tibetans not to rent them out to migrants. These efforts failed, as the result of an overdetermined and mutually constitutive set of political-economic, cultural-political, and social-spatial forces that have allowed migrants to outcompete local Tibetans.

Migrants do not act as the bearers of development in the form of technology transfer that state officials claim them to be. The reproduction of socio-spatial distance between Han migrants and local villagers not only precludes the transfer of vegetable cultivation skills, but also makes it easier for the migrants to pass on the risk of vegetable farming to local villagers through unenforceable contracts and the option of simply running away. The migrant farmers also do not act as vectors of development since the income they earn does not stay in the TAR: it is almost entirely sent home as remittances. While in Tibet, the migrants live frugally and build their own mud brick houses, adding little to the circulation of value within the region. Yet they see themselves as contributing significantly to the development of Tibet, drawing on a spatial imaginary of *suzhi* that posits the east as the direction from which development comes; people from more "developed" areas are assumed to absorb this quality of place, making them more developed subjects. The Han see Tibet as underdeveloped and underurbanized. Even as they are convinced of their own contribution to Tibet's development, they believe that the state has bypassed their own hometowns, and thus resent state largesse in the form of subsidies poured into Tibet, not recognizing the extent to which these subsidies flow out almost as quickly as they stream in. Instead, they wonder why the Tibetans are not more grateful for development.

Third, among the many visible expenditures of state development money that Han migrants witness in the changing Tibetan landscape have been Lhasa's rapid urbanization, and starting in the middle of the first decade of the twenty-first century, the gargantuan project of constructing Comfortable Houses across peri-urban and rural Tibet. Middle-class Tibetans have been able to purchase new, spacious homes made desirable through representations bearing little resemblance to Tibet's material and cultural landscapes. At the same time urban planning, deployed as a technical act of development, and accumulation by dispossession have resulted in land expropriation and displacement, as well as a profoundly disorienting rearrangement of the socio-spatial contours of everyday life for peri-urban farmers.

Like migration, Comfortable Housing has been viewed in diametrically opposed ways: as a pure gift, and as a project of involuntary resettlement and Maoist-style socialist engineering. Neither view is accurate. Like Tibetan nonparticipation in vegetable farming, the implementation of the program has been one in which Tibetans exercise agency in a way that appears to contradict their assumed interests, demonstrating that subject positions have multiple, not singular, interests. Such contradictions emerge within hegemonic projects, as Gramsci suggested with his term "contradictory consciousness." Tibetan participants in the program fear the indebtedness that must be repaid through loyalty, but they have also been shaped by development as a biopolitical project to be subjects for whom a free subsidy for a new house is difficult to pass up.

As present and poison, the gift captures the contradictions of housing in particular and development more generally as both desirable and frightening for the relationships and obligations it entails. For Tibetans in Lhasa, the gift of development has brought both access to more commodities and a growing sense of themselves as *ra ma lug,* "neither goat nor sheep," no longer known, in a sense, to themselves. The gift of development housing is accompanied by a monetary debt that is transmuted into a deeper debt of loyalty, one that must be constantly performed at the articulation point of sovereign power and biopower. Moreover, any reluctance to perform appreciation and indebtedness becomes a sign of ingratitude; thus Tibetans speak about fearing monetary indebtedness, even when they clearly have the financial means to pay for their new houses. In both the production of the state effect and the visible changes of the material landscape, the gift of development is a spatial process, producing new forms of space and territory.

Taming Tibet has endeavored to deepen our understanding of development in several respects. To briefly summarize, I mention five points. First, I have argued that rather than dismiss claims of development as gift, we should take them seriously. The analytic of the gift is useful for interrogating development beyond interstate relations and foreign aid. The grammar of the gift posits an intersubjective relationship between the state as giver and its citizens as recipients; it thus works to produce the effect of the state as a reified, unitary actor with an ontological presence. This reification of the state calls into being the recognition of a relationship of belonging and thus works to consolidate state space as territory.

Second, I have argued for the importance of culturally specific idioms as a key to understanding experiences of development as a project and process that is not everywhere the same, and as materially important in the shaping of political-economic outcomes. It is crucial, then, to map out how the cultural politics and the political economy of development constitute each other. This entanglement must be considered as various projects continue to be devised in the name of improvement. The trope of Tibetan indolence is produced at the conjuncture of a response to the highly dependent and distorted economic structure of the TAR, culturally constructed notions of work and leisure, and the performance of a Tibetan identity distinct from that of the Han. This, in turn, shapes desires, aspirations, and convictions about self that inform everyday decisions about participation in new economic opportunities and labor markets, reproducing broader patterns of economic marginalization. Cultural politics are a force as significant as rationalities of rule in outcomes and future possibilities.

Third, I have demonstrated the power of an ethnographic approach to development, territorialization, and the production of landscape. Arguing for analytical specificity is not a resort to infinite variability or radical contingency, but rather the recognition that common patterns, whether of racism or tropes of indolence, are produced in specific places with their own sedimentations of history and memory. The role of ethnography is not merely to fill in the empirical details of grand narratives, whether of development, capitalism, or state power but rather, as Karl Marx put it, to "advance to the concrete,"[1] producing concepts adequate to messy actualities of socio-spatial formations.

Fourth, I have suggested that tracing agency and power in the production of material landscapes helps us see how development produces contradictory subjects and complex subject positions. Finally, I have argued that development and landscape transformation are central to processes of state territorialization. Migrant vegetable farming and Comfortable Houses form a trajectory of state incorporation and territorialization that, beginning with the establishment of the state farms in the 1950s, transformed nature in part through the recruitment of Tibetan participants. The transformation of the material landscape has helped advance the project of making the current boundaries of the PRC seem the proper and naturalized geographical container for Tibet and Tibetans.

Criticizing government-in-exile calls for a "truly autonomous" "Greater Tibet," Chinese intellectuals have deployed the specter of ethnic cleansing, asking: Would such a Tibet be defined as a place reserved only for ethnic Tibetans? What would happen to the Chinese living there? Would they be violently removed? From one perspective, this stance on the relationship between people and territory appears more progressive and promising than nationalist claims of "Tibet for Tibetans," a "sedentarist metaphysics" that maps peoples and cultures onto national soils, bounded spaces on a map bordered by other equally neat and isomorphic entities.[2] Yet in the aftermath of 2008, Tibetans trying to engage in mundane activities outside of Tibetan areas—checking into hotels or hailing taxis, for example—were frequently positioned as "out of place" and objects of suspicion. Though perhaps not completely resolvable, such contradictions of belonging and exclusion, and the need for a more accommodating spatiality and imagination of territory, must be addressed to reduce future violence and suffering.

Afterword

Fire

Between 2011 and the time of this writing in the spring of 2013, the Tibetan plateau witnessed a series of more than one hundred self-immolations. Unprecedented in Tibetan political history, these grisly acts of protest and sacrifice against increasingly repressive forms of rule were quickly labeled "terrorism" by state authorities, and the monks, nuns, and lay men and women who have set themselves aflame, were declared losers as well as terrorists. This is perhaps unsurprising, given the challenge these self-immolations pose to state territorialization. Terror and territory are intertwined: maintaining a bounded space of territory requires the constant mobilization of threat.[1] In this new formation, the perception of anything that threatens to undo the hard work of territorialization is declared a form of terror, even in the absence of any harm to innocent others.

The state claims for itself not only the role of legitimate caretaker, fostering proper forms of life, but also the role of arbiter of death. Individuals have no right to kill themselves; only the state can give them the right to be punished or killed. What appears terrifying, then, is a death unregulated by the nation-state, "the illusion of an uncoerced interiority that can withstand the force of institutional discipline,"[2] that destabilizes the foundations of the state effect. The state of emergency enacted throughout Tibetan areas since 2008, particularly in response to the violence in Lhasa, interpellates Tibetans as always already guilty. This denies them the right to act politically, which as Hannah Arendt suggested, is the basis of the possibility of being individual and thus human.[3] In this sense, self-immolation is a fiery reclamation of sovereignty over one's own self, of the possibility of being human. Biological life is taken in an assertion of a political life.

In December 2012 the state responded to this assertion by introducing legislation criminalizing self-immolations in Tibetan areas, thus rendering plainly visible the origin of the law in violence. Stating categorically and without evidence that the self-immolations were the result of "premediated coordination and organization of antagonistic forces inside and outside of China in a plot to split the state, damage the unity of the nationalities, and disrupt the social order," the legal opinion by China's highest court, highest prosecutorial office and Ministry of Police made it a crime to self-immolate. Moreover, it made it a crime of intentional homicide to "organize, plan, incite, coerce, lure, abet, or assist" others in self-immolation, and even to "illegally carry gasoline into a public place or on public transportation" for self-immolation,[4] thus making even easier the casting of the wide net of guilt that already hangs over all Tibetans. This criminalization of self-immolation not only reaffirms that only the state has the right to make live and make die, but also exposes what Walter Benjamin argued to be the inseparability of law-preserving and lawmaking violence. Rather than merely upholding the rule of law, as it claims, this legislation contains within it a defensive element that seeks to seize hold of a form of violence that threatens the state by being outside of the law.[5]

The epicenter of the burnings has been in eastern Tibet, particularly Ngawa, in Sichuan Province. In Lhasa, after two young men from eastern Tibet set themselves on fire in front of the Jokhang Temple, the state apparatus enacted a new security drive to increase checks of identification cards and expel hundreds of Tibetans from the eastern part of the plateau, including those with valid business permits who had resided and run businesses in Lhasa for years. At the Eighteenth Chinese Communist Party Congress held in Beijing in November 2012, officials insisted that Lhasa is "the happiest city in China," while guards stood outside on Tiananmen Square armed with fire extinguishers, in case anyone should try to light themselves on fire. The spatiality of the state has recently been reinforced through the imposition of further tightened security, surveillance, and mobility restrictions including new checkpoints along roads in Tibetan areas, particularly those leading to Lhasa, as well as the recall of all Tibetan passports in the TAR. Paramilitary patrols have added fire extinguishers to their arsenal of weapons, to safeguard the right of the state to decide who should live and who should die (and how). At the same time, development proceeds apace, with new projects and promises of prosperity, urbanization, sustainability, and stability, along with further measures to instill gratitude. These dynamics have deepened rather than fundamentally changed the configurations of power already in place, including the privileged coupling of sovereign power with biopower since 2008.

Indeed, the intensification of the entanglement between fostering life through development and the assertion of power over death was laid bare in the official response to self-immolations in Rebgong, Qinghai Province.[6] Seven self-immolations followed in the nine days after an official decree blamed the Dalai Lama for using the "cloak of religion" to incite self-immolations as well as protests in which thousands of middle-school students called for "equality of nationalities and freedom of languages" and the return of the Dalai Lama. Starkly disclosing the heavy debt of loyalty incurred by the unfree gift of development, the decree called for the immediate and permanent cancellation of all welfare benefits, disaster relief aid, and all other livelihood and public benefit programs not only to self-immolators' families, but also to any lay person, monk, or nun who visited these family members to console or grieve with them, or who made donations to the family members. Those who make visits to console or who donate money must be reprimanded and, if they do not properly see the error of their ways, the decree says, the public security apparatus must "severely strike" against them. Villages from which anyone who self-immolates hail are also to have all state-funded development projects, either underway or planned, immediately canceled, and any town or township with numerous incidents becomes ineligible to receive state projects for three years.

These self-immolations occurred not only in response to the state of siege imposed on Tibetan areas after 2008 but also within the context of a broader political crackdown across China that began in 2011, with the rounding up of lawyers, writers, and activists in an attempt to secure "stability" out of fear of the threat posed by events in North Africa and by scattered internet calls for a "Jasmine Revolution." Claims in state media that the famous artist Ai Weiwei had come too close to the "red line of Chinese law," and warnings that law cannot be used as a shield by those who want to make trouble, that "no law can protect" such people, again call to mind Walter Benjamin's reflections on the origins of law in violence and its distance from justice. The nervousness of the Nervous System, the permanent state of emergency that has long characterized Tibet, erupts at times on a much broader scale, reminding us of why the margins are a useful vantage point from which to consider the logics of state power.

The disciplinary institutions of power/knowledge mobilized in efforts to secure "stability" also include those of academic Tibetan studies. Like the birth out of the Cold War of area studies in the United States, Tibetan studies in the PRC was born out of a specific geopolitical imperative: to secure the loyalty of Tibetans and the stability of the country. The tasks of these institutions include reading and translating foreign scholarly works on Tibet, whereupon they are often classified as internal documents, deemed too subversive for ordinary PRC citizens to lay their eyes on because they deviate from sanctioned narratives of historical belonging and gratitude. Within this disciplinary framework, development must be framed as the pure gift, benevolence without power. The ontologization of the state and the work of producing territory are naturalized and demand invisibility. There is thus much uncertainty about the ways in which a book such as this will be received, and with what consequences. In the face of these unknowns and of the tragedy of self-immolations, the only option is to maintain, as Antonio Gramsci suggested, a pessimism of the intellect and an optimism of the will.

Notes

Preface

1. Howard French, "In Tibetan Areas, Parallel Worlds Now Collide," *New York Times,* March 20, 2008. www.nytimes.com/2008/03/20/world/asia/20tibet.html.

2. chinatibet.people.com.cn/96065/6623277.html.

Introduction

1. See also Barnett 2010 for a discussion of the Chinese perspective on gift giving in Sino-Tibetan historical relations. My emphasis here is on the particularities of the project of development as a gift and its role in constituting the "state effect," or the experience of the state as thing-like and having an ontological presence.

2. PRC State Council 2001.

3. Wainwright 2008, 21. See also Brenner and Elden 2009.

4. For discussions challenging the realist assumptions regarding territory and processes of state territorialization, see Agnew 1994; Brenner 1999; Bryan 2012; Elden 2007a, 2010a, 2010b; Vandergeest and Peluso 1995; and Wainwright and Robertson 2003.

5. Patshang 1973; Samuel 1993; Sørensen 1994, 131–33. Avalokitesvara prays, "May this barbarous borderland, moreover, become the field of conversion [done] by me," and Tibet becomes his "field of conversion" [*zhing khams*] (Sørensen 1994, 97–98). The multiple resonances of taming can be seen in Jäschke's (1968 [1881], 21, in Samuel 1993, 219) definition of *'dul ba*: "(1) to tame, to break in [of horses]; to subdue, conquer, vanquish [of enemies], sometimes even to kill, to annihilate; (2) to till, to cultivate, waste land; to civilize, a nation, which with the Buddhist is the same as to convert, frq.; to educate, to discipline, to punish."

6. Michel Foucault (1980, 195) describes *dispotif*, or "apparatus," as "a kind of formation, so to speak, that at a given historical moment has as its major function the response to an urgency. The apparatus therefore has a dominant strategic function." Giorgio Agamben (2009, 14) proposes an even more extensive conceptualization of an apparatus as "anything that has in some way the capacity to capture, orient, determine, intercept, model, control or secure the gestures, behaiors, opinions or discourses of living beings," of which development is surely an exemplar.

7. "Looking at Tibet in a New Light," *People's Daily*, May 16, 1994, p. 1.

8. Mukerji 1997, 1. Mukerji's study of the relationship between the garden of Versailles and the growth of French state power highlights how territorial control is effected through the landscape. However, her study focuses primarily on elite culture, with little attention to the labor of ordinary people who constructed the gardens of state power. See also Karan 1976.

9. On agency see Mahmood 2001.

10. Daniels 1989.

11. Barnes and Duncan 1992; Cosgrove 1994; Cosgrove and Daniels 1988.

12. Don Mitchell 1996, 2002; Olwig 1996, 2002; Zukin 1991.

13. Mitchell 1996, 28.

14. Mitchell 1996, 32–33; see Latour 1987 and Callon 1986.

15. Gramsci 1999 (1971); Hall 1980, 1987; Hart 2002a; Moore 2005.

16. Althusser 1995 (1969), 104, 113.

17. Smith 1998, 111.

18. Cowen and Shenton 1996; Lawson 2007; Wainwright 2008.

19. Cowen and Shenton 1996; Gidwani 2008; Hart 2001, 2004, 2010; Lawson 2007; Li 2007; Polanyi 1957 (1944).

20. Pandian 2009, 7, 11.

21. Wainwright 2008, 12; Gidwani 2008, 100–101.

22. Gidwani 2008, 100–101.

23. Gramsci 1999 (1971); Hall 1987, 1996 (1986); Willis 1981 (1977); Williams 1977. See also Crehan 2002.

24. Gramsci 1999 (1971), 419; see also 321–34 and 420–22.

25. See also Gidwani 2008, xiv, who brings Gramsci's use of "consent" and Foucault's formulation of governmentality together in this way; Li 2007, 25, by contrast suggests that the "conduct of conduct" and "consent" refer to different types of power-laden practices with different degrees of visibility: Foucault's governmentality with practices of subject formation of which subjects are themselves unaware, and Gramsci's consent with more visible practices that trigger conscious reactions.

26. Watts 2003.

27. Chatterjee 2006; Gidwani 2008; Li 2007; Ludden 1992; Wainwright 2008.

28. Foucault 1991, 102, 2003 (1976), 241, 46–47; Moore 2005.

29. Long translated as "nationality," *minzu* (which was first used in China in the early twentieth century, by way of Japan) has since the 2000s been translated increasingly as "ethnic group" or simply left untranslated, as in the renaming of the Minzu University in Beijing (once the Central University for Nationalities), in an attempt to separate it from the idea of the nation associated with its own state. In the 1950s, state work groups attempted to identify separate *minzu* through Stalinist criteria of common language, territory, economic life, and psychological makeup, or culture.

30. See Bulag 2002b and Schein 2000.

31. Mauss 1990 (1924, 28), 1990 (1950).

32. Godelier 1999; Korf 2007; Mauss 1990 (1924); Woods 2003.

33. Emerson 1997 (1844); Godelier 1999; Woods 2003.

34. Bourdieu 1997; Silk 2004.

35. Bourdieu 1990, 122–34; Korf et al. 2010. See also Rankin 2004.

36. Hattori 2001, 640.

37. It is not my intention here to review the very extensive corpus of anthropological work on the gift; see among many others Firth 1983; Graeber 2001; Sahlins 1972; Schrift 1997; Yan 1996, and Yang 1994.

38. Hattori 2001; Kapoor 2008; Korf 2007; Korf et al. 2010; Silk 2004; Silva 2008; Stirrat 2006; Stirrat and Henkel 1997; Woods 2003.

39. Hattori 2001, 634–5.

40. See Abrams 1988; Gidwani 2008; Gupta 1995; Hansen and Stepputat 2001; Mitchell 1991, 1999; Secor 2007a; and Taussig 1992.

41. Silva 2008, 110; Kapoor 2008; Osteen 2002; Woods 2003.

42. Derrida 1997 (1992), 137.

43. Derrida 1997 (1992), 127.

44. Li 1999.

45. Boulnois 2003.

46. Kham encompasses, roughly speaking, Dechen (Ch.: Diqing) Prefecture in Yunnan Province, Kardze (Ch.: Ganzi) Prefecture in western Sichuan Province, Yushu Prefecture in Qinghai province, and Chamdo Prefecture in the TAR. Amdo includes Ngaba Prefecture in Sichuan, and parts of Gansu, and much of Qinghai Province. After the breakup of the Tibetan Empire in the ninth century, Amdo and Kham retained close cultural and religious links to central Tibet but were politically organized as small kingdoms and tribes nominally under fluctuating Chinese and Tibetan authority but actually controlled by local leaders who often held political allegiance to neither Lhasa nor Beijing. The division of Tibetan cultural geography into U-Tsang, Kham, and Amdo is relatively new. An earlier scheme conceived of the major regions of Ngari Korsum, U-Tsang, and Mdo-Kham. The modern TAR border was established when the Tibetan government in Lhasa lost control of most of these eastern areas to the Manchu Empire in the middle of the eighteenth century. The Tibetan government never accepted these losses as permanent, and the cultural and religious ties between these areas remained strong, as people continued to make pilgrimages to Lhasa for both religion and trade.

47. Samuel 1982, 1993.

48. Kapstein 1998; Shakya 1993.

49. In addition, some land was allocated directly to peasants in return for tax payments and corvée labor for the government transportation network, and some land was worked by laborers who did not receive a share of the yield. On the organization of land in Tibet and the political system in place in the early twentieth century, including figures on landholding, see Carrasco 1959 and Goldstein 1989.

50. There is considerable debate over whether *mi ser* should be translated into English as "serfs" or "peasants," as well as whether the term "feudal" should be applied to the Tibetan economic and political system. On this issue see Coleman 1998; Goldstein 1986; Kolås 2003; and Miller 1987. Chinese historiographers call Tibetan social organization a "feudal-serf" system but Western scholars have been divided, partly by different definitions of serfdom and on the extent to which taxpayers had autonomy from their lords. Taxpayers were called *khral pa*, and "small households" were called *dud chung*, literally "small smoke."

51. For example *tshe g.yog* were hereditary servants; *nang bran* were house servants.

52. This large number of runaways prompted the Tibetan government to create a new rule that allowed those who had not been caught within three years to register as "human lease" with the newly created Agricultural Office. See Coleman 1998; Goldstein 1968.

53. In eastern China, the term *Chengguanqu* (translated as "region of city" in the TAR Statistical Yearbooks) is often understood to be a completely urbanized area, whose residents have nonagricultural household registrations. In Lhasa, however, the actual urbanized area covers less area than the four rural townships that are also part of the *Chengguanqu*.

54. This is itself a changing notion (particularly for older Tibetans who have watched the city expand dramatically over the decades), but it refers roughly to the area closest to the center of the old city (the Barkor around the Jokhang) as well as *Xijiao*, the large stretch of built-up area west of the Potala Palace. Administratively, these areas are those parts of the *Chengguanqu* that do not belong to one of the four rural townships and whose residents are registered to neighborhood committees (*jumin weiyuanhui*) rather than village committees (*cunmin weiyuanhui*).

55. "Looking at Tibet in a New Light." *People's Daily*, May 16, 1994, BBC SWB (British Broadcasting Corporation, Summary of World Broadcasts), FE/2010/G.

56. Das and Poole 2004, 4.

57. Agamben 1998; Das and Poole 2004.

1. State Space

1. "Kyi kyi so so! (*skyid skyid gsol gsol*)" is typically shouted before "lha rgyal lo," and implies happiness and propitation of deities. "Gyi hee hee!" does not have a particular meaning but is a common vocalization of excitement.

2. Certeau 1984, 98. See also Bourdieu 2000, 131.

3. Huber 1999.

4. Kapstein 1998.

5. See Makley 2003 on the gendered aspects of circumambulation as a Tibetan spatial practice.

6. Lefebvre 2003, 87; Secor 2007a.

7. Brenner and Elden 2009, 364, 367.

8. Abrams 1988, 58. See also Foucault 2008; Gupta 1995; Hansen and Stepputat 2001; Mitchell 1991; and Secor 2007a.

9. Mitchell 1991, 92; see Foucault 1995 (1977).

10. Certeau 1984, 35–37.

11. Foucault 1995 (1977), 201.

12. Agamben 1998, 8–10, 28.

13. Agamben 1998, 115; Coleman and Grove 2009; Mitchell 2006; Patton 2007, 218; Pratt 2005; Sanchez 2004.

14. Agamben 1998, 28–29.

15. Quote from *No. 16 Barkor South Street*, documentary film by Duan Jin-Chuan, 1996, Tibetan Culture Communication Company.

16. See Mountz 2004.

17. See Barnett 1994 for an extensive analysis of the symbolic struggles over this ceremony.

18. "Harsher Measures to Enforce Ban on Dalai Lama Birthday Celebrations," TIN (Tibet Information Network), August 6, 1999.

19. http://www.huffingtonpost.com/rebecca-novick/chinas-propaganda-in-tibe_b_142642.html; http://www.tchrd.org/press/2001/pr20010713.html.

20. Agamben 1998, 27.

21. http://www.chinatoday.com.cn/ctenglish/se/txt/2009–07/30/content_209854.htm.

22. Secor 2007a, 49.

23. Das and Poole 2004.

24. Secor 2007a, 42.

25. Barnett 2006b, 2012.

26. Mitchell 1991, 93.

27. I draw here on parallels with Sanchez's (2004) discussion of the Portland "prostitution-free zone" and the prostitute as a figure of "excluded exclusion." As she notes, such bans are strategies of spatial governmentality. All technologies of governmentality are spatial, but some strategies make use of explicit spatial organization such as planning and zoning.

28. Fischer 2005, 73.

29. Barnett 2006b.

30. http://www.cctv.com/english/20080318/101140.shtml.

31. Secor 2007a, 33.

32. See Barnett 1998, 2006a, 2006b; Schwartz 1994. The domain of the State Security Bureau or *Anquanju* (the Ministry of State Security, *Anquanbu*, at the national level), includes both foreign intelligence and domestic security. Although offices are found all over China, its presence is particularly heavy in Lhasa. It is said to be very difficult to join. Party membership is a prerequisite, as are political background checks not only of the candidate but also of his or her family members and spouse.

33. Foucault 1995 (1977), 187.

34. *Sagadawa* is also the name for the entire month, but the fifteenth of the month (which usually corresponds to late May or June in the Western calendar) in particular commemorates the birth, enlightenment, and *Parinirvana* (Departed in Bliss) Day of the Shakyamuni Buddha.

35. Secor 2007b, 49.

36. Barnett 2006b, 2012. Barnett (2012, 84) notes that a written document was finally published in 2012 that confirmed the existence of the restriction on students and government salaried workers circumambulating the Lingkor during Sagadawa, and by implication, on other religious practices.

37. Barnett (2006b and 2012) notes that there is a similar ban in Xinjiang, but that there it is explicit and publicly posted, whereas in Tibet there had been no admission of the restriction until 2012. Furthermore, he notes that this ban is different from the ban on having photographs of the Dalai Lama; the latter has been the subject of considerable public commentary including repeated official vilification of the Dalai Lama as a rationale for the ban.

38. Barnett 2006b.

39. Agamben 1998, 104.

40. Benjamin 1996 (1978); Das and Poole 2004; Secor 2007b; Taussig 1992.

41. Agamben 1998, 28.

42. "Tibet: Anniversary of an Uprising," radio interview with Robert Barnett, http://audiovideo.economist.com/?fr_story=66793fb0d49b320d4b67addd7498463 1e52b2c7d&rf=bm.

43. Yang 1994, 20–21.

44. This was in reference to the brewing international controversy at the time over the proposed World Bank Western Poverty Alleviation Project in Qinghai Province, which would resettle Han and Hui (Chinese Muslim) farmers to a Tibetan region.

45. Certeau 1984, 96.

2. *Cultivating Control*

1. Shakya 1999, 93–94. The Chinese troops included two thousand men led by Wang Qimei from Chamdo, 3000 led by General Zhang Guohua and another three thousand who came with General Tan Guansan (political commissar of the 18th Army Corps). Their ponies, yaks, and camels also had to be grazed and fed.

2. Shakya 1999, 96, 99–100, 117.

3. Goldstein 2007, 256–57 mentions the opening up of farmland but not the state farms.

4. In between the July First and August First State Farms there was also a very small state farm called the Qingban State Farm, established by troops from Qinghai.

5. American journalist Anna Louise Strong who visited the area in 1959, after seven years of reclamation, described the land as "half flooded, the other half boulders and sand" (Bista 1979, 79).

6. From 1951 to 1959, the CCP paid for everything they bought in the TAR in *dayuan*, since Chinese paper currency was not accepted by Tibetans. *Dayuan* were accepted because they could be remelted as silver and resold. The large-scale use of *dayuan* eventually undermined Tibetan currency by making it worthless (Shakya 1999, 94–95).

7. Xizang Nongkeng Zhuangkuang Writing Group 1986, 5.

8. Xizang Nongkeng Zhuangkuang Writing Group 1986, 4.

9. One *fen* is one-tenth of a *mu*; one *mu* is one-fifteenth of a hectare. The Chinese version of the words about not taking local resources, *bu chi di fang*, literally means "don't eat the local place" (Agricultural Research Institute 1992).

10. Rohlf 1999, 252.
11. Williams 2002.
12. Shapiro 2001.
13. Xizang Nongkeng Zhuangkuang Writing Group 1986, 4.
14. Xizang Nongkeng Zhuangkuang Writing Group 1986.
15. http://202.84.17.22/xizhang/zazhi/2001-3/eng/p17.htm.
16. See Samuel 1993, 218–22 and Ekvall 1968, 92–93.
17. Xizang Nongkeng Zhuangkuang Writing Group 1986, 406.
18. Shapiro 2001, 107.
19. Debord 1994 (1967), 64.
20. Debord 1994 (1967), 64.
21. Bista 1979, 82.
22. *sa dang 'thab, gnam dang 'thab, gral rim 'thab rtsod mthar phyin byed dgos.*
23. Others were sent to Jang Tsala Karpo, a borax mine in the high-altitude Jangtang region of northern Tibet (in Nagchu). After the Najin plant was completed, those who were strongest and those classified as not reformed were sent to the mine.
24. This included branches in Chushur and Tolung as well as the main farm in Lhasa (Yeh 2008).
25. Later, many of these prisoners were also sent to the Zhölpa State Farm in Nyingtri, which was then under the control of the Agricultural Reclamation Bureau, where they participated in logging. Of those who stayed on the main branch of the August First State Farm, those who displayed "proper behavior" were allowed to continue as formal workers starting around 1964.
26. See Yeh 2009a for a detailed environmental history of the Lhalu wetland.
27. *chi yi nung khrang bzo pa byas pa las sla po mi 'dug/dbu rtse nyi shar ldig sgra dgos kyis/ lcags kyi mid pa dgos kyis/zangs kyi mchu to dgos kyis.*
28. Shakya 1999, 116.
29. Xizang Nongkeng Zhuangkuang Writing Group 1986, 4–6.
30. Xizang Nongkeng Zhuangkuang Writing Group 1986, 4–6.
31. Xizang Nongkeng Zhuangkuang Writing Group 1986, 6.
32. Agricultural Research Institute 1992.
33. This is one of the two major disputed borders between India and China; the other is between Ngari and Ladakh. The MacMahon Line was drawn by Sir Henry MacMahon and Lochen Shatra, the Tibetan representative to the Simla Conference in 1914. See Shakya 1999.
34. Tian Bao was appointed to a high military post (Second Political Commissar of the Tibet Military District) and later served as TAR governor.
35. Agricultural Research Institute 1992.
36. Bista 1979, 79–80.
37. Workers on the August First State Farm reported the use of the first glass-pane greenhouses as being between 1956 and 1965. Plastic greenhouses such as the ones that became common in peri-urban villages in the 1990s were not introduced until 1980–82.
38. "Liberation Brings New Life to Tibetans," *China Daily*, May 24, 2001.
39. Yang Xi, "From Serf to Actor—a Tibetan Life," March 19, 2009, http://www.china.org.cn/china/tibet_democratic_reform/content_17470663.htm.
40. Fighting monks (Wylie: *rdab rdob*) were monks in larger monasteries who were responsible for protecting the monastery and did not have to study scriptures.
41. According to the Seventeen Point Agreement, the Tibetan army was supposed to be integrated into the PLA. However, all but three regiments were disbanded. These regiments remained in Lhasa; their reorganization was a point of contention between the Tibetan government and PLA leadership (see Shakya 1999).

42. From the founding of the August First State Farm until 1953, the soldiers were on high alert, and were not allowed to take vacations, rest, or leave the farm. After 1953, the drafted soldiers (*yiwu bing*) were allowed to leave if they had already served for three years, but the volunteer soldiers (*ziyuan bing*) were not allowed to leave.

43. *Changqi jian zang, bianjiang weijia.* Some PLA soldiers did try to run away from the farm; if caught they were treated as prisoners of war. Some soldiers were allowed to return home in 1957–58. Another wave returned during the first "internal transfer" (Ch.: *neidiao*) in 1972. Also in 1972, many new soldiers were sent to the different branches of the August First State Farm as well as to other state farms under the TAR Agricultural Reclamation Bureau.

44. *Shenggen, kaihua, jieguo.* The Tibetan cadre who told me this said, "This policy was to help the soldiers occupy Tibet. It not only destroyed Tibet but also the lives of those poor PLA soldiers."

45. *Xizang Xizang san nian yi huan, san nian bu huan yao dang he shang.*

46. Chinese-Tibetan marriages became less common after the mid-1960s.

47. Labrang (Wylie: bla brang) refers to the household corporation of a lama. Ramoche Temple was built roughly the same time as the Jokhang Temple and is just north of the Barkhor area. Ramoche also refers to the neighborhood around the temple.

48. Liu was state president of the PRC until Mao attacked him as the "leader of the capitalist roaders" in 1966.

49. See Makley 2007, 103–4, 133–34.

50. Aziz 1987; Bell 1928; Willis 1987.

51. Gyatso and Havnevik 2005; Makley 2003, 2007; McGranahan 2010.

52. Keller 1998; Massell 1974.

53. Makley 2007, 90–93, 116.

54. A measure of seed volume that also refers to the area sown with that quantity of seed.

55. They do not eat fish because fish are associated with *klu* (*nagas*), underwater serpentine deities. Before the 1950s, villagers in Kyichuling, who lived on a monastic estate, were forbidden to raise chickens and pigs because they were considered to be unclean. (See also Bell 1928, 232.) Also, smaller animals were avoided following the logic that killing one large animal for consumption was morally preferable to killing several smaller ones.

56. Both of these were new terms created for the classification of class positions. In the "old society" servants in this village were called *g.yog po* rather than *bran g.yog*.

57. Among the earliest ones were Bangdo Commune in Tagtse, Tongkha Commune in Tolung Dechen County, and a commune in Phenpo.

58. Toward the end of the collective period, when policies began to loosen, the sideline brigade also participated in construction, truck driving, and brewing *chang* for sale in Lhasa.

59. During most of the collective period, there was only one farming production brigade in Kyichuling, but toward the end, two separate teams were formed, in order to foster competition.

60. Later state farms, such as the Phenpo State Farm, were also not as privileged as the August First State Farm.

61. The much sparser population density also meant that communes in Tibet had significantly fewer people than in other regions. In the TAR there was generally just one level of production brigade, rather than two levels as was common elsewhere.

62. Instead, the brigade assigned one person to sell all households' potatoes and radishes in Lhasa. That person received work points for this labor, and divided the profit among all of the villagers.

63. Estimates I was given for the basic grain ration in peri-urban Lhasa ranged from 115–175 kg/person per year; 150 kg (11 *khal*, the unit used at the time) for agricultural laborers is a reasonable estimate. The seed grain, stalks for fodder, and basic grain ration were referred to together as the "three retains." On local grain reserves throughout China, see Oi 1989.

64. Tib.: *rgyal gces gzhung 'bru*; Ch.: *aiguo gongliang*. In Kyichuling, the tax was roughly 10 *khal* (280 pounds) of grain per person, and was always collected in barley. Oi 1989, 50–51 notes that in China, the agricultural tax together with the basic quota of "surplus" grain was called "tax and sales responsibility" (*zhenggou renweu*). In addition to the basic quota sale of grain to the state there were also over-quota sales, which unlike the quota sales, had no predetermined annual targets but rather were based on "negotiation." Throughout the early 1950s, Korean War, and efforts to "resist America" the amount of money paid for over-quota and quota sales was the same. Because peasants were expected to sell due to their patriotism, this was called "patriotic surplus grain" (*aiguo yuliang*). Note that this was different in the TAR, where the tax itself was called *aiguo gongliang* or "patriotic government share grain" and the surplus was simply called *yuliang* or *phud tshong*.

65. The figure was arrived at by totaling the monetary value of grain production, income from sideline work, and income from livestock production and subtracting expenditures on agricultural inputs (chemical fertilizers, etc.), grain tax, public welfare money, public investment money (spent on irrigation ditches, tractors, etc.), and cadre salaries.

66. Makley 2003, 609.

67. Rofel 1999, 132.

68. By 2001, the population of the village had increased to 380.

69. For example, a four-person household received roughly 12.8 *mu* of land divided into six to twelve plots around the village.

70. In Kyichuling during the early 2000s, those whose household registrations had changed could either give their land back to the village or pay rent on it. The rent was set at 150 RMB per *mu* until migrant greenhouse vegetable farming became common, at which point it was raised to half of the average rent that Chinese farmers paid for their vegetable plots (400 to 450 RMB per *mu*).

71. In the late 1990s, the farm rented out its land at three different prices: the lowest figure for formal workers, a slightly higher one for "temporary workers" whose household registrations were with the farm, and the highest figure for outsiders whose household registrations were not local. The latter are all Han migrants. Although Tibetan formal workers still paid the lowest rent, the absolute amount they paid roughly tripled from 1986 to 2000. Tibetan farmers were forbidden from renting out land from the farm and then rerenting at a higher price to migrants. Furthermore, formal workers who had not yet reached retirement age were required to rent the land or otherwise pay a fee. As a result, most Tibetans who had not retired dropped out of vegetable farming, allowing the farm to rent out the land at the higher figure to Han migrants.

3. Vectors of Development

1. In 1989, work units and military units had a total of 1,900 *mu* (193 hectares) of land under vegetable cultivation throughout the TAR. Xiao 1994, 632.

2. Tibetans use this term interchangeably with *rgya nag*, to refer to any non-Tibetan part of the PRC. Usage of the term is dependent on geographic and ethnic context.

3. Murphy 2006, 7.

4. PRC 2000 Census, Table 7-2. Sichuan has the most sending migrants to both the TAR and Lhasa Municipality, followed by Gansu.

5. For example http://www.wistib.org/. Part of the issue is the definition of Tibet—the PRC government considers only the TAR to be Tibet whereas exiles include Tibetan parts of Yunnan, Qinghai, Sichuan, and Gansu, sometimes including areas that have long been ethni-

cally mixed such as Qinghai's capital, Xining. The government-in-exile has toned down its rhetoric by redefining "population transfer" in accordance with a statement by the UN Commission on Human Rights, in which "the State's role [in population transfer] may be active or passive ... involv[ing] financial subsidies, planning, public information, or other judicial action (Central Tibetan Administration 2000).

6. Fischer 2008, 632. For example http://www.tibetsun.com/elsewhere/2010/04/14/not-everyone-from-switzerland-adores-the-dalai-lama/.

7. Yan 2000.

8. Naughton 1995; Oi 1989.

9. Solinger 1999, 51–53.

10. Chan and Buckingham 2008 argue that the 2005 reforms, which some have misinterpreted as an abolition of the system, actually made permanent migration to cities harder than before.

11. Hansen 1999, 2007.

12. Huang 1995.

13. Iredale, Bilik, and Su 2001.

14. See Shakya 1999 and Wang 1994.

15. See Schwartz 1994.

16. Barnett 1998, 2006a.

17. Clarke 1998.

18. *Tibet Daily*, February 4, 1994.

19. Xinhua News Agency, January 4, 1993; FBIS (Foreign Broadcast Information Service).

20. The Department of Industry and Commerce reported that the number of individual businesses grew from 489 in 1980 to 41,830 in 1993, with a registered capital of over 170 million RMB. "Roundup on Tibet's Private Sector Economy," *Tibet Daily*, February 4, 1994, pp. 1, 4, BBC SWB, March 2, 1994, FE/1935/G.

21. http://news.xinhuanet.com/english/2009-12/30/content_12727769.htm.

22. http://www.yuanzang.com/xw/list.asp?id=227.

23. Shakya 1999.

24. Hu 2003.

25. November 28, 1994. Tibet People's Broadcasting Station, Lhasa, in Chinese, BBC SWB, FE/2170/G, December 5, 1994. The SWB translation uses the confusing English term "hinterlander" to refer to people from Han China; here I have used *neidi* to avoid confusion.

26. PRC State Council 2001.

27. Hu 2003 found in her study that 70 percent of each year's newly arrived migrants in Lhasa left after one or two years, while 5–10 percent stayed five years or more. Vegetable farmers generally stay longer than one to two years, and a few have stayed for twenty years or longer. In Ma and Lhundrup's (2008, 19–20) survey of Lhasa migrants, most reported planning to stay in Lhasa for one or two years (18.5 percent and 21.9 percent), though 12.5 percent reported planning to stay for ten years. Iredale et al. 2001 report that migrants stay for five to six years on average.

28. This includes both the built-up urban area as well as four townships that were still largely agricultural in 2000.

29. See Yeh and Henderson 2008.

30. Fischer 2008a, 647.

31. Ma and Lhundrup 2008, 15–16.

32. A city street office (*jiedao banshichu*) is a subdivision of an urban ward (*qu*), equivalent in the administrative hierarchy to a town (*zhen*, an urban unit) or township (*xiang*, a rural unit), both of which are subdivisions of counties (*xian*).

33. See Fischer 2008a, 36.

34. See Fischer 2005, 2008a for much more extensive discussions of the political economy of development in Tibet.

35. PRC State Council 2001.

36. "The west" was defined as Xinjiang, Tibet, Ningxia, Inner Mongolia, and Guangxi Autonomous Regions; Chongqing Municipality; and Qinghai, Gansu, Shaanxi, Sichuan, Yunnan, and Guizhou Provinces. Note that Inner Mongolia stretches all the way to China's very eastern limit. Later a Korean autonomous prefecture in Jilin in China's far northeast was added, suggesting that "the west" was more of a metaphorical than a geographical concept. In many ways "the west" became associated with minority areas (Oakes 2007, 245).

37. Xinhua News Agency. "China Leader Hails Qinghai-Tibet Railway as a Major Step for Western Development," October 25, 2005, *BBC Monitoring International Reports*.

38. Goodman 2004; Holbig 2004; Lai 2003; Oakes 2004, 2007; Shih 2004.

39. Fischer 2009, 39.

40. "China Pumps 310 Bln into Tibet's Development in 9 Years," http://in.chineseembassy.org/eng/focus/t653680.htm.

41. Fischer 2009, 42–43.

42. Fischer 2005.

43. Fischer 2005, 73; 2008a.

44. Fischer 2012.

45. Dreyer 2003; Fischer 2005; Hu 2003; Sharlho 1992; Wang and Bai 1991.

46. Fischer 2008a, 47–48.

47. Fischer 2008a, 50.

48. Barnett 2006a.

49. "Car Ownership Boom Means Traffic Jams in Once-Tranquil Tibet," Associated Press, November 7, 2007, http://motoring.asiaone.com/Motoring/News/Story/A1Story20071114-36736.html.

50. Fischer 2005, 2009.

51. Solinger 1999, 71–72.

52. Chan 2007, 397.

53. This is consistent with Solinger's (1999) findings about migration sending areas across China more generally.

54. The "three rural problems" (*sannong wenti*) refers to rural livelihoods of peasants (*nongmin*), rural society (*nongcun*), and (rural) agricultural production (*nongye*).

55. For more details about the building of the railway see Lustgarten 2008.

56. Solinger 1999; Yan 2003; Zhang 2001.

57. Anagnost 2004, 193.

58. Hu and Salazar 2008, 2.

59. Lefebvre 1991 (1974).

60. Yan 2008, 114.

61. Yan 2003, 496.

62. Yan 2003, 506–7.

63. Yan 2008, 130.

64. Fischer 2012, 17, notes that while per capita expenditure on education in 2010 was higher than in nearby provinces, this reflects the difference in the cost of education supply in the sparsely populated TAR; higher urban wages; and its top-heavy education structure.

65. Ma and Lhundrup 2008, 15 n. 16, also report the phenomenon of "university exam migrants" who find a way to temporarily transfer their household registrations to Lhasa for the purpose of college entrance exams. *Guanxi* refers to relationships, personalized networks of influence in particular.

66. Taxes for farmers and nomads in the TAR were canceled after Hu Yaobang's 1980 trip to the TAR. However, they paid taxes throughout the collective period.

67. See also Fischer 2008b.
68. Ferguson 1990, 20.

Signs of Lhasa

1. See Yurchak 2006 on the unmooring of constative from performative dimensions of speech acts, as well as on the "quotient of ideological density" (57).

4. The Micropolitics of Marginalization

1. "Tibet Maintains Abundant Winter Vegetable Supply," Xinhua News Agency, February 3, 1995, FBIS CHI-95–024.
2. Andersen, Cooke, and Wills 1995, 119.
3. The cases of the Lubu and Hebalin cooperatives were different for historical reasons. Tibetanized descendants of Han (Lubu) and Chinese Muslim (Hebalin) soldiers settled in these neighborhoods during the Qing dynasty and cultivated vegetables. See Yeh 2009b.
4. Barley and wheat prices fell significantly with the lifting of some government controls over the grain procurement and distribution system. By the late 1990s market prices were lower than state purchase prices for "surplus grain," which was transformed from an economic burden during the collective period to a state subsidy. Residents of peri-urban villages reported that sales of "surplus grain" had become voluntary (*rang mos*) between 1996 and 1999. If the quality of the grain did not meet new standards set by the county, the county could refuse to purchase any grain at all, which frequently happened. In peri-urban villages in the late 1990s, this created an additional incentive to lease land to Han migrants.
Rough calculations for winter wheat in 2000 suggested that, assuming it would sell at the highest market price, it would yield a gross (not net) profit of 592 RMB/*mu*, less than the average 800 RMB/*mu* paid by Han farmers for rentals. A typical gross profit for barley would be 305 RMB/*mu* as against 800 RMB/*mu*. See Yeh 2003 for more details.
5. Williams 1974, 124; Williams 1977, 88.
6. Moore 2005, 11.
7. In 2005, the exchange rate was roughly 8 RMB to the US dollar.
8. Compare this to the rental amounts that the Tibetan villagers earn, which began at 250 RMB/*mu*/year in 1985, quadrupled to 800–1,000 RMB/*mu*/year by 2001, and then stayed roughly constant through at least 2008. Rentals are significantly higher on the state farms, but there they include steel-frame greenhouses, so that the migrants do not have to invest in building and rebuilding the structures. Migrants in peri-urban villages also tend to have some land that is not in greenhouses, whereas on the state farms, all rented land is for greenhouse cultivation. Thus, those who rent on state farms cultivate on less land overall.
9. Vegetable prices also vary seasonally: highest in winter and early spring, and lowest in the summer months when supply is greatest.
10. If a Han household wants to rent land from more than one Tibetan household (as is often the case), one Tibetan household sometimes takes the lead to sign a single contract on behalf of all of the Tibetan households.
11. Coronil 1997; Guthman 2004; Harvey 1982.
12. Coronil 1997, 48.
13. Coronil 1997, 47–48.
14. Despite being told that contracts were standardized in one particular village, I saw that two households had entirely different contracts. In some villages, particularly in Tulong Dechen

County, the village committee rather than individual households rented out contiguous fields comprised of multiple households' land. In those cases, the villagers are not involved and the committee divides up the rent to households at the end of each year.

15. See Fischer 2008b for similar examples. Fischer argues that Tibetan cultural preferences are enabled by a higher subsistence capacity—the generally greater amount of land that Tibetans have compared to Han farmers—and thus ability to act on these preferences.

16. On the state farms Han migrants rent prefabricated steel-frame greenhouses at a much higher price (3,500 RMB/*mu* for rental of greenhouse against 1,000 RMB/*mu* ground rent), but do not need to purchase bamboo poles.

17. Prices increased from 0.5 RMB a pole in 1996, to 2–2.5 RMB in 2000, and 3.5 RMB the following year. Chinese farmers complained that this dramatic price increase was due to environmental protection measures in Nyingtri.

18. "Xinhua on Vegetable Markets in Lhasa," BBC SWB, June 4, 1994, FE/2014/G.

19. Andersen, Cooke, and Wills 1995.

20. Gidwani 2008, 214.

21. Gidwani 2008, 142.

22. Freidberg 2001.

23. Gidwani 2008, 143. See also Butler 1997 and Moore 2005.

24. Tibetans also use night soil, but usually compost it with straw and ashes for a year, whereas Han farmers don't compost so long. One Tibetan claimed, "they put it right on the fields."

25. Bourdieu 1998 (1977), 80.

26. This was the case from 1997 through 2002, the last time I visited the farm. By 2007 this entire area had been built up.

27. These dynamics have begun to change in recent years, as vegetarianism has been promoted by the influential religious figures Khenpo Tsultrim Lodroe and Khenpo Sodargye, both former students of Khenpo Jigme Phuntsok, who played a major role in the revitalization of Tibetan Buddhism after the Cultural Revolution with the founding of the Larung Gar Buddhist Institute in Serthar County, Sichuan. Khenpo Tsultrim Lodroe's and Khenpo Sodargye's Buddhist modernist promotion of vegetarianism has gone hand-in-hand with other movements including asking herders to stop selling their livestock to slaughterhouses and to stop wearing clothes with trims made of pelts of endangered animals.

28. These stupas (*chos rten*) to propitiate birth and place deities were destroyed during the Cultural Revolution, but later rebuilt on their former locations.

29. Liechty 1996; Raffles 2002.

30. Wylie: *skyes lha*. This term can refer both to a deity associated with one's date of birth, or more commonly, and as it is used here, to the god that presides over the place of one's birth. Makley 2013.

31. Raffles 1999, 339; also Rodman 1992.

32. Certeau 1984, 97–98.

33. Massey 1994, 168, 264–65.

34. The festival was called *nyal tro*, a local name for what is perhaps a local festival; I did not hear of it elsewhere. The Tibetan New Year, determined by a lunar calendar, falls between January and March.

35. On imperialist nostalgia see Rosaldo 1989.

5. Indolence and the Cultural Politics of Development

1. "Looking at Tibet in a New Light," *People's Daily*, May 16, 1994.

2. *People's Daily*, March 27, 2000.

3. Perreault 2003.

4. Escobar 1995; Esteva 1992; Ferguson 1990; Sachs 1992.

5. Bebbington 2000; Blaikie 2000; Hart 2001, 2004; Li 1999; Sivaramakrishnan and Agrawal 2003.

6. Gupta 1998; Perreault 2003; Pigg 1992; Radcliffe and Laurie 2006.

7. Moore 2000, 2005.

8. John Pomfret, "Tibetans Reach a Crossroads," *New York Times*, July 16, 1999.

9. Merlan 1998, 333–34, 197.

10. Adams 1996, 511.

11. Butler 1997; Moore 1996.

12. Gramsci 1999 (1971), 323.

13. Hall 1988, 43.

14. Willis 1981 (1977), 119.

15. There are two issues here: one theoretical, about how speech should be analytically considered; the second, methodological, is sometimes framed as "How do you know that 'lazy' isn't just a convenient way to dismiss the researcher?" In Lhasa, the discourse of indolence is a whole complex of statements not limited to formal interviews or even, according to many informants, the presence of an outside researcher.

16. Butler 1990, 185.

17. In Bell 1998, 165.

18. Herbert 2000.

19. Butler 1990, 165.

20. Bell 1928, 40–41.

21. Hall 1988, 55.

22. Weber 1958 (1905), 49–59.

23. In the Sigalovada sutra in the *Digha Nikaya*, for example, the Buddha teaches: "Sleeping by day/Wandering all around untimely. ... These things destroy a person .../... Gathering wealth as bees do honey/And heaping it up like an ant hill/ Once wealth is accumulated/ Family and household life may follow. .../... Energetic, not lazy ... Such a person attains glory." http://accesstoinsight.org/canon/sutta/digha/dn-31-ksyo.html. Benavides notes that in a Buddhist story about beginnings, it is the laziness of primordial beings that begets work, and work that causes scarcity; work is both a curse and blessing. "Work as production ... appears as degrading, as something from which one must distance oneself; and if one cannot distance oneself from it in reality, one must at least cleanse oneself from it as much as one can." At the same time, the act of giving brings merit, and donating to the monastic community requires accumulation and hence productive work (Benavides 2005, 79, 87).

24. Bell 1928, 264; Harrer 1953.

25. On alternative Buddhist development projects see Makley 2007 and Gaerrang 2012.

26. Gidwani 2008, 213; emphasis in original.

27. Gidwani 2008, 217.

28. Gidwani 2008, 229. See also Timothy Mitchell 2002 on the question of thinking and writing about capitalism without attributing to it an inherent power or internal rationality. This view of the "para-sitic" existence of capitalism clarifies the close association between capitalism and development without fully reducing or subsuming one to the other.

29. Croll 1994; Liu 2000; Rofel 1999.

30. Liu 2000, 12.

31. Croll 1994, 22; Rofel 1999, 132–33.

32. On *suku,* see Rofel 1999, 138–39.

33. Around Lhasa, twelve *khal* would have been equivalent to roughly 336 pounds.

34. Rofel 1999, 135.

35. Rofel 1999, 129.

36. Germano 1998, 55.
37. Adams 2005, 235.
38. TIN 1999.
39. Hall 1996 (1986), 435.

MICHAEL JACKSON AS LHASA

1. Williams 2009.

6. "BUILD A CIVILIZED CITY"

1. "da grong khyer rang chags shag."
2. Blondeau and Gyatso 2003, 26.
3. Larsen and Sinding-Larsen 2001; Liu 1988; Ma 1991.
4. "lha sa rgya che ba'i sgang la, ra mo che snon 'bel rgyab."
5. Li 2005, 18–19.
6. Because I am discussing etymology (where spelling is important), I use Wylie transliteration in this section.
7. Zhang 2003, 411.
8. Dungdkar 2002, 573–74.
9. Dungdkar 2002, 2167–68.
10. Goldstein, Shelling, and Surkhang 2001, 205.
11. Tibetan from Patshang 1973, 114; English translation in Sørensen 1994, 131. According to a popular Tibetan legend, which first appeared in post–tenth-century Buddhist works, Tibetans are descended from the union of an ape and a rock-ogress, said to be emanations of the *bodhisattva* Avalokitesvara and the goddess Tara.
12. One might ask why *grong* is not contrasted here against pastoralist spaces. *Grong* can be used in terms that refer to pastoral (*'brog*), as well as farming (*zhing*) areas. The difficulty in finding a single term that captures the opposite of *grong* (a place with humans and dwellings) is precisely the point here: that it is not a structuring dichotomy.
13. Williams 1973, 307.
14. Williams 1976, 55–57.
15. Sørensen 1994, 133. In Tibetan: "de nas thang thams brje la zhing byas, grong khyer mang po rtsigs" (Patshang 1973, 117).
16. While *zhing/'brog* (agricultural/pastoral) is also a binary of sorts, it is not conceptually dichotomous in the same way as city/country or lay/monastic, given both the widespread existence of *sa ma 'brog* (agropastoralists) as well as the relative weakness of hierarchical mapping of qualities such as purity, respect, morality, and civilization in *zhing/'brog* as compared to the lay versus the monastic dichotomy.
17. Fitzgerald 2002, 26; Ma 2005, 482.
18. Chang 1977, 99. See also discussions in Skinner 1977, particularly by Wright (1977) as well as a dissenting view by Mote (1977).
19. Gaubatz 1996; Knapp 2000, 7.
20. Wright 1977, 34; Xu 2000.
21. Wright 1977, 34.
22. Mann 1984.
23. Chan 1994; Coulter and Ivory 1982; Henderson 2004; Naughton 1995; Pannell 2002.

24. Cartier 2002, 2003, 62; Ma 2002.
25. Hsing 2010.
26. Bulag 2002a, 212.
27. Ma 2005, 477; Shen 2005, 49–50.
28. Friedmann 2005.
29. Hsing 2010; Logan 2008; Wu 2009.
30. Hsing 2010, 182–83; Zhang 2010, 39.
31. Hsing 2010; Lin 2009.
32. Harvey 2003; Hsing 2010.
33. Zhang 2010.
34. Bulag 2002a, 198, 202; also Bulag 2006.
35. Gelek and Li 1997, 191–92, 201.
36. Li 2005, 20, 22–24.
37. Li 2005, 18.
38. China Intercontinental Communication Center, and Tibet International Cultural Film and Television Programs Company, *Celebrating the 50th Anniversary of the Peaceful Liberation of Tibet* (China Intercontinental Audio-Video Press, 2001).
39. For more details see Yeh and Henderson 2008, as well as http://www.xizang.gov.cn/getCommonContent.do?contentId=342222.
40. Bulag 2002a, 225.
41. For a general analysis of Tibetan cadres in Tibet, see Conner and Barnett 1997. However, they do not deal with cadres below the county level.
42. Kate Saunders, "Impact of Urbanization in Rural Areas of Tibet Autonomous Region" (International Campaign for Tibet, 2 October, 2003); Human Rights Watch, "Fewer Tibetans on Lhasa's Key Ruling Bodies" (November 7, 2006).
43. Official statements that in the year 2000, the urban population of Lhasa Municipality (total population of 470,000) had reached 230,000 refer not to the number of residents in the *Chengguanqu* or urban district, but rather to the total population living in the six city street offices and nine urban towns across the entire prefecture. A comparison with figures for 1990 thus shows that fully 30 percent of the reported urban growth at the time was a result of the reclassification of townships as towns. For more details see Yeh and Henderson 2008.
44. Zhang 2010, 73.
45. See Barnett 2006a for more on architectural styles in Lhasa.
46. Barnett 2006a, 72–74, 98. In 1987, not counting temporary migrants, there were 27,500 native Lhasa residents living in the old urban district around the Barkor, another 33,300 Tibetans (along with 37,800 Han) living in work unit housing, and 8,000 Tibetans living in nearby suburbs (Ma 1991, 822).
47. This is due in part to the relative sizes of urban cores, as well as perhaps to the Jokhang Temple's listing in 2000 as a World Heritage Site, which imposes some building restrictions in its immediate vicinity.
48. Barnett (2006a, 91–92) describes this as the hybrid "New Tibetan" style.
49. See also Zhang 2010, 66, 93.
50. See Fraser 2000 and Zhang 2010, 95.
51. See Hsing 2010 and Zhang 2006, 2010. Urban plans across China are often based on inflated urban population and economic growth projections.
52. The planning area includes four towns and townships of Tolung Dechen County, Nyedang Township of Chushur County, and the entire area from one kilometer to the west to one kilometer to the east of Lhagong Highway between Lhasa and Gongkar Airport, for a total of 1,480 square kilometers.
53. Holston 1989.

54. Kabir Heimsath, personal communication.

55. Hsing 2010, 123.

56. Xi Jan Zhang, "Lasa Shi Chengzhong Cun Gaizao: Qi yi yuan gaijian Gama Gongsang Xiao Qu" [Lhasa Municipality reconstruction of villages in the city: 700 million yuan to reconstruct the Karma Kunsang residential area], Xinhua News Agency, December 17, 2009, http://tibet.cctv.com/20091217/103604.shmtl.

57. "Advertisement for the Reconstruction of TAR Lhasa Municipality Chengguan District Karma Kunsang Village in a City Project" (in Chinese), June 30, 2010, http://www.lasa.gov.cn/Item/12968.aspx.

58. See for example Bi 2008, 149.

59. Penkyi 2007.

60. Roughly 21,000 USD/acre at the exchange rate at the time. This is significantly more than some other villagers in Tolung Dechen County have received (12,000 RMB/*mu* for loss of land to the Qinghai-Tibet Railway) but less than villages in Najin Township who lost their land to urbanization (for example, 40,000 RMB/*mu* for villagers displaced by the new campus of Tibet University).

61. Perry 2011, 42, citing Deng and Deng 2007.

62. Hsing 2010, 107–108.

63. The largest house was 181 square meters in area plus a courtyard of roughly 100 square meters, with an insider's price of 180,000 RMB (roughly 26,000 U.S. dollars). A second model was slightly smaller, with an insider's price of 140,000 RMB. There were only ten of the third model, a much smaller 110-square-meter house built for families that qualified as being officially impoverished, who were required to pay only 5,000 RMB.

64. Penkyi 2007.

65. Ironically, one of the villages included in the new scheme was the one that had previously had the successful all-female Tibetan vegetable cooperative described in chapter 4.

66. Hsing 2010, 197.

67. Makley 2013, 696. See also Blondeau and Steinkeller 1996.

68. The stupa is named either Drolma Namsum or Namgyal Chörten, depending on whom I asked. According to one story, a long time ago there were three Drolmas (Taras, female bodhisattva-goddesses) who were coming from Tsang (a western part of Tibet including Shigatse) to visit the Jokhang Temple on pilgrimage. They arrived at Chushur (just south and west of Tolung Dechen) at sunset when a robber came upon them. The first fled to where the Drolma Lhakhang shrine is located, at the site of a large Buddha painting at Nedang (on the road between Lhasa and Gongkar Airport). The second fled to Sera Monastery. The last was wounded by the robber's dagger and made it as far as this village in Dongkar, near Dongkar Fort before dying; the stupa, according to this tale, was put up to commemorate her.

69. Cartier 2001.

70. Hsing 2010, 99.

71. Hsing 2010, 102.

72. http://www.lsda.gov.cn/show.php?id=136.

73. They were slated to receive 30,000 RMB/*mu* of which 2000 RMB/*mu* would be kept by the village.

74. A "natural village" (*ziran cun*) is a hamlet or traditional unit of settlement, whereas an "administrative village" (*xingzheng cun*) is an administrative unit, usually made up of several natural villages.

75. Zheng Lin Yang, "Lasa Chengguanqu: Ta Shang Anju Xiaokang Lu" [Lhasa Chengguanqu: Stepping on the road to peaceful life and prosperous living], Tibet Daily, June 29, 2010.

76. See Yeh and Henderson 2008.
77. Lefebvre 1991 (1974).

7. Engineering Indebtedness and Image

1. "Armed Police Power Plant Builders on Snowy Plateau," http://english.chinamil.com.cn/site2/special-reports/2009–04/30/content_1746386.htm.
2. http://www.tibet.com/eco/eco4.html.
3. http://www.xz.xinhuanet.com/zhuanti/2005–08/27/content_4987934.htm; http://www.tibetinfor.com/news/2004–12–19/N0120041219125459.htm; http://news.sina.com.cn/c/2005–01–04/11184710827s.shtml.
4. http://news.xinhuanet.com/english/2009–03/02/content_10927923.htm.
5. "Tibet Meets Comfortable Housing Project Goal Ahead of Schedule" January 14, 2010, http://chinatibet.people.com.cn/6867585.html; "All Tibet's Farmers, Herdsmen to Move in Affordable Houses by 2010," December 1, 2009, http://chinatibet.people.com.cn/6829088.html.
6. "Pilgrims and Progress," *Economist,* February 6, 2010, pp. 43–44.
7. Tim Johnson, "China Orders Resettlement of Thousands of Tibetans," McClatchy Newspapers, May 3, 2007, http://www.mcclatchydc.com/2007/05/03/16232/china-orders-resettlement-of-thousands.html.
8. Email from Professor Goldstein to World Tibet News, May 8, 2007, see http://sft.radicaldesigns.org/article.php?id=1034.
9. Goldstein, Childs, and Wangdui 2010; Robin 2009, 58; Scott 1999.
10. Appadurai 1986, 19; Firth 1983, 101; Makley 2006.
11. Makley 2006, 9.
12. Douglas 1990, viii.
13. See Firth 1959; Graeber 2001; Lévi-Strauss 1997 (1950); Mauss 1990 (1950); Parry 1985; Sahlins 1972; Weiner 1985; and Yan 1996.
14. Balanced reciprocity is present in relationships of greater social distance; gifts are of similar value, and expectations of giving and receiving are better defined. Negative reciprocity refers to attempts to obtain something for nothing, through gambling, theft, trickery, or seizure; in a sense, this type of interaction between people or groups at great social distance is not reciprocity at all.
15. Sahlins 1972, 191–210.
16. See Harrell 1995 and Heberer 2001.
17. See Makley 2007.
18. Parry 1985. The ideology of the pure gift can be exemplified by private giving to the NGO world, where donors and recipients are unknown to each other, social ties are not created, and no obligation to the giver is created. Nevertheless, the aid chains through which such gifts are propagated entangle the receipt of the gift with conditionality, leading them to become a form of patronage or control. Korf et al. 2010; Mosse 2005; Stirrat and Henkel 1997.
19. Gregory 1982, 41.
20. Carrier 1995, 149, cited in Osteen 2002, 21.
21. Parry 1985, 469.
22. Kapoor 2008.
23. Silva 2008, 25.
24. However, see Li 1999 and Vandergeest 1991.
25. Derrida 1997 (1992), 127.
26. Li 1999.
27. Mauss 1990 (1950), 74–75.

28. Roth 2002, 124.
29. Debord 1994 (1967), 57.
30. Adams 2010, 97.
31. Debord 1994 (1967), 24.
32. Debord 1994 (1967), 44.
33. Guo et al. 2009.
34. Day 2008; Day and Hale 2007; He 2007.
35. Perry 2011, 36.
36. Perry 2008, 2011.
37. Wu 2007, cited in Perry 2011, 41.
38. See chapter 6. Deng and Deng 2007, cited in Perry 2011, 42.
39. *Anju gongcheng* (Tib.: *bde sdod rnam grangs*) is usually translated as Comfortable Housing, but could also be translated as "tranquil/peaceful living project"
40. As discussed in chapter 6, the term *anju gongcheng* was also used in Lhasa to refer to early retirement homes and is now used colloquially to refer to private row housing. Most rural Tibetans refer to the TAR Comfortable Housing project that began in 2006 (which is quite different) simply as *rnam grangs*, or "the project."
41. Yang, An, and Zhou 2007, 31.
42. http://chinatibet.people.com.cn/6829088.html; http://www.xxmy.gov.cn/asp/showdetail.asp?id=7760.
43. Ecological migration (*shengtai yimin*), often implemented in conjunction with "converting pastures to grasslands" (*tuimu huancao*), particularly in the Sanjiangyuan area of Qinghai province, moves herders and their livestock entirely off the grasslands in the name of environmental protection. In the case of Comfortable Housing, pastoralists are simply provided with subsidies to build houses. Implementation varies widely. In a small number of cases, where pastoralists do not already have houses at their home bases of winter pasture, new houses are built. In other cases, the houses are made of concrete to replace mud brick construction. In still other cases, new houses are built by the sides of major roads and families split up, with children and one parent or grandparents living along roads, while others stay on the grasslands to herd livestock. Finally, in some unpopular cases, as in one case in Amdo County, TAR, herders are moved to concentrated settlements far from their pastures; these tend to be the least welcome, but even in these cases, in contrast to ecological migration, livestock are not sold. Chinese media reports tend to exaggerate the scope of these programs, with headlines such as "Nagchu Plans for 80% of Nomads to Have Left the Pastoral Life in 2 Years" (http://www.xz.xinhuanet.com/xizangyaowen/2007-09/08/content_11088083.htm) which imply that herders will no longer be herders, but this is not the actual content of the project. All forms of housing (ranging from ecological migration to simple building of housing on winter pastures) are often conflated in media reports.
44. Zheng 2007, 59–60.
45. Yang, An, and Zhou 2007.
46. For pastoral sedentarization, the TAR government provided 15,000 RMB per household; 25,000 RMB per household for those resettled out of areas of endemic disease; 12,000 RMB for border households; 25,000 RMB for households classified as being in absolute poverty; and 12,000 RMB for those designated as impoverished households.
47. In Lhasa Municipality, those resettled from Kashin-Beck areas received 35,000 RMB and herders received 19,000 RMB. Tolung Dechen County contributed another 10,000 RMB per household, for a total of 24,000 RMB for each farming household there, and 35,000 RMB per pastoral household (Yang, An, and Zhou 2007).
48. See Miranda Wu, "Housing Project Changes Remarkably Tibetan Rural Areas," (China Tibet Information Center, September 8, 2009), http://eng.tibet.cn/news/today/200909/

t20090908_500585.htm; China Tibet Online, "All Tibet's Farmers, Herdsmen to Move in Affordable Houses by 2010," http://chinatibet.people.com.cn/6829088.html; and also Robin 2009, 58.

49. Other sources put the total at about 2.7 billion RMB (Yang, An, and Zhou 2007).

50. Jiangyong et al. 2006.

51. Goldstein, Childs, and Wangdui 2010; Bi 2008, 150. Goldstein et al. found that in three villages in Shigatse, the Comfortable Housing subsidy accounted for only between 7.4 and 9.7 percent of total expenditures, while bank loans accounted for 24.2–30.5 percent, private loans accounted for 18.9–22.1 percent, and savings accounted for 40.9–46.3 percent (Geoff Childs, personal communication).

52. Based on my interviews, including in Tolung Dechen County areas near Lhasa. According to government figures, across the *Chengguanqu*, 41 percent of the investment came from the regional, municipal, county (the *Chengguanqu* is a county-level unit), township, and village governments combined, while 32 percent of the investment came from the villagers, 12 percent from bank loans and the rest from villagers' labor. http://news.sohu.com/20081109/n260529055.shtml.

53. Geoff Childs, personal communication. Note that official figures include the value of local labor contributions, but it is not clear how this is calculated.

54. *yi qian ze qian, yi jian ze jian, yi gai ze gai.*

55. http://www.gov.cn/wszb/zhibo82/content_654471.htm, June 20, 2007. See Yang, An, and Zhou 2007, 34.

56. Yang, An, and Zhou 2007, 33.

57. Timothy Mitchell 2002, 192, 202.

58. "Party Chief Brings Tibet New Homes," *China Daily*, March 15, 2007, http://www.china.org.cn/english/government/203051.htm.

59. Zheng 2007, 56.

60. Yang, An, and Zhou 2007, 26. Comfortable Housing also encompasses a focus on the provision of rural infrastructure, in particular for drinking water, roads, telephones, and television. The number one catalyst for bringing about the desired goals of the New Socialist Countryside, however, is housing.

61. "Tightly grasp goals, attack difficulty and overcome hardship, resolutely grasp implementation, and stress special characteristics, in order to achieve phased achievements in the Comfortable Housing Project for the farmers and herders of the entire municipality." Speech at the meeting of the Leading Small Group of Comfortable Housing of Lhasa Municipality, February 11, 2009.

62. Yan 2008, 114. Yan argues that *suzhi* represents a new form of human value. Just as value for Marx is an abstracted form that allows for exchange and commensurability across heterogeneous forms of labor, so too *suzhi* is an abstraction of human subjectivity that makes it commensurable for development. "The representation and valuation of human subjectivity through *suzhi* is achieved through the processes of abstraction and radical suppression of heterogeneity existing among individuals and populations, much as 'value' operates as an abstraction and reduction of the radical heterogeneity of concrete and individual aspects of labor" (Yan 2008, 119).

63. Speech at the meeting of the Leading Small Group of Comfortable Housing of Lhasa Municipality, February 11, 2009, pp. 3, 12.

64. Speech at the meeting of the Leading Small Group of Comfortable Housing of Lhasa Municipality, February 11, 2009, p. 12.

65. Yang, An, and Zhou 2007, 28.

66. Korf 2007; Korf et al. 2010; Stirrat 2006.

67. Jiangyong et al. 2006, 29. "China Agricultural Bank TAR Branch Method for managing loans for the Comfortable Housing Project for Farmers and Herders," http://www.xizang.gov.cn/getCommonContent.do?contentId=345297.

68. http://www.xizang.gov.cn/getCommonContent.do?contentId=357463.

69. See Zhang (2010, 64–65) on Han urban residents' anxiety about debt in Kunming. Li and Yi (2007) find, based on national data as well as housing survey data in Guangzhou, that in general people in China are still reluctant to use mortgage finance where it is available, preferring to draw on their savings; on average mortgage loans contribute 20.5 percent of total expenditures on home purchases across China. However, Goldstein, Childs, and Wangdui (2010, 67) report that in Shigatse "As a result of the younger generation's confidence, the majority of household heads who had built houses and were surveyed in 2009 did not worry about being able to repay their ABC loans." Geoff Childs suggests that one possible explanation for the difference is demographic structure. In Shigatse a disproportionate percentage of the population is in their twenties, an age at which they have both the greatest off-farm wage-earning opportunities and the greatest degree of confidence. There is also a resurgence of fraternal polyandry which keeps labor (and earnings from labor) within the household (personal communication). I did not find this kind of optimism in villages near Lhasa. The concerns expressed by the Agricultural Bank of China as well as by Chinese scholars about risk to banks, discussed below, also suggest that this optimism is not found across the TAR.

70. They cite the influx of Tibetan migrants from other areas, such as Kham or Amdo, as potential buyers or renters. Rules about demolishing old houses are quite varied. In rural Shigatse, villagers have no desire to rebuild anywhere but on their original locations because they do not want to take up extra farmland (Geoff Childs, personal communication).

71. See Hsing 2010, 159–65, as well as http://news.xinhuanet.com/house/2007-06/07/content_6210625.htm.

72. Yang, An, and Zhou 2007, 33.

73. Bi 2008, 150.

74. Jiangyong et al. 2006, 29.

75. Bi 2008, 150.

76. Geoff Childs, personal communication.

77. Goldstein, Childs, and Wangdui 2010, 66.

78. Rates of 12 to 18 percent were reported to me. See Jiangyong et al 2006, 29.

79. http://news.sina.com.cn/c/2005-01-04/11184710827s.shtml, my emphasis.

80. http://www.buildcc.com/html/24/n-140824.html, my emphasis; http://www.yoyocn.cn/info/tibet/14140.html.

81. Families with 1–5 members were required to build on 17-by-29-meter areas, or 493 square meters. Households with 6–7 members had a slightly larger target area, and a still greater area was set for households with 8–9 members.

82. Families classified as "a bit better than poor" received a higher per capita subsidy, though were only allowed to take out a 30,000 RMB loan. A few families classified as the "very poor" received houses worth 40,000–50,000 RMB with no loans.

83. Villagers were told that if they did not build two stories, they would not receive the 25,000 RMB subsidy. Officially designated poverty households were allowed to build only one floor, but none of these are visible from the street.

84. http://zt.tibet.cn/web/sjgc/sjgc070307/20070200738162726.htm, my emphasis.

85. In addition to housing, Peton was also the target of several other New Socialist Countryside projects, including biogas digesters and subsidized pig raising.

86. Bi 2008, 150.

87. Jiangyong et al. 2006.

88. Goldstein, Childs, and Wangdui (2010) note similarly in Shigatse that more households wanted subsidies than could be accommodated, and that it was clear that the Comfortable Housing Project in that area had fallen short of the government's goal of 80 percent completion (since then, the government has claimed to have reached 100 percent of the goal by the end of 2010).

89. http://www.hrw.org/en/news/2006/12/19/tibet-china-must-end-rural-reconstruction-campaign.

90. Goldstein, Childs, and Wangdui 2010, 68.

91. http://www.xz.xinhuanet.com/zhuanti/2008-01/16/content_12235766.htm.

92. Bi 2008; Jiangyong et al. 2006; Yang, An, and Zhou 2007.

93. This is true even if, as Goldstein, Childs, and Wangdui (2010) argue, many villagers are familiar with loans for productive assets such as trucks. In Han China as well, home mortgages provoke significant anxiety, even among the privileged middle class (Li and Yi 2007; Zhang 2010.

94. Goldstein, Childs, and Wangdui 2010, 72.

95. Jiangyong et al 2006.

96. Li 2007, 9.

Conclusion

1. Hart 2004; Marx 1990 (1887).

2. Gupta and Ferguson 1997; Malkki 1997; Yan and Spivak 2007.

Afterword

1. Elden 2007b.

2. Asad 2007, 91.

3. Arendt 1970, 64.

4. http://gn.gansudaily.com.cn/system/2012/12/03/013508017.shtml.

5. Benjamin 1996 (1978), 281.

6. http://panchinese.blogspot.com/2012/11/6.html. Thanks to Charlene Makley for pointing me to this link.

References

Abrams, Philip. 1988. "Notes on the Difficulty of Studying the State." *Journal of Historical Sociology* 1 (1): 58–89.

Adams, Laura. 2010. *The Spectacular State: Culture and National Identity in Uzbekistan.* Durham, N.C.: Duke University Press.

Adams, Vincanne. 1996. "Karaoke as Modern Lhasa, Tibet: Western Encounters with Cultural Politics." *Cultural Anthropology* 11 (4): 510–46.

______. 2005. "Moral Orgasm and Productive Sex: Tantrism Faces Fertility Control in Lhasa, Tibet (China)." In *Sex in Development: Science, Sexuality, and Morality in Global Perspective*, edited by Vincanne Adams and Stacey Lee Pigg, 207–40. Durham, N.C.: Duke University Press.

Agamben, Giorgio. 1998. *Homo Sacer: Sovereign Power and Bare Life.* Stanford, Calif.: Stanford University Press.

______. 2009. *What Is an Apparatus? And Other Essays.* Stanford, Calif: Stanford University Press.

Agnew, John. 1994. "The Territorial Trap: The Geographical Assumptions of International Relations Theory." *Review of International Political Economy* 1 (1): 53–80.

Agricultural Research Institute. 1992. *Gaikuang: Xizang Zizhiqu sishinian fazhan. Nongye kexue yanjiu suo. Qiyi nongye shiyan cang 1952.7.1–1992.7.1* [A brief introduction: Tibet Autonomous Region's forty years of development. Agricultural Research Institute. July First Agricultural Experimental Farm, July 1, 1952–July 1, 1992]. Lhasa, TAR: TAR Agricultural Science and Technology Publishers.

Alatas, Syed Hussain. 1977. *The Myth of the Lazy Native: Study of the Image of Malays, Filipinos and Javanese from the 16th to the 20th Century and Its Functions in the Ideology of Colonial Capitalism.* London: Frank Cass.

Althusser, Louis. 1995 (1969). "Contradiction and Overdetermination: Notes for an Investigation." In *For Marx*, 87–128. New York: Verso.

Anagnost, Ann. 2004. "The Corporeal Politics of Quality (Suzhi)." *Public Culture* 16 (2): 189–208.

Andersen, Anders, Sarah Cooke, and Michael Wills. 1995. *New Majority: Chinese Population Transfer into Tibet.* London: Free Tibet Campaign.

Appadurai, Arjun. 1986. "Introduction: Commodities and the Politics of Value." In *The Social Life of Things: Commodities in Cultural Perspective*, edited by Arjun Appadurai, 3–63. Cambridge: Cambridge University Press.

Arendt, Hannah. 1970. *On Violence.* New York: Harcourt Brace Javonovich.

Asad, Talal. 2007. *On Suicide Bombing.* New York: Columbia University Press.

Aziz, Barbara Nimri. 1987. "Moving Towards a Sociology of Tibet." In *Feminine Ground: Essays on Women and Tibet*, edited by Janice Willis. Ithaca, N.Y.: Snow Lion Publications.

Barnes, Trevor, and James Duncan. 1992. *Writing Worlds: Discourse, Text and Metaphor in the Representation of Landscapes*. London: Routledge.

Barnett, Robert. 1994. "Symbols and Protests: The Iconography of Demonstrations in Tibet, 1987–1990." In *Resistance and Reform in Tibet*, edited by Robert Barnett, 238–58. Bloomington: Indiana University Press.

_______. 1998. Untitled essay. In *The Tibetans: A Struggle to Survive*, photographer Steve Lehman, 178–96. New York: Umbrage Editions.

_______. 2006a. *Lhasa: Streets with Memories*. New York: Columbia University Press.

_______. 2006b. "Modernity, Religion and Urban Space in Contemporary Lhasa." Paper presented at the Annual Meeting of the Association of Asian Studies, San Francisco.

_______. 2010. "Tibet." In *Politics in China: An Introduction*, edited by William Joseph. New York: Oxford University Press.

_______. 2012. "Restrictions and their Anomalies: The Third Forum and the Regulation of Religion in Tibet." *Journal of Current Chinese Affairs* 41 (4): 45–107.

Bataille, Georges. 1989. *The Accursed Share,* vol. 1: *Consumption*. New York: Zone Books.

Bebbington, Anthony. 2000. "Reencountering Development: Livelihood Transitions and Place Transformations in the Andes." *Annals of the Association of American Geographers* 90 (3): 495–520.

Bell, Sir Charles Alfred. 1928. *The People of Tibet*. Oxford: Clarendon Press.

Bell, Vikki. 1998. "On Speech, Race and Melancholia: An Interview with Judith Butler." In *Performativity & Belonging*, edited by Vikki Bell, 163–74. Thousand Oaks, Calif.: Sage.

Benavides, Gustavo. 2005. "Economy." In *Critical Terms for the Study of Buddhism*, edited by Donald Lopez, 77–102. Chicago: University of Chicago Press.

Benjamin, Walter. 1996 (1978). "Critique of Violence." In *Reflections: Essays, Aphorisms, Autobiographical Writings*, edited by P. Demetez, 277–301. New York: Harcourt Brace Jovanovich.

Bi, Hua. 2008. "Xizang shehui zhuyi xinnongcun jianshe de xin jinzhan—Anju Gongcheng" [New progress in the construction of Tibet's new socialist countryside—Comfortable Housing]. *Zhongguo Zangxue* [China Tibetan studies] 81:145–50.

Bista, Dor Bahadur. 1979. *Report from Lhasa*. Kathmandu: Sajra Parkashan.

Blaikie, Piers. 2000. "Development: Post, Anti-, and Populist: A Critical Review." *Environment and Planning A* 32 (6): 1033–50.

Blondeau, Anne-Marie, and Yonten Gyatso. 2003. "Lhasa, Legend and History." In *Lhasa in the Seventeenth Century: The Capital of the Dalai Lamas*, edited by Françoise Pommaret, 15–38. Boston: Brill.

Blondeau, Anne-Marie, and Ernst Steinkeller. 1996. *Reflections of the Mountain: Essays on the History and Social Meaning of the Mountain Cult in Tibet and the Himalaya*. Vienna: Verlag der Österreichischen Akademie der Wissenschaften.

Boulnois, Luce. 2003. "Gold, Wool and Musk: Trade in Lhasa in the Seventeenth Century." In *Lhasa in the Seventeenth Century: The Capital of the Dalai Lamas*, edited by Françoise Pommaret, 133–56. Boston: Brill.

Bourdieu, Pierre. 1990. *The Logic of Practice*. Translated by Richard Nice. Stanford, Calif.: Stanford University Press.

———. 1997. "Marginalia: Some Additional Notes on the Gift." In *The Logic of the Gift: Toward an Ethic of Generosity*, edited by Alan D. Schrift, 231–41. New York: Routledge.

———. 1998 (1977). *Outline of a Theory of Practice*. Translated by Richard Nice. Cambridge: Cambridge University Press.

———. 2000. *Pascalian Meditations*. Stanford, Calif.: Stanford University Press.

Brenner, Neil. 1999. "Beyond State-Centrism? Space, Territoriality and Geographical Scale in Globalization Studies." *Theory and Society* 28 (1): 39–78.

Brenner, Neil, and Stuart Elden. 2009. "Henri Lefebvre on State, Space, Territory." *International Political Sociology* 3:353–77.

Bryan, Joe. 2012. "Rethinking Territory: Social Justice and Neoliberalism in Latin America's Territorial Turn." *Geography Compass* 6 (4): 215–26.

Bulag, Uradyn. 2002a. "From Yeke-juu League to Ordos Municipality: Settler Colonialism and Alter/native Urbanization in Inner Mongolia." *Provincial China* 7 (2): 196–234.

———. 2002b. *The Mongols at China's Edge: History and the Politics of National Unity*. Boulder: Rowman and Littlefield.

———. 2006. "Municipalization and Ethnopolitics in Inner Mongolia." In *Mongols from Country to City: Floating Boundaries, Pastoralism and City Life in the Mongol Lands*, edited by Ole Bruun and Li Narangoa, 56–81. Copenhagen: Nordic Institute of Asian Studies.

Butler, Judith. 1990. *Gender Trouble: Feminism and the Subversion of Identity*. New York: Routledge.

———. 1997. "Merely Cultural." *Social Text* 52/53: 265–77.

Callon, Michel. 1986. "Some Elements of a Sociology of Translation: Domestication of Scallops and the Fishermen of St. Brieux Bay." In *Power, Action, Belief: A New Sociology of Knowledge?* edited by John Law, 196–229. New York: Routledge.

Carrasco, Pedro. 1959. *Land and Polity in Tibet*. Seattle: University of Washington Press.

Carrier, James G. 1995. *Gifts and Commodities: Exchange and Western Capitalism since 1700*. New York: Routledge.

Cartier, Carolyn. 2001. "'Zone Fever,' the Arable Land Debate, and Real Estate Speculation: China's Evolving Land Use Regime and Its Geographical Contradictions." *Journal of Contemporary China* 10 (28): 445–69.

———. 2002. "Transnational Urbanism in the Reform-Era Chinese City: Landscapes from Shenzhen." *Urban Studies* 39 (9): 1513–32.

———. 2003. "Symbolic City/Regions and Gendered Identity Formation in South China." *Provincial China* 8 (1): 60–77.

Central Tibetan Administration. 2000. *Tibet 2000: Environment and Development Issues*. Dharamsala, India: DIIR.

Certeau, Michel de. 1984. *The Practice of Everyday Life*. Translated by Steve Rendall. Berkeley: University of California Press.

Chan, Kam Wing. 1994. *Cities with Invisible Walls: Reinterpreting Urbanization in Post-1949 China*. New York: Oxford University Press.

_______. 2007. "Misconceptions and Complexities in the Study of China's Cities: Definitions, Statistics and Implications." *Eurasian Geography and Economics* 48 (4): 383–412.

Chan, Kam Wing, and Will Buckingham. 2008. "Is China Abolishing the Hukou System?" *China Quarterly* 195:582–606.

Chang, Sen-dou. 1977. "The Morphology of Walled Capitals." In *The City in Late Imperial China*, edited by G. William Skinner, 75–100. Stanford, Calif.: Stanford University Press.

Chatterjee, Partha. 2006. *The Politics of the Governed: Reflections on Popular Politics in Most of the World*. New York: Columbia University Press.

Clarke, Graham E. 1998. "Development, Society and Environment in Tibet." In *Development, Society and Environment in Tibet: Papers Presented at a Panel of the 7th Seminar of the International Association for Tibetan Studies, Graz 1995*, edited by Graham Clarke, 1–46. Vienna: Verlag der Österreichischen Akademie der Wisenschaften.

Coleman, Matthew, and Kevin Grove. 2009. "Biopolitics, Biopower and the Return of Sovereignty." *Environment and Planning D: Society and Space* 27:489–507.

Coleman, William. 1998. "Writing Tibetan History: The Discourses of Feudalism and Serfdom in Chinese and Western Historiography." M.A. thesis, University of Hawai'i, Honolulu.

Conner, Victoria, and Robert Barnett. 1997. *Leaders in Tibet: A Directory*. London: Tibet Information Network.

Coronil, Fernando. 1997. *The Magical State: Nature, Money, and Modernity in Venezuela*. Chicago: University of Chicago Press.

Cosgrove, Denis. 1994. *Social Formation and Symbolic Landscape*. Madison: University of Wisconsin Press.

Cosgrove, Denis, and Stephen Daniels. 1988. *The Iconography of Landscape*. Cambridge: Cambridge University Press.

Coulter, John, and Paul Ivory. 1982. "The Rural-Urban Dichotomy in China: A Case Study of the Mid-Yellow River Region Using Remote Sensing Data." *Australian Journal of Chinese Affairs* 7:37–53.

Cowen, Michael P., and Robert Shenton. 1996. *Doctrines of Development*. New York: Routledge.

Crehan, Kate. 2002. *Gramsci, Culture, and Anthropology*. Berkeley: University of California Press.

Croll, Elisabeth. 1994. *From Heaven to Earth: Images and Experiences of Development*. New York: Routledge.

Daniels, Stephen. 1989. "Marxism, Culture and the Duplicity of Landscape." In *New Models in Geography*, vol. 2, edited by Richard Peet and Nigel Thrift, 196–220. London: Unwin Hyman.

Das, Veena, and Deborah Poole. 2004. "State and Its Margins: Comparative Ethnographies." In *Anthropology in the Margins of the State*, edited by Veena Das and Deborah Poole, 3–34. Santa Fe: School of American Research Press.

Day, Alexander. 2008. "The End of the Peasant? New Rural Reconstruction in China." *boundary 2* 35 (2): 49–73.

Day, Alexander, and Matthew A. Hale. 2007. "Guest Editor's Introduction." *Chinese Sociology and Anthropology* 39 (4): 3–9.
Debord, Guy. 1994 (1967). *Society of the Spectacle*. Translated by Donald Nicholson-Smith. New York: Zone Books.
Deng, Weihua, and Huaning Deng. 2007. "Jianshe Xinnongcun jinfang 'wei chengshihua yuejin'" [Constructing a New Socialist Countryside while guarding against a "fake urbanization leap forward"]. *Xibu caikuai* [Western finance and accounting] 6:73–74.
Derrida, Jacques. 1997 (1992). "The Time of the King." In *The Logic of the Gift*, edited by A. D. Schrift, 121–47. New York: Routledge. Excerpted from *Given Time*, University of Chicago Press.
Douglas, Mary. 1990. "Foreword: No Free Gifts." In *The Gift: The Form and Reason for Exchange in Archaic Societies*. New York: Norton.
Dreyer, June. 2003. "Economic Development in Tibet under the People's Republic of China." *Journal of Contemporary China* 12 (36): 411–30.
Dungdkar, Blo Bzang 'Phrin Las. 2002. In *Dung dkar tshig mdzod chen mo* [The big dictionary of Dungkar]. Beijing: Krung go'i Bod rig pa dpe skrun khang [China Tibetan culture publishing house].
Ekvall, Robert. 1968. *Fields on the Hoof: Nexus of Tibetan Nomadic Pastoralism*. New York: Holt, Rinehart and Winston.
Elden, Stuart. 2007a. "Governmentality, Calculation, Territory." *Environment and Planning D: Society and Space* 25 (3): 562–80.
______. 2007b. "Terror and Territory." *Antipode* 39 (5): 821–54.
______. 2010a. "Land, Terrain, Territory." *Progress in Human Geography* 34 (6): 799–817.
______. 2010b. "Thinking Territory Historically." *Geopolitics* 15 (4): 757–61.
Emerson, Ralph Waldo. 1997 (1844). "Gifts." In *The Logic of the Gift: Toward an Ethic of Generosity*, edited by Alan D. Schrift, 25–27. New York: Routledge.
Escobar, Arturo. 1995. *Encountering Development: The Making and Unmaking of the Third World*. Princeton, N.J.: Princeton University Press.
Esteva, Carlos. 1992. "Development." In *The Development Dictionary: A Guide to Knowledge as Power*, edited by Wolfgang Sachs, 6–25. London: Zed Books.
Ferguson, James. 1990. *The Anti-Politics Machine: "Development," Depoliticization and Bureaucratic Power in Lesotho*. Minneapolis: University of Minnesota Press.
Firth, Raymond. 1959. *Economics of the Zealand Maori*. Wellington: Government Printer.
______. 1983. "Magnitudes and Values in Kula Exchange." In *The Kula: New Perspectives on Massim Exchange*, edited by J. W. Leach and E. Leach, 89–102. Cambridge: Cambridge University Press.
Fischer, Andrew Martin. 2005. *State Growth and Social Exclusion in Tibet: Challenges of Recent Economic Growth*. Copenhagen: NIAS Press.
______. 2008a. "'Population Invasion' versus Urban Exclusion in the Tibetan Areas of Western China." *Population and Development Review* 34 (4): 631–62.
______. 2008b. "Subsistence and Rural Livelihood Strategies in Tibet under Rapid Economic and Social Transition." *Journal of the International Association of Tibetan Studies* 4:1–49. http://www.thlib.org?tid=T5569.

______. 2009. "The Political Economy of Boomerang Aid in China's Tibet." *China Perspectives* 2009 (3): 38–55.

______. 2012. "The Revenge of Fiscal Maoism in China's Tibet." *International Institute of Social Studies Working Paper* No. 547:1–32.

Fitzgerald, John. 2002. "The Province in History." In *Rethinking China's Provinces*, edited by John Fitzgerald, 11–40. New York: Routledge.

Foucault, Michel. 1980. "The Confessions of the Flesh." *In Power/Knowledge: Selected Interviews and Other Writings, 1972–1977*, edited by Colin Gordon, 194–228. New York: Pantheon Books.

______.1991. "Governmentality." In *The Foucault Effect: Studies in Governmentality*, edited by Graham Burchell, Colin Gordon, and Peter Miller, 87–104. Chicago: University of Chicago Press.

______. 1995 (1977). *Discipline and Punish: The Birth of the Prison*. New York: Pantheon.

______. 2003 (1976). *Society Must Be Defended: Lectures at the Collège de France, 1975–1976*. New York: Picador.

______. 2008. *The Birth of Biopolitics: Lectures at the Collège de France, 1978–1979*. New York: Picador.

Fraser, David. 2000. "Inventing Oasis: Luxury Housing Advertisements and Reconfiguring Domestic Space in Shanghai." In *The Consumer Revolution in Urban China*, edited by Deborah S. Davis, 25–53. Berkeley: University of California Press.

Freidberg, Susanne. 2001. "Gardening on the Edge: The Social Conditions of Unsustainability on an African Urban Periphery." *Annals of the Association of American Geographers* 91 (3): 349–69.

Friedmann, John. 2005. *China's Urban Transition*. Minneapolis: University of Minnesota Press.

Gaerrang. 2012. "Alternative Development on the Tibetan Plateau: The Case of the Slaughter Renunciation Movement." Ph.D. diss., University of Colorado Boulder.

Gaubatz, Piper. 1996. *Beyond the Great Wall: Urban Form and Transformation on the Chinese Frontier*. Stanford, Calif.: Stanford University Press.

Gelek, and Tao Li. 1997. "Rural Urbanization in China's Tibetan Region: Dulongdeqing County as a Typical Example." In *Farewell to Peasant China: Rural Urbanization and Social Change in the Late Twentieth Century*, edited by Gregory Guldin, 183–208. Armonk, N.Y.: M. E. Sharpe.

Germano, David. 1998. "Re-membering the Dismembered Body of Tibet: Contemporary Tibetan Visionary Movements in the People's Republic of China." In *Buddhism in Contemporary Tibet: Religious Revival and Cultural Identity*, edited by Melvyn Goldstein and Matthew Kapstein, 53–94. Berkeley: University of California Press.

Gidwani, Vinay. 2008. *Capital, Interrupted: Agrarian Development and the Politics of Work in India*. Minneapolis: University of Minnesota Press.

Godelier, Maurice. 1999. *The Enigma of the Gift*. Chicago: University of Chicago Press.

Goldstein, Melvyn. 1968. "An Anthropological Study of the Tibetan Political System." Ph.D. diss., University of Washington.

_______. 1986. "Reexamining Choice, Dependency and Command in the Tibetan Social System: 'Tax Appendages' and Other Landless Serfs." *Tibet Journal* 11 (4): 79–113.

_______. 1989. *A History of Modern Tibet, 1913–1951: The Demise of the Lamaist State*. Berkeley: University of California Press.

_______. 2007. *A History of Modern Tibet*, vol. 2: *The Calm Before the Storm, 1951–1955*. Berkeley: University of California Press.

Goldstein, Melvyn, Geoff Childs, and Puchung Wangdui. 2010. "Beijing's 'People First' Development Initiative for the Tibet Autonomous Region's Rural Sector—A Case Study from the Shigatse Area." *China Journal* 63:59–78.

Goldstein, Melvyn, T. N. Shelling, and J. T. Surkhang. 2001. *The New Tibetan-English Dictionary of Modern Tibetan*. Berkeley: University of California Press.

Goodman, David S. G. 2004. "The Campaign to 'Open up the West': National, Provincial-level, and Local Perspectives." In *The Campaign to 'Open up the West'*, edited by David S. G. Goodman, 3–20. Cambridge: Cambridge University Press.

Graeber, David. 2001. *Toward an Anthropological Theory of Value: The False Coin of Our Own Dreams*. New York: Palgrave.

Gramsci, Antonio. 1999 (1971). *Selections from the Prison Notebooks*. Translated by Quintin Hoare and Geoffrey Nowell-Smith. New York: International Publishers.

Gregory, Christopher A. 1982. *Gifts and Commodities*. London: Academic Press.

Guo, X., Z. Yu, T. M. Schmit, B. M. Henhan, and D. Li. 2009. "Evaluation of the New Socialist Countryside Development in China." *China Agricultural Economic Review* 1 (3): 314–26.

Gupta, Akhil. 1995. "Blurred Boundaries: The Discourse of Corruption, The Culture of Politics and the Imagined State." *American Ethnologist* 22 (2): 375–402.

_______. 1998. *Postcolonial Developments: Agriculture in the Making of Modern India*. Durham, N.C.: Duke University Press.

Gupta, Akhil, and James Ferguson. 1997. *Culture, Power, Place: Explorations in Critical Anthropology*. Durham, N.C.: Duke University Press.

Guthman, Julie. 2004. "Back to the Land: The Paradox of Organic Food Standards." *Environment and Planning A* 36:511–28.

Gyatso, Janet, and Hanna Havnevik. 2005. "Introduction." In *Women in Tibet*, edited by Janet Gyatso and Hanna Havnevik. New York: Columbia University Press.

Hall, Stuart. 1980. "Race, Articulation and Societies Structured in Dominance." In *Sociological Theories: Race and Colonialism*, 305–45. Paris: UNESCO.

_______. 1987. "Gramsci and Us." *Marxism Today*, June: 16–21.

_______. 1988. "The Toad in the Garden: Thatcherism among the Theorists." In *Marxism and the Interpretation of Culture*, edited by C Nelson and L Grossberg, 35–74. Champaign: University of Illinois Press.

_______. 1996 (1986). "Gramsci's Relevance for the Study of Race and Ethnicity." In *Stuart Hall: Critical Dialogues in Cultural Studies*, edited by David Morley and Kuan-Hsing Chen, 411–40. New York: Routledge.

Hansen, Mette. 1999. "The Call of Mao or Money? Han Chinese Settlers on China's Southwestern Borders." *China Quarterly* 158:394–414.

______. 2007. *Frontier People: Han Settlers in Minority Areas of China.* Vancouver: UBC Press.

Hansen, Thomas Blom, and Finn Stepputat. 2001. *States of Imagination: Ethnographic Explorations of the Postcolonial State.* Durham, N.C.: Duke University Press.

Harrell, Stevan. 1995. "Introduction: Civilizing Projects and the Reaction to Them." In *Cultural Encounters on China's Ethnic Frontiers*, edited by Stevan Harrell, 3–36. Seattle: University of Washington Press.

Harrer, Heinrich. 1953. *Seven Years in Tibet.* Translated by Richard Graves. London: Rupert Hart-Davis.

Hart, Gillian. 2001. "Development Critiques in the 1990s: Culs de Sac and Promising Paths." *Progress in Human Geography* 25 (4): 649–58.

______. 2002a. *Disabling Globalization: Places of Power in Post-Apartheid South Africa.* Berkeley: University of California Press.

______. 2002b. "Geography and Development: Development/s beyond Neoliberalism? Power, Culture, Political Economy." *Progress in Human Geography* 26 (6): 812–22.

______. 2004. "Geography and Development: Critical Ethnographies." *Progress in Human Geography* 28 (1): 91–100.

______. 2010. "D/developments after the Meltdown." *Antipode* 41:117–41.

Harvey, David. 1982. *Limits to Capital.* Chicago: University of Chicago Press.

______. 2003. *The New Imperialism.* Oxford: Oxford University Press.

Hattori, Tomohisa. 2001. "Reconceptualizing Foreign Aid." *Review of International Political Economy* 8 (4): 633–60.

He, Xuefeng. 2007. "New Rural Construction and the Chinese Path." *Chinese Sociology and Anthropology* 39 (4): 26–38.

Heberer, Thomas. 2001. "Old Tibet a Hell on Earth? The Myth of Tibet and Tibetans in Chinese Art and Propaganda." In *Imagining Tibet: Perceptions, Projections, and Fantasies*, edited by Thierry Dodin and Heinz Räther, 111–50. Somerville, Mass.: Wisdom Publications.

Henderson, Mark. 2004. "Spatial Contexts of Urbanization and Land Conservation in China." Ph.D. diss., University of California, Berkeley.

Herbert, Steven. 2000. "For Ethnography." *Progress in Human Geography* 24 (4): 550–68.

Holbig, Heike 2004. "The Emergence of the Campaign to Open up the West: Ideological Formation, Central Decision-making and the Role of the Provinces." *China Quarterly* 178:335–57.

Holston, James. 1989. *The Modernist City: An Anthropological Critique of Brasilia.* Chicago: University of Chicago Press.

Hsing, You-tien. 2010. *The Great Urban Transformation: Politics of Land and Property in China.* New York: Oxford University Press.

Hu, Xiaojiang. 2003. "The Little Shops of Lhasa, Tibet: Migrant Businesses and the Formation of Markets in a Transitional Economy." Ph.D. diss., Harvard University.

Hu, Xiaojiang, and Miguel A. Salazar. 2008. "Ethnicity, Rurality and Status: Hukou and the Institutional and Cultural Determinants of Social Status in Tibet." *China Journal* 60:1–21.

Huang, Yasheng. 1995. "China's Cadre Transfer Policy toward Tibet in the 1980s." *Modern China* 21 (2): 184–204.

Huber, Toni. 1999. "Putting the Gnas Back in Gnas-skor: Rethinking Tibetan Pilgrimage Practice." In *Sacred Spaces and Powerful Places in Tibetan Culture: A Collection of Essays*, edited by Toni Huber, 77–104. Dharamsala, India: Library of Tibetan Works and Archives.

Iredale, Robyn, Naran Bilik, and Wang Su. 2001. *Contemporary Minority Migration, Education, and Ethnicity in China*. Cheltenham: Edward Elgar Publishing.

Jäschke, Heinrich A. 1968 (1881). *A Tibetan-English Dictionary with Special Reference to the Prevailing Dialects*. London: Routledge.

Jiangyong, Tanke, and People's Bank Linzhi Prefecture Branch Research Group. 2006. "Shishi nongmumin Anju Gongcheng dui Linzhi jingji jinrong chansheng de xiaoying" [The effects of the implementation of Comfortable Housing for farmers and nomads on the economy and finance of Linzhi Prefecture]. *Xinan jinrong* [Southwest finance] 302:28–29.

Kapoor, Ilan. 2008. *The Postcolonial Politics of Development*. New York: Routledge.

Kapstein, Matthew. 1998. "Concluding Reflections." In *Buddhism in Contemporary Tibet: Religious Revival and Cultural Identity*, edited by Melvyn Goldstein and Matthew Kapstein, 139–51. Berkeley: University of California Press.

Karan, Pradyumna P. 1976. *The Changing Face of Tibet: The Impact of Chinese Communist Ideology on the Landscape*. Lexington, Ky.: University Press of Kentucky.

Keller, Shoshana. 1998. "Trapped between State and Society: Women's Liberation and Islam in Soviet Uzbekistan, 1926–1941." *Journal of Women's History* 10 (1): 20–44.

Knapp, Ronald G. 2000. *China's Walled Cities*. Oxford: Oxford University Press.

Kolås, Åshild. 2003. " 'Class' in Tibet: Creating Social Order before and during the Mao Era." *Identities: Global Studies in Culture and Power* 10:181–200.

Korf, Benedikt. 2007. "Antinomies of Generosity: Moral Geographies and Post-Tsunami Aid in Southeast Asia." *Geoforum* 38:366–78.

Korf, Benedikt, Shahul Habullah, Pia Hollenbach, and Bart Kelm. 2010. "The Gift of Disaster: The Commodification of Good Intentions in Post-Tsunami Sri Lanka." *Disasters* 34, suppl. 1: 60–77.

Lai, Hongyi. 2003. "National Security and Unity, and China's Western Development Program." *Provincial China* 8 (2): 118–43.

Larsen, Knud, and Amund Sinding-Larsen. 2001. *The Lhasa Atlas: Traditional Tibetan Architecture and Townscape*. Boston: Shambala.

Latour, Bruno. 1987. *Science in Action: How to Follow Scientists and Engineers through Society*. Cambridge, Mass.: MIT Press.

Lawson, Victoria. 2007. *Making Development Geography*. New York: Hodder Arnold.

Lefebvre, Henri. 1991 (1974). *The Production of Space*. Translated by Donald Nicholson-Smith. Malden, Mass.: Blackwell.

———. 2003. "Space and the State." In *State/Space*, edited by Neil Brenner, Bob Jessop, Martin Jones, and Gordon Macleod, 84–100. Oxford: Blackwell.

Lévi-Strauss, Claude. 1997 (1950). "Selections from Introduction to the Work of Marcel Mauss." In *The Logic of the Gift: Toward an Ethic of Generosity*, edited by Alan D. Schrift, 45–69. New York: Routledge.
Li, Si-ming, and Zheng Yi. 2007. "Financing Home Purchase in China, with Special Reference to Guangzhou." *Housing Studies* 22 (3): 409–25.
Li, Tania. 1999. "Compromising Power: Development, Culture, and Rule in Indonesia." *Cultural Anthropology* 14 (3): 295–322.
______. 2007. *The Will to Improve: Development, Governmentality, and the Practice of Politics*. Durham, N.C.: Duke University Press.
Li, Tao. 2005. "Tibetan Rural Urbanization and the Desakota Model." *Perspectives* 6 (1): 18–25.
Liechty, Mark. 1996. "Kathmandu as Translocality: Multiple Places in a Nepali Space." In *The Geography of Identity*, edited by Patricia Yaeger, 98–130. Ann Arbor: University of Michigan Press.
Lin, George, C. S. 2009. *Developing China: Land, Politics and Social Conditions*. New York: Routledge.
Liu, Rui. 1988. *Zhongguo renkou: Xizang fence* [China's population: Tibet volume]. Beijing: Zhongguo caizheng jingji chubanshe [China finance and economy publishing house].
Liu, Xin. 2000. *In One's Own Shadow: An Ethnographic Account of the Condition of Post-Reform Rural China*. Berkeley: University of California Press.
Logan, John R. 2008. *Urban China in Transition*. Oxford: Blackwell.
Ludden, David. 1992. "India's Development Regime." In *Colonialism and Culture*, edited by Nicholas B. Dirks. Ann Arbor: University of Michigan Press.
Lustgarten, Abrahm. 2008. *China's Great Train: Beijing's Drive West and the Campaign to Remake Tibet*. New York: Times Books.
Ma, Laurence J. C. 2002. "Urban Transformation in China, 1949–2000: A Review and Research Agenda." *Environment and Planning A* 34:1545–69.
______. 2005. "Urban Administrative Restructuring, Changing Scale Relations, and Local Economic Development in China." *Political Geography* 24:477–97.
Ma, Rong. 1991. "Han and Tibetan Residential Patterns in Lhasa." *China Quarterly* 128:814–36.
Ma, Rong, and Tanzen Lhundrup. 2008. "Temporary Migrants in Lhasa in 2005." *Journal of the International Association of Tibetan Studies* 4 (December 2008): 1–42. http://www.thlib.org?tid=T5561.
Mahmood, Saba. 2001. "Feminist Theory, Embodiment, and the Docile Agent: Some Reflections on the Egyptian Islamic Revival." *Cultural Anthropology* 16 (2): 202–36.
Makley, Charlene. 2003. "Gendered Boundaries in Motion: Space and Identity on the Sino-Tibetan Frontier." *American Ethnologist* 30 (4): 597–619.
______. 2006. Competing Conversions: Gendered Development Encounters among Tibetans in Qinghai. Paper presented at the Annual Meeting of the Association of Asian Studies, San Francisco.
______. 2007. *The Violence of Liberation: Gender and Tibetan Buddhist Revival in Post-Mao China*. Berkeley: University of California Press.

———. 2013. "The Politics of Presence: Voice, Deity Possession, and Dilemmas of Development Among Tibetans in the PRC." *Comparative Studies in Society and History* 55 (3): 665–700.

Malkki, Liisa. H. 1997. "National Geographic: The Rooting of Peoples and the Territorialization of National Identity among Scholars and Refugees." In *Culture, Power, Place: Explorations in Critical Anthropology*, edited by Akhil Gupta and James Ferguson, 52–74. Durham, N.C.: Duke University Press.

Mann, Susan. 1984. "Urbanization and Historical Change in China." *Modern China* 10 (1): 79–113.

Marx, Karl. 1990 (1887). *Capital*, vol. 1: *A Critique of Political Economy*. Translated by Ben Fowkes. New York: Penguin.

Massell, Gregory J. 1974. *The Surrogate Proletariat: Moslem Women and Revolutionary Strategies in Soviet Central Asia, 1919–1929*. Princeton, N.J.: Princeton University Press.

Massey, Doreen. 1994. *Space, Place, and Gender*. Minneapolis: University of Minnesota Press.

Mauss, Marcel. 1990 (1924). "Gift, Gift." In *The Logic of the Gift: Toward an Ethic of Generosity*, edited by Alan D. Schrift, 28–32. New York: Routledge.

———. 1990 (1950). *The Gift: The Form and Reason for Exchange in Archaic Societies*. New York: Norton.

McGranahan, Carole. 2010. "Narrative Dispossession: Tibet and the Gendered Logics of Historical Possibility." *Comparative Studies in Society and History* 52 (4): 768–97.

Merlan, Francesca. 1998. *Caging the Rainbow: Place, Politics, and Aborigines in a North Australian Town*. Honolulu: University of Hawai'i Press.

Miller, Beatrice. 1987. "A Response to Goldstein's 'Reexamining Choice, Dependency and Command in the Tibetan Social System.'" *Tibet Journal* 12 (2): 65–67.

Mitchell, Don. 1996. *The Lie of the Land: Migrant Workers and the California Landscape*. Minneapolis: University of Minnesota Press.

———. 2002. "Cultural Landscapes: The Dialectical Landscape—Recent Landscape Research in Human Geography." *Progress in Human Geography* 26 (3): 381–89.

Mitchell, Katharyne. 2006. "Geographies of Identity: The New Exceptionalism." *Progress in Human Geography* 30:95–106.

Mitchell, Timothy. 1991. "The Limits of the State: Beyond Statist Approaches and Their Critics." *American Political Science Review* 85 (1): 77–96.

———. 1999. "Society, Economy and the State Effect." In *State/Culture: State Formation After the Cultural Turn*, edited by George Steinmertz, 76–97. Ithaca, N.Y.: Cornell University Press.

———. 2002. *Rule of Experts: Egypt, Techno-Politics, Modernity*. Berkeley: University of California Press.

Moore, Donald S. 1996. "Marxism, Culture, and Political Ecology: Environmental Struggles in Zimbabwe's Eastern Highlands." In *Liberation Ecologies: Environment, Development, Social Movements*, edited by Richard Peet and Michael Watts, 125–47. New York: Routledge.

_______. 2000. "The Crucible of Cultural Politics: Reworking 'Development' in Zimbabwe's Eastern Highlands." *American Ethnologist* 26 (3): 654–89.

_______. 2005. *Suffering for Territory: Race, Place, and Power in Zimbabwe.* Durham, N.C.: Duke University Press.

Mosse, David. 2005. *Cultivating Development: An Ethnography of Aid Policy and Practice.* Ann Arbor, Mich.: Pluto Press.

Mote, F. W. 1977. "The Transformation of Nanking, 1350–1400." In *The City in Late Imperial China*, edited by G. William Skinner, 101–54. Stanford, Calif.: Stanford University Press.

Mountz, Alison. 2004. "Embodying the Nation-State: Canada's Response to Human Smuggling." *Political Geography* 23 (3): 323–45.

Mukerji, Chandra. 1997. *Territorial Ambitions and the Gardens of Versailles.* Cambridge: Cambridge University Press.

Mumford, Lewis. 1961. *The City in History: Its Origins, Its Transformations, and Its Prospects.* New York: Harcourt, Brace and World.

Murphy, Rachel. 2006. *Domestic Migrant Remittances in China: Channels, Distribution and Livelihoods.* IOM Migration Research Series. New York: United Nations Press.

Naughton, Barry. 1995. "Cities in the Chinese Economic System: Changing Roles and Conditions in Autonomy." In *Urban Spaces in Contemporary China: The Potential for Autonomy and Community in Post-Mao China*, edited by Deborah S. Davis, Richard Kraus, Barry Naughton, and Elizabeth Perry, 61–89. Cambridge: Cambridge University Press.

Oakes, Timothy. 2004. "Building a Southern Dynamo: Guizhou and State Power." In *China's Campaign to 'Open up the West': National, Provincial, and Local Perspectives*, edited by David S. G. Goodman, 153–73. Cambridge: Cambridge University Press.

_______. 2007. "Welcome to Paradise! A Sino-U.S. Joint Venture Project." In *China's Transformations: The Stories beyond the Headlines*, edited by Lionel Jensen and Timothy Weston, 240–64. Boulder: Rowman & Littlefield.

Oi, Jean. 1989. *State and Peasant in Contemporary China: The Political Economy of Village Government.* Berkeley: University of California Press.

Olwig, Kenneth. 1996. "Recovering the Substantive Nature of Landscape." *Annals of the Association of American Geographers* 86 (4): 630–53.

_______. 2002. *Landscape, Nature, and the Body Politic: From Britain's Renaissance to America's New World.* Madison: University of Wisconsin Press.

Osteen, Mark. 2002. "Introduction: Questions of the Gift." In *The Question of the Gift: Essays across Disciplines*, edited by Mark Osteen, 1–42. New York: Routledge.

Pandian, Anand. 2009. *Crooked Stalks: Cultivating Virtue in South India.* Durham, N.C.: Duke University Press.

Pannell, Clifton W. 2002. "China's Continuing Urban Transition." *Environment and Planning A* 34 (9): 1571–89.

Parry, Jonathan. 1985. "*The Gift*, the Indian Gift and the 'Indian Gift.'" *Man* 21:453–73.

Patshang, Lama Sonam Gyaltsen. 1973. *Rgyal rab gsal ba'i me long* [A history of Tibet during the period of the Royal Lha Dynasty]. Dolnaji, India: Tibetan Bonpo Monastic Centre.

Patton, Paul. 2007. "Agamben and Foucault on Biopower and Biopolitics." In *Giorgio Agamben: Sovereignty and Life*, edited by Matthew Calarco and Steven DeCaroli, 203–18. Stanford, Calif.: Stanford University Press.

Penkyi. 2007. "Comfortable Housing and Happy Lives of Tibetan Farmers and Herders." *China Tibet Magazine*, March 2.

Perreault, Thomas. 2003. "A People with our Own Identity: Toward a Cultural Politics of Development in Ecuadorian Amazonia." *Environment and Planning D: Society and Space* 21 (5): 583–606.

Perry, Elizabeth J. 2008. "Chinese Conceptions of 'Rights': From Mencius to Mao—and Now." *Perspectives on Politics* 6 (1): 37–50.

______. 2011. "From Mass Campaigns to Managed Campaigns: 'Constructing a New Socialist Countryside.'" In *Mao's Invisible Hand: Political Foundations of Adaptive Governance in China*, edited by Sebastian Heilmann and Elizabeth J. Perry, 30–61. Cambridge, Mass.: Harvard University Press.

Pigg, Stacey Lee. 1992. "Inventing Social Categories through Place: Social Representations and Development in Nepal." *Comparative Studies in Society and History* 34 (3): 491–513.

Polanyi, Karl. 1957 (1944). *The Great Transformation: The Political and Economic Origins of Our Time*. Boston: Beacon Press.

Pratt, Geraldine. 2005. "Abandoned Women and Spaces of the Exception." *Antipode* 37 (5): 1052–78.

PRC 2000 Census. All China Marketing Research Company. 2003. *Zhongguo 2000 xian ji ren kou pu cha zhi liao* [China 2000 county population census]. Beijing: All China Marketing Research Co.

PRC State Council. 2001. *White Paper on Tibet's March toward Modernization*. http://www.china-embassy.org/eng/zt/zgxz/News20About%20Tibet/t37001.htm.

Radcliffe, Sarah A, and Nina Laurie. 2006. "Culture and Development: Taking Culture Seriously in Development for Andean Indigenous People." *Environment and Planning D: Society and Space* 24:231–48.

Raffles, Hugh. 1999. "'Local Theory': Nature and the Making of an Amazonian Place." *Cultural Anthropology* 14 (3): 323–60.

______. 2002. *In Amazonia: A Natural History*. Princeton, N.J.: Princeton University Press.

Rankin, Katharine N. 2004. *The Cultural Politics of Markets: Economic Liberalization and Social Change in Nepal*. Toronto: University of Toronto Press.

Robin, Françoise. 2009. "The 'Socialist New Villages' in the Tibetan Autonomous Region: Reshaping the Rural Landscape and Controlling Its Inhabitants." *China Perspectives* 2009 (3): 56–65.

Rodman, Margaret C. 1992. "Empowering Place: Multilocality and Multivocality." *American Anthropologist* 94:640–56.

Rofel, Lisa. 1999. *Other Modernities: Gendered Yearnings in China after Socialism*. Berkeley: University of California Press.

Rohlf, Gregory. 1999. "Agricultural Resettlement to the Sino-Tibetan Frontier, 1950–1962." Ph.D. diss., University of Iowa.

Rosaldo, Renato. 1989. *Culture & Truth: The Remaking of Social Analysis*. Boston: Beacon Press.

Roth, Christopher F. 2002. "Goods, Names, and Selves: Rethinking the Tsimshian Potlatch." *American Ethnologist* 29 (1): 123–50.

Sachs, Wolfgang. 1992. *The Development Dictionary: A Guide to Knowledge as Power*. London: Zed Books.

Sahlins, Marshall. 1972. *Stone Age Economics*. New York: Aldine Atherton.

Samuel, Geoffrey. 1982. "Tibet as a Stateless Society and Some Islamic Parallels." *Journal of Asian Studies* 41 (2): 215–29.

_______. 1993. *Civilized Shamans: Buddhism in Tibetan Societies*. Washington, D.C.: Smithsonian Institution Press.

Sanchez, Lisa E. 2004. "The Global E-rotic Subject, the Ban, and the Prostitute-Free Zone: Sex Work and the Theory of Differential Exclusion." *Environment and Planning D: Society and Space* 22:861–83.

Schama, Simon. 1995. Landscape and Memory. New York: Vintage Books.

Schein, Louisa. 2000. *Minority Rules: The Miao and the Feminine in China's Cultural Politics*. Durham, N.C.: Duke University Press.

Schrift, Alan D. 1997. *The Logic of the Gift: Toward an Ethic of Generosity*. New York: Routledge.

Schwartz, Ronald. 1994. *Circle of Protest: Political Ritual in the Tibetan Uprising*. New York: Columbia University Press.

Scott, James. 1999. *Seeing Like a State: How Certain Schemes to Improve the Human Condition Have Failed*. New Haven, Conn.: Yale University Press.

Secor, Anna. 2007a. "Between Longing and Despair: State, Space, and Subjectivity in Turkey." *Environment and Planning D: Society and Space* 25:33–52.

_______. 2007b. " 'An Unrecognizable Condition Has Arrived.' " In *Violent Geographies: Fear, Terror, and Political Violence*, edited by Derek Gregory and Allen Pred, 37–54. New York: Routledge.

Shakya, Tsering. 1993. "Whither the Tsampa Eaters?" *Himal* 6 (5): 8–15.

_______. 1999. *The Dragon in the Land of the Snows: A History of Modern Tibet Since 1947*. New York: Columbia University Press.

Shapiro, Judith. 2001. *Mao's War against Nature*. Cambridge: Cambridge University Press.

Sharlho, Tseten Wangchuk. 1992. "China's Reforms in Tibet: Issues and Dilemmas." *Journal of Contemporary China* 1 (1): 34–60.

Shen, Jianfa. 2005. "Space, Scale, and the State: Reorganizing Urban Space in China" In *Restructuring the Chinese City: Changing Society, Economy and Space*, edited by Laurence J. C. Ma and Fulong Wu, 39–58. New York: Routledge.

Shih, Victor. 2004. "Development, the Second Time Around: The Political Logic of Developing Western China." *Journal of East Asian Studies* 4 (3): 427–51.

Silk, John. 2004. "Caring at a Distance: Gift Theory, Aid Chains and Social Movement." *Social & Cultural Geography* 5 (2): 229–51.

Silva, Kelly Cristiane da. 2008. "AID as Gift: An Initial Approach." *Mana* 14 (1): 141–71.

Sivaramakrishnan, K., and Arun Agrawal. 2003. *Regional Modernities: The Cultural Politics of Development in India*. New Delhi: Oxford University Press.

Skinner, G. William. 1977. *The City in Late Imperial China*. Stanford, Calif.: Stanford University Press.

Smith, Anna Marie. 1998. *Laclau and Mouffe: The Radical Democratic Imaginary*. New York: Routledge.

Solinger, Dorothy. 1999. *Contesting Citizenship in Urban China: Peasant Migrants, the State, and the Logic of the Market*. Berkeley: University of California Press.

Sørensen, Per K. 1994. *The Mirror Illuminating the Royal Genealogies: An Annotated Translation of the XIVth Century Tibetan Chronicle: "rGyal rabs gsal ba'i me long."* Wiesbaden: Harrassowitz Verlag.

Stirrat, Jock. 2006. "Competitive Humanitarianism: Relief and the Tsunami in Sri Lanka." *Anthropology Today* 22 (5): 11–16.

Stirrat, Roderick L., and Heiko Henkel. 1997. "The Development Gift: The Problem of Reciprocity in the NGO World." *Annals of the American Academy of Political and Social Science* 443:66–80.

Taussig, Michael. 1992. *The Nervous System*. New York: Routledge.

TIN (Tibet Information Network). 1996. *Cutting off the Serpent's Head: Tightening Control in Tibet, 1994–95*. London: Tibet Information Network.

———. 1999. *Social Evils: Prostitution and Pornography in Lhasa*. London: Tibet Information Network.

Vandergeest, Peter. 1991. "Gifts and Rights: Cautionary Notes on Community Self-Help in Thailand." *Development and Change* 22:421–43.

Vandergeest, Peter, and Nancy Lee Peluso. 1995. "Territorialization and State Power in Thailand." *Theory and Society* 24:385–426.

Wainwright, Joel. 2008. *Decolonizing Development: Colonial Power and the Maya*. Oxford: Blackwell.

Wainwright, Joel, and Morgan Robertson. 2003. "Territorialization, Science and the Colonial State: The Case of Highway 55 in Minnesota." *Cultural Geographies* 10:196–217.

Wang, Xiaoqiang, and Nanfeng Bai. 1991. *Poverty of Plenty*. New York: St. Martin's Press.

Wang, Yao. 1994. "Hu Yaobang's Visit to Tibet, May 22–31, 1980." In *Resistance and Reform in Tibet*, edited by Robert Barnett, 285–89. Bloomington: Indiana University Press.

Watts, Michael. 2003. "Development and Governmentality." *Singapore Journal of Tropical Geography* 24 (1): 6–34.

Weber, Max. 1958 (1905). *The Protestant Ethic and the Spirit of Capitalism*. New York: Charles Scribner's Sons.

Weiner, Annette B. 1985. "Inalienable Wealth." *American Ethnologist* 12 (2): 210–27.

Williams, Dee Mack. 2002. *Beyond Great Walls: Environment, Identity, and Development on the Chinese Grasslands of Inner Mongolia*. Stanford, Calif.: Stanford University Press.

Williams, Patricia J. 2009. "Mirror Man." *The Nation*, July 20.

Williams, Raymond. 1973. *The Country and the City*. New York: Oxford University Press.

———. 1974. *Television: Technology and Cultural Forms*. London: Fontana.

———. 1976. *Keywords: A Vocabulary of Culture and Society*. New York: Oxford University Press.

———. 1977. *Marxism and Literature*. Oxford: Oxford University Press.

———. 1991. "Base and Superstructure in Marxist Cultural Theory." In *Rethinking Popular Culture: Contemporary Perspectives in Cultural Studies*, edited by Chandra Mukerji and Michael Schudson, 407–23. Berkeley: University of California Press.

Willis, Janice. 1987. *Feminine Ground: Essays on Women and Tibet*. Ithaca, N.Y.: Snow Lion Publications.

Willis, Paul. 1981 (1977). *Learning to Labor: How Working Class Kids Get Working Class Jobs*. New York: Columbia University Press.

Woods, Tim. 2003. "Giving and Receiving: Nuruddin Farah's Gifts, or the Postcolonial Logic of Third World Aid." *Journal of Commonwealth Literature* 38:91–112.

Wright, Arthur F. 1977. "The Cosmology of the Chinese City." In *The City in Late Imperial China*, edited by G. William Skinner, 33–74. Stanford, Calif.: Stanford University Press.

Wu, Fulong. 2009. *China's Emerging Cities: The Making of New Urbanism*. New York: Routledge.

Wu, Shan. 2007. "Wei jianshe xin nongcun ganbu jaioshi xiaxiang (bamiao)" [Cadre teachers sent down to the villages to "tug at roots" in order to construct a new countryside]. *Xiangzhen luntan* [Township and village forum] 18:13–15.

Xiao, Huaiyuan. 1994. *Xizang nongye jiegou yu liangshi liutong* [Tibet's agricultural structure and grain circulation]. Beijing: China Tibet Publishing House.

Xizang Nongkeng Zhuangkuang Writing Group. 1986. *Xizang nongkeng zhuangkang* [The situation of agricultural reclamation in Tibet]. Lhasa.

Xu, Yinong. 2000. *The Chinese City in Space and Time: The Development of Urban Form in Suzhou*. Honolulu: University of Hawai'i Press.

Yan, Hairong. 2003. "Neoliberal Governmentality and Neohumanism: Organizing Suzhi/Value Flow through Labor Recruitment Networks." *Cultural Anthropology* 18 (4): 492–523.

———. 2008. *New Masters, New Servants: Migration, Development, and Women Workers in China*. Durham, N.C.: Duke University Press.

Yan, Hairong, and Gayatri C. Spivak. 2007. "Position without Identity: An Interview with Gayatri Chakravorty Spivak." *positions: east asia cultures critique* 15 (2): 429–48.

Yan, Hao. 2000. "Tibetan Population in China: Myths and Facts Re-examined." *Asian Ethnicity* 1 (1): 11–35.

Yan, Yunxiang. 1996. *The Flow of Gifts: Reciprocity and Social Networks in a Chinese Village*. Stanford, Calif.: Stanford University Press.

Yang, Mayfair Mei-hui. 1994. *Gifts, Favors, and Banquets: The Art of Social Relationships in China*. Ithaca, N.Y.: Cornell University Press.

Yang, Minghong, Qiyi An, and Zheng Zhou. 2007. "Xizang 'Anju Gongcheng' jianshe: Jiyu gonggong chanpin shijue de fenxi [Tibet's construction of Comfortable Housing: Analysis from the perspective of public goods)." *Zhongguo Zangxue* [China Tibetan studies] 78:25–34.

Yeh, Emily T. 2008. "Modernity, Memory, and Agricultural Modernization in Central Tibet, 1950–1980." In *Tibetan Modernities: Notes from the Field on*

Cultural and Social Change, edited by Robert Barnett and Ronald Schwartz, 37–72. Boston: Brill.

_______. 2009a. "From Wasteland to Wetland? Nature and Nation in China's Tibet." *Environmental History* 14 (1): 103–37.

_______. 2009b. "Living Together in Lhasa: Ethnic Relations, Coercive Amity, and Subaltern Cosmopolitanism." In *The Other Global City*, edited by Shail Mayaram, 54–85. Durham, N.C.: Duke University Press.

Yeh, Emily T., and Mark Henderson. 2008. "Interpreting Urbanization in Tibet: Administrative Scales and Discourses of Modernization." *Journal of the International Association of Tibetan Studies* 4:1–44. http://www.thlib.org/collections/texts/jiats/#jiats=/04/yeh/.

Yurchak, Alexei. 2006. *Everything Was Forever, Until It Was No More: The Last Soviet Generation.* Princeton, N.J.: Princeton University Press.

Zhang, Li. 2001. *Strangers in the City: Reconfigurations of Space, Power, and Social Networks within China's Floating Population.* Stanford, Calif.: Stanford University Press.

_______. 2006. "Contesting Spatial Modernity in Late-Socialist China." *Current Anthropology* 47 (3): 461–84.

_______. 2010. *In Search of Paradise: Middle-Class Living in a Chinese Metropolis.* Ithaca, N.Y.: Cornell University Press.

Zhang, Yisun. 2003. *Bod rgya tshig mdzod chen mo* [Great Tibetan-Chinese dictionary]. Beijing: Mi rigs par khang [Nationalities Publishing House].

Zheng, Zhou. 2007. "Anju Gongcheng yu Xizang shehuizhuyi Xinnongcun Jianshe" [Comfortable Housing and the construction of the New Socialist Countryside in Tibet]. *Heilongjiang minzu congkan* [Heilongjiang nationality collection] 100:56–62.

Zukin, Sharon. 1991. *Landscapes of Power: From Detroit to Disneyland.* Berkeley: University of California Press.

Index

Page numbers in *italics* refer to illustrations.

Abrams, Philip, 32
accountability, 47–49
accumulation by dispossession, 207, 211; land expropriation and, 25, 197, 202, 266
Adams, Vincanne, 166
Agamben, Giorgio, 273n6; on the state of exception, 33–34, 41
agency, 8–9, 168; and cultural politics, 13; of states, 15; Tibetan, 49, 83, 91, 159, 265
Agricultural Bank of China (ABC), 244–45, 292n69
agricultural/pastoral *(zhing/'brog)* binary, 286n16
Agricultural Reclamation Department, 72–73
Agriculture and Animal Husbandry Department (AAHD), 108–10
Aid-Tibet programs, 101–2, 186, 231
Alatas, Syed, 186–87
alcohol consumption, 96, 182, 225
Althusser, Louis, 11
altitude sickness, 64–65
Amdo County, 18, 290n43, 292n46
appearance *(nampa)*, 102, 236; economy of, 4, 263; and gift of development, 247, 251–53. *See also* image engineering
Arendt, Hannah, 269
August First State Farm: branches and production, 72; decollectivization, 89–90; establishment of, 61–62; food shortage, 87; grain yields, 62; Han youth volunteers, 82; land rentals, 90, 280n71; location (map), 23; management of, 72, 89; retired workers, 79–80, 90; Tibetan participation in, 130; vegetable cultivation, 71–73; wetland reclamation, 69; women at, 81–83; workers and reformed prisoners, 67–69, 278n25
Avalokitesvara, 5, 198, 273n5, 286n11

backwardness: and development, 164, 241, 244, 263; of Lhasa, 181; of Tibetans, 264–65; urbanization as a solution to, 8
bans. *See* restrictions and bans

Barnett, Robert, 38, 41, 277nn36–37
Bataille, Georges, 231
Bell, Charles, 170, 174
Benjamin, Walter, 29, 34, 270–71
Benpa Chungdak, 191–92
"big wind cooperative," 85
biopower, 13, 263, 267, 270
bodily movement, 30–32, 35
Bourdieu, Pierre, 15, 17, 145–46
boycotts, 13, 131
Buddhism: practice, 83–84, 160; and science, 148; sutras, 172, 285n23; Tibetan landscape and, 5–6; vegetarianism, 284n27; work ethics and, 171–74
Bulag, Uradyn, 203–4
business development, 102–3; licenses, 101
Butler, Judith, 168

cadres: Aid-Tibet, 101–2; income, 107, 206, 265; performance, 253; retirement housing for, 205–6; as town-level leaders, 100; transfers to Tibet, 100
calendar, Tibetan, 49–50, 284n34
capital, 175; accumulation, 115, 197, 204, 212, 265; for greenhouse costs, 140; land and, 134–35
capitalism: China's insertion into, 237; development and, 11, 175, 264; "para-sitic" existence of, 285n28; spectacle of, 236; and Tibetan Buddhist work ethic, 171–75
Certeau, Michel de, 30, 33, 155
chai ("demolish" or "raze"), 217
chain migration, 111
Chengdu, 41, 97, 205, 226
chengshi ("city"), 199–200
chengzhongcun ("villages in the city"), 210–11
Chen Kuiyuan, 96, 103, 164
Chen Yi, 74, 75, 82
Chen Yonggui, 66
Childs, Geoff, 232, 240, 245, 257, 292n69, 293n93; on Comfortable Housing subsidies, 258, 291n51, 292n88

China. *See* People's Republic of China (PRC)
China Tibet Magazine, 212, 214–15
Chinese Communist Party (CCP): eightieth anniversary celebration of, 26–28; land expropriation, 219–21; modernization of Tibet, 71; negotiations with Tibetan government, 20; rural development, 232, 236, 243; Tibetan closeness to, 243; Tibetan membership, 77, 82–83
Chinese Constitution, 37, 40
Chinese farmers. *See* Han migrants; migrant farmers
Chinese *(Zhonghua)* nation, 14, 234
chupas (Tibetan robes), 77, 228
circumambulation, 30–32; restrictions, 39–40; routes in Lhasa, 17, 31, 198
citizenship, 34, 261; rights of, 38
city and country, conceptions of, 198–200; and ethnic autonomy, 203
city street offices *(jiedao banshichu),* 104, 281n32
civilization, 2, 6; Chinese, 200; and nation making, 241
class: labels, 68, 86; and labor, 145; spatialization of, 202, 205, 227
coercion and consent, 257; Gramsci's use of, 12–13, 274n25
collectivization, 20, 61; land-leasing policy, 202; nostalgia and anti-nostalgia for, 177–79; ownership rights, 89
Comfortable Housing Project *(anju gongcheng),* 8, 25, 290nn39–40; building within one's means, 254–55, 259; conditions of program, 240; contradictions of, 267; controversy, 232–33, 256–57; emphasis on new housing, 242–43; farmers' investments in, 239–40, 244; government investments and subsidies, 232, 239, 244, 249, 251–56, 291nn51–52; growth since 2008, 262; income generated from, 257–58; loans and debt, 244–46, 248–49, 251–53, 258–60, 292n82; materials and labor, 247, 252, 254–58; objective of, 206, 238, 292n88; participation and reaction to, 253–54, 259–60; Peton model village, 251–53; provisions for livestock, 250; renovation and remodeling, 239–41, 251–52; village appearance improvement projects, 246–51, *249, 250*; voluntary participation in, 240, 258–60. *See also* New Socialist Countryside
common sense and good sense, 12–13, 166–67, 170; and indolence, 187
communes, 6, 61–62, 85; in Kyichuling village, 87–88
compassion, 171
consciousness, contradictory, 12–13, 166–67, 267
construction workers, 97–98, 107, 142, 257
cooperatives, 237, 283n3; urban farming, 97, 108–9, 111, 130–31
Cosgrove, Denis, 9
cultural genocide, ix, 99
cultural history: Chinese, 199–200, 264; Tibetan, 197–99
cultural politics: of development, 9, 12–13, 24–25, 164, 267; of identity, 119, 147, 215; and inequalities, 132; and marginalization, 139; of work, 61, 145–46, 160

Dalai Lama, Fifth, 17, 197
Dalai Lama, Fourteenth, 243, 270; birthday celebrations, 36, 45, 50; bodyguards, 78; criticism of, ix, 58–59; exile, 20, 35; forbidden images of, 262, 277n37; "obstacle years" of, 260
Damba village, 80–81
Daniels, Stephen, 9
dap dop ("fighting monks"), 78
Das, Veena, 21
dayuan, 62, 68, 277n6
Debord, Guy, 66, 231, 236
debt. *See* indebtedness
decollectivization, 61–62; land used for agriculture, 109, 111, 138; opportunities provided by, 108
Deng Xiaoping, 105, 201, 217; Southern Tour (1992), 3, 100, 102, 164
Derrida, Jacques, 16–17, 234
deterritorialization and reterritorialization, 216–17
development: and becoming spoiled, 180, 187; of capitalism, 11, 175, 264; cities as a metonym for, 183, 201–2; concept of, 11; critiques of, 164; cultural politics of, 9, 12–13, 24–25, 123, 164; as a hegemonic project, 8, 10, 12, 159, 166, 260–61; Hu Jintao on, 163–64; image of, 244; Lhasa signs and slogans on, 126–28, 164; marketing, 213; "people first," 232, 263; projects and strategies, 102, 124, 164, 186, 232, 234–35, 271; spatialization of, 211–12; spectacle of, 236, 251, 253, 263; state favoritism toward, 121–22; uneven, 119; as a Western narrative, 264. *See also* economic development; gift of development; Lhasa urbanization; self-development; urbanization
Dharma companions *(chö trog),* 31
disciplinary power, 33, 36, 38; and control of space, 32, 51, 235
disease, endemic, 238–39, 290n46

disenchantment and acceptance condition, 166
displacement, 197, 211, 266. *See also* resettlement
dispositions, 10, 145–47, 160
dispossession, 11. *See also* accumulation by dispossession
distinction, forms of, 145–48, 160
dog eating, 85–86, 89
Dongkar Town, 195, 210, 224, 237; resettlement of residents, 212–18
Douglas, Mary, 233
drought, 46

ecological living, 207–9, *208*
ecological migration *(shengtai yimin)*, 290n43
economic development, 3, 6, 173, 175; Comfortable Housing Project and, 257; Lhasa signs on, 127–28; role of migration in, 7, 99, 114; rural, 242; socio-, 243–44, 246; of TAR, 187; urbanization and, 203
education, 282n64; for Han migrants, 120–21, 147, 282n65; inequalities, 160; rural, 236–37; for state farm workers, 80–81
emasculation, 61, 84
embodied practices, 31, 40, 154–55
equality, 37, 41; differential treatment and, 41–42; gender, 88
estates, 19, 85
ethnic groups. See *minzu* (nationalities or ethnic groups)
ethnic relations, 79–80, 268; autonomy, 203–4; prejudice, 116
ethnography, role of, 268
exceptionalism, 33–34, 265
exclusion and inclusion, 21, 261, 265, 268, 276n27; zones in Lhasa, 38
exile, 280n5; of the Dalai Lama, 20, 35; Tibetan historiography, 61, 63
expropriation. *See* land expropriation

fear of politics, 24, 34, 49; surveillance and, 43, 46–47
Ferguson, James, 124
fertilizers, chemical: free or subsidized, 88, 110; in greenhouses, 134, 139–40; spoiling effects of, 183–87; and taste of food, 151, 185, 187; Tibetan reluctance toward, 147–48, 168
food shortages, 60–61, 85–87
foreign aid, 14–15, 234
formal workers, 68, 80, 278n25, 280n71
Foucault, Michel, 32, 39; biopower, 13; *dispotif,* 273n6; governmentality, 274n25
free gift, 233–34, 244, 262. *See also* gift of development; pure gift
gender roles, 61, 84; in labor, 91, 142, 149–51, 167, 174, 265
Germano, David, 181
Gidwani, Vinay, 12, 145, 175
gift, grammar of the, 16, 234–35, 263, 267
Gift, The (Mauss), 15–16, 233, 235
gift giving: asymmetry in, 15; of *khataks,* 3–4; reciprocity and, 233–34, 289n14; recognition and, 16–17, 261. *See also* gratitude
gift of development: appearance and, 247, 251–53; gratitude for, 3, 5–6, 203, 231, 235; Han migrants as bearers of, 99, 123, 129, 186; and loyalty, 262, 267, 270; new housing and, 25, 231–33, 244, 259, 261, 263, 267; as present and poison, 15, 17, 187, 233, 261, 267; receipt of, 14–17, 234–35, 261; and space, 267; for TAR fortieth anniversary, 231, 246, *248*. *See also* free gift; gratitude; pure gift
Goldstein, Melvyn, 232, 240, 245, 257, 292n69, 293n93; on Comfortable Housing subsidies, 258, 291n51, 292n88
government employees, 206, 262; accountability of officials, 48–49; restrictions, 39–40
grain cultivation: land purchases for, 62–63; rations, 279n63; supply for PLA, 60–61; surplus, 88, 131, 141, 280n64, 283n4; winter wheat and barley, 87–88, 170, 283n4; yields, 62
Grain Procurement Board, 60
Gramsci, Antonio, 170, 271; analysis of situations, 10–11; contradictory consciousness, 12–13, 166, 267; hegemony concept, 12; use of consent, 13, 274n25
gratitude: for Chinese liberation, 83; debt of, 262–63, 267; as a demand, 2; expectations of, 8, 244, 261; for gift of development, 3, 5–6, 203, 231, 235; for Han assistance, 71; for housing, 224, 243; for loan forgiveness, 248; performance of, 95, 224, 227, 246, 261; for wasteland reclamation, 66. *See also* gift of development
Gratitude Education *(gan en jiao yu)* campaign, 8
Greater Tibet, 18
greenhouses: chemical use in, 139–40, 147–48; cultivation skills, 109, 147–49; early structures, 71, 73, 278n37; inputs and costs, 140; plastic, 8, 90–91, 93, 108, 278n37; renting of, 7, 130–31, 134, 284n16; spatial patterning of, 151, *152*, *153*; subsidized or free, 130, 266; Tibetan views of, 146–47

Green Revolution, 87
grong khyer etymology, 198–99
guanxi (relationships), 121, 144, 282n65
guilt, 37, 41, 269–70; by association, 49, 57; as fate, 43, 229; nervousness with, 42, 230
Guo Kaizhong, 108–9
gyami (Chinese person), 104, 156. *See also* Han migrants

Hall, Stuart, 10, 12, 186
Han migrants: as agents of development, 99, 103, 122–24, 266; dominance in economic activities, 4, 6, 98, 107–8; education, 120–21, 147, 282n65; embodied practices, 154–55; as "floating population," 100, 102–3, 115; housing, 151, *152*, 153, 206; income, 113–14; from Mianyang Municipality, 111–12; population totals in Lhasa, 103–4, *104*, *105*; rural, 116; from Shuangliu County, 108–10; superiority, 14; temporary settlement, 103, 153; as tour guides, 102; transfers, 98–99, 121; in vegetable sales, 143–45; views of Tibet, 121–25; from Yuhe Town, 112–14. *See also* migrant farmers
Hattori, Tomohisa, 15
hegemony: cultural formations and, 10; and development, 12; economic, 231, 236; Gramsci's concept of, 12–13; landscape transformation and, 67; state farms and, 73, 85; of states, 263
hierarchy: administrative, 200–201, 226, 281n32; gendered, 84; in gift giving, 235; social, 233
homo economicus, 12, 159
house-building projects: debt from, 9, 25, 244–46; Lhasa-Gongkar Road House Renovation, 238, 246; private housing, 206–9; resettlement housing, 214–15, 218–20, *219*, 222–25; retirement homes *(tuixiu fang),* 204–6, 227; rural, 237–39; villager reaction to, 195–97. *See also* Comfortable Housing Project
household registration system. See *hukou* system
Household Responsibility System, 89, 113, 131, 133, 138
housing: *anju* or "comfortable," 206–7, 220; apartment buildings, 222–24; compensation for, 214, 216, 218, 221–22; demolition *(chai),* 212, 217, 252; Han and Tibetan comparison of, 151, *152*, 153, 250; market, 245; modeling and remodeling *(zhuangxiu),* 205, 214–15, 223; reform, 202; renting and selling, 244–45, 250; rural and peri-urban, 206, 232, 238, 245, 261; work unit, 202, 205–7, 238, 287n46. *See also* Comfortable Housing Project; house-building projects
Hu, Xiaojiang, 116, 281n27
Hui migrants (Chinese Muslim): carpenters, 220–21; total population of Lhasa, 104, *104*
Hu Jintao, 27, 106, 248; crackdown on martial law, 26, 100, 246; on development, 163–64
hukou system, 115, 121, 280n70; non/agricultural registrations, 99–100; rural-urban divide of, 116, 201; splitting registration, 216, 254, 260
human-nature relationship, 6, 66; socialist vision of, 24
Human Rights Watch, 257
humor, 95–96
hunger, 85–87, 179
Hu Yaobang, 100, 282n66
hybridity, 192–93

identification cards (ID), 27; checks, 35, 41–42, 270; and discrimination, 41, 58
identity/identities: Chinese, 264; collective, 145; cultural politics of, 119, 147, 215; and development, 10; of Han and Tibetan men, 150–51, 160; and labor practices, 170; making, 170; Tibetan, 31, 36, 51, 194; Tibetan cultural, 10–12, 18–19, 160, 187
illiteracy, 120, 148
image engineering *(xingxiang gongcheng),* 263; of housing on main roads, 246–51, *249*, 258
imaginaries: environmental, 63–65, 69, 176, 208; geographical, 116; place, 121; spatial, 266; of underdevelopment, 244
indebtedness: anxiety about, 9, 258, 262–63, 292n69; of Comfortable Housing Project, 244–46; engineering, 233, 262; loyalty and, 248, 262–63, 267, 270
indolence, 9, 91, 267, 285n15; and image of "lazy native," 186–87; lack of development and, 164–66; Lhasa as a contributor to, 182; as speech acts, 167, 187; the Tibetan landscape and, 176–77; Tibetan self-criticism and, 167–69; underemployment and, 180–81, 225–26; work ethics and, 7, 170–74
infrastructure projects, 102, 105; funding, 124; Qinghai-Tibet Railway construction, 106, 208. *See also* Comfortable Housing Project; New Socialist Countryside
intellectuals, Chinese, 99, 200, 268

Jackson, Michael, *191*, 192–94
Jiang Zemin, 96, 105, 182

Johnson, Tim, 232
Jokhang Temple, 17, 279n47, 287n47; as a pilgrimage site, 1, 197
July First State Farm: decline in Tibetan participation, 130; decollectivization, 89; establishment of, 61–62; female workers, 77–78, 80–84; food shortage, 87; greenhouses, 73; health care, 80; high-level military visits to, 74, *75*; location (map), *23*; official history, 72; pensions, 90; retired workers, 62, 70, 79–80; scientific functions of, 73, 90; worker advancement, 74–75

Kham, 18, 76, 181, 275n46
Khampas, 76, 78
khataks, 3–4
kyemen (low birth), 84
Kyichuling village (pseud.), 279n55, 279n59, 280n70; accounts of collective past, 177–79; committee, 225; communes, 87–88; decollectivization, 89; food shortage, 85–86; land reforms, 85; land subleasing, 131, 180; resettlement of villagers, 220, 222–25; social-spatial distribution of, 151, *152*, 153–56; work scarcity, 225–26

labor: on communes/collectives, 6, 86–89, 177–79; control, 91; gender roles, 91, 142, 149–51, 167; at greenhouses, 141–43; markets, 119, 132, 142, 227; migration, 113; naturalization of, 9; off-farm, 142; practices, 6, 170; and production of landscape, 9, 61; quality of, 61; socialist, 62, 90–91; theory of value, 134. *See also* state farms; work ethics
land expropriation: accumulation by dispossession and, 25, 197, 202, 266; CCP and, 219–20; in China, 202; of farmland, 4, 25, 209, 212, 218, 288n60; livelihoods and, 225, 227; for new housing development, 195–97; petitions against, 210, 218. *See also* resettlement; urbanization
land grabs, 211–13, 217, 224, 237. *See also* land expropriation
land reclamation, 72; of wastelands and wetlands, *55*, 64–67, 69
land renting/subleasing: absolute *vs.* differential theory of, 134–35; contracts and prices, 133–38, 266, 283n10, 283n14, 284n17; contradiction in, 10; income from, 131–32; landlords as laborers, 143; policies for collectives, 202; social relations of, 139; spatial patterning of, 138; for vegetable cultivation, 7–8, 90, 109, 131
landscape: built, 25, 236, 263; duplicity of, 9; material, 5, 8, 91, 267–68; peri-urban, 8, *93*, 195; physical connection of, 30–31; rural, 233; struggles over, 9–10; and territorialization, 5–6; Tibetan and Han conceptions of, 176–77; urban, *189*, 207, 211–12, 218, 226–27
landscape transformation: agriculture and, 61, 91; contributing factors of, 24, 265–66; market reforms and, 91; material practices of, 8; peri-urban and rural, 261; and state territorialization, 6, 91, 268; and urbanization, 6. *See also* land reclamation
language barriers, 157–58
Latour, Bruno, 9
lay-monastic dichotomy, 199, 286n16
Learn from Dazhai Campaign, *55*, 66–67, 91
Lefebvre, Henri, 32, 116, 226
leisure, 173–74
Lhalu wetland, 69
Lhasa: arrival of migrant farmers, 108–15, 281n27; Central Urban District, 209–10; cultural and political importance, 18–19, 21, 200; founding of, 197; geography of, 17, 198; improvement efforts, 4, 8; Lhasa *Chengguanqu,* 21, *23*, 103–4, *104*, 210, 275n53; Michael Jackson as, 192–94; migrant numbers, 103–4; military presence in, 34; parks, 176; population figures, 103, *104*, 197–98, 287n46; private enterprises, 101; prostitution, 182–83; signs of, 126–28; tea houses, 44–45; term usage, 21, 275n54; township meeting, 52–53; unemployment and underemployment in, 149, 181; wealth and poverty, 107; Yuthok Rd, 4. *See also* Lhasa neighborhoods; Lhasa urbanization
Lhasa Economic and Technological Development Zone, 195, 212, 217, *219*
Lhasa Municipality, 73, 198; administrative units, 21, *23*; Comfortable Housing Project, 238, 240, 290n47; population totals (2000), 104, *105*, 204, 287n43
Lhasa neighborhoods: Barkor, 17, 39, 42, 198, 206, 228–29; Karma Kunsang, 42, 58, 210–11; Lhalu, 4, 132, 181, 210; "little Sichuan," 24, 98, 103, 123–24, 265; Ramoche, 198, 279n47
Lhasa urbanization: cultural confusion and, 193–94; Economic and Technological Development Zone, 195, 212, 217–18, *219*; geographic extent of, 203–4; master plan for, 209–12, 287n52; new housing, 196–97; private housing, 206–8, *208*; rapid development, 226, 266; spoiling effects of, 181–82, 187, 201
Li, Tania, 261

listening, 52–53
loans: anxiety about, 253, 258, 293n93; forgiveness, 248; for housing projects, 9, 205, 244–46; for Peton village housing, 251–53; for vegetable cultivation, 140; for village appearance improvement, 248–49
loyalty, 248, 262–63, 267, 270–71

Makley, Charlene, 83–84, 233
Maoist period, 32, 95, 181, 236–37; labor practices, 69, 177, 179; state farms, 61, 63, 85; women's liberation, 88
Mao Zedong, 3, 66, 201
marginalization: and being spoiled, 181; cultural politics and, 139; distinction and, 160; of rural Tibetans, 116; Tibetan contribution to, 227; and vegetable cultivation, 145–46, 158–59, 187
margins, 21
martial law, 33, 35, 100, 246
Marx, Karl, 268, 291n62
Marxism, 11, 132
Mauss, Marcel: on "archaic" societies, 233–34; on the gift, 15–16, 233; on potlatch gift exchange, 235
Merlan, Francesca, 166
Mianyang Municipality: out-migration, 111–12; returned migrants, 118. *See also* Yuhe Town, Mianyang
migrant farmers: arrival in Lhasa, 108–15, 265, 281n27; dominance in vegetable cultivation, 130–31; from Gansu Province, 220; greenhouse operations, 140–43; land rentals and contracts, 7, 89, 133–39, 266; outsider status, 151, 159; profits and income, 133, 135, 266; relations with Tibetans, 151, 153–56. *See also* Han migrants; vegetable cultivation
minzu (nationalities or ethnic groups), 14, 18, 37, 274n29; on ID cards, 41; urbanization and autonomy, 202–4
mi ser, 19–20, 275n50
Mitchell, Don, 9–10
Mitchell, Timothy, 241
mobility: gender, 77, 84; personal, 76, 90; restrictions on, 38, 42, 10[illegible], 265, 270; social, 80; state control of, 33, 35–36, 39
modernity, 11, 227; urbanization and, 181, 200, 202
Moore, Donald, 132
moral economy, 139, 151
Mukerji, Chandra, 8, 273n8

Najin Township, 108–9, 206, 210, 288n60; Peton village, 251–53, 292n85. *See also* Red Star Village
nationalism, Chinese, 14
nationalities. See *minzu* (nationalities or ethnic groups)
National Work Forums, 101–3, 105
nation-state: hierarchy, 264; naturalization of, 2; recognition of, 235, 262; as a stable subject, 16; territory and, 5, 116, 262; Tibet exclusion/inclusion in the, 69, 265
naturalization: of Han migrants, 99; of labor, 9; of nation-state, 2; of the PRC, 91; of Tibetan belonging, 5, 8
natural village, definition of, 288n74
nature: conquest of, 61, 64–66, 91, 265; in state formation, 24, 90; transformation of, 69, 88, 208, 268
neoliberal ideology, 7, 24, 99, 101, 265
nervousness, 29, 271; with guilt, 42, 230; of power, 49; of the state, 27, 35, 38
New Rural Reconstruction Movement, 237
New Socialist Countryside: ambivalence about, 258; as a development gift, 261; emphasis on new housing, 241, 263; goals for Tibet, 242; and land expropriation, 212–13; plan and implementation, 236–38. *See also* Comfortable Housing Project
nostalgia: for collective Maoist period, 177–79; imperialist, 158

Open Up the West *(Xibu da kaifa)*, 3–4, 8, 97, 103, 105; Qinghai-Tibet Railway construction, 106, 208
Opium Wars, 2, 236
opportunistic space-time, 49–50
overdetermination concept, 11, 129, 132

parent-child relationship, 233–34
passports, 37–38, 270
pastoral sedentarization *(mumin dingju)*, 238–39, 290n43, 290n46
peaceful liberation, 1, 4, 20, 74; fiftieth anniversary celebration, 26–28, 36, 203–4
peasants: "civilizing," 241; class categories of, 68, 86; land expropriation, 202; mobility, 76
People's Daily, 21, 164
People's Liberation Army (PLA): behavior, 79–80; control in Tibet, 72; food for, 6, 60–61, 63, 70–72, 91; land purchases, 62–63; Logistics Department, 69, 76, 78; marriage to Tibetan women, 79; pressured to stay in Tibet, 79, 279n42; respect for Tibetan traditions, 71, 78–79; wasteland reclamation, 64–67; working on state farms, 67–68, 279n43
People's Republic of China (PRC): attempts to secure stability, 271; control over Tibet, 24, 74; difference from the West, 264; eastern seaboard, 116, 264; economy of coastal regions, 105, 112; ethnic governance within, 18; ethnic minority areas, 202–3; migration, 99–100,

102–3; multinational state designation *(duo minzu guojia)*, 13–14; population increase, 201; sovereignty, 2–3, 18, 26; as a spatial container for Tibet, 5, 123, 159, 235, 265, 268; Special Economic Zones, 217; uneven development in, 119; urbanization, 181, 197, 201–2, 216
peripheries, 21
Peton village (pseud.), 251–53, 292n85
Phenpo State Farm, 67, 86, 178, 279n60
picnicking, 174
piecework, 145
pilgrims and pilgrimage *(nèkor)*: at Drolma Ri, 29–30; at Jokhang Temple, 1, 228; physical-place connection of, 30–31; at Potala Palace, 27–28; as a spatial practice, 31–32, 40, 51
place making, 30, 40, 51, 154–55
place(s): Lhasa as, 124; quality and, 117–19, 121, 266; space and, 132, 155; in Tibetan cultural history, 198
poetry, 65, 70
policing, 34, 41, 43; arrests, 229–30, 262
"political" category, 46–47, 50, 229; boundaries of, 34, 48–49
political economy: and cultural politics, 120, 132, 139; of development, 12, 24–25, 51, 119, 166, 267; marginalization and, 175; of reform, 180
political practices, 32
politics of fear, 24, 34, 43, 49, 263
Poole, Deborah, 21
population transfer, 265, 281n5
postdevelopment, 164
Potala Palace, 17, 27–28, 192–94, 223
poverty, 220; alleviation strategies, 124, 149, 238–39, 257; in Lhasa, 107
power: in gift exchange, 233; and hegemony, 12; image and, 236; in land renting, 135; landscapes and, 10; over life and death, 270; social, 15, 135; surveillance and, 33. *See also* disciplinary power; sovereign power; state power
preventive detention, 43
primitive accumulation, 218, 221
production: capitalist value, 11–12; of landscapes, 5, 9–10, 61, 167; of "little Sichuan," 124–25; of state power, 32, 37, 41; of state space, 24, 32, 49, 51; of urban landscape, 25, 207, 211–12, 218, 226–27
"prosperous borders and wealthy households" project, 238–39
prosperous *(xiaokang)* society, 163, 209
prostitution, 182–83, 276n27
protests of 2008, ix–x, 37, 159, 262; aftermath of, 41, 57–59, 228–30, 268; state power and, 13, 19, 49
Public Security Bureau (PSB), 36, 38, 103–4, 157
pure gift: contradiction of, 233; development as, 14–15; ideology of, 234, 289n18; recognition and, 16

Qinghai Province, 239, 275n46, 277n44, 298n5; Rebgong, 233, 270
Qinghai-Tibet Railway, 4, 106, 208, 253; slogans for, 127
quality *(suzhi)*, 24, 226, 291n62; of Han migrants *vs.* Tibetans, 99, 117–20, 125; of migrant body, 115, 119; national value-coding of, 116–17; raising the level of, 242–43; spatial imaginary of, 266

racism, 181, 186, 268
ra ma lug ("neither goat nor sheep"), 192, 194, 267
Ramoche Temple, 17, 279n47
real estate industry: in China, 202; companies, 205–8, 211–12; growth, 217; reform, 238
reciprocity, 233–34, 289n14
red, symbolism of color, 193
Red Star Village, 108, *189*; location (map), 23; Tangchen natural village, 224–25; urbanization of, 220–22. *See also* Kyichuling village
religious practices: attacks on, 67; bans and restrictions on, 3, 38–40; and science, 147–48; of state farm workers, 82–83; twenty-ninth day ritual, 49–50; and work ethics, 171–74. *See also* Buddhism; circumambulation; pilgrims and pilgrimage *(nèkor)*
relocation, 216, 221, 251. *See also* resettlement
remittances, 98, 113, 123, 133, 266
representations of Tibetans, 61, 119; as being spoiled, 166–67, 179, 187; as indolent, 163, 165–69; state favoritism and, 121–22
resettlement: housing, 213–15, 218–20, *219*, 222–25, 288n63; pastoral, 238–39; programs, 48–49, 212; of Red Star villagers, 220–25; and religious/social disconnection, 215–16, 226; rental and income strategies of, 216; voluntary, 240. *See also* land expropriation
restrictions and bans: during the Beijing Olympics, 58–59; ethnic differentiation of, 40; impossibility of, 41; on mobility, 38, 101, 265, 270; on public celebrations, 35–37; on students and government workers, 38–40, 277n36
retail markets, 143–44
retirement communities, 205–6
rights: of citizenship, 38; differential, 42; equal, 37; housing, 245, 249; human, 99, 243; to kill, 269; land, 19, 89, 210;

rights (*continued*)
property, 153, 159, 205; to territory, 105; use, 133, 135, 138, 143, 187, 245
risk taking, 43–44
road expansion, 195, 212, 231, 246
Robin, Françoise, 232–33
runaways, 20, 265, 275n52; to avoid paying rent, 135–37
rural development, 236–37, 241, 261. *See also* Comfortable Housing Project; New Socialist Countryside
rural-urban migration, 201, 209

Sagadawa, 40, 42, 277n34
Sahlin, Marshall, 233
Salazar, Miguel A., 116
Schama, Simon, 60
schooling. *See* education
science: religious practices and, 147–48; and technology transfer event, 161–62; Tibetan knowledge of, 147–49, 183–84
scientific agriculture, 6, 73, 183–84
Scott, James, 232
Secor, Anna, 37, 40
security, 41, 228–29, 270; threats to, 47
self, conceptions of, 5, 11–12
self-cultivation, 163, 174, 187, 242
self-development, 165, 175, 209; new housing and, 25, 242, 246, 252, 263
self-immolations, 269–71
sem (minds), 70, 172–73, 225
sensitive issues, 48–49
Serf (Nongnu), 75
serfdom, 2–3, 275n50
Seventeen Point Agreement, 20, 60, 85, 278n41; fiftieth anniversary celebration of, 26–28
Shigatse, 29, 198, 292nn69–70; Comfortable Housing Project in, 232, 240, 245, 257, 291n51, 292n88
Shuangliu County, 108–12, 133
Sichuan, 275n46; agricultural taxes, 121; Chengdu, 41, 97, 205, 226; out-migration, 98, 111–15, 123–24, 280n4; sellers from, 144; Tibet as more developed than, 122, 125. *See also* Han migrants
signs, 126–28
sin *(dig pa),* 171
Sino-Tibetan relationship, 2, 90
skills, lack of, 147–49, 169
skill transfer, 109–10, 124, 130, 151
slogans and songs: on the conquest of nature, 63–67; on development, 164; on greenhouses, 73; "Lhasa Bar" song, 18–19; PLA, 71, 79; on technology, 161. *See also* signs
small households *(dud chung),* 19–20, 76, 179, 275n50
socialist market economy, 3, 103, 151
sociality, 31, 40, 49, 155
social relations, 15, 123–24, 235, 265; capitalist, 9, 99; Han-Tibetan, 156–58; within land renting, 139; and spatial patterns and practices, 151, *152*, 153–55, 226
social status, 149
Songtsen Gampo, 1–2, 17, 62, 197
sovereign power, 13, 235, 263, 267, 270; Agamben's theory of, 33–34, 41; coercive forms of, 24; control over space and, 50–51. *See also* state power
sovereignty: challenges of, 243; Chinese, 1–3, 20, 26, 73, 231; over one's self, 269; rejection of, 224, 263; territorial, 14, 18, 47, 218, 224
Soviet Union, 84
space: control over, 32–33, 49, 50, 53; of exclusion, 21; experience of, 212, 215, 226; gift of development and, 267; of the home, 42, 44–45, 263; living, 202, 205, 221, 227; and place, 132, 155; production of state, 24, 32, 49, 51; public and private, 44–45; restrictions on, 35–40; rural-urban divide and, 116, 226; social, 116, 164, 226; state power and, 32–33, 39, 43; and territory, 5, 200, 262, 267, 269
spatial practices, 226; of religious practices, 30–32, 40
spectacle: concentrated, 66, 236; of development, 236, 251, 253, 263; gifts as, 235–36; society of the, 231; and state territorialization, 233
speech acts, 8, 131, 167, 187
splittism and "splittists," 1, 3, 14, 34, 218; captured on signs, 126
spoiling or being spoiled, 166–67; by alcohol, 225–26; effects of chemical fertilizers, 183–87; indolence as a result of, 179, 187; Lhasa's influence on, 181–82, 187, 201; urbanization and, 203; youth as, 180–81
state (the), 15–16; and citizen, 16, 234, 236, 261, 263; claims on life and death, 269; development as gift and, 16–17, 235, 263; effect, 16, 32–33, 37–38, 53, 267, 273n1; and free money, 259, 262; hegemony, 263; and market, 209; societies, 234; spatiality of, 32–34, 39, 50–51, 270. *See also* state incorporation; state power; state territorialization
state farms: female workers, 24, 61, 77–78, 80–84, 91; founding of, 61–63; naming convention, 62; recruitment, 6, 9, 61, 76–77, 268; state control of, 90–91; stories of early workers, 76–77; territorialization and, 24, 61–62, 70, 74,

84–85, 90; transformation of wasteland for, 64–67. *See also* August First State Farm; July First State Farm
state incorporation: gendered nature of, 61, 84; gratitude concept and, 2–3; role of migrants in, 123, 159; role of state farms in, 6, 61, 76, 90; through development, 21; Tibetan history and, 1–2; vegetable farming and, 268
state of emergency, 24, 33, 51, 269, 271; Benjamin on, 29, 34
state of exception, 32–33, 41, 51, 235
state-owned industries, 201
state power, 27, 35, 271, 273n8; accountability and, 49; building of, 49, 83; coercion and, 13, 84; control and, 32–33, 39, 43; development and, 14, 175; nature and, 61; production of, 32, 41
State Security Bureau, 39, 41, 43, 100, 276n32; plainclothes officers, 44–45
state territorialization: control and, 63; development as, 193; gender and, 91, 265; gift of development and, 17, 234, 264; Han migration and, 99, 159; labor and, 61–62; landscape transformation and, 6, 91, 268; marginalization and peripheralization and, 21; market reforms and, 91; as a process, 5, 25; role of housing in, 233, 243; self-immolations and, 269; state farms as sites of, 24, 61–62, 70, 74, 84–85, 90; of Tibetan landscape, 5–6; urbanization and, 193–94, 197, 227
stupas, 154, 216–17, 284n28, 288n68
superstition, 67, 73, 148, 160–61
surveillance and self-surveillance, 228–29; fear and, 39, 43, 46–47; systems, 39; and taking precautions, 44–45
suzhi. *See* quality *(suzhi)*
symbolic domination, 15, 234

taming *('dul ba)*, 5–6, 32, 65, 267, 273n5
Tangchen village, 220–22, 224–25
Taussig, Michael, 29, 42
taxpayers *(khral pa)*, 19–20, 62, 275n50
tea houses, 44–45
technology transfer, 129, 147, 266; events and strategies, 131, 161–62
temporary migrants, 99, 103
temporary wage laborers *(xiao gong)*, 62, 67, 80
territorialization. *See* state territorialization
terrorism, 269
"Three Go Down to the Countryside, The" (*sange xiaxiang*), 161–62
Tibet, definition of, 280n5
Tibetan government, 18–20, 275n46, 275n52; land sales, 62–64
Tibetan-Mongol relationship, 2
Tibetan studies, 271
Tibet Autonomous Region (TAR): administrative regions, 18, 20–21, 22; aid and subsidies, 24, 106–7, 123, 187; as belonging to China, 8, 18, 38, 262–65; cultural history, 197–99; and difference, 264; economic reforms, 100–101; education system, 120–21; fortieth anniversary of, 127, 195, 231, 246, 248, 251; GDP and economy, 105–7, 123; geographical extent, 18, 275n46; grasslands, 63–64; house-building program, 237–41, 256; loan program, 244–45; migration to, 98, 100–101, 112–15; origin story, 5–6, 65, 199, 286n11; Party secretaries, 48, 52, 74; population figures, 99, 103–4, *104*; suspension of laws, 33; temporary migrants, 99, 103; thirtieth anniversary of, 27, 36, 74; town and township growth, 204; urbanization, 197, 200, 203–4, 261; wealth, 237; as a zone of exception, 43, 186, 238
Tolung Dechen County: land deals, 212–13, 288n60; migrant farmers, 110; resettlement of villagers, 212–15, 240; total population (2000), *104*; urbanization in, 203; vegetable cultivation, 149–51; village appearance improvement project, 248–50
tourists, 45–46, 98, 103, 229; tour guides, 102
Transplantation (Benpa Chungdak), *191*, 192–94
Trunglha village, 36–37, 46
Trunglha Yarsol, 36
tsampa, 18, 68; as survival food, 74, 86; used in ritual, 29–30, 36

unemployment and underemployment, 44, 149, 181, 225–26
unity and harmony: disruption of, 269; of nationalities or ethnic groups, 14, 58, 73, 106; of Tibetan identity, 18; between Tibetans and Han, 136
urban expansion, 8, 134, 202, 209, 216, 251
urbanism, 25, 200
urbanization: administrative, 201, 204; in China, 181, 197, 201–2, 216; as development, 202–3, 209, 220, 226–27; and ethnic autonomy, 202–3; land expropriation and, 4, 202, 212–13, 218–20; landscape transformation and, 6; of Red Star Village, 220–25; religious/social disruption of, 215–16, 226; resettlement, 213–19; as a solution to backwardness, 8; spatial experience

urbanization (*continued*)
of, 211, 215; spoiling effect of, 203; and state territorialization, 193–94, 197, 227; in TAR, 197, 200, 203–4, 261. *See also* land expropriation; Lhasa urbanization
urban-rural division: in China, 200; meaning and etymology, 197, 199; and quality, 117; salary disparity, 107, 186; space, 116; urbanization and, 204; work habits, 168, 182

vegetable cultivation: deliberate creation of, 266; development of Lhasa industry, 108–9; gendering of, 149–51, 160, 174; government projects, 149–50; Han domination in, 130, 138, 168; land distribution, 138; new crop varieties, 87–88, 91; prices, 133, 283n9; profits and income, 133, 135, 283n8; sellers, 143–44; Tibetan non/participation in, 24, 124, 129–32, 145–47, 159; urbanization and, 197. *See also* fertilizers, chemical; grain cultivation; land renting/subleasing
vegetarianism, 151, 284n27
"village in the city" designation, 210–11
violence: fear of, 34; law in, 269–71; at public celebrations, 57; threat of, 13–14
visibility, 33–34, 43. *See also* surveillance and self-surveillance

wages: for cadres, 107, 206, 265; disparities, 120, 122; fixed, 87; out-migrant incomes, 113–14, 133; point system, 87–88; for Tibetan laborers, 143; urban *vs.* rural, 107
Wainwright, Joel, 11
Wangdu (actor), 75–76
Wangdui, Puchung, 232, 240, 245, 257, 292n69, 293n93; on Comfortable Housing subsidies, 258, 291n51, 292n88
wasteland *(huangdi)*, 55, 63; reclamation of, 64–67
wealth: accumulation of, 173, 235; Buddhist principles and, 172–74; TAR ranking for, 237
Weber, Max, 171, 173
Wencheng, Princess, 1–2
Williams, Patricia, 194
Williams, Raymond, 10–12, 129, 132
women: harassment, 78, 84; liberation of, 88; state farm workers, 61, 77–84, 91; status in society, 84; in vegetable cultivation, 150–51, 174. *See also* gender roles
work ethics: and cultural conceptions, 170–71; Han-Tibetan comparison, 166–69; influence of landscape on, 176–77
work units, 35, 97, 115, 280n1; housing, 202, 205–7, 238, 287n46; promotion of science and technology, 161–62

xiaokang living: model homes and village, 189, 223–24; standard of, 246

Yan, Hairong, 116, 291n62
Yang, Mayfair, 43
youth: employment prospects, 154, 180–81; state farm volunteers, 72, 82
You-tien Hsing, 210
Yuhe Town, Mianyang, 112–13, 123; government, 114, 133; Yutai village, 11, 113–14

Zhang Guohua, 60, 74, 277n1
Zhang Qingli, 224, 235, 241

Studies of the Weatherhead East Asian Institute

Columbia University

Selected Titles

(Complete list at http://www.columbia.edu/cu/weai/weatherhead-studies.html.)

The Nature of the Beasts: Empire and Exhibition at the Tokyo Imperial Zoo, by Ian J. Miller. University of California Press, 2012.

Redacted: The Archives of Censorship in Postwar Japan, by Jonathan E. Abel. University of California Press, 2012.

Asia for the Asians: China in the Lives of Five Meiji Japanese, by Paula Harrell. MerwinAsia, 2012.

The Art of Censorship in Postwar Japan, by Kirsten Cather. University of Hawai'i Press, 2012.

Occupying Power: Sex Workers and Servicemen in Postwar Japan, by Sarah Kovner. Stanford University Press, 2012.

Empire of Dogs: Canines, Japan, and the Making of the Modern Imperial World, by Aaron Herald Skabelund. Cornell University Press, 2011.

Russo-Japanese Relations, 1905-17: From Enemies to Allies, by Peter Berton. Routledge, 2011.

Realms of Literacy: Early Japan and the History of Writing, by David Lurie. Harvard University Asia Series, 2011.

Planning for Empire: Reform Bureaucrats and the Japanese Wartime State, by Janis Mimura. Cornell University Press, 2011.

Passage to Manhood: Youth Migration, Heroin, and AIDS in Southwest China, by Shao-hua Liu. Stanford University Press, 2010.

Imperial Japan at its Zenith: The Wartime Celebration of the Empire's 2,600th Anniversary, by Kenneth J. Ruoff. Cornell University Press, 2010.

Behind the Gate: Inventing Students in Beijing, by Fabio Lanza. Columbia University Press, 2010.

Postwar History Education in Japan and the Germanys: Guilty Lessons, by Julian Dierkes. Routledge, 2010.

The Aesthetics of Japanese Fascism, by Alan Tansman. University of California Press, 2009.

The Growth Idea: Purpose and Prosperity in Postwar Japan, by Scott O'Bryan. University of Hawai'i Press, 2009.

National History and the World of Nations: Capital, State, and the Rhetoric of History in Japan, France, and the United States, by Christopher Hill. Duke University Press, 2008.

Leprosy in China: A History, by Angela Ki Che Leung. Columbia University Press, 2008.

Kingdom of Beauty: Mingei and the Politics of Folk Art in Imperial Japan, by Kim Brandt. Duke University Press, 2007.

Mediasphere Shanghai: The Aesthetics of Cultural Production, by Alexander Des Forges. University of Hawai'i Press, 2007.

Modern Passings: Death Rites, Politics, and Social Change in Imperial Japan, by Andrew Bernstein. University of Hawai'i Press, 2006.

The Making of the "Rape of Nanjing": The History and Memory of the Nanjing Massacre in Japan, China, and the United States, by Takashi Yoshida. Oxford University Press, 2006.